READINGS IN THE THEORY OF EDUCATIONAL SYSTEMS

Sociology

Editor

PERCY S. COHEN

Professor of Sociology in
the London School of Economics and
Political Science

READINGS IN THE THEORY
OF EDUCATIONAL SYSTEMS

EDITED BY

Earl Hopper

Lecturer in Sociology in the
London School of Economics and Political Science

HUTCHINSON UNIVERSITY LIBRARY
LONDON

HUTCHINSON & CO (*Publishers*) LTD
3 Fitzroy Square, London W1

London Melbourne Sydney Auckland
Wellington Johannesburg Cape Town
and agencies throughout the world

First published 1971

*This book has been set in Times type, printed in Great Britain
on smooth wove paper by Anchor Press, and
bound by Wm. Brendon, both of Tiptree, Essex*
ISBN 0 09 109230 2 (cased)
0 09 109231 0 (paper)

For Ilya Neustadt

CONTENTS

ACKNOWLEDGMENTS

I should like to acknowledge Penguin Education for 'A cross-cultural outline of education' by Jules Henry; Doubleday & Co. Inc., for 'Social selection in the Welfare State', by T. H. Marshall; Cambridge University Press for 'Domination and assertion in educational systems' based on *Social Conflict and Educational Change, 1780–1850* by Margaret Scotford-Archer and Michalina Vaughan; the American Sociological Association for 'Sponsored and contest mobility and the school system' by Ralph Turner, and for 'The political functions of the educational system' by Harmon Zeigler and Wayne Peak; The British Sociological Association for 'The management of knowledge: a critique of the use of typologies in educational sociology' by Ioan Davies; Dennis Smith for 'Selection and knowledge management in education systems' and 'Power, ideology and the transmission of knowledge: an exploratory essay'; Pierre Bourdieu for 'Systems of education and systems of thought'; Basil Bernstein for 'On the classification and framing of educational knowledge'; and A. H. Halsey for 'Theoretical advance and empirical challenge.'

I am indebted to Linda Walker for her assistance in the preparation of the typescript of this book.

E.H.

FOREWORD

Educational systems can be studied either as institutions and organisations, or as processes of cultural transmission: hence, the sociology
of education has stemmed from two rather distinct sources and has
often taken two rather distinct forms. In the first place, there have
been studies of the way in which educational systems have affected
and, in turn, been influenced by such factors as class structure,
social mobility, ethnic assimilation, and so on (see Chapters 1–5).
At the other extreme, there have been studies which, stemming
from the sociology of knowledge, have concentrated on the communication of ideas, skills, knowledge, values and categories of thought,
which either contribute to the maintenance of given cultural and
social systems or else encourage innovatory tendencies in them
(see Chapters 6 and 8). Between these two extremes lie the studies
of particular educational organisations which are focussed on formal
and informal structures (of, for example, schools), while also looking
at the process of cultural transmission as an aspect of these; and, of
course, there have been those rare studies, which have attempted to
bridge the analysis of social structure and of culture via the examination of symbolism and, especially, of language (see Chapters 8, 9, 10).
Fortunately and, to a large extent, as a result of the work of Professor
Basil Bernstein, these two currents are now flowing more and more
together, although, of course, there is still room in this sub-discipline
for choice of emphasis (see Chapters 7 and 11).

All educational systems in modern societies have at least two pairs
of functions. First, as in traditional societies, they communicate
the cultures or sub-cultures which already exist and which will, at

least in part, continue to exist, thereby reinforcing social systems or sub-systems; however, in addition, they also promote innovatory tendencies, which means that they must provide both the skills and the motivation to change at least some parts of cultural and social systems, or to add to them. Secondly, they create or encourage motivation for success and mobility, while, at the same time, encouraging acceptance of existing systems on the part of at least some of their members. No educational system can do these things without creating tensions and conflicts: thus conservative and inno-vatory forces may become politically polarised, while motivation for success may not be confined to those who are fortunate enough to enjoy it. Furthermore, what persists as part of an on-going culture or sub-culture—for example, the structure of language—may inhibit innovation or stunt the growth of ambition. The recog-nition of these tensions excites the curiosity and, possibly, also the moral indignation of social scientists; and out of this, if we are fortunate, more interesting social analyses emerge (see Appendix II).

Concomitant with the elaboration of the theory and the attempt to build theoretical bridges between different parts of the sociology of education, there has also been a good deal of progress in research and increasing success in relating research directly to the theoretical propositions which inform it and which are, in turn, modified by it (see Chapter 12). As part of this development there is a growing concern with the comparative study of types of educational system seen both in organisational and in cultural terms.

The articles in this volume reflect all of these tendencies and tensions and, so that they can do this more effectively, they are arranged in 'logical' rather than in chronological order. It is hoped that they will appeal not only to the graduate student or to the under-graduate specialist in sociology, but also to other students of society and of educational problems and, indeed, to a wider public of those interested in modern social life. They are all examples of a truly maturing sociology, in which theory and empirical observation are brought increasingly into fruitful confrontation with one another.

PERCY S. COHEN
London School of Economics
March 1971

I

NOTES ON STRATIFICATION EDUCATION AND

MOBILITY IN INDUSTRIAL SOCIETIES*

Earl Hopper

I

1. The basic unit of stratification is the nuclear family. This unit usually consists of a husband and wife and their offspring. The nuclear family usually resides in one household, at least until the offspring become employed, leave for university, enter the armed services, etc. Sometimes other relatives, such as an aged grandparent, may reside with the nuclear family. Although marked variations in this pattern exist both within and among advanced industrial societies, most observers agree that it is the dominant pattern, particularly when seen in comparison with the family structure of most pre-industrial, tribal societies.[1]

2. Configurations of nuclear families comprise the strata of industrial societies. The term 'strata' is used because the configurations are hierarchically ranked according to the power of the members of the constituent families to control their own and others' life chances, or life fates, in various spheres of activity. Their power is usually determined by the position of the head of the family within hierarchies of stratified power. These hierarchies are located in the three most comprehensive spheres of interest and activity in an industrial society: the 'economic', 'status', and 'political'. The configurations

* This paper makes explicit my own assumptions, perspectives, and language concerning stratification and mobility processes. It was written initially as an appendix to a monograph concerning the subjective consequences of social mobility in England and the United States, some aspects of which are discussed in Appendix II. But I have found it useful for teaching purposes, especially with advanced undergraduates. I have refrained from elaborate bibliographical references; most of the relevant literature can be found in R. Bendix and S. M. Lipset (Eds.), *Class, Status and Power*, second edition, London, Free Press, 1966.

of families which share similar positions of power in these hierarchies are called, respectively, 'classes', 'status groups', and 'parties'.

3. These groupings can also be ordered in terms of the degree of consciousness their members have of being a part of the groupings. Political parties are formally organised, and represent the more or less explicit articulation of interests and values. Because joining them is a matter of choice, their members are likely to have a high degree of consciousness concerning the fact of membership and identity as members. Depending on the current political issues and other aspects of the political system, their consciousness of party will vary in degree and intensity. Parties may be compared with respect to each other at a given time and to themselves over time with respect to their degree and intensity of group consciousness. Henceforth, I shall not discuss political parties or political hierarchies of power; they require an approach which is different from the one which follows.

Classes and status groups also vary in their degree of group consciousness, both over time and among themselves. Status groups are likely to have a higher degree of group consciousness than are classes. In fact, the degree of class consciousness which characterizes a given economic collectivity is likely to depend upon the extent to which its members are also members of the same status group. Classes, however, may, under certain conditions, have so little group consciousness that they do not warrant the connotation of 'community'. 'Class awareness' exists, but 'class consciousness' does not. Classes which are not communities are more accurately called 'economic collectivities'. But, depending on the context of the argument in which the terms are used, 'class' and 'economic collectivity' refer to the same unit; it is appropriate to use 'class' to refer to economic collectivities with at least a moderate degree of group consciousness.

4. When one refers to 'class', one is usually concerned with 'class situation'. This refers to the 'opportunities (of the members of a class) to gain sustenance and income through the possession of property or skill (in the market place) but also the life experiences arising from the way in which such opportunities are organised, e.g., the necessity of complying with the discipline of a capitalist proprietor's workshop'.[2] In short, aspects of economic power which must be considered in the specification of a class are wealth, income, economic security, and various aspects of the work condition, all of which affect the power of families to control their life chances in the market place. And in most industrial societies to control one's own life chances is also to control the life chances of others.

5. When one refers to 'status group', one is usually concerned with the 'status situation' of the group's members. This refers 'not only to . . . their chances of receiving "positive or negative social honour", but also those life chances that result from the status prerogatives of such groups', such as the opportunity to own certain types of property, to pursue certain types of occupations, to gain access to the most advantageous mobility routes, etc. Status groups are distinguished by the 'life-styles' of their member families, and by the degree of deference which they demand and the degree of respect which they bestow. To some extent status groups and status situations will be based on a given locality, and not necessarily on the 'society as a whole'. But some evidence suggests that a national prestige ordering of such groups develops as a society industrializes.

The power over life chances provided by class situation is obvious. The power provided by status situation is more subtle. Perhaps the key point is that status distinctions appear to be harmless, but they function to signify location in the stratification system. They implicate the 'potential power' which could be brought into play if necessary. Yet, more direct means of employing status situation as a power resource may be cited. For example, businesses usually regard 'good will' as an invaluable intangible asset, and the prestige of their executives is an excellent source of good will. This is particularly true of those types of business which depend on a high degree of trust on the part of the client, such as banking, law, real estate, etc. In other words, all else being equal, a man from a high status group will have an easier time getting a job and being a success at it than a man from a less prestigious background. Two additional examples will suffice: the ability of high status families to influence the course of legal justice over the minor offences of their members; and the ability of a 'gentleman' to secure a bank loan, even when his economic resources hardly justify his receiving it.

6. Supplements to the concept of 'status group' are 'core status group' and 'peripheral status group'.[3] The structure of status groups in an industrial society is not simple. At almost every echelon of the status hierarchy, the predominant status group is likely to be characterized by internal networks of esteem and influence. Such internal structures are of little interest to members of higher and lower status groups, but are crucial to the life styles and status power of the members of the group in question. From the point of view of the members of a given status group, it is possible to consider these internal variations in terms of 'hierarchy'. But from the point of view of the wider society, it is more helpful to think in terms of 'cores' and 'peripheries'. In a given status group, the

members of the core have more status power than the members of the periphery; they set the status norms and the life-style of the group, and adjudicate concerning the status behaviour and status positions of more peripheral members. The members of the periphery conform to these norms and life-styles, and their positions depend on the adjudication of the core.

The degree of social distance between the core and periphery of a status group is problematic, and will be mentioned later in the context of status rigidity. The relations between membership in a core or periphery and upward or downward mobility is also problematic. In general, however, mobility between or among status groups is unlikely to proceed from core to core, but to be mediated through one or more peripheral status groups.

7. Most families in advanced industrial societies tend to have positions in the economic hierarchy which are similar to their positions in the status hierarchy. Configurations of such families are called 'social classes', and the strata in an industrial society are likely to be social classes.

The main reason for a general tendency towards congruence between classes and status groups in industrial societies is the development of a complex, highly differentiated occupational system, the units of which can be ranked in terms of a number of concrete, hierarchical properties of both classes and status situations. On the one hand, the occupation of an individual will reflect his education, values, and previous personal associates; on the other hand, it will strongly influence his current personal associates, income, job security, working conditions, the wealth which he can accumulate, and the life style which he can afford and choose. In addition, and this aspect is usually over-emphasized by those who equivocate occupational rankings with social class rankings, the occupations themselves contribute to the social honour bestowed upon the occupant, independently of these other more specific dimensions of economic and status power which the occupations may reflect and produce. This is also why the occupational hierarchy becomes the best single index of social class position.[4] In sum, to the extent that class and status situations depend on occupational position, regardless of the structure and biases of the mechanisms for allocating such positions, the society is likely to be stratified by social classes.

8. Thus far, occupations have been considered only from a 'vertical' perspective, i.e., in terms of their economic and status rewards, and, hence, in terms of their position in an occupational 'hierarchy'. With respect to studies of stratification, this occupational hierarchy has explanatory and indicatory value for the

economic and status hierarchies, and for a hierarchy of social classes. But occupations may be treated in terms of many other problems and processes. For example, they may also be considered from a 'horizontal' perspective, i.e., they may be classified in terms of situs. A 'situs' is a category of occupations which is differentiated from other categories according to any number of criteria other than or in addition to economic and status bestowal values. For example, whereas manual work in a manufacturing industry differs from clerical work in the same industry in terms of economic and status criteria, it also differs from manual work in service or agricultural industries in terms of situs criteria, e.g., 'indoor' vs. 'outdoor' work, contact with objects vs. contact with people, etc. The occupations within situses can, of course, be ranked in terms of their economic and status rewards. By definition, some of the occupations in one situs will bestow economic and status rewards which are identical to those bestowed by some of the occupations in another situs; but in order that one situs be differentiated from another, it is not necessary for all the occupations in one to be identical in this respect to all the occupations in another. One situs might contain a number of occupations which are either or both higher and lower in economic and status rewards than the occupations in another situs. And the occupations in one situs might all be either higher or lower in economic and status rewards than the occupations in another, but nonetheless be equivalent to all the occupations in still a third situs. Consequently, situses as such are also ranked with respect to the economic and status hierarchies, but such a ranking is difficult to ascertain, and is likely to be of value only in special circumstances.

Among the many reasons why the recognition of situses is important in studies of stratification and mobility is that they vary with respect to such properties as opportunities to develop mobility orientations and to become mobile, and potentials for the formation of comparative reference groups and membership groups based on the occupation.

9. With respect to the problems of selection through educational systems, a number of political and economic trends inherent in industrialization processes (particularly apparent in England) make the status situation of social classes more important than the class situation. There has been an increase in the economic power of the lowest classes, especially when they have been able to organize for political purposes. Indeed, this has often been associated with the extension of the franchise: although their rise in economic power appears to have preceded their rise in political power, the latter has certainly reinforced the former. The spread of citizenship has also

been associated with the institutionalization of economic conflict; by containing economic disputes within the negotiating apparatus of the existing formal and legitimate political institutions, the visibility of class conflict, as well as its spontaneous and potentially violent character, have been reduced. Relative to unskilled and skilled white collar and black-coated workers, the increased bargaining power of manual workers has improved other aspects of their class situation, such as working conditions, job security, retirement benefits, vacation pay, bonus schemes, etc. The trade unionization of the lower middle class can be explained partly in terms of a response to these developments, and partly in terms of their own changing class situation. The proportion of the labour force engaged in manual work has decreased, and the proportion engaged in urban, non-manual, tertiary occupations has increased. In terms of economic power, therefore, it is increasingly difficult to distinguish between the upper levels of the lowest class and the lowest levels of the middle class.[5]

All of these trends have increased the utility of conceptualizing economic power in terms of a finely graded hierarchy, a continuum, as it were, with a decreasing number of breaks, and a smaller and smaller amount of 'economic space' among them. Insofar as occupation is the main source of class situation for the majority of people the reduction of large gaps in economic space between clusters of occupations, and the rise in class situation of the members of those occupations which are the lowest in the economic hierarchy, have *reduced* the degree to which class situation can function as a source of group consciousness, i.e., the degree to which an economic collectivity can be called a 'class'. And the reduction of visible, spontaneous, and violent inter-class conflict has reduced the intensity of intra-class cohesion. Consequently, it is likely that both the propensity to *choose* a class as an object of identification and the degree to which class can be *taken* as an object of identification have been reduced.

At the same time, the growing cohesion of status groups under the pressures of increased economic mobility of both a group and an individual kind has increased the importance of status situation. As class interests are negotiated within the context of a legitimate authority structure as manifested in political and quasi-political institutions, status groups take on an increasingly important role in preserving consensus and cohesion in the society as a whole. Although many of the economic and political trends which affect the structure of the economic hierarchy also affect the minimum level of status in the society, the number of status groups, the amount of social distance between them, the visibility of status group boundaries, and the structure of the general status hierarchy all change much more slowly.

One indication of the growing importance of status situation is that it is often the major source of 'bias' in the increasingly centralized and standardized educational system. At virtually all levels of 'natural ability' and at most levels of the educational system, the status situation of parents markedly determines how well their children do in school. Consequently, the status situation of the parents is likely to influence the educational selection of their children, and hence, their occupational allocation, and their eventual class and status situations. Although the parents' class situation also affects the eventual occupational position of their children, the existence of institutionalized recruitment procedures of the educational system tend to make the informal effects of their status situation more important than those of their class situation.

The main distinguishing properties of social classes can be best understood, therefore, in terms of status situation. *But this is in no way to deny that classes exist, reinforce the maintenance of status group boundaries, and in the long run are the main source of status group formation.*

10. Thus, given the importance of social class stratification, but also the relatively greater importance of status group differences compared with class differences (especially at the boundaries of the social classes), the *descriptive* utility of the separate concepts 'class' and 'status group' decreases. However, at the same time, their *analytical* utility, their ability to guide one's observations to different aspects of a situation in which both class and status elements are almost inextricably intermeshed, increases. Indeed, even though social class stratification exists, a number of important processes cannot be fully explained or clearly identified unless these analytical tools are retained.

By utilising the analytical tools of 'economic and status hierarchies of power', 'class', and 'status group', one can identify and partially explain the simultaneous existence of tendencies towards cohesion as well as towards conflict within a stratification system consisting of social classes. [6]

Although both class and status situations are power resources, even when they refer to different aspects of a situation in which both appear to be inextricably interconnected, class situation reflects, for the most part, power which is *not legitimized*. It is not that economic power is illegitimate. In and of itself economic power implies only the ability to control one's own economic alternatives and resources; and, in a market-economy, this implies the control of the economic alternatives and resources of others. People do not voluntarily relinquish their economic power and their economic self-sufficiency. Nowhere do poor people think that it is right and proper that they should be poor and others rich. But insofar as the distribution of economic power is seen to be based on laws and norms concerning economic activity and the economic system, which usually are derived from the status system, few members of a society are likely to regard it as illegitimate.

The status hierarchy of power is based primarily on internalized, voluntary cooperation. Status situations reflect legitimate power. People bestow status power; it is not simply taken. It works through the normative subordination and superordination of members of different status groups. And although status usurpation may occur, this is primarily likely under conditions of rapid social change in which the criteria for making status evaluations also change.

On this basis, the 'economic *power* hierarchy' can be distinguished from the 'status *authority* hierarchy'. Families are stratified according to both hierarchies, and, by virtue of social class stratification, a given family's class position is likely to be commensurate with its status position. But when people relate to those outside their class or status group, they are likely to define the context of their relationship as either primarily 'economic' or primarily 'status', and to feel and behave accordingly. Although both contexts are sources of interests and values on the part of the actors, the status context is a source of interests which are regarded as legitimate. Consequently, the status hierarchy and the norms upon which it is based are likely to be a manifestation, as well as a source, of social cohesion among status groups; but the economic hierarchy is more likely to be a manifestation, as well as a source, of social conflict among classes. In general, therefore, social stratification is not only a source of social integration; it is also a source of conflict.

It is, however, too simple to argue that the economic hierarchy in an industrial society is always the source and manifestation of conflict, and the status hierarchy always the source and manifestation of consensus. Apart from the fact that status usurpation can and does occur under certain circumstances, it is important to consider how certain properties of a status hierarchy can affect its consensus and conflict functions. Of special importance in this connection is 'status rigidity'.

11. Status rigidity refers to the following properties of the status hierarchy and its relationships to the stratification system: (1) the degree to which status groups are mutually exclusive in their inter-

relationships and memberships; (2) the degree to which the life styles associated with each status group are distinctive and extensive such that they are difficult to shed as well as to acquire, especially after childhood; (3) the degree of social distance between adjacent status groups, between any one echelon in the hierarchy and any other, and between the core and peripheral status groups at any given echelon; (4) the degree to which it is possible to legitimize a newly acquired economic position by entering with speed and ease the core of the commensurate status group; (5) the degree to which various occupations or sets of them are governed and regulated by certain status groups, with special reference to recruitment and promotion; (6) the degree to which the educational system is governed and regulated so that certain status groups are favoured with respect to the processes of educational selection and training. A status system can be more rigid in some respects than in others. One segment of a system can be more rigid than another, with respect to any number of these properties. And one system can in general be more rigid than another system.

The relationship between status rigidity and certain patterns of conflict and discontent is usually manifest in various processes of mobility, and especially in certain phases of these processes. Of special interest are its effects on mobility orientations, mobility potentials, expectations of adult economic and status positions and of occupational roles, and on the kinds of interpersonal relationships which characterize the educational and occupational careers of various categories of mobile people. Too little is known about status rigidity to permit ready generalizations. But some evidence suggests that when the degree of status rigidity is either 'very high' or 'very low', the status hierarchy is likely to function primarily as a source of social integration; and when the degree of status rigidity is 'moderate', it is likely to generate conflict as well as integration. The relationship is curvilinear. The degree of status rigidity can be called 'moderate' when it is high enough to retard status mobility but low enough to permit economic mobility. Under such conditions, the status hierarchy is likely to lose some of its legitimacy, and the hierarchy of economic power, in turn, is likely to be defined as 'less fair'.

12. It follows that there can be and usually are many exceptions to the general pattern of class and status group congruence. In such cases the concept 'social class' loses both its descriptive and its analytical utility, and one must again differentiate 'class' from 'status group'. The exceptions are sufficiently numerous and non-random to warrant special consideration. At the outset, however,

one must state that where 'status incongruence' exists, change is likely to be occurring or to have recently occurred in the criteria for status evaluation, in the occupational structure, in the distribution of people within the occupational hierarchy, and/or in the economic hierarchy.

In general terms, 'status incongruence' denotes that the rankings which a position bestows and/or receives on various hierarchies of power are not all equally high or low. It usually implies that a discrepancy exists between the power bestowed by the position in one context of activity and the power it bestows in another. A number of more or less interchangeable synonyms have been used to refer to status incongruence: status incongruency, lack of status crystallization, status inconsistency, lack of status harmony, low rank-equalization, etc.

When used in this sense, the term 'status' refers to any ranked position with normatively, and possibly legally, defined rights and duties, and not only to a ranked position in the status hierarchy of a society. The fact that 'status' and 'status incongruence' have come to refer mainly to the stratification hierarchies of a society (that is, to include both 'status position' and 'economic position', as I have used the terms above) probably reflects the general congruence between the two hierarchies in industrial societies. When using the concept of status incongruence in this way, however, one should specify the particular hierarchies involved. In other words, positions may be characterized by congruence or incongruence with respect to any number and kind of hierarchies. I am mainly concerned with the general hierarchies of stratification, i.e., the hierarchies of economic and status power, and with the more concrete hierarchies which comprise them, e.g., income and working conditions, on the one hand, and occupational prestige, on the other. It is worth mentioning that a position might bestow economic rewards which are generally congruent with its status rewards, but nonetheless bestow various economic rewards and status rewards, each set of which are themselves incongruent internally, and vice versa.

Although status incongruence or congruence usually refers to a property of a position, it can also refer to a property of a person. For example, an occupation can be considered as a position. To refer to the status incongruence of an occupation is to indicate that it bestows rewards in one hierarchy which are either higher or lower than the rewards which it bestows in another. It follows that a person who holds an incongruent occupation will be in an incongruent personal position; but a person who holds a congruent occupation might also be in an incongruent personal position. Occupations are not the only source of status and economic rankings. It is necessary to consider various other personal characteristics, which, although they are properties of persons and not of positions, derive their meaning and value from social organization and inter-personal expectations. For example, with respect to the status hierarchy, such properties as skin colour, amount of education, and even intelligence are likely to bestow status rewards independently. Each is likely to affect a person's occupational recruitment and allocation.

An important example is incongruence between a person's educational ranking as a status characteristic and the general status bestowal value of his occupation; if he has a lower educational ranking than that held by most of the people in his occupation, he may not be treated by others as if he were entitled to the full status bestowal value of his occupation; but, at the same time, he may experience satisfaction at having obtained an occupational position which exceeds what he might have expected to achieve on the basis of his educational ranking alone. Another example of personal status incongruence is that produced by membership in an ethnic group which bestows negative social honour, such as to be a Black in the United States or in England. To be a Black in either society sets limits on the status which can be obtained; no matter how much money a Black makes and no matter what the status bestowal of his occupation, there is a point in the status hierarchy which he cannot exceed. Of course, ethnic groups may have their own internal system of stratification which only partly coincides with that of the society generally; in this case, a Black might have an incongruent position in the larger society but a congruent one in his own group.

This raises the further point that status incongruence can refer to a property of a group as well as to a property of a position and of a person. For example, an entire ethnic group may be characterized by status incongruence. This is especially so when the distinguishing characteristics of the ethnic group are visible, such as skin colour. But whenever the distinguishing characteristic of the group has status bestowal value, it may involve the group in status incongruence, e.g., the status bestowal value of being Jewish will contribute to the status incongruence of a Jew's stratification position (but the status bestowal value of being Jewish varies with time and place). A member of a group which is characterized by status incongruence will also be in an incongruent personal position; however, a member of a group which is characterized by status congruence might nonetheless have an incongruent personal position on the basis of other criteria.

It is important to recognize that 'status incongruence' does not refer to the psychological condition of 'subjective identification' with the members of a class or status group which is either higher or lower than the class or status group in which one is regarded as an 'objective member'. The evidence suggests, however, that under certain conditions such a psychological response is common among those who are in positions characterized by status incongruence. In such cases, it is important to determine which statuses are mainly responsible for the person's identifications, and which for his memberships, as well as which patterns of incongruence violate the expectations of other people concerning the characteristics of the position in question.

In brief, a person's class position may not coincide with his class identifications, just as his status position may not coincide with his status identifications. The absence of an agreement between identifications and membership is an interesting phenomenon, which is often patterned among many people and not just a random personal occurrence, and which has structural as well as psychological antecedents and consequences.[7]

13. One way in which an occupation develops the characteristic of incongruence is that it may become necessary to pay the occupants more money when the occupation itself has negative status connotations, yet 'must be' done, e.g., assembly-line work; or to pay less when the job has positive status connotations, e.g., school teaching. Another source of status incongruence is that a core membership of a status group is likely to form over the generations; even when the occupational structure changes and economic circumstances are altered drastically, these cores often establish themselves within the new occupational hierarchy as relatively cohesive groups. Their status situation often becomes a characteristic of a given occupation, even though the criteria for status evaluation may change shortly after the occupational structure is altered. Consequently, certain occupations have come to be associated with a degree of positive or negative social honour, even though their apparent economic value to the society does not appear to be commensurate with their status bestowal value, and vice versa, e.g., a Professor of Classics at Cambridge, and certain types of assembly-line workers.

It is also true, however, that the core members of highly ranked status groups within the old status and economic hierarchies have usually been able to re-establish themselves as members of highly ranked status groups within the new hierarchies. In such cases they have been able to maintain their previous status authority, and to provide status continuity by absorbing selected members of the rising classes who were still constrained by the old status norms. In short, they are able to exploit their previous status authority, and to participate in the market in such a way as to utilize it as a form of capital, e.g., by going into Banking, the Law Courts, etc.

14. This consideration of concepts for the analysis of various properties of stratification in industrial societies would be incomplete without at least a comment on marginality. The concept of 'marginality' refers to a situation in which a person is not a full member of a well organized and supportive group, and, more precisely, that he is on the 'margin' of the social spaces of the groups involved. It is usually associated with social isolation and cultural estrangement, and under certain conditions, self estrangement and loss of personal identity. Observers who are themselves members of core status groups in the established and predominant status hierarchy often assume that all 'outsiders' are in marginal situations. However, this is not necessarily so. One sociologist who was concerned with the indiscriminate use of the concept has argued:

If (1) the so-called 'marginal' individual is conditioned by his existence on the borders of two cultures from birth, if (2) he shares the existence and conditioning process with a large number of individuals in his primary group, if (3) his years of early growth, maturation, and even adulthood find him participating in institutional activities manned largely by other marginal individuals like himself, and finally, if (4) his marginal position results in no major blockages or frustrations of his learned expectations and desires, then he is not a true 'marginal' individual in the defined sense, but is a participant member of a *marginal* culture, every bit as real and complete to him as is the non-marginal culture to the non-marginal man.[8]

In other words, when people recognize that they have certain characteristics in common, they often form their own supportive networks. When their common characteristics are visible, such as skin colour, or when they are 'voluntary', such as religion, this tendency is likely to be strong. Jews and Blacks, for example, have often formed their own sub-cultural networks, characterized by their own internal system of stratification, which is only partly articulated with that of the host society. Such people do not necessarily become 'marginal'. But when the members of such groups try to leave them and to enter other groups, marginality is likely to arise, and the conventional definition of marginal man is likely to hold: 'neither fish nor fowl'.

15. Before turning to a discussion of mobility processes, it would be helpful to mention a few hypotheses concerning the relationships among status rigidity, status incongruence, membership in a peripheral as opposed to a core status group, and marginality. By

definition, the greater the degree of status rigidity, the greater the degree of social distance between adjacent status groups, and between the periphery and the core of any given status group. In a society which permits and even encourages economic and occupational mobility, the greater the degree of status rigidity, the greater the extent and amount of positional, personal, and group forms of status incongruence, and the more is it likely that status incongruence will be associated with membership of a peripheral as opposed to a core status group. It is sometimes assumed that status incongruence and peripheral status group membership are characterized by marginality. This is likely to be so, however, only under certain conditions. When people in these situations have nothing in common other than their status incongruence and peripheral status position, they are more likely to become marginal; and the greater the degree of status rigidity, the greater the intensity and amount of their marginality.

II

Thus far the term 'mobility' has been used indiscriminately to mean, quite simply, the movement of a person or group from one ranked position in a given hierarchy or set of hierarchies to another ranked position in the same one or set of hierarchies. It is now necessary to consider the process more systematically. I have found it convenient to discuss mobility in terms of a number of its properties: unit, time span, direction, hierarchy, distance, and speed.[9]

(1) Unit

In industrial societies, sociologists are usually concerned with the mobility of an individual with respect to his position at a given time relative to the position he held at a previous time. However, because the nuclear family is usually treated as the basic unit of the stratification system (i.e. people become members of families of procreation) sociologists are also concerned with the mobility of groups, i.e., family units. Other types of groups can be mobile, but such processes are more common in non-industrial societies. For example, large and complex kinship groups are, under certain conditions, mobile as entire units; an individual member of a unit may move to a new position before other members, but he is unlikely to consider himself or to be considered by others as a full member of his new position until various other members of his kinship unit have also been mobile accordingly. In such a case the individual who is mobile first and furthest is likely to maintain his involvement and identification with his less mobile kin for a much longer time than is his individual counterpart in an industrial society. A more familiar example of group mobility is the movement of one stratum in a hierarchy relative to other strata in the same hierarchy, such as caste or subcaste mobility in India. In industrial societies, however, it is not uncommon for entire ethnic groups to be mobile relative to other ethnic groups, e.g., Irish Americans compared with Italian Americans, of Japanese Americans compared with Greek Americans, or Puerto Ricans compared with Negroes; in England it is likely that a similar process is occurring with Cypriots compared with Pakistanis. Group mobility in industrial societies, whether in small units such as a family or large ones such as ethnic groups, is almost always ascertained in terms of the mobility of individuals, specifically of individuals who are the heads of their households.

(2) *Time span*

In the first instance, mobility can usefully be classified as inter-generational or intra-generational. *Inter-generational* mobility refers to movement from a ranked position which a person inherits as a child to another ranked position which a person achieves in the course of his career. In most industrial societies, at least those in the West, a person begins his mobility from positions inherited from his father, who is the head of his own family of procreation but also of the person's family of orientation. Of course, some positions, or properties of them, are also inherited through the maternal line. Further, inter-generational mobility may refer to movement over more than two generations. One can use, for example, the peak position of a grandfather as the base line. In other words, a mobility profile may be constructed over several generations.

Intra-generational mobility refers to movement from a ranked position which a person has achieved in the course of his career to another ranked position which he has achieved at a later point in time. I do not consider as a mobility process a person's movement into an ascribed position which does not become available to him until he reaches a certain predetermined position in his life cycle, e.g., inheriting a title at a given age.

It is difficult but crucial to distinguish between inter- and intra-generational mobility. Although two generational comparisons are sufficient for most purposes, it is necessary to decide at what age to measure a person's position, and at what age to measure his father's position. If, for example, one takes the father's position at the birth of his son, one excludes the possibility that during the first decade of the son's life the father may yet achieve his own peak position,

And it is likely that for many research problems the father's peak position during the childhood of the son is more relevant than his position at the son's birth. Similarly, one must decide whether the peak position of the son or some other point within his own range of intra-generational achievements is required.

There is some evidence which indicates that during this century men have reached their peak occupational positions at approximately 35 years of age. Consequently, it would appear most useful if the full span of inter-generational mobility were indicated by the differences between the father's position at his 35th year and the son's position at his 35th year. Intra-generational mobility, in the first instance, could then be indicated by the differences among achieved positions within that range.

In addition to the phase in the personal and family life-cycle, it is useful to consider a person's mobility relative to that of his age cohort, and, under certain conditions and for certain problems, relative to that of his siblings. Due to demographic variables (such as differential fertility and morbidity at various levels of a given hierarchy), changes in the economic structure (such as economic growth generally, differentiation of occupations, the development of new occupations, etc.), and/or to patterns of immigration and emigration (such as Irish and Pakistanis coming to England as well as the brain-drain and moves to Australia), mobility may not produce changes in a person's position relative to that of his cohort or siblings, yet still produce changes relative to his father and/ or grandfather.

At present the available evidence does not permit generalizations concerning the social or personal consequences of mobility which is relative to a person's cohort or siblings as compared with those of mobility which is not. Insofar as interpersonal relationships are likely to be altered considerably during the period of mobility, whether or not a person's cohort are also mobile (e.g., a person's mobility process is likely to be 'idiosyncratic'), the difference between the two types of mobility processes may not be as great as would appear at first thought. Of course, in this connection, mobility relative to a person's siblings in a context in which the mobility of large kinship units is usual is more likely to demand special treatment.

(3) Direction

Mobility can be vertical, i.e., movement from one position to another which is either higher or lower in one or more hierarchies of power. Thus far I have been concerned only with vertical mobility.

But mobility can also be horizontal, i.e., from a position in one situs to a position in another which does not differ from the first in any but situs criteria. Mobility can also be both vertical and horizontal simultaneously, i.e., from a position in one situs to a position in another which is also either higher or lower in either or both economic and status rewards.

(4) *Hierarchy*

To the extent that various hierarchies of stratification are integrated (i.e., the criteria of power in any one hierarchy are either the same as or readily exchanged for the criteria of power in any other hierarchy), a person who is mobile in any one hierarchy will be mobile simultaneously in any other. When, for example, a stratification system consists primarily of social classes, the economic and status hierarchies are integrated, and, thus, mobility refers to a change in a person's or group's social class position. However, to the extent that various hierarchies are not integrated (i.e., the system contains certain patterns of status incongruence), it is possible for a person to be mobile in any one hierarchy but non-mobile in any other. For example, when the status and economic hierarchies are not integrated, a person can be mobile in the status hierarchy but non-mobile in the economic hierarchy, and vice versa.

The concept of 'occupational mobility' subsumes processes of this kind, and can, therefore, often be misleading. In industrial societies a person's occupation is the best single index of his social class position, and usually of both his economic and his status position. Because economic and status positions are determined by many factors in addition to occupation, and although occupation is closely related to such factors, occupation is not the only index of economic and status positions, and it is less than perfect with respect to each. This is especially so in other than large scale descriptive studies of the distribution of a population within the stratification system. Consequently, it should be recognized more widely than is so at present that under some circumstances occupational mobility is likely to indicate social class mobility, and, hence, both economic and status mobility; but under other circumstances it is likely to indicate only economic mobility or only status mobility or varying amounts of each. For example, a manual worker might take a white collar job and thereby improve his position in the status hierarchy, but remain non-mobile or even become downwardly mobile in the economic hierarchy. Similarly, a manual worker may raise his economic position through rises in income and improvements in working conditions, but remain a manual worker; in this case, he becomes upwardly mobile in the economic hierarchy, but non-mobile in the status hierarchy. In sum, status mobility and especially economic mobility can occur either separately or together, whether or not a person has changed his occupation.

The existence of peripheral and core status groups at various echelons in the status hierarchy is another reason why the concept of occupational mobility must be used with care. The relatively permanent core status groups become associated with various ranges or sets of occupations; membership of these respective cores represents the *potential* prestige of these associated occupations, but not the *actual* prestige of all the occupations. To hold a given occupation, therefore, is not automatically to obtain the potential prestige of the relevant core status group. Until a person becomes a member of the relevant core, he does not realize the potential prestige of the associated occupation, and he is likely to experience a discrepancy between his potential and his actual prestige. Similarly, a person from a given core status group who takes an occupation which is usually associated with a core status group at a lower echelon does not necessarily receive the actual prestige associated with his occupation. He may be able to maintain membership in his initial core status group, especially when the status hierarchy is characterized by rigidity. In short, it is necessary to look beyond a person's occupation, and not to confuse its indicatory value of membership in the status hierarchy with the membership itself.

The process of realizing potential prestige is most accurately described as the process of 'status legitimization'. It consists not only of raising one's status position to a level which approximates one's new economic position (a process which may or may not depend on one or more changes in an occupation), but also of realizing the potential prestige to which one has become 'entitled' through having changed one's occupation by becoming a full member of the relevant core status groups. In other words, status legitimization is a special case of status mobility generally. This legitimization process is not complete until all groups in the status hierarchy, both core and peripheral, rank the newcomer with as much consensus and in the same way as they would a non-mobile person in the same economic and occupational positions. It should be recognized that depending on a person's economic and occupational mobility, his process of status legitimization may involve either movement between status groups at different points in the status hierarchy or movement from a periphery to a core at only one status echelon, or both.

(5) *Distance*

The distance of mobility refers to the amount of status or social distance between a person's initial and adult status positions, or to the amount of economic distance between a person's initial and adult economic positions, or to both. Neither sociologists nor economists have invented a scale of social and economic distance for any one society, let alone a scale which could be used with two or more societies. We are able to measure status and economic positions, and especially the latter, in an ordinal way (i.e., we can rank them relative to one another), but we cannot say with much confidence that a move between any two ranks covers the same amount of status and economic distance as a move between any other two ranks. Consequently, for an actor or for the society, the meaning of mobility between any one set of ranks may differ from the meaning of mobility between any other set, and the consequences of the former are not necessarily those of the latter.

It is helpful, therefore, to distinguish at least between inter- and intra-class mobility with respect to ranks in the economic hierarchy, and between inter- and intra-status group mobility with respect to ranks in the status hierarchy. For status mobility, movement within either a periphery or a core can also be distinguished from movement from a periphery into a core and from a core into a periphery, within a given status group or between two or more of them. Of course, the distance of a person's mobility in any one hierarchy may be more than, equivalent to, or less than the distance of his mobility in any other.

One reason why even this approximate ordinal ranking may have little utility is that whether or not the status and/or economic distance between any one set of ranks differs from the distances between any other set of ranks, a comparison of the distance of one set with that of the other will necessarily involve the more fundamental comparison of the ranks themselves. For example, a comparison of the distance between the Lowest Social Class and the Lower Middle Social Class with the distance between the Lowest Social Class and the Upper-Middle Social Class permits the obvious observation that the former is less than the latter. But one must also take account of the fact that the adult position in the former pattern is in the Lower-Middle Social Class, and in the latter in the Upper-Middle. It is impossible to distinguish the effects of distance from those of the Social Classes themselves. It is likely that each pattern of mobility must be treated as an attribute, and comparisons among them interpreted in a very tentative way, partly in terms of distance and partly in terms of the component social classes.

(6) *Speed*

The speed of mobility refers to how long a person takes to move from one position to another. Generally, the greater the distance between any two positions, the longer the time the mobility will take. But this is not necessarily so; the speed depends on many other factors, and especially on the route. For example, it may take a person with little formal education longer to move from the Lowest Social Class to the Lower-Middle Social Class than it takes a person who has graduated from university to move from the Lowest Social Class to the Upper-Middle Social Class. Speed, then, is a property of a 'pattern of mobility or of non-mobility', and not of any one of its components.

III

Before mentioning a few hypotheses and observed empirical generalizations concerning mobility, status incongruence, membership in a peripheral as opposed to a core status group, marginality, and status rigidity, it is first necessary to distinguish mobility from several other processes, and to introduce the concept of 'life-trajectory', 'pattern of mobility and of non-mobility', and 'mobility route'.

(1) *Life-trajectory*

A 'life-trajectory' is a structured pathway through the society which an actor follows as he completes his life-cycle. At first thought, it would seem that an industrial society, because of its scale and complexity, has an almost infinite number of such pathways. Actually, due to the bureaucratization of educational and occupational roles and recruitment processes, the number of life-trajectories in an industrial society is relatively limited. Nonetheless, in addition to such obvious and overriding properties as occupational and educational routes, it is possible to specify many others, such as: the structure of the family of orientation (i.e., size, birth order, sex composition, and marital status of parents); ecology (i.e., the degree of urbanization of place of birth and early residence, density of population, and such neighbourhood conditions as housing, schooling, and delinquency rates); and the structure of the family of procreation (i.e., marital status, spouse mobility, number of children, etc.). Clearly, life-trajectories can be studied from many points of view, and with respect to many different research problems.

(2) *Pattern of Mobility or of Non-mobility*

A 'pattern of mobility or of non-mobility' is itself only one aspect or part of a life-trajectory. To define and identify a pattern of mobility or of non-mobility in an industrial society, at least the following four properties of life-trajectories must be selected: initial social class position, adult social class position, educational amount, and educational route. Each property can itself be considered in terms of a range of values, e.g., with respect to initial social class position, there are at least five social classes in England and the United States; and with respect to educational amounts, there are at least six formal steps after the minimum school leaving age in England, and at least as many informal ones in the United States. Consequently, a surprisingly large number of patterns can be identified from even a minimum number of values for these four properties. At a given period of time, such patterns can be compared with one another with respect both to other of their structural properties, and to the personal characteristics of the actors who have been constrained by them; and over a given period of time, they may be compared with themselves, both with respect to these factors and to those which might emerge as the society (of which they are themselves a part) continues to change.

(3) *Occupational Routes, Mobility Routes and Non-mobility Routes*

'Patterns of mobility and of non-mobility', 'educational routes', 'occupational routes', and 'mobility routes' are sometimes used in a confusing way. In all societies there are routes for the upwardly and downwardly mobile; such routes lead to various levels in the economic and status hierarchies, and are usually organised so that the mobile can acquire certain skills and other qualities which they will need in their adult positions, but which they could not have acquired either from their families of orientation or from others who are non-mobile from the same initial social class. In industrial societies, most occupations, and, hence, most economic and status positions, are filled by various mixtures of the mobile and non-mobile, and most routes to these occupations and positions are taken by various mixtures of the mobile and non-mobile. Of course, in some societies certain occupations attract primarily either the mobile or the non-mobile, and, hence, one might consider their respective recruitment routes as 'mobility routes' or as 'non-mobility routes'. Perhaps the Church, the Military and even Banks are, at particular times, examples of such mobility routes, while at other times they serve as examples of non-mobility routes.

(4) *Educational Routes, Mobility Routes and Non-mobility Routes*

In industrial societies it is the educational system which is concerned with the selection, training, and allocation of personnel to their adult occupational, economic, and status positions. The routes which both the mobile and the non-mobile take to their adult positions are organized within the context of the educational system. Consequently, although for some purposes it is meaningful to view the educational system and certain educational routes as the 'main channels for mobility', for others it is equally meaningful to view them as the 'main channels for non-mobility'; similarly, the educational system may be seen as a set of institutions which generate this kind of change in the society, or which contribute to its permanence and stability, or as a mixture of both. However, certain educational routes often become associated with particular initial social class positions, adult social class positions, and combinations of the two. When an educational route is characterized predominantly by a pattern of mobility or a pattern of non-mobility, it is reasonable to refer to it as a mobility route or as a non-mobility route, e.g., grammar schools or major public schools.

In this connection, it would be helpful to clarify the distinction between 'educational amount' and 'educational route'. A person who graduates from the University of Leicester has the same *amount* of education as a person who graduates from the University of Cambridge. Both will have spent the same number of years within the education system, and both will have the same formal qualifications. But they will have taken different educational *routes*. If the two routes were to involve the same sets of experience and the same types of preparation for adult social class positions, then a distinction between the two routes would have only nominal value. However, many aspects of one's life experiences depend on one's educational route. This is not to suggest that the effects of variation in the amount of education are less important. But failure to recognize the independent effects of educational routes, especially within a highly differentiated and specialized educational system, disguises the variation which exists in mobility experiences, and in the experiences of maturation generally. By way of illustration, it is worth noting that the distinction should also be made with respect to education in the United States. Although the educational routes there are not as formally differentiated and specialized as are the routes in England, one cannot deny that graduation from Harvard University represents a route which is very different from that represented by graduation from the University of Missouri. This is seldom recognized in the literature on social stratification and education.

(5) *Life-cycle, and career*

Another aspect or part of a life-trajectory is a 'life-cycle'. A life-cycle is usually viewed in terms of the physiological and psychological stages through which men progress from birth to death. It may also be viewed in terms of the role sets which are characteristic of each stage, and of the progressions between them. These are structural considerations, which have been treated primarily by anthropologists working in non-industrial societies: the passage-rite is perhaps the best known example. Both mobile and non-mobile people progress through their life-cycles, and in most societies the roles which characterize these various stages and progressions among them are not a function of mobility or non-mobility.

'Career' is a more general term which refers to a structured pathway among positions and roles which are ranked in terms of any given dimension, which may or may not be hierarchically structured. For example, one refers to an educational career, an occupational career, a family career, a moral career and a friendship career. Both mobile and non-mobile people have many types of career. They may be similar with respect to some careers, and different with respect to others. For example, the family of procreation careers of mobile people do not differ much from those of the non-mobile; but, obviously, the occupational careers of certain groups of mobile people differ from those of certain groups of non-mobile people, as well as from certain other groups of mobile people.

Careers may be compared with respect to many interesting properties, e.g., the 'orderliness and disorderliness' of friendship, residence, and occupational careers. The relationships between the orderliness and disorderliness of these careers and various patterns of mobility and of non-mobility have yet to be explored adequately.

A few hypotheses are now in order. The greater the degree of status rigidity, the more likely is mobility to be associated with personal status incongruence, usually in the form of an economic rank which exceeds a status rank. However, non-mobile people can also be in status incongruent personal positions. For example, a person can inherit an incongruent position from his father and be unable to reduce the incongruence during the course of his career; similarly, a person can inherit an incongruent position in the Lower-Middle Social Class, graduate from University, and nonetheless acquire an occupation which bestows a position in the Lower-

Middle Social Class, and, thus, be non-mobile in a status incongruent personal position.

The greater the degree of status rigidity, the more likely is mobility
to be associated with membership in peripheral as opposed to core
status groups. However, some non-mobile people may also be in
peripheral status groups.

Marginality is not automatically determined by mobility, and
thus, both mobile and non-mobile people may be in marginal
positions. However, the greater the degree of status rigidity, the
more likely are status incongruence and membership in peripheral
status groups to be associated with marginality. And, hence, to the
extent that non-mobile people have such positions, they are likely
to be characterized by marginality. But the greater the degree of
status rigidity: the more likely are mobile people especially to be
in status incongruent and peripheral positions; and the more likely
is the process of status legitimization to be difficult and lengthy.
Hence, the greater the degree of status rigidity, the more likely are
mobile people especially to be characterized by marginality.

1. The arguments concerning the effects of industrialization on family structure
often hide a simple fact: whether or not the nuclear family forms which exist in
the currently advanced industrial societies were produced by industrialization
processes, whenever industrialization *does* occur, there are marked tendencies
toward the reduction of the importance of the family system and toward the
emergence of a more simple kinship pattern. In other words, when the functions
of the extended family are reduced, there is a tendency for its member nuclear
units to become more important relative to the extensions. One of the most
important industrialization processes making for this pattern is the development
of a relatively autonomous occupational hierarchy in which the head of each
nuclear family is placed.

2. See J. H. Goldthorpe and D. Lockwood, 'Affluence and the British Class
Structure', *Sociological Review*, July, 1962.

3. The notions of 'core and peripheral status groups' are my own. But they are
implicit in N. Elias and J. L. Scotson, *The Established and the Outsiders*, London,
1965, and in Joel Smith, William H. Form, and Greg P. Stone, 'Local Intimacy
in a Middle Sized City', *A.J.S.*, 1954.

4. It is sometimes overlooked that in the first instance the meaning of an
occupational hierarchy is based on the properties and functions of occupations
in the society, and that the 'hierarchy' is a methodological construction based on
the properties of occupations. To study the occupational hierarchy in this sense
is primarily to illuminate the economic and status hierarchies, and not vice
versa.

5. One would ordinarily want to add the following paragraph, but I think that
it is more a statement of technological ideology than an empirical generalization.

In addition, the demands of the economy have made it increasingly necessary
for the labour force in general to receive a higher level of education. It has

become necessary to utilize all the 'natural talent' available. The application of norms of substantive rationality to the location, training, and recruitment of people with different types and amounts of 'natural talent' has *tended* to increase occupational mobility towards the limits established by the distribution of 'natural talent' in the society. Although the patterns of bias are still marked, especially with respect to certain class boundaries, the institutionalization of the educational system as the channel for mobility and the increasingly widespread belief that *class* bias is inimical to the principles of rationality upon which an industrial society is organized, have to a noticeable extent both decreased the rigidity of *class* boundaries and impeded their reformation.

It is still difficult to tell to what extent this is a hopeful assumption as opposed to an accurate description. Certainly the fact that mobility is now channelled through the educational system makes it more obvious, and, thus, it is rather too easy to argue that mobility is on the increase. But, at the same time, this is not the main point. I am arguing that whether or not mobility rates have changed, such rates are now more a function of status situation than of class situation, and that status situation no longer depends enough on class situation to permit one to be predicted from the other.

6. T. Parsons, 'A Revised Analytical Approach to the Theory of Social Stratification', in R. Bendix and S. M. Lipset (eds.), *Class, Status and Power*, Glencoe, 1954. Parsons, who defines social stratification as a system by which family units are ranked according to their 'social honour', or prestige, and who thus sees it primarily as the society's main source of integration, is unable to handle such a process within his conceptual framework.

7. It is worth pointing out in this connection that because status groups, status membership, and the status hierarchy are based on 'subjective' processes, i.e., the mental and emotional phenomena of values, norms, and beliefs, they are in no way less 'real' than classes, class membership, and the economic hierarchy. Although the latter are based on economic rewards which are relatively easy to measure and, in some cases, to see and to touch, they are not necessarily more constraining on a person's actions than the former.

This is why I am not in favour of the view which sees stratification in terms of 'subjective stratification' and 'objective stratification'. Nor do I think that there is much sense in the view that because status evaluations emanate from individuals, they are primarily psychological in origin. Clearly, people learn about the status system, and although other of their psychological properties may affect their need to identify with it and to use it in certain ways, it also exists 'outside' the psychic processes of any one person or group of persons.

8. Milton M. Goldberg, 'A Qualification of the Marginal Man Theory', *American Sociological Review*, 6, February 1941, pp. 52–8.

9. I am indebted to Clive Ashworth of the Department of Sociology, the University of Leicester, for his helpful comments on this section.

2

SOCIAL SELECTION IN THE WELFARE STATE[1]

T. H. Marshall

I will begin by defining my terms. There need be little ambiguity about 'social selection'. I take it to refer to the processes by which individuals are sifted, sorted and distributed into the various positions in the social system which can be distinguished one from another by their function, status, or place in the social hierarchy. I shall be considering, in this lecture, social selection through the educational system.

The Welfare State is a tougher proposition, because it would be difficult to find any definition acceptable both to its friends and to its enemies—or even to all its friends. Fortunately I needn't try to define it; I have only to explain what are the characteristics of the Welfare State which seem to me to provide a distinctive setting to the problem of social selection. I take the most relevant aspects of the Welfare State, in this context, to be the following.

First, its intense individualism. The claim of the individual to welfare is sacred and irrefutable and partakes of the character of a natural right. It would, no doubt, figure in the new Declaration of the Rights of Man if the supporters of the Welfare State were minded to issue anything so pithily dramatic. It would replace property in those early French and American Testaments which speak of life, liberty and property; this trinity now becomes life, liberty and welfare. It is to be found among the Four Freedoms in the guise of 'Freedom from Want'—but that is too negative a version. The welfare of

[1] The Galton Lecture delivered at a meeting of the Eugenics Society on 18 February 1953; reprinted from *Class, Citizenship and Social Development* (Garden City, N.Y.: Doubleday and Co., Inc., 1964), pp. 236–255, by permission of the author and the publisher.

the Welfare State is more positive and has more substance. It was lurking in the Declaration of Independence, which listed the inalienable rights of man as 'Life, Liberty and the Pursuit of Happiness'. Happiness is a positive concept closely related to welfare, but the citizen of the Welfare State does not merely have the right to pursue welfare; he has the right to receive it, even if the pursuit has not been particularly hot. And so we promise to each child an education suited to its individual qualities, we try to make the punishment (or treatment) fit the individual criminal rather than the crime, we hold that in all but the simplest of the social services individual case study and family case work should precede and accompany the giving of advice or assistance, and we uphold the principle of equal opportunity, which is perhaps the most completely individualistic of all.

But if we put individualism first, we must put collectivism second. The Welfare State is the responsible promoter and guardian of the welfare of the whole community, which is something more complex than the sum total of the welfare of all its individual members arrived at by simple addition. The claims of the individual must always be defined and limited so as to fit into the complex and balanced pattern of the welfare of the community, and that is why the right to welfare can never have the full stature of a natural right. The harmonizing of individual rights with the common good is a problem which faces all human societies.

In trying to solve it, the Welfare State must choose means which are in harmony with its principles. It believes in planning—not of everything but over a wide area. It must therefore clearly formulate its objectives and carefully select its methods with a full sense of its power and its responsibility. It believes in equality, and its plans must therefore start from the assumption that every person is potentially a candidate for every position in society. This complicates matters; it is easier to cope with things if society is divided into a number of non-competing social classes. It believes in personal liberty because, as I choose to define it, it is a democratic form of society. So although, of course, like all States, it uses some compulsion, it must rely on individual choice and motivation for the fulfilment of its purpose in all their details.

How do these principles apply to selection through the educational system? The general social good, in this context, requires a balanced supply of persons with different skills and aptitudes who have been so trained as to maximize the contribution they can make to the common welfare. We have, in recent years, seen the Welfare State estimating the need for natural scientists, social scientists and technicians, for doctors, teachers and nurses, and then trying to stimulate the educational system to produce what is required. It must also be careful to see that the national resources are used economically and to the best advantage, that there is no waste of individual capacities, by denying them the chance of development and use, and no waste of money and effort, by giving education and training to those who cannot get enough out of them to justify the cost.

On the other side, the side of individualism, is the right of each child to receive an education suited to its character and abilities. It is peculiar, in that the child cannot exercise the right for itself, because it is not expected to know what its character and abilities are. Nor can its parents wholly represent its interests, because they cannot be certain of knowing either. But they have a rather ambiguous right at least to have their wishes considered, and in some circumstances to have them granted. The status of parental rights in the English educational system is somewhat obscure at the moment. There is no reason to assume that the independent operation of the two principles, of individual rights and general social needs, would lead to the same results. The State has the responsibility of harmonizing the one with the other.

So far I have merely been trying to explain the general meaning which I have discovered in the title of this lecture. As I have already said, I shall first limit this broad field by concentrating on selection through the educational system. I shall then limit it further to the two following aspects of the problem. I shall look first at the selection of children for secondary education and try to see what is involved in bringing it into harmony with the principles of the Welfare State. I choose this particular point in the selection process partly because of its intrinsic and often decisive importance, and partly because so much has recently been written about it. I shall look in the second place rather at the social structure and consider how far it is possible to achieve the aims of the Welfare State in this field—particularly the aim of equal opportunity—in a society in which there still exists considerable inequality of wealth and social status. In doing this I shall be able to draw on some of the still unpublished results of researches carried out at the London School of Economics over the past four years, chiefly with the aid of a generous grant from the Nuffield Foundation.

Selection for secondary schools

We are all, I expect, aware that for some time past educationists (both teachers and administrators) and psychologists and statisticians (I sometimes find it hard to distinguish the one from the other) have been hurling themselves at the problem of selection for secondary schools with a determination and a ferocity of purpose which are positively terrifying. A good general survey of the campaign can, I think, be extracted from four sources. There is first the Report of the Scottish Council for Research in Education, *Selection of Secondary Education*, presented by William McClelland in 1942. This is an impressive document which might be described as a bold and challenging advance by the forces of pure science and exact measurement. It was met and held in check by a counter-attack delivered by the National Union of Teachers in its Report *Transfer from Primary to Secondary Schools*, published in 1949. Meanwhile there had opened, in June 1947, a friendly contest conducted under strict tournament rules in *The British Journal of Educational Psychology*, in the form of the 'Symposium of the Selection of Pupils for Different Types of Secondary Schools', which continued until February 1950. It was richly informative, and contained a little bit of everything. Finally we have the two Interim Reports of the Committee of the National Foundation of Educational Research: *The Allocation of Primary School Leavers to Courses of Secondary Education*, published in 1950 and 1952. It is too soon to say exactly what position this new detachment will take up on the battlefield, but the wording of its title is highly significant when compared with that of the Symposium. 'Selection' has been replaced by 'Allocation' and 'types of secondary school' by 'courses of secondary education'.

The first point to note is that, in this matter of selection for secondary education, the State is in full command of the whole situation. It provides the primary schools which prepare children for the examination, it designs the secondary school system for which they are being selected, and therefore determines the categories into which they are to be sorted, and it invents and administers the tests. Such power is dangerous. It is easy in these circumstances to make sure that one will find what one is looking for, and it is, no doubt, gratifying to discover that one's artistic masterpiece had been faithfully copied by Nature. I find it unfortunate that, just as there are three main types of secondary school, so there are three types of ability with which educational psychologists juggle—g or general, t or technical and k or spatial. I am afraid people may come to regard this as evidence of collusion, when in fact, of course, the two trinities do not correspond.

The second point to note is that the principles of the 1944 Act, which I take to be the principles of the Welfare State, have not yet been put into effect. The Act, according to the N.U.T. Report, 'has given the problem of transference from the primary to the secondary school an entirely new form', which necessitates a thorough reassessment of our old methods of selection (p. 16). The profound change referred to is that from competitive selection of a few for higher things to allocation of all to suitable schools, or, as Kenneth Lindsay phrased it nearly twenty years before the Act, from 'selection by elimination' to 'selection by differentiation'.[1] When allocation is working fully, says the N.U.T., 'the situation ought not to arise in which it is impossible to send a child to the school most suited to his needs because there is no place available for him in a school of this kind' (p. 20). We are still a long way from this, and 'for the time being the sole certain indication for a modern school is unsuitability for a grammar or technical school' (p. 18).

I see danger lurking here too. If too long a time passes during which an ideal cannot be realized, it may become unrealizable—a myth, as it were, which has lost contact with the world of experience and which has never been through the testing which must lie between the blueprint and the finished machine. There is a danger, too, that we may imagine we are preparing the instruments for use in the new operation when in fact we are only perfecting those which are suited for use in the old. In the first Interim Report of the National Foundation there occurs the sentence: 'It is the procedure of competitive entry to grammar schools that has been responsible for the undue importance which has been attached to objective tests and to external examinations' (p. 62). Note 'external examinations', for there is something pretty fundamental there.

But the principle of allocation is not a new idea. It was implicit in the Act of 1918, which stated that sufficient provision must be made to ensure that no children are 'debarred from receiving the benefits of any form of education by which they are capable of profiting through inability to pay fees', and it has been steadily developing since that date. And the importance attached to objective tests and external examinations is not an old phenomenon which happens to have survived into the new age. It has grown side by side with the growth of the idea of allocation, and continued to grow after the passing of the 1944 Act.

The movement in the field of ideas towards allocation instead of selection, and the movement in the field of practice towards uniform general standardized testing, have been contemporaneous. I think, too, that any reader of the Symposium must be struck by the intense

[1] *Social Progress and Educational Waste*, p. 28.

interest shown in the possibility of devising objective tests accurate enough to be used for allocation on the basis of special aptitudes, as well as for selection on the basis of general ability. There are, of course, signs of movement in other directions among education authorities, such as the greater use made of cumulative school records and so on; and, as regards the Symposium, it must not be overlooked that Sir Cyril Burt opened boldly with the statement that the problem was 'administrative rather than psychological'.[1] This sounded very much like the old-fashioned rebuking the new-fangled, and no doubt some psychologists thought that he was letting the side down.

In all this I seem to see evidence of a clash between what I earlier referred to as the collectivist and individualist elements in the Welfare State. Allocation, interpreted along N.U.T. lines, represents unqualified individualism. The right of each child to receive the education best suited to its unique individual needs should not be inhibited by reference to the cost of providing the necessary schools and teachers nor to the demand in society at large for particular numbers of persons educated and trained in particular ways. But to the collectivist principle these limiting factors arise from rights of the community as a whole, which the Welfare State cannot ignore. And they may favour a provision of grammar school places which is less than the provision needed to accommodate all who could benefit from a grammar school education. As long as this happens, competitive selection will remain with us. How long that will be, I do not propose to guess. But, when selection is competitive, the authorities must reach a decision somehow, using the best means at their disposal. And they must be able to enforce the decision negatively (that is to say, the decision not to admit) against the wishes of the parent. When faced with the necessity of filling the last five places in a grammar school from twenty applicants, all backed by ambitious and determined parents, you may feel that the best means of selection are either to follow the mark order or to toss up. The public may prefer you to follow the marks, even though you know that in this border zone the verdict of the marks has no real validity. So the use of imperfect selection methods can be justified by the inadequacy of the educational system, as judged by the ideal of allocation.

But in my view, if allocation replaced selection, then no amount of improvement would make the tests sufficiently exact to carry the weight of decisions enforceable against parental wishes. For the question to be answered in each case would not be: 'Is this child

[1] *The British Journal of Educational Psychology*, Vol. XVII, June 1947, p. 57.

better suited to a grammar school than the other applicants? If so, we must tell the others we are full up.' But: 'What, as judged by absolute standards and without reference to competing claims, is the education best suited to this child's needs?' I feel convinced that, in the majority of cases, questions in this form will remain unanswerable by tests and examinations—unanswerable, that is, with the degree of assurance necessary before the answer can be made the basis of administrative action. So we should find, I think, that instead of allocation in the sense of the definitive assignment of each child to an appropriate school or course, we should have something more like an advisory service which left the responsibility of decision to the parents. And that, I understand, is what happens now in so far as the principle of allocation already enters into our system. And in support of the view that it *should* be so, I can quote, from the Symposium, Mr. Dempster of Southampton, who writes: 'The wishes of the parents are possibly the best guide at present available to selectors in deciding between grammar and technical school education.'[1]

This sounds in many ways a very attractive prospect, though we ought to know a little more about how parental wishes work before we acclaim it, and I shall have something to say on that later. But I fancy it conflicts with another aspect of the collectivist element in the Welfare State. The principle I have in mind is the one which says that all should be judged by the same procedure, as impartially and impersonally as possible, that favouritism and privilege must be eradicated, and also the effects of differing social environments on the critical turning-points in life. So far so good. The principle must be allowed to have full weight. There is one obvious point at which it favours objective tests. Because children come to their examination at 11 + from schools and neighbourhoods of very different quality, they cannot be judged by their attainments only; an attempt must be made to discover natural abilities which may have been frustrated by circumstances but may still be able to come to fruition if given a fair chance. But latent capacities are concealed, and something more scientific than a teacher's judgement or a school record is needed to reveal them.

But the collectivist principle goes farther, and sometimes assumes shapes which are more open to question. The doctrine of fair shares and equal opportunity sounds admirable, but it may become so distorted as to merit the cynical comment that fair shares means 'if we can't all have it, nobody shall', and that equal opportunity

[1] *The British Journal of Educational Psychology*, Vol. XVIII, November 1948, p. 130.

means 'we must all have an equal chance of showing that we are all equally clever'. And the present situation may encourage this type of distortion, if it leads us to regard competitive selection as a necessary evil. If the Welfare State is to bring its two principles into harmony it must conceive of the basic equality of all as human beings and fellow-citizens in a way which leaves room for the recognition that all are not equally gifted nor capable of rendering equally valuable services to the community, that equal opportunity means an equal chance to reveal differences, some of which are superiorities, and that these differences need for their development different types of education, some of which may legitimately be regarded as higher than others. The notion, therefore, that selection, even competitive selection, can be eliminated from our educational system seems to me to be a pipe-dream and not even a Utopian one.

Obstacles to equal opportunity

I will defer making any general comment until I have considered my second question, to which I now turn. This relates to another dilemma or antithesis inherent in the principles and structure of the Welfare State. It is the problem of establishing equal opportunity without abolishing social and economic inequality. I say this is inherent in the nature of the Welfare State because it is my opinion—which I do not propose to argue here—that the Welfare State, as we know it, must necessarily preserve a measure of economic inequality. This problem, therefore, is a permanent and not a transitory one.

One of the most striking passages in Kenneth Lindsay's well-known and far-sighted study of this question in the inter-war period is the quotation from Lord Birkenhead which runs: 'There is now a complete ladder from the elementary school to the university, and the number of scholarships from the elementary to the secondary school is not limited, awards being made to all children who show capacity to profit.'[1] This fantastic illusion was blown sky-high by Lindsay's book, and later studies showed that equality of educational opportunity was still a distant ideal at the outbreak of World War II. The research carried out at L.S.E. during the past four years, to which I have already referred, has drawn in more firmly the outlines of the picture and added some details. We can see pretty clearly what the situation was when the Welfare State took over and what were the obstacles it had to overcome.

This research included a 10,000 sample survey of persons aged

[1] Kenneth Lindsay: *Social Progress and Educational Waste*, p. 9.

18 and over in Great Britain in 1949. Mobility was examined on the basis of the seven-point scale of occupational status, widely known as the Hall-Jones scale, which had been prepared for this study. Groups 1 and 2 include the professional and managerial occupations, and groups 3 and 4 the supervisory and clerical— to give a rough idea of their character. Together they comprised about 30 per cent. of the sample, which can be called the middle-class section (the upper class is too small to appear in a sample of this size). Group 5, including routine non-manual and skilled manual jobs, was a very large one comprising 40 per cent., while groups 6 and 7, semi-skilled and unskilled manual, provided approximately another 30 per cent. Of the general picture I will say little; I would rather wait for the papers to be published with full statistical tables. But one or two points may be noted. We find that the social forces holding a son to the occupational group of his father are significantly strongest in groups 1 and 2 and weakest in group 5. We can summarize crudely by saying that money and influence count for most at the top, and life's chances lie most widely open, for good or ill, in the melting-pot in the middle of the scale. This is interesting, because it is at this middle point in the scale that we might expect to find many families ambitious for their children's future and ready to forgo their earnings while they get secondary and further education, but not in a position to pay fees. It is precisely among such families that the building of an educational ladder is likely to have the greatest effect.

The second point of relevance in the general picture is that the returns show what to many may be a surprising amount of downward movement. There is a common saying, which in the United States has had the force of a political dogma, that 'there is plenty of room at the top'. And one remembers benevolent members of the upper layers of society who have strongly advocated the building of a social and educational ladder under the impression, apparently that it could carry one-way traffic only, and that the ascent of the deserving from below would not have to be accompanied by a descent on the part of any of their own children to make room for the newcomers. But if we take all the male subjects in the sample, we find that 35·2 per cent. had the same occupational status as their father, 29·3 per cent. had risen and 35·5 per cent. had fallen. These figures probably exaggerate the falls because they include the young men in the sample who had not yet reached their final occupational level, and, of course, they tell us nothing of the distance risen or fallen, which is an important factor. The believers in one-way traffic thought the upper- and middle-class jobs were increasing faster than jobs in general, while upper- and middle-class families were producing fewer children than families in general. But it seems clear, and the 1951 census sample confirms this, that this was true, as regards middle-class jobs in general, only of women's employment. The proportion of occupied men in such jobs showed no significant increase from 1911 to 1951, while the proportion of occupied women in such jobs rose approximately from 24·5 per cent. to 45·5 per cent. There was some increase in clerical jobs for men, but even here the spectacular advance was in the employment of women. In 1947, to quote one illustrative case, of those leaving secondary grammar schools at the age of sixteen to go straight into jobs, just about 43 per cent. of the boys went into the 'clerical and professional' category and of the girls 68 per cent., or, if nursing is included, nearly 77 per cent. Since there was an expansion of grammar schools during this period, and since grammar schools were largely an avenue to middle-class jobs, these facts are interesting. There may have been many boys who hitched their wagon to a white collar without realizing that their most serious competitors were their own sisters.

The educational data in the survey confirm and extend the picture presented in 1926 by Kenneth Lindsay. The most interesting general lesson to be drawn is that it is harder than one might suppose to ensure that the new opportunities created go to the people for whom they are intended, provided the fundamental principles of a free democracy are preserved. The survey covered the period of the introduction and expansion of the Free Place system in secondary schools, and its successor, the Special Place system, and it is possible to compare the experience of the first wave of entrants following the Act of 1902 (those born from 1890 to 1899) with the last pre-war wave (those born from 1920 to 1929). In the period covered by this comparison the percentage of boys in families belonging to the top three occupational groups who went to grammar schools rose from 38·4 to 45·7, and the corresponding figures for group 5 (the skilled manual and routine non-manual workers) are 4·1 and 10·7. The percentage increase for the working-class group is much greater than for the middle-class group, but the inequality that remains is enormous. And it is still greater if one includes boarding schools. The reason for this was not only that the total provision was insufficient, but also that a considerable part of the benefit went to the middle classes. It is true that the proportion of children in grammar schools who are occupying free places increases as you go down the social scale. But the proportion of the whole company of children of an occupational group who hold free places in grammar schools is highest at the top, 13·2 per cent. in status groups 1 and 2 (upper middle class) and 5 per cent. in group 5 (upper working class). I have picked these pieces of information from the analysis which Mrs. Floud has made of this part of the survey and which contains many more points of equal interest.

My point is this. It may look at first sight as if the *bourgeoisie* had, as usual, filched what should have gone to the workers. But, in the circumstances, that was bound to happen in a free democracy and is bound to go on happening in the Welfare State. For the Welfare State is not the dictatorship of the proletariat and is not pledged to liquidate the *bourgeoisie*. Of course more and more middle-class families made use of the public elementary schools as the quality of these improved, and of course more and more of them competed for admission to secondary schools through free and special places. And since the children were backed by a better educational tradition and stronger parental support, because more of their families could afford to forgo the earnings of the children, because they came from more comfortable homes, where it was easier to work, and from smaller families, they were certain to be more successful. And when it came to deciding as to remission of fees for special places, many of the middle-class families had a genuine claim. Today, with the 100 per cent. free place system in maintained schools, there can be no question of discriminating against middle-class families, and the competitive advantages of social and economic status can operate without check. Other inquiries conducted at the L.S.E., either within or in close relation to the main project, have begun to throw some light on the nature and extent of these competitive advantages.[1]

That there is a greater preponderance of working-class children in the modern schools today and of middle-class children in the grammar schools is a fact which no one is likely to dispute. In an article in the March 1953 issue of *The British Journal of Sociology*, Messrs Halsey and Gardner produce evidence to show that, in the London areas they studied, this uneven distribution could not be attributed solely to the intelligence of the children, but must be in large part the result of social forces. When, for instance, comparison was made of two groups with the same mean I.Q., one of which had been assigned to a grammar school and the other to a modern school, it was found that the middle classes were heavily over-represented and the working classes, especially the unskilled families, heavily under-represented in the grammar school group. It is

[1] The work has been done by Dr. Hilde Himmelweit, Mr Martin and their associates. Since the information has been collected in intensive local studies it cannot be used for generalization of any kind as yet.

also interesting that of working-class children in grammar schools in the areas studied 63 per cent. came from small families with one or two children and 37 per cent. from larger families with three or more. Among working-class children in modern schools the proportions were almost exactly the reverse, and among middle-class children there was no significant relation between type of school and size of family. No known correlation between fertility and intelligence could possible explain this, and it is clear that powerful social influences are at work. And they show themselves in other ways. A similar, though less marked, correlation with size of family appears when we ask how much thought parents give to their children's school career, how much interest they show in their work and progress, and how ambitious they feel about their future. Here, then, is a social factor causing what might be called 'unfairness' in social selection about which the Welfare State can do very little. Positive action, by improving the physical conditions in poorer families and by stimulating greater interest and ambition among apathetic parents, can only be a very slow process. Family differences will continue to have their influence as long as the family is the basic cell in the social structure.

Social ambition and educational achievement

The interest of parents may be shown by their giving thought to the matter of secondary schooling for their children. In one county area parents of children about to sit for the examination for secondary schools were asked whether they had thought a lot, a little or not at all about the matter. The proportion claiming to have thought a lot declined steadily as one moved down the social scale and was little over a third among the unskilled workers. But the preference for a grammar school education, though it showed the same trend, did not fall so low. The lowest proportion preferring the grammar school was 43·4 per cent. and the highest preferring the modern school 23·9 per cent.—these figures being those for unskilled workers. But over two-thirds of the unskilled worker parents preferring the grammar school did not want their child to stay there after the age of sixteen. Their ambitions were limited. And about half the professional and a quarter of the clerical families said that if their child did not get a grammar school place they would not send it to a modern school.

The picture is slightly distressing. It suggests that those who care about education, and some who do not care much, almost automatically aspire to a grammar school for their children; but the aspirations may vary from the desire of a steady job, with good prospects, to be entered at sixteen, to the hope of admission to a university and a professional career. There cannot be much homogeneity of purpose in a grammar school population. And, looking at the other side of the picture, we find a low opinion of the modern school which to many appears as a catastrophe and a disgrace. Talk of 'parity of esteem' is a little premature.

Now these likes and dislikes owe something, no doubt, to real or supposed differences in the quality of education received in the different types of school. But I doubt whether most parents are following the advice of the N.U.T. to concentrate on the 'present educational needs of the child' and not to think too much 'what these needs may be at some later stage in his development'.[1] They are thinking of what the school may lead to in the way of employment or further education, and perhaps of what it stands for in terms of social prestige. This last point is one on which it is extremely hard to get reliable information, since much of the mental processes involved may be only semi-conscious. If social status is not offered by the questioner as a possible reason for aiming at a particular school or job, it is not likely to be put down spontaneously; if it is offered, it may score a fair number of votes, but less than such job attributes as good prospects, security and interesting work. Another cause of difficulty is the lack of uniformity in the use of class names. People differ widely in the way they classify themselves or typical occupations as middle or working class, and it is clear that the term 'lower middle class' is becoming abhorrent. But, in spite of this, there is fairly close agreement as to the order in which jobs should be ranked, even though there is disagreement as to the social class to which they should be assigned.

The material dealing with job ambitions is too complicated to be briefly surveyed in an intelligible form. So I shall confine myself to two points. In a sample of adults in two urban areas who were asked what occupation they would like their son to enter, more than a fifth of the working-class subjects chose a profession and less than 8 per cent. a clerical job; the commonest choice (about 36 per cent.) was for a skilled trade. The figures are not complete, as a good many said their son must choose for himself. In the middle-class section of the sample, clerical jobs were even less popular, and the total vote for independent business was practically negligible. A similar dislike of the sound of clerical and office jobs was found by Dr Jahoda among school-leavers in Lancashire—that is to say, among

[1] Report of the National Union of Teachers: *Transfer from Primary to Secondary Schools*, p. 20.

the boys. The girls put office work at the top of the list. When boys were asked what jobs they most definitely rejected, office work was the one most often chosen, but half of those who named it did so because they did not think they were qualified for it.[1] It would be very rash to jump to conclusions from such fragmentary evidence, but it does seem possible that office work is losing its charm. It is often described as dull and monotonous and perhaps the rise in wages for manual work and familiarity with conditions of full employment are robbing it of some of its other former attractions.

The second point of interest is the clear evidence, at present confined to one area, that working-class boys who get into grammar schools have very high expectations that they will rise in the world, while middle-class boys in modern schools are inclined to expect to fall below the position of their parents. No less than 63 per cent. of the boys of lower working-class origin in grammar schools expected to rise at least two steps on a five-point status scale above their fathers; only 12 per cent. of their comrades in the modern schools were equally ambitious. But, if we measure the rise by the boys' own estimate of it and not by objective standards, the percentage falls from 63 to 21. This inquiry was reported in Dr Himmelweit's article in *The British Journal of Sociology*, June 1952. It suggests that the boys themselves feel that selection for secondary schooling has a decisive effect on future careers, and that boys from the humbler working-class families who get into grammar schools may overrate their chances without fully realizing how ambitious their success has made them. So long as this is the case, 'parity of esteem' is hardly possible.

Effects of social distance

My last point relates to the possible effects of social distance on life in a grammar school. Grammar schools, one might say, have a tradition, an educational atmosphere, and contacts with the world outside which have for some time past belonged to the way of life of the middle classes. And the middle classes are over-represented in the school population, even though the skilled working-class families may supply the largest absolute numbers. If, then, we introduce boys and girls from outside this circle, can they fit in? Can they become sufficiently assimilated to enter into the life of the school and get out of it what it has to give, and yet retain enough of their identity to break down, in the course of time, any class barriers which

[1] *Occupational Psychology*, Vol. xxvi, pp. 132–134.

exist, and thus make the way easier for their successors, and for the Welfare State? Much study is needed before this question can be fully answered. We have evidence to show that middle-class boys in grammar schools (in the area studied) do better on average in class examinations in pretty well all subjects than working-class boys, and that, when teachers are asked to rank the boys in their class in terms of such things as industry, responsibility, interest in school affairs, good behaviour, and popularity, the middle-class boys do definitely better than the rest. And working-class boys are inclined to care less about their marks and to take less part in general school activities, and yet, as we have seen, they expect great results from their grammar school status when the time comes for them to get a job. On the other hand may not a school have an assimilating influence and mould its members into a more homogeneous group than they were to start with, thus producing in reality the category of children which until then existed only in the imagination of the selectors? That is a question which points the way to a fascinating piece of research which has hardly yet been begun.

The Americans have similar problems today, and there is much evidence of status-consciousness in the high schools of the United States. The book *Who Shall Be Educated?*, by Lloyd Warner, (Havighurst and Loeb 1946), is a revelation on this point. We hear a junior high school principal say: 'You generally find the children from the best families do the best work. The children from the lower class seem to be not as capable as the others,' and on this the authors comment that 'this correlation holds true. There is a strong relationship between social status and rank in school.' A teacher then says that there is a lot of class feeling in the schools. 'Sections [i.e. streams] are supposed to be made up just on the basis of records in school but it isn't [*sic*] and everybody knows it isn't. I know right in my own A section I have children who ought to be in B section, but they are little socialites and so they stay in A', and there is much more in the same strain (p. 73). But the problem there is allocation between streams or courses, rather than between schools.

It was on this general question that Sir Cyril Burt made one of his most challenging remarks. 'A realistic policy', he wrote, 'must take frankly into consideration the fact that a child coming from this or that type of home may as a result be quite unsuited for a type of education, occupation or profession, which lies at an excessive 'social distance' from those of his parents and friends.'[1] Whereupon Dr Alexander descended on him like a ton of bricks, saying that no Authority could act on the view 'that the present social circumstances

[1] *The British Journal of Educational Psychology*, Vol. XVII, June 1947, p. 67.

of a child should be a criterion limiting his future opportunity.'[1] Undoubtedly he is right. No Authority can act on the principle that social circumstances must limit educational opportunity, but in fact they do, and the accepted methods of educational selection cannot wholly prevent this. The remedy lies in the reduction of 'social distance'.

Conclusions

I must now try to sum up. The Welfare State, as I see it, is in danger of tying itself in knots in an attempt to do things which are self-contradictory. One example, I submit, is the proposal to assign children to different schools, largely on the basis of general ability, and then to pretend that the schools are all of equal status. If this means that we shall take equal trouble to make all schools as good as possible, treat all the children with equal respect and try to make them all equally happy, I heartily endorse the idea. But the notion of parity of esteem does not always stop there; and I feel it really is necessary to assert that some children are more able than others, that some forms of education are higher than others, and that some occupations demand qualities that are rarer than others and need longer and more skilled training to come to full maturity, and that they will therefore probably continue to enjoy higher social prestige.

I conclude that competitive selection through the educational system must remain with us to a considerable extent. The Welfare State is bound to pick the children of high ability for higher education and for higher jobs, and to do this with the interests of the community as well as the rights of the children in mind. But the more use it can at the same time make of allocation to courses suited to special tastes and abilities the better. It further seems to me that, for the purpose of selection on grounds of general ability, the objective tests are already accurate enough to do all that we should ever ask of them to do, while, so far as 'allocation' is concerned, they will never be able to give a decisive verdict in more than a minority of cases, although they can be of great value in helping to decide what advice to give.

So I agree with Sir Cyril Burt that the problem which now faces us is more administrative than psychological. There is less to be gained by trying to perfect the tests and examinations than by thinking how to shape the structure of our educational and employment systems. It is better to minimize the effects of our decisions in doubtful cases than to imagine that, if we only try hard enough,

[1] Ibid., November 1947, p. 123.

we can ensure that all our decisions in such cases are correct. The word 'correct' has no meaning in this context; it is a bureaucratic fiction borrowed from the office where there is a correct file for every document.

By 'minimize the effects of our decisions' I mean refrain from adding unnecessary and artificial consequences to acts whose real meaning and necessary consequences I have been urging that we should frankly recognize. A system of direction into distinct 'types of secondary school' rather than 'courses of secondary education' (to use the titles I quoted earlier) must, I think, intensify rather than minimize the consequences. I am aware of the educational arguments on the other side, but do not intend to enter into a controversy for which I have no equipment. The other point at which artificial consequences may be added is the point of passage from education to employment. The snobbery of the educational label, certificate or degree when, as often, the prestige of the title bears little or no relation to the value of the content, is a pernicious thing against which I should like to wage a major war.

There is another matter on which the Welfare State can easily try to follow contradictory principles. It relates to occupational prestige, social class and the distribution of power in society. All I can do is to throw one or two raw ideas at your heads as a parting gift.

Although the Welfare State must, I believe, recognize some measure of economic inequality as legitimate and acceptable, its principles are opposed to rigid class divisions, and to anything which favours the preservation or formation of sharply distinguished culture patterns at different social levels. The segregation when at school of those destined for different social levels is bound to have some effect of this kind and is acceptable only if there are irrefutable arguments on the other side. Further, a system which sorts children by general ability and then passes them through appropriate schools to appropriate grades of employment will intensify the homogeneity within each occupational status group and the differences between groups. And, in so far as intelligence is hereditary and as educational chances are influenced by family background (and I have produced evidence to show that they are), the correlation between social class and type of school will become closer among the children.

Finally, the Welfare State, more than most forms of democracy, cannot tolerate a governing class. Leadership and power are exercised from many stations in life, by politicians, judges, ecclesiastics, business men, trade unionists, intellectuals and others. If these were all selected in childhood and groomed in the same stable, we should have what Raymond Aron calls the characteristic feature of a totalitarian society—a unified *élite*.[1] These leaders must really belong to and represent in a distinctive way the circles in and through which their power is exercised. We need politicians from all classes and occupational levels, and it is good that some captains of industry should have started life at the bench, and that trade unions should be led by genuine members, men of outstanding general ability who have climbed a ladder other than the educational one. It is important to preserve these other ladders, and it is fortunate that the selection net has some pretty big holes in it. It is fortunate too, perhaps, that human affairs cannot be handled with perfect mechanical precision, even in the Welfare State.

[1] *The British Journal of Sociology*, March 1950, p. 10.

3

DOMINATION AND ASSERTION IN EDUCATIONAL SYSTEMS*

Margaret Scotford-Archer & Michalina Vaughan

Through comparative study of the development of English and French education in the first half of the nineteenth century, it became clear that no theory which endorsed one or more of the following assumptions could account for such institutional change at the macro-sociological level:

(a) That complex institutional relations between education and social structure are exclusive to the post-industrial period (incompatible with French data).

(b) That some aspect of economic development is directly responsible for reducing the autonomy of education (incompatible with English data).

(c) That institutional secularization is closely related to industrialization (incompatible with both).

Furthermore a theory capable of interpreting educational change in this context must take into account the existence of profound educational conflict without either assimilating the parties involved to conflicting social classes (Marxist tendency) or attributing to the values involved some order of ascendancy and subordination according to social needs (structural-functionalist tendency). Because it complies with this criterion, an extension of the Weberian framework is a more useful approach to developing a theory of educational change in pre-state 'systems'.

From Max Weber

While Weber does not develop a systematic theory of education

* Based on *Social Conflict and Educational Change, 1780–1850*, to be published by CUP in 1971. An early version of this text was published in *European Journal of Sociology*, IX (1968), pp. 1–11.

in his work, his studies of bureaucracy, religion and status provide the main elements from which it can be extracted. Thus in his discussion of Confucianism, he suggests a tripartite classification of educational types based on the two characteristics of control and content of instruction:

CLASSIFYING CHARACTERISTICS	TYPE OF EDUCATIONAL SYSTEM		
	A	B	C
Content	Heroic/ magical	Cultivation	Specialized expert training
Control	Charismatic	Traditional	Rational-bureaucratic

Source: H. H. Gerth and C. Wright Mills, Eds., *From Max Weber*, London 1967, p. 240–44 and 426–34.

At one polar extreme, the education which corresponds to the charismatic structure of domination seeks to awaken various latent possibilities—heroic qualities or magical gifts, for these can neither be inculcated by teaching nor developed by training. The intermediate pattern 'attempts to educate a cultivated type of man, whose nature depends on the decisive stratum's respective ideal of cultivation'.[1] The traditional group who dominates this form of education may be either religious or secular. At the other extreme, the bureaucratic structure of domination develops 'specialized and expert schooling (which) attempts to *train* the pupil for practical usefulness for administrative purposes—in the organization of public authorities, business offices, workshops, scientific or industrial laboratories, disciplined armies'.[2] All three are ideal types which may overlap and rarely occur in a pure form.

Weber attributes the transition from 'cultivation' to 'specialized expert training' to 'the irresistibly expanding bureaucratization of all public relations of authority'.[3] However, while this expansion is presented as unavoidable, it can be delayed and modified by either the prevalence of a democratic ideology hostile to meritocratic selection and to the status distinctions it entails, or by an intensification of in-service training as a substitute for educational reform. Weber himself acknowledged that in establishing the compatibility between bureaucratic structure and specialized education he has not provided a complete theory of educational change. Thus the processes by which domination over education is removed from the Church

and this institution becomes integrated with the bureaucratic structure are left unclear. 'Behind all the present discussions of the foundations of the educational system, the struggle of the "specialized
type of man" against the older type of "cultivated man" is *hidden
at some decisive point*.'[4] The essential aspect of educational change
is to be found in conflict, in 'struggle' between groups and between
ideas. It is to this interplay of groups and ideas within the social
structure that Weber attributes institutional change—the contribution of both these elements being regarded as partially independent.
Such interaction is inextricably bound up with a process of struggle
for domination in society.[5] Either a dominant group and its ideology
seek to retain their position by controlling other groups and by
attempting to eradicate their ideas through the universalization of
its own. Or alternatively the supremacy of a dominant group and its
ideology is being successfully challenged by competing groups
advancing different ideas.

Various types of groups can achieve institutional domination—
ranging from classes and status groups to political groupings,
organizations and associations. Such groups may overlap and may
be characterized as voluntary or compulsory, as communal or aggre-
gate. This plurality negates the polarization of conflict posited by
Marx, as well as its uniquely economic content, and is therefore
better able to account for the multiple forms of educational conflict.
The essential characteristic of any group dominating an institution or
a society is the possession of a monopoly. Hence the economically
dominant class enjoys unique opportunities for capital accumula-
tion by virtue of its monopoly of property,[6] but this is merely a
special case of the acquisition of a monopoly in an economic context.
'Monopoly exists as soon as a group imposes a closed-door policy,
within variable limits, in order to enhance its opportunities as against
those on the outside. . . . The idea of monopoly, therefore, should not
be taken in the current polemical and ideological sense, as used by
those whose purpose is to discredit a certain form of capitalism.
For the trend toward monopoly is not bound up with any particular historical, economic and social structure.'[7] The very existence of
status groups is dependent upon the monopolization of attributes,
albeit valued on irrational grounds, which confer upon their members the exclusive right to social honour. 'Stratification by status
goes hand in hand with monopolization of ideal and material goods
or opportunities, in a manner we have come to know as typical.
Besides the specific status honour, which always rests upon distance
and exclusiveness, we find all sorts of material monopolies. . . . This
monopolization occurs positively when the status group is exclus-

ively entitled to own and manage them; and negatively when, in order to maintain its specific way of life, the status group must *not* own and manage them.'[8] Similarly the definition given to a State is based upon a monopoly: 'a compulsory political association with a continuous organization will be called a "State" if, and in so far as, its administrative staff successfully claims the monopolization of the legitimate use of physical force in the enforcement of its authority'.[9] In all these cases, the monopoly on which domination is based should be distinguished from further monopolization derived from it. Domination unavoidably results in constraints and the counterpart of the monopoly enjoyed by some is the exclusion of others. The imposition of constraints and the enforcement of exclusion are the objects of social control which is, when unsuccessful, the source of conflict in relation to specific institutions. In both cases, conflict may consist in either Communal or Social action.[10]

However, while monopolies can be successfully exploited through reliance on force, domination will be more secure and more efficient if a general justifying ideology can be invoked by the dominating and accepted by the subordinate group, thus transforming power into authority. In fact Weber uses the terms 'authority' and 'domination' as largely synonymous and differentiates them from the power arising from an unlegitimated monopoly.[11] 'Thus Weber emphasized both the organization that implements and the beliefs that sustain a given system. ... His study of domination stresses the importance of group formation *and* of beliefs. In Weber's view beliefs in the legitimacy of a system of domination are not merely philosophical matters. They can contribute to the stability of an authoritarian relationship, and they indicate very real differences between systems of domination.'[12] Not only can ideas serve to consolidate domination, but also to further the assertive claims of a competing group. 'Each society is a composite of positively or negatively privileged status groups that are engaged in efforts to preserve or enhance their present "style of life" by means of social distance and exclusiveness and by the monopolization of economic opportunities. In order to understand the stability and dynamics of a society we should attempt to understand these efforts in relation to the ideas and values that are prevalent in the society; or, conversely, for every given idea or value that we observe we should seek out the status group whose material and ideal way of life it seeks to enhance.'[13] While they are far from being determined by material environment, the ideas adopted by a particular group are influenced by it and are necessarily related to the interests at stake. As groups compete for domination either in society or over an institution, so their ideas clash and any universally accepted ethic merely represents the outcome of past struggles.

Thus conflict is the obverse aspect of control over a social institution and both are part of a continuous process of interplay between the interests and ideas of competing groups, summarized as follows:

PHASES OF PROCESS FROM ASSERTION T_1 TO ASSERTION T_2			
ASSERTION T_1	TRANSITION	DOMINATION	ASSERTION T_2
Status group A & its ideas compete with other groups & ideas	Status group A gains power & seeks to institutionalize its ideas	Status group A becomes dominant & its ideas universal	Status group B & its ideas challenge dominant group A & ideas

This table is an over-simplification of the process, since assertion does not necessarily culminate in domination, which in turn can prove remarkably stable and resist counter-assertion for centuries. Similarly periods of transition may be very long.

While retrospectively the interplay of groups and their ideas competing for domination over educational institutions can be reconstructed on the basis of Weber's notions of monopoly and ideology, these do not allow for any predictive statement and do not constitute a theory of change. His historical studies describe the unfolding of conflict culminating either in the overthrowal or in the continuation of domination over an institution. A theory with predictive power would need to specify and quantify the main prerequisites of successful domination and successful assertion. In the following pages it is hoped to supplement the elements supplied by Weber to specify more closely the factors involved in successful domination and assertion. This can perhaps be seen as a mid-way stage between his formulation and the development of a predictive theory of institutional change.

Towards a theory of educational change

Seeking to extend Weber's insights into institutional change at the macro level is inextricably related to a study of the structural relations of education. This derives from the simple, but often forgotten, fact that education has always been characterized by low autonomy as a social institution. The earliest types of informal instruction were integrated with the family and tribe while the emergence of formal education throughout Europe involved its integration with religion. This means that it would be exceptional to detect in history a group dominating education which itself was strictly 'educational'—in the same sense that at different times the groups dominating religious, legal and military institutions have often been the clerical, juridical and army elites. The very fact that the concept of giving education 'for its own sake' emerged so late in European history witnesses to its subordination to other social institutions and to the aims of their dominant groups.

Because of the low historical autonomy of formal instruction, a theory of educational change of necessity goes beyond this institution to the extent to which it is integrated with others. Similarly, the groups dominating education will not be narrowly educational any more than those which challenge them through assertion. While the main concern is to specify the factors ensuring the domination of a group over the social institution of education, these may at times coincide with those required for social domination—defined as domination over the main institutions of society. However, when education is semi-autonomous (i.e. largely unintegrated with such institutions), the group dominating it will tend to be distinct from the ruling group in society. Correspondingly, assertion need not then involve attacks upon the ruling group and may even be aided by it, where the goals of assertion are perceived as approximating more closely to its own needs than those of the dominant group.

It should also be remembered that the notion of an educational system, involving hierarchically integrated levels of institutions, is comparatively recent. Before such a system is established, domination may be pluralistic, different groups controlling different levels or types of institutions. In this case, various levels may be integrated with a variety of social institutions, and assertive groups may attempt to gain control over one rather than all levels. Thus it is only when an integrated educational system exists that domination must be unitary, although of course a single group can control all levels without these being regarded, or operating, as a system in the usual sense of the word.

In this brief discussion of education and its relationships to social structure, the area in which concepts of domination and assertion are applicable has also been defined. As has been seen, when an educational system exists, the dominant group must be unitary and, when the factors required for its domination coincide with those ensuring social domination, the discussion of educational control in these terms ceases to be relevant. In other words, when an educational system becomes integrated with the State, it is irrelevant to discuss domination and assertion, since both activities become subsumed under a broader model of changes in political power of different groups and parties.

It must be underlined that the possession of political power by a group is not synonymous with their educational domination, since education may not be integrated to the State for two major reasons. Firstly, the dominant political group may see no advantages to be derived from controlling education. They may either view the education dispensed by a separate dominant group as perfectly adequate—as most political elites during the middle ages considered instruction given by the Church—or they may be willing to allow educational control to be decided by the free interplay of domination and assertion. There are certain advantages accruing to the State from the latter policy in that competing groups may considerably extend educational provisions in the process, and do so from their own funds. Secondly, the political elite may seek to integrate education with the State, but lack the facilities required for deposing the existing dominant group and constituting a State educational system. Therefore it is only upon the emergence of such a system that changes in political power subsume those of domination and assertion.

Following Max Weber, domination in this context has been defined as the opportunity to have a command concerning education obeyed by a given group of persons. By assertion is meant the sum of efforts made by another group—denied the opportunity of making commands concerning education—to challenge the existing form of domination. The dominant group is successful both when it remains unchallenged and when it overcomes challenge. Although the former situation is characterized by the absence of educational conflict, it is not necessarily identical with the unanimity described as consensus. Prolonged educational stability corresponds to the lasting domination of a particular group and the successful resolution of conflict in its favour. While minor forms of educational change may be initiated independently by the dominant group in accordance with its changing interests, major changes in goals and content result from the conflict between dominant and assertive groups—either through the success of the latter or the concessions gained by the former. However, the changing structural relations of education with other social institutions usually result from successful assertion against an existing form of domination. It is therefore by investigating the main prerequisites of successful domination and assertion that one can account for educational stability and change at the macro-sociological level.

A group whose domination over education proves lasting is characterized by three main factors. Firstly, the dominant group must possess a *monopoly* of certain scarce resources in society, scarcity being relative to time and place. Monopoly is used in the Weberian sense and does not carry exclusively economic connotations. When education is semi-autonomous, this monopoly will be connected with owning and providing the facilities—material and human—for imparting instruction. However, when education is multiply integrated with other social institutions, the resources monopolized will tend to become less specifically educational, but it is not until an educational system is fully integrated with the State that the monopoly required for its domination coincides with the legal right of control vested in the governing political group or party. Here of course this group will not own or provide educational facilities either corporately or through its members.

The second feature of successful domination is that, for monopolies to be fully advantageous, they must be allied to *constraints* ensuring the acquiescence of other groups to their existence and exercise. Such constraints may range from economic or legal sanctions to the use of coercive or repressive force. While these constraints need not be specifically educational, their consequences reinforce domination over this institution. Again, the more integrated education is with other social institutions, the more general will be the types of constraints employed. The nature of the dominant group's monopoly will act as a predisposition towards the types of negative sanctions available and employed. Hence a Church, unless established, will tend to rely solely on symbolic constraints to protect its educational domination. Some constraints, however, are common or available to all dominant groups and these are constituted by the ways in which educational institutions themselves can be manipulated. Discrimination against other groups or their exclusion from education, the use of instruction for indoctrination and the imposition of non-academic requirements for entry or examination can all serve to consolidate the domination of a particular group by promoting its supporters and penalising its potential critics or those likely to challenge its monopoly. Legal constraints will only be available to those groups either whose educational domination is sanctioned by the State or who themselves also control the State machinery. While methods of constraint need not actually be employed, it is unlikely for a group to remain dominant over time without at least threatening to use such methods. It would be even more rare to identify a dominant group not manipulating the educational institutions to reinforce its own position.

Thirdly, a complementary *ideology*, legitimating the monopolistic claims of a group and justifying pressures for the maintenance of its domination, is indispensable to gaining the willing conformity rather than the forced compliance of others. It is always in the interest of the dominant group to gain willing collaboration from those they dominate, since this ensures greater efficiency as well as stability. The universalization of an ideology will transform a system of control by power into one of legitimate authority. A dominant group can be legitimated by reference to any type of ideology, but—following Weber—the justifying ideas endorsed by such a group will be consonant with its interests and with its monopoly. The very fact of control over educational institutions facilities the dissemination of an ideology; however, it is rare to find a newly dominant group relying on this method alone, since its results are too long-term. Buttressing the position of dominant groups, ideologies either replace the use of constraint or, if they are less successful, justify its employment.

In outlining the three factors, *Monopoly, Constraints* and *Ideology*, an attempt has been made to specify the necessary conditions for successful institutional domination. Successful domination is measured by the ability to resolve conflict or quell opposition, and therefore to endure. While only monopoly appears essential to the *achievement* of domination, constraint and ideology seem vital to its *maintenance*. Indeed, the latter two elements may in some cases only be developed or acquired after a group has become dominant. For example, it is rare for a status group to possess any formal powers of constraint until it has established its control over a particular institution. Similarly, other groups, such as military ones, do not develop or at least refine an ideology until domination has been established. Monopoly is also related to the other two factors in that it always affects, though it does not determine, the forms taken by constraint and ideology, and in turn is supported by them. In addition, Constraint and Ideology will tend to be mutually reinforcing where the dominant group is successful—the type of constraints employed will be compatible with at least the fundamental ideological postulates, while the ideology will seek to legitimate not only the dominant group, but also the methods it uses or may have to use to maintain its position. These relationships can be expressed as in Fig. 1.

It should be stressed that the connecting lines represent influences, not determinants, and that these factors, even when interrelated in this ideal form, are probably far from constituting the sufficient conditions of successful domination.

Conflict over a social institution need not prove ultimately damaging to the dominant group or modify the targets of its policy. Constraints and ideological pressures may be sufficient to contain or eliminate opposition. If they fail to do so, changed institutional relations will be the outcome. Obviously, change within the institution is not always produced by inter-group conflict within a society

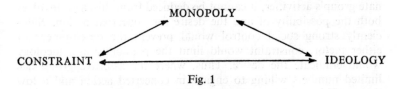

Fig. 1

—it may be prompted by forces external to it or by natural phenomena, or be initiated independently by the dominant group itself. However, excluding these cases, institutional change will be effected through conflict with an opposing group possessing certain attributes. Again, only the necessary conditions of successful assertion are advanced. Any form of assertion by a group implies a position of subordination within the institution concerned—successful challengers to the dominant group must overcome the three factors on which its supremacy rests. To assert itself successfully, the subordinate group must engage in activities *instrumental* in devaluing the existing monopoly, either by restricting or by replacing it. Thus the instrumental activities of an assertive group are defined as the sum of actions in which it can or does engage to devalue the particular monopoly on which domination is based in the given institution. This devaluation can take two forms: substitution or restriction. The former consists in replacing the scarce resource which the institutionally dominant group monopolized by an alternative resource or by discovering another source of supply. Where education is a semi-autonomous social institution, and consequently the dominant group's monopoly is largely educational, this substitution takes the form of providing alternative educational facilities. Where education is highly integrated with other institutions, and consequently the dominant group's monopoly is largely supra-educational, substitution can occur in a greater variety of fields, according to the area in which this monopoly is located.

However, instrumental activities alone do not suffice for successful assertion. A group must not only engage in them, but should also possess *bargaining power* to be successful. Bargaining power is an alternative to the use of violence and yet implies a degree of organization which would make revolt effective, if reform were denied. The prospect of success or failure is related to the two components of bargaining power—numerical strength and organization. The conjunction of these two elements is indispensable to the success of pressures upon the dominant group, in order to make it relinquish some of the advantages related to its position. Although bargaining power is dependent upon the instrumental character of the subordinate group's activities, it cannot be deduced from this, as it involves both the possibility of and the desire for concerted action. Sufficiently strong social control would prevent the development of either factor, constraint would limit the possibility and ideology would eradicate the desire. Thus, where the assertive group has limited numbers willing to engage in concerted action and a low degree of internal organization, while the dominant group has a strong and highly organized portion of its membership engaged in applying constraints, domination is likely to prove stable. Numerical and organizational variations in both groups partially account for their relative degrees of success. However, this interplay is influenced by the alliances either group can form in order to acquire wider support for either domination or assertion.

Finally, the ideology of the dominant group has to be challenged and replaced by a separate philosophy legitimating the claims and activities of the assertive group. Hence this new *ideology* must be both a negation and an affirmation. Acceptance of such a counter-ideology by an assertive group will be related to its interests and will influence the form taken by its instrumental activities, as well as the degree of intensity of its members' participation.

These three factors, *Instrumental Activities, Bargaining Power* and *Ideology*, are necessary, rather than sufficient, conditions of successful assertion. While some advantages may be gained from the existence of the first two, ideology is required both to inform the movement of its goals and to provide its members with a justification for the use of the bargaining power at their disposal. By definition, the development of an assertive ideology implies a recession in the philosophy informing social control, since this means that the latter is no longer universal. Such a recession results in a weakening of constraint, as the legitimation of assertive bargaining power strengthens opposition to the monopolistic group. Thus, in assertive action, instrumental activities, bargaining power and supportive ideology are related as in Fig. 2.

The outcome of a confrontation between a dominant and an assertive group depends upon the balance of factors present on both sides. There are two limiting cases: an unchallenged domination under which none of the factors of assertion exist in other groups and, on the other hand, a situation in which the three factors of domination are matched by the three factors of assertion. These extremes correspond to institutional stability and to overt institutional conflict. They also probably represent the limits of the predictive power deriving from this preliminary attempt at a theory of

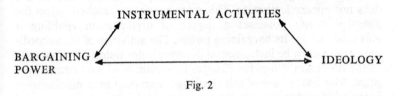

Fig. 2

educational change. When only some of the factors of successful assertion exist, for instance when the dominant group dependent on a particular monopoly possesses both means of constraint and an ideology, while the assertive group has only ideology, the outcome is clearly in favour of the former. Organized conflict rather than uncoordinated violence will result from a situation in which the three factors of domination are confronted by those of assertion. Such phases can be illustrated in the manner shown in Fig. 3.

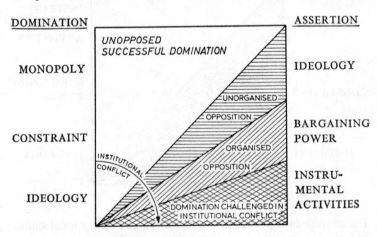

Fig. 3

When institutional domination is challenged, the first factor to weaken is ideology. This is self-evident since the existence of such a challenge implies that the dominant ideology no longer provides a universally acceptable legitimation of the status quo. However, the full crystallization of an alternative ideology need neither precede nor accompany this negation; while there may be a time-lag, this will not be a long one, since assertive activities require justification, both to those who engage in them and to onlookers. The second respect in which domination weakens is the power of constraint, which is no longer feared and increasingly challenged once its use does not appear legitimate. This stage cannot be reached unless the assertive group possesses a degree of organization enabling it effectively to use its bargaining power. The activities of the subordinate group must be instrumental in severely devaluing the monopoly of the dominant group for changes in institutional relations to take place. The final phase of this challenge is marked by a modification in the relationship between the monopoly of the dominant group and its institutional position. Depending on the restrictive or substitutive character of the assertive group's instrumental activities, their success will consist in either reducing or replacing this institutional domination. In the former case, educational change will result; in the latter, a change in institutional relations is also likely to occur. These relationships can be expressed in the manner shown in Figure 4.

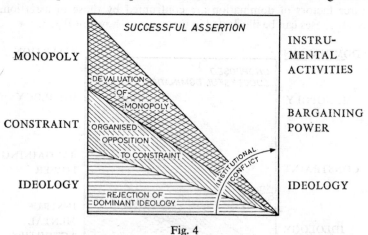

Fig. 4

The relationships posited above to account for institutional stability and change constitute no more than hypotheses requiring to be tested by reference to events. Furthermore, this discussion of domination and assertion, in only seeking to outline necessary, not sufficient, conditions for educational change, is far from constituting a fully predictive set of hypotheses.

In addition, special attention should be paid to *ideology* to account for the form and content given to education by the dominant group. Its interests could be served and its position maintained by a variety of institutional arrangements and practices, and the actual choice between them is not dictated by the nature of the group's monopoly. Similarly, the claims of an assertive group in respect to the content of educational reforms advocated are not fully determined by the nature of their instrumental activities. In both cases, it is by reference to the ideologies held that the more specific aspects of educational policy are defined.

Thus ideology is not only a component of successful domination and assertion, but also defines the means by which educational goals can be implemented. Therefore it not only functions as a source of legitimation for domination and assertion, but also as a wider educational philosophy for the dominant and assertive group. Bearing these points in mind, the ideology adopted by either type of group can be said to serve three distinct purposes—those of *legitimation*, *negation* and *specification*.

As has been seen, both the dominant and assertive groups must seek to *legitimate* their position to their followers as well as to a wider audience. This involves an appeal to certain principles consonant with the interests the group represents, but not derived automatically from them. Secondly, the same principles must be extended to constitute a *negation* of the sources of legitimation advanced by other groups. With an assertive group, this happens immediately since the claims of domination must be undermined before challenge is possible. It is because of this that assertive groups in their earliest stages may concentrate almost exclusively upon negation, that is upon unmasking or condemning the interests concealed by the ideology of the dominant group. However, a group whose domination has been unopposed over a long period may only begin to develop this negative function in proportion to the attacks launched at it. This is why the typical response of a well-established dominant group to new assertion is an immediate reformulation of its ideology, intended to strengthen its source of legitimation by extending it to negate the claims of other groups. Thirdly, a *specification* of the blue-print to be implemented within educational establishments, their goals, curricula and intake, must be derived from the same ideological principles.

References

1. H. H. Gerth & C. Wright Mills, Eds, *From Max Weber*, op. cit., pp. 426–7.
2. id., p. 426.
3. id., p. 243.
4. id., p. 243.
5. cf. M. Weber, *Basic Concepts in Sociology* (London, 1962), p. 117: 'By domination is meant the opportunity to have a command of a given specified content obeyed by a given group of persons.'
6. H. H. Gerth & C. Wright Mills, *From Max Weber*, op. cit., p. 181.
7. J. Freund, *The Sociology of Max Weber*, London 1968, p. 154–5.
8. H. H. Gerth & C. Wright Mills, *From Max Weber*, op. cit., p. 190–1.
9. M. Weber, *Basic Concepts in Sociology*, op. cit., p. 119.
10. cf. H. H. Gerth & C. Wright Mills, *From Max Weber*, op. cit., p. 183: 'Communal action refers to that action which is oriented to the feeling of the actors that they belong together. Societal action, on the other hand, is oriented to a rationally motivated adjustment of interests.'
11. cf. R. Bendix, *Max Weber. An Intellectual Portrait*, London 1960, p. 296, footnote 16.
12. id., p. 297.
13. id., p. 267.

4

SPONSORED AND CONTEST MOBILITY AND
THE SCHOOL SYSTEM*

Ralph H. Turner

This paper suggests a framework for relating certain differences between American and English systems of education to the prevailing norms of upward mobility in each country. Others have noted the tendency of educational systems to support prevailing schemes of stratificaton, but this discussion concerns specifically the manner in which the *accepted mode of upward mobility* shapes the school system directly and indirectly through its effects on the values which implement social control.

Two ideal-typical normative patterns of upward mobility are described and their ramifications in the general patterns of stratification and social control are suggested. In addition to showing relationships among a number of differences between American and English schooling, the ideal types have broader implications than those developed in this paper; they suggest a major dimension of stratification which might be profitably incorporated into a variety of studies in social class; and they readily can be applied in further comparisons between other countries.

THE NATURE OF ORGANIZING NORMS

Many investigators have concerned themselves with rates of upward mobility in specific countries or internationally,[1] and with

* This is an expanded version of a paper presented at the Fourth World Congress of Sociology, 1958, and abstracted in the *Transactions* of the Congress. Special indebtedness should be expressed to Jean Floud and Hilde Himmelweit for helping to acquaint the author with the English school system.

[1] A comprehensive summary of such studies appears in Seymour M. Lipset and Reinhard Bendix, *Social Mobility in Industrial Society*, Berkeley and Los Angeles: University of California Press, 1959.

the manner in which school systems facilitate or impede such mobility.[2] But preoccupation with the *extent* of mobility has precluded equal attention to the predominant *modes* of mobility. The central assumption underlying this paper is that within a formally open class system that provides for mass education the organizing folk norm which defines the accepted mode of upward mobility is a crucial factor in shaping the school system, and may be even more crucial than the extent of upward mobility. In England and the United States there appear to be different organizing folk norms, here termed *sponsored mobility* and *contest mobility*, respectively. *Contest* mobility is a system in which elite[3] status is the prize in an open contest and is taken by the aspirants' own efforts. While the 'contest' is governed by some rules of fair play, the contestants have wide latitude in the strategies they may employ. Since the 'prize' of successful upward mobility is not in the hands of an established elite to give out, the latter can not determine who shall attain it and who shall not. Under *sponsored* mobility elite recruits are chosen by the established elite or their agents, and elite status is *given* on the basis of some criterion of supposed merit and cannot be *taken* by any amount of effort or strategy. Upward mobility is like entry into a private club where each candidate must be 'sponsored' by one or more of the members. Ultimately the members grant or deny upward mobility on the basis of whether they judge the candidate to have those qualities they wish to see in fellow members.

Before elaborating this distinction, it should be noted that these systems of mobility are ideal types designed to clarify observed differences in the predominantly similar English and American systems of stratification and education. But as organizing norms these principles are assumed to be present at least implicitly in people's thinking, guiding their judgments of what is appropriate

[2] *Cf.* C. A. Anderson, 'The Social Status of University Students in Relation to Type of Economy: An International Comparison,' *Transactions of the Third World Congress of Sociology*, London, 1956, Vol. V, pp. 51–63; J. E. Floud, *Social Class and Educational Opportunity*, London: Heinemann, 1956; W. L. Warner, R. J. Havighurst, and M. B. Loeb, *Who Shall be Educated?*, New York: Harper, 1944.

[3] Reference is made throughout the paper to 'elite' and 'masses'. The generalizations, however, are intended to apply throughout the stratification continuum to relations between members of a given class and the class or classes above it. Statements about mobility are intended in general to apply to mobility from manual to middle-class levels, lower-middle to upper-middle class, and so on, as well as into the strictly elite groups. The simplified expressions avoid the repeated use of cumbersome and involved statements which might otherwise be required.

on many specific matters. Such organizing norms do not correspond perfectly with the objective characteristics of the societies in which they exist, nor are they completely independent of them. From the complex interplay of social and economic conditions and ideologies people in a society develop a highly simplified conception of the way in which events take place. This conception of the 'natural' is translated into a norm—the 'natural' becomes what 'ought' to be— and in turn imposes a strain toward consistency upon relevant aspects of the society. Thus the norm acts back upon the objective conditions to which it refers and has ramifying effects upon directly and indirectly related features of the society.[4]

In brief, the conception of an ideal-typical organizing norm involves the following propositions: (1) The ideal types are not fully exemplified in practice since they are normative systems, and no normative system can be devised so as to cope with all empirical exigencies. (2) Predominant norms usually compete with less ascendant norms engendered by changes and inconsistencies in the underlying social structure. (3) Though not fully explicit, organizing folk norms are reflected in specific value judgments. Those judgments which the relevant people regard as having a convincing ring to them, irrespective of the logic expressed, or which seem to require no extended argumentation may be presumed to reflect the prevailing folk norms. (4) The predominant organizing norms in one segment of society are functionally related to those in other segments.

Two final qualifications concerning the scope of this paper: First, the organizing folk norm of upward mobility affects the school system because one of the latter's functions is the facilitation of mobility. Since this is only one of several social functions of the school, and not the most important function in the societies under examination, only a very partial accounting of the whole set of forces making for similarities and differences in the school systems of United States and England is possible here. Only those differences which directly or indirectly reflect the performance of the mobility function are noted. Second, the concern of this paper is with the current dynamics of the situation in the two countries rather than with their historical development.

[4] The normative element in an organizing norm goes beyond Max Weber's *ideal type*, conveying more of the sense of Durkheim's *collective representation*; cf. Ralph H. Turner, 'The Normative Coherence of Folk Concepts', *Research Studies of the State College of Washington*, 25 (1957), pp. 127–136. Charles Wagley has developed a similar concept which he calls 'ideal pattern' in his as yet unpublished work on Brazilian kinship. See also Howard Becker, 'Constructive Typology in the Social Sciences', *American Sociological Review*, 5 (February, 1940), pp. 40–55.

DISTINCTIONS BETWEEN THE TWO NORMS

Contest mobility is like a sporting event in which many compete for a few recognized prizes. The contest is judged to be fair only if all the players compete on an equal footing. Victory must be won solely by one's own efforts. The most satisfactory outcome is not necessarily a victory of the most able, but of the most deserving. The tortoise who defeats the hare is a folk-prototype of the deserving sportsman. Enterprise, initiative, perseverance, and craft are admirable qualities if they allow the person who is initially at a disadvantage to triumph. Even clever manipulation of the rules may be admired if it helps the contestant who is smaller or less muscular or less rapid to win. Applied to mobility, the contest norm means that victory by a person of moderate intelligence accomplished through the use of common sense, craft, enterprise, daring, and successful risk-taking[5] is more appreciated than victory by the most intelligent or the best educated.

Sponsored mobility, in contrast, rejects the pattern of the contest and favours a controlled selection process. In this process the elite or their agents, deemed to be best qualified to judge merit, choose individuals for elite status who have the appropriate qualities. Individuals do not win or seize elite status; mobility is rather a process of sponsored induction into the elite.

Pareto had this sort of mobility in mind when he suggested that a governing class might dispose of persons potentially dangerous to it by admitting them to elite membership, provided that the recruits change character by adopting elite attitudes and interests.[6] Danger to the ruling class would seldom be the major criterion for choice of elite recruits. But Pareto assumed that the established elite would select whom they wished to enter their ranks and would inculcate the attitudes and interests of the established elite in the recruits.

The governing objective of contest mobility is to give elite status to those who earn it, while the goal of sponsored mobility is to make the best use of the talents in society by sorting persons into their proper niches. In different societies the conditions of competitive

[5] Geoffrey Gorer remarks on the favourable evaluation of the successful gamble in American culture: 'Gambling is also a respected and important component in many business ventures. Conspicuous improvement in a man's financial position is generally attributed to a lucky combination of industry, skill, and gambling, though the successful gambler prefers to refer to his gambling as "vision".' *The American People*, New York: Norton, 1948, p. 178.

[6] Vilfredo Pareto, *The Mind and Society,* New York: Harcourt, Brace, 1935, Vol. 4, p. 1796.

struggle may reward quite different attributes, and sponsored mobility may select individuals on the basis of such diverse qualities as intelligence or visionary capability, but the difference in principle remains the same.[7]

Under the contest system society at large establishes and interprets the criteria of elite status. If one wishes to have his status recognized he must display certain credentials which identify his class to those about him. The credentials must be highly visible and require no special skill for their assessment, since credentials are presented to the masses. Material possession and mass popularity are altogether appropriate credentials in this respect, and any special skill which produces a tangible product and which can easily be assessed by the untrained will do. The nature of sponsored mobility precludes these procedures, but assigns to credentials instead the function of identifying elite members to one another.[8] Accordingly, the ideal credentials are special skills that require the trained discrimination of the elite for their recognition. In this case, intellectual, literary, or artistic excellencies, which can be appraised only by those trained to appreciate them, are fully suitable credentials. Concentration on such skills lessens the likelihood that an interloper will succeed in claiming the right to elite membership on grounds of the popular evaluation of his competence.

In the sporting event there is special admiration for the slow starter who makes a dramatic finish, and many of the rules are designed to insure that the race should not be declared over until it has run its full course. Contest mobility incorporates this disapproval of premature judgments and of anything that gives special advantage to those who are ahead at any point in the race. Under sponsored mobility, fairly early selection of only the number of persons necessary to fill anticipated vacancies in the elite is desirable. Early selection allows time to prepare the recruits for their elite position. Aptitudes, inherent capacities, and spiritual gifts can be assessed fairly early in

[7] Many writers have noted that different kinds of societies facilitate the rise of different kinds of personalities, either in the stratification hierarchy or in other ways. *Cf.* Jessie Bernard, *American Community Behavior*, New York: Dryden, 1949, p. 205. A particularly interesting statement is Martindale's exploration of 'favoured personality' types in sacred and secular societies. Don Martindale and Elio Monachesi, *Elements of Sociology*, New York: Harper, 1951, pp. 312–378.

[8] At one time in the United States a good many owners of expensive British Jaguar automobiles carried large signs on the cars identifying the make. Such a display would have been unthinkable under a sponsored mobility system since the Jaguar owner would not care for the esteem of persons too uninformed to tell a Jaguar from a less prestigious automobile.

life by techniques ranging from divination to the most sophisticated psychological test, and the more naive the subjects at the time of selection the less likely are their talents to be blurred by differential learning or conspiracy to defeat the test. Since elitists take the initiative in training recruits, they are more interested in the latters' capabilities than in what they will do with them on their own, and they are concerned that no one else should first have an opportunity to train the recruits' talents in the wrong direction. Contest mobility tends to delay the final award as long as practicable to permit a fair race; sponsored mobility tends to place the time of recruitment as early in life as practicable to insure control over selection and training.

Systems of sponsored mobility develop most readily in societies with but a single elite or with a recognized elite hierarchy. When multiple elites compete among themselves the mobility process tends to take the contest pattern since no group is able to command control of recruitment. Sponsored mobility further depends upon a social structure that fosters monopoly of elite credentials. Lack of such monopoly undercuts sponsorship and control of the recruitment process. Monopoly of credentials in turn is typically a product of societies with well entrenched traditional aristocracies employing such credentials as family line and bestowable title which are intrinsically subject to monopoly, or of societies organized on large-scale bureaucratic lines permitting centralized control of upward social movement.

English society has been described as the juxtaposition of two systems of stratification, the urban industrial class system and the surviving aristocratic system. While the sponsored mobility pattern reflects the logic of the latter, our impression is that it pervades popular thinking rather than merely coexisting with the logic of industrial stratification. Patterns imported into an established culture tend to be reshaped, as they are assimilated, into consistency with the established culture. Thus it may be that changes in stratification associated with industrialization have led to alterations in the rates, the specific means, and the rules of mobility, but that these changes have been guided by the but lightly challenged organizing norm of sponsored mobility.

SOCIAL CONTROL AND THE TWO NORMS

Every society must cope with the problem of maintaining loyalty to its social system and does so in part through norms and values, only some of which vary by class position. Norms and values especially prevalent within a given class must direct behavior into channels that support the total system, while those that transcend strata must support the general class differential. The way in which upward mobility takes place determines in part the kinds of norms and values that serve the indicated purposes of social control in each class and throughout the society.

The most conspicuous control problem is that of ensuring loyalty in the disadvantaged classes toward a system in which their members receive less than a proportional share of society's goods. In a system of contest mobility this is accomplished by a combination of futuristic orientation, the norm of ambition, and a general sense of fellowship with the elite. Each individual is encouraged to think of himself as competing for an elite position so that loyalty to the system and conventional attitudes are cultivated in the process of preparation for this possibility. It is essential that this futuristic orientation be kept alive by delaying a sense of final irreparable failure to reach elite status until attitudes are well established. By thinking of himself in the successful future the elite aspirant forms considerable identification with elitists, and evidence that they are merely ordinary human beings like himself helps to reinforce this identification as well as to keep alive the conviction that he himself may someday succeed in like manner. To forestall rebellion among the disadvantaged majority, then, a contest system must avoid absolute points of selection for mobility and immobility and must delay clear recognition of the realities of the situation until the individual is too committed to the system to change radically. A futuristic orientation cannot, of course, be inculcated successfully in all members of lower strata, but sufficient internalization of a norm of ambition tends to leave the unambitious as individual deviants and to forestall the latters' formation of a genuine subcultural group able to offer collective threat to the established system. Where this kind of control system operates rather effectively it is notable that organized or gang deviancy is more likely to take the form of an attack upon the conventional or moral order rather than upon the class system itself. Thus the United States has its 'beatniks'[9] who repudiate ambition and most worldly values and its delinquent and criminal gangs who try to evade the limitations imposed by conventional means,[10] but very few active revolutionaries.

These social controls are inappropriate in a system of sponsorship since the elite recruits are chosen from above. The principal threat

[9] See, e.g., Lawrence Lipton, *The Holy Barbarians*, New York: Messner, 1959.
[10] *Cf.* Albert K. Cohen, *Delinquent Boys: The Culture of the Gang*, Glencoe, Ill.: Free Press, 1955.

to the system would lie in the existence of a strong group the members of whom sought to *take* elite positions themselves. Control under this system is maintained by training the 'masses' to regard themselves as relatively incompetent to manage society, by restricting access to the skills and manners of the elite, and by cultivating belief in the superior competence of the elite. The earlier that selection of the elite recruits is made the sooner others can be taught to accept their inferiority and to make 'realistic' rather than phantasy plans. Early selection prevents raising the hopes of large numbers of people who might otherwise become the discontented leaders of a class challenging the sovereignty of the established elite. If it is assumed that the difference in competence between masses and elite is seldom so great as to support the usual differences in the advantages accruing to each,[11] then the differences must be artificially augmented by dicouraging acquisition of elite skills by the masses. Thus a sense of mystery about the elite is a common device for supporting in the masses the illusion of a much greater hiatus of competence than in fact exists.

While elitists are unlikely to reject a system that benefits them, they must still be restrained from taking such advantage of their favorable situation as to jeopardize the entire elite. Under the sponsorship system the elite recruits—who are selected early, freed from the strain of competitive struggle, and kept under close supervision—may be thoroughly indoctrinated in elite culture. A norm of paternalism towards inferiors may be inculcated, a heightened sensitivity to the good opinion of fellow elitists and elite recruits may be cultivated, and the appreciation of the more complex forms of aesthetic, literary, intellectual and sporting activities may be taught. Norms of courtesy and altruism can easily be maintained under sponsorship since elite recruits are not required to compete for their standing and since the elite may deny high standing to those who strive for position by 'unseemly' methods. The system of sponsorship provides an almost perfect setting for the development of an elite culture characterized by a sense of responsibility for 'inferiors' and for preservation of the 'finer things' of life.

Elite control in the contest system is more difficult since there is no controlled induction and apprenticeship. The principal regulation seems to lie in the insecurity of elite position. In a sense there is no 'final arrival' because each person may be displaced by newcomers throughout his life. The limited control of high standing from above

[11] D. V. Glass, editor, *Social Mobility in Britain*, Glencoe, Ill.: Free Press, 1954, pp. 144–145, reports studies showing only small variations in intelligence between occupational levels.

prevents the clear delimitation of levels in the class system, so that success itself becomes relative: each success, rather than an accomplishment, serves to qualify the participant for competition at the next higher level.[12] The restraints upon the behavior of a person of high standing, therefore, are principally those applicable to a contestant who must not risk the 'ganging up' of other contestants, and who must pay some attention to the masses who are frequently in a position to impose penalties upon him. But any special norm of paternalism is hard to establish since there is no dependable procedure for examining the means by which one achieves elite credentials. While mass esteem is an effective brake upon over-exploitation of position, it rewards scrupulously ethical and altruistic behavior much less than evidence of fellow-feeling with the masses themselves.

Under both systems, unscrupulous or disreputable persons may become or remain members of the elite, but for different reasons. In contest mobility, popular tolerance of a little craftiness in the successful newcomer, together with the fact that he does not have to undergo the close scrutiny of the old elite, leaves considerable leeway for unscrupulous success. In sponsored mobility, the unpromising recruit reflects unfavorably on the judgments of his sponsors and threatens the myth of elite omniscience; consequently he may be tolerated and others may 'cover up' for his deficiencies in order to protect the unified front of the elite to the outer world.

Certain of the general values and norms of any society reflect emulation of elite values by the masses. Under sponsored mobility, a good deal of the protective attitudes toward and interest in classical subjects percolates to the masses. Under contest mobility, however, there is not the same degree of homogeneity of moral, aesthetic, and intellectual values to be emulated, so that the conspicuous attribute of the elite is its high level of material consumption—emulation itself follows this course. There is neither effective incentive nor punishment for the elitist who fails to interest himself in promoting the arts of literary excellence, or who continues to maintain the vulgar manners and mode of speech of his class origin. The elite has relatively less power and the masses relatively more power to punish or reward a man for his adoption or disregard of any special elite culture. The great importance of accent and of grammatical excellence in the attainment of high status in England as contrasted with the twangs and drawls and grammatical ineptitude among American elites is the most striking example of this difference. In a contest system, the class order does not function to support the

12 Gorer, *op. cit.*, pp. 172–187.

quality of aesthetic, literary, and intellectual activities; only those well versed in such matters are qualified to distinguish authentic products from cheap imitations. Unless those who claim superiority in these areas are forced to submit their credentials to the elite for evaluation, poor quality is often honored equally with high quality and class prestige does not serve to maintain an effective norm of high quality.

This is not to imply that there are no groups in a 'contest' society devoted to the protection and fostering of high standards in art, music, literature, and intellectual pursuits, but that such standards lack the support of the class system which is frequently found when sponsored mobility prevails. In California, the selection by official welcoming committees of a torch singer to entertain a visiting king and queen and 'cancan' dancers to entertain Mr. Khrushchev illustrates how American elites can assume that high prestige and popular taste go together.

FORMAL EDUCATION

Returning to the conception of an organizing ideal norm, we assume that to the extent to which one such norm of upward mobility is prevalent in a society there are constant strains to shape the educational system into conformity with that norm. These strains operate in two fashions: directly, by blinding people to alternatives and coloring their judgments of successful and unsuccessful solutions to recurring educational problems; indirectly, through the functional interrelationships between school systems and the class structure, systems of social control, and other features of the social structure which are neglected in this paper.

The most obvious application of the distinction between sponsored and contest mobility norms affords a partial explanation for the different policies of student selection in the English and American secondary schools. Although American high school students follow different courses of study and a few attend specialized schools, a major educational preoccupation has been to avoid any sharp social separation between the superior and inferior students and to keep the channels of movement between courses of study as open as possible. Recent criticisms of the way in which superior students may be thereby held back in their development usually are nevertheless qualified by the insistence that these students must not be withdrawn from the mainstream of student life.[13] Such segregation offends the sense of fairness implicit in the contest norm and also

[13] See, e.g., *Los Angeles Times*, May 4, 1959, Part I, p. 24.

arouses the fear that the elite and future elite will lose their sense of fellowship with the masses. Perhaps the most important point, however, is that schooling is presented as an opportunity, and making use of it depends primarily on the student's own initiative and enterprise.

The English system has undergone a succession of liberalizing changes during this century, but all of them have retained the attempt to sort out early in the educational program the promising from the unpromising so that the former may be segregated and given a special form of training to fit them for higher standing in their adult years. Under the Education Act of 1944, a minority of students has been selected each year by means of a battery of examinations popularly known as 'eleven plus,' supplemented in varying degrees by grade school records and personal interviews, for admission to grammar schools.[14] The remaining students attend secondary modern or technical schools in which the opportunities to prepare for college or to train for the more prestigeful occupations are minimal. The grammar schools supply what by comparative standards is a high quality of college preparatory education. Of course, such a scheme embodies the logic of sponsorship, with early selection of those destined for middle-class and higher-status occupations, and specialized training to prepare each group for its destined class position. This plan facilitates considerable mobility, and recent research reveals surprisingly little bias against children from manual laboring-class families in the selection for grammar school, when related to measured intelligence.[15] It is altogether possible that adequate comparative study would show a closer correlation of school success with measured intelligence and a lesser correlation between school success and family background in England than in the United States. While selection of superior students for mobility opportunity is probably more efficient under such a system, the obstacles for persons not so selected of 'making the grade' on the basis of their own initiative or enterprise are probably correspondingly greater.

That the contrasting effects of the two systems accord with the social control patterns under the two mobility norms is indicated

[14] The nature and operation of the 'eleven plus' system are fully reviewed in a report by a committee of the British Psychological Society and in a report of extensive research into the adequacy of selection methods. See P. E. Vernon, editor, *Secondary School Selection: A British Psychological Inquiry*, London: Methuen, 1957; and Alfred Yates and D. A. Pidgeon, *Admission to Grammar Schools*, London: Newnes Educational Publishing Co., 1957.

[15] J. E. Floud, A. H. Halsey, and F. M. Martin, *Social Class and Educational Opportunity*, London: Heinemann, 1956.

by studies of student ambitions in the United States and in England. Researchers in the United States consistently show that the general level of occupational aspiration reported by high school students is quite unrealistic in relation to the actual distribution of job opportunities. Comparative study in England shows much less 'phantasy' aspiration, and specifically indicates a reduction in aspirations among students not selected following the 'eleven-plus' examination.[16] One of the by-products of the sponsorship system is the fact that at least some students from middle-class families whose parents cannot afford to send them to private schools suffer severe personal adjustment problems when they are assigned to secondary modern schools on the basis if this selection procedure.[17]

This well-known difference between the British sorting at an early age of students into grammar and modern schools and the American comprehensive high school and junior college is the clearest application of the distinction under discussion. But the organizing norms penetrate more deeply into the school systems than is initially apparent. The most telling observation regarding the direct normative operation of these principles would be evidence to support the author's impression that major critics of educational procedures within each country do not usually transcend the logic of their respective mobility norms. Thus the British debate about the best method for getting people sorted according to ability, without proposing that elite station should be open to whosoever can ascend to it. Although fear of 'sputnik' in the United States introduced a flurry of suggestions for sponsored mobility schemes, the long-standing concern of school critics has been the failure to motivate students adequately. Preoccupation with motivation appears to be an intellectual application of the folk idea that people should *win* their station in society by personal enterprise.

The functional operation of a strain toward consistency with the organizing norms of upward mobility may be illustrated by several other features of the school systems in the two countries. First, the value placed upon education itself differs under the two norms. Under sponsored mobility, schooling is valued for its cultivation of elite culture, and those forms of schooling directed toward

[16] Mary D. Wilson documents the reduction in aspirations characterizing students in British secondary modern schools and notes the contrast with American studies revealing much more 'unrealistic' aspirations; see 'The Vocational Preferences of Secondary Modern School-children,' *British Journal of Educational Psychology*, 23 (1953), pp. 97–113. See also Ralph H. Turner, 'The Changing Ideology of Success,' *Transactions of the Third World Congress of Sociology, 1956*, London, Vol. V, esp. p. 37.

[17] Pointed out by Hilde Himmelweit in private communication.

such cultivation are more highly valued than others. Education of the non-elite is difficult to justify clearly and tends to be half-hearted, while maximum educational resources are concentrated on 'those who can benefit most from them'—in practice, this means those who can learn the elite culture. The secondary modern schools in England have regularly suffered from less adequate financial provision, a higher student-teacher ratio, fewer well trained teachers, and a general lack of prestige in comparison with the grammar schools.[18] Under contest mobility in the United States, education is valued as a means of getting ahead, but the contents of education are not highly valued in their own right. Over a century ago Tocqueville commented on the absence of an hereditary class 'by which the labors of the intellect are held in honor.' He remarked that consequently a 'middling standard is fixed in America for human knowledge.'[19] And there persists in some measure the suspicion of the educated man as one who may have gotten ahead without really earning his position. In spite of recent criticisms of lax standards in American schools, it is in keeping with the general mobility pattern that a Gallup Poll taken in April, 1958, reports that school principals are much more likely to make such criticisms than parents. While 90 per cent of the principals thought that '. . . our schools today demand too little work from the students,' only 51 per cent of the parents thought so, with 33 per cent saying that the work was about right and six per cent that schools demanded too much work.[20]

Second, the logic of preparation for a contest prevails in United States schools, and emphasizes keeping everyone in the running until the final stages. In primary and secondary schools the assumption tends to be made that those who are learning satisfactorily need little special attention while the less successful require help to be sure that they remain in the contest and may compete for the final stakes. As recently as December, 1958, a nationwide Gallup Poll gave evidence that this attitude had not been radically altered by the

[18] Less adequate financial provision and a higher student-teacher ratio are mentioned as obstacles to parity of secondary modern schools with grammar schools in *The Times Educational Supplement*, February 22, 1957, p. 241. On difficulties in achieving prestige comparable with grammar schools, see G. Baron, 'Secondary Education in Britain: Some Present-Day Trends,' *Teachers College Record*, 57 (January, 1956), pp. 211–221; and O. Banks, *Parity and Prestige in English Secondary Education*, London: Routledge and Kegan Paul, 1955. See also Vernon, *op. cit.*, pp. 19–22.

[19] Alexis de Tocqueville, *Democracy in America*, New York: Knopf, 1945, Vol. I, p. 52.

[20] An earlier Gallup Poll has disclosed that 62 per cent of the parents opposed stiffened college entrance requirements while only 27 per cent favored them. Reported in *Time*, April 14, 1958, p. 45.

international situation. When asked whether or not teachers should devote extra time to the bright students, 26 per cent of the respondents replied 'yes' and 67 per cent, 'no.' But the responses changed to 86 per cent 'yes' and only nine per cent 'no' when the question was asked concerning 'slow students.[21]

In western states the junior college offers many students a 'second chance' to qualify for university, and all state universities have some provision for substandard high school students to earn admission.

The university itself is run like the true contest: standards are set competitively, students are forced to pass a series of trials each semester, and only a minority of the entrants achieve the prize of graduation. This pattern contrasts sharply with the English system in which selection is supposed to be relatively complete before entrance to university, and students may be subject to no testing whatsoever for the first year or more of university study. Although university completion rates have not been estimated accurately in either country, some figures are indicative of the contrast. In American institutions of higher learning in 1957–1958, the ratio of bachelor's and first-professional degrees to the number of first-time degree-credit enrollments in the fall four years earlier was reported to be 0·610 for men and 0·488 for women.[22] The indicated 39 and 51 per cent drop-out rates are probably underestimates because transfers from two-year junior colleges swell the number of degrees without being included in first-time enrollments. In England, a study of the careers of individual students reports that in University College, London, almost 82 per cent of entering students between 1948 and 1951 eventually graduated with a degree. A similar study a few years earlier at the University of Liverpool shows a comparative figure of almost 87 per cent.[23] Under contest mobility, the object is to train as many as possible in the skills necessary for elite status so as to give everyone a chance to maintain competition at the highest pitch. Under sponsored mobility, the objective is to indoctrinate elite culture in only those who presumably will enter the elite, lest there grow a dangerous number of 'angry young men' who have elite skills without elite station.

Third, systems of mobility significantly affect educational content. Induction into elite culture under sponsored mobility is consistent

[21] Reported in the *Los Angeles Times*, December 17, 1958, Part I, p. 16.

[22] U.S. Department of Health, Education and Welfare, Office of Education, *Earned Degrees Conferred by Higher Education Institutions, 1957–1958*, Washington, D.C.: Government Printing Office, 1959, p. 3.

[23] Nicholas Malleson, 'Student Performance at University College, London, 1948–1951,' *Universities Quarterly*, 12 (May, 1958), pp. 283–319.

with an emphasis on school *esprit de corps* which is employed to cultivate norms of intra-class loyalty and elite tastes and manners. Similarly, formal schooling built about highly specialized study in fields wholly of intellectual or aesthetic concern and of no 'practical' value serves the purpose of elite culture. Under contest mobility in the United States, in spite of frequent faculty endorsement of 'liberal education,' schooling tends to be evaluated in terms of its practical benefits and to become, beyond the elementary level, chiefly vocational. Education does not so much provide what is good in itself as those skills, especially vocational skills, presumed to be necessary in the competition for the real prizes of life.

These contrasts are reflected in the different national attitudes toward university students who are gainfully employed while in school. More students in the United States than in Britain are employed part-time, and relatively fewer of the American students receive subsidies toward subsistence and living expenses. The most generous programs of state aid in the United States, except those applying to veterans and other special groups, do not normally cover expenses other than tuition and institutional fees. British maintenance grants are designed to cover full living expenses, taking into account parental ability to pay.[24] Under sponsored mobility, gainful employment serves no apprenticeship or testing function, and is thought merely to prevent students from gaining the full benefit of their schooling. L. J. Parry speaks of the general opposition to student employment and asserts that English university authorities almost unanimously hold that '. . . if a person must work for financial reasons, he should never spend more than four weeks on such work during the whole year.'[25]

Under contest mobility, success in school work is not viewed as a sufficient test of practical merit, but must be supplemented by a test in the world of practical affairs. Thus in didactic folk tales the professional engineer also proves himself to be a superior mechanic, the business tycoon a skilful behind-the-counter salesman. By 'working his way through school' the enterprising student 'earns' his education in the fullest sense, keeps in touch with the practical world, and gains an apprenticeship into vocational life. Students are often urged to seek part-time employment, even when there is

[24] See, e.g., C. A. Quattlebaum, *Federal Aid to Students for Higher Education*, Washington, D.C.: Government Printing Office, 1956; and 'Grants to Students: University and Training Colleges,' *The Times Educational Supplement*, May 6, 1955, p. 446.

[25] 'Students' Expenses,' *The Times Educational Supplement*, May 6, 1955, p. 447.

no financial need, and in some instances schools include paid employment as a requirement for graduation. As one observer describes the typical American view, a student willing to work part-time is a 'better bet' than 'the equally bright student who receives all of his financial support from others.'[26]

Finally, training in 'social adjustment' is peculiar to the system of contest mobility. The reason for this emphasis is clear when it is understood that adjustment training presumably prepares students to cope with situations for which there are no rules of intercourse or for which the rules are unknown, but in which the good opinions of others cannot be wholly ignored. Under sponsored mobility, elite recruits are inducted into a homogeneous stratum within which there is consensus regarding the rules, and within which they succeed socially by mastering these rules. Under contest mobility, the elite aspirant must relate himself both to the established elite and to the masses, who follow different rules, and the elite itself is not sufficiently homogeneous to evolve consensual rules of intercourse. Furthermore, in the contest the rules may vary according to the background of the competitor, so that each aspirant must successfully deal with persons playing the game with slightly different rules. Consequently, adjustment training is increasingly considered to be one of the important skills imparted by the school system.[27] That the emphasis on such training has had genuine popular support is indicated by a 1945 *Fortune* poll in which a national sample of adults was asked to select the one or two things that would be very important for a son of theirs to get out of college. Over 87 per cent chose 'Ability to get along with and understand people'; and this answer was the second most frequently chosen as the *very* most important thing to get out of college.[28] In this respect, British education may provide better preparation for participation in an orderly and controlled world, while American education may prepare students more adequately for a less ordered situation. The reputedly superior ability of 'Yankees' to get things done seems to imply such ability.

To this point the discussion has centred on the tax-supported school systems in both countries, but the different place and em-

[26] R. H. Eckelberry, 'College Jobs for College Students,' *Journal of Higher Education*, 27 (March, 1956), p. 174.

[27] Adjustment training is not a necessary accompaniment of contest mobility. The shift during the last half century toward the increased importance of social acceptability as an elite credential has brought such training into correspondingly greater prominence.

[28] Reported in Hadley Cantril, editor, *Public Opinion 1935–1946*, Princeton: Princeton University Press, 1951, p. 186.

phasis of the privately supported secondary schools can also be related to the distinction between sponsored and contest mobility. Since private secondary schools in both countries are principally vehicles for transmitting the marks of high family status, their mobility function is quite tangential. Under contest mobility, the private schools presumably should have little or no mobility function. On the other hand, if there is to be mobility in a sponsored system, the privately controlled school populated largely with the children of elite parents would be the ideal device through which to induct selectees from lower levels into elite status. By means of a scholarship program, promising members of lesser classes could be chosen early for recruitment. The English 'public' schools, in fact, have incorporated into their charters provisions to insure that a few boys from lesser classes will enter each year. Getting one's child into a 'public' school, or even into one of the less prestigeful private schools, assumes an importance in England relatively unknown in the United States. If the children cannot win scholarships the parents often make extreme financial sacrifices in order to pay the cost of this relatively exclusive education.[29]

How much of a role private secondary schools have played in mobility in either country is difficult to determine. American studies of social mobility usually omit information on private *versus* tax-supported secondary school attendance, and English studies showing the advantage of 'public' school attendance generally fail to distinguish between the mobile and the nonmobile in this respect. However, during the nineteenth century the English 'public' schools were used by *nouveaux riches* members of the manufacturing classes to enable their sons to achieve unqualified elite status.[30] In one sense, the rise of the manufacturing classes through free enterprise introduced a large measure of contest mobility which threatened to destroy the traditional sponsorship system. But by using the 'public' schools in this fashion they bowed to the legitimacy of the traditional system—an implicit acknowledgement that upward mobility was not complete without sponsored induction. Dennis Brogan speaks of the task of the 'public' schools in the nineteenth century as 'the job of marrying the old English social order to the new.'[31]

With respect to mobility, the parallel between the tax-supported

[29] For one account of the place of 'public' schools in the English educational system, see Dennis Brogan, *The English People*, New York: Knopf, 1943, pp. 18–56.

[30] A. H. Halsey of Birmingham University has called my attention to the importance of this fact.

[31] *Op. cit.*, pp. 24–25.

grammar schools and the 'public' schools in England is of interest. The former in important respects have been patterned after the latter, adopting their view of mobility but making it a much larger part of their total function. Generally the grammar schools are the vehicle for sponsored mobility throughout the middle ranges of the class system, modelled after the pattern of the 'public' schools which remain the agencies for sponsored mobility into the elite.

EFFECTS OF MOBILITY ON PERSONALITY

Brief note may be made of the importance of the distinction between sponsored and contest mobility with relation to the supposed effects of upward mobility on personality development. Not a great deal is yet known about the 'mobile personality' nor about the specific features of importance to the personality in the mobility experience.[32] However, today three aspects of this experience are most frequently stressed: first, the stress or tension involved in striving for status higher than that of others under more difficult conditions than they; second, the complication of interpersonal relations introduced by the necessity to abandon lower-level friends in favor of uncertain acceptance into higher-level circles; third, the problem of working out an adequate personal scheme of values in the face of movement between classes marked by somewhat variant or even contradictory value systems.[33] The impact of each of these three mobility problems, it is suggested, differs depending upon whether the pattern is that of the contest or of sponsorship.

Under the sponsorship system, recruits are selected early, segregated from their class peers, grouped with other recruits and with youth from the class to which they are moving, and trained specifically for membership in this class. Since the selection is made early, the mobility experience should be relatively free from the strain that comes with a series of elimination tests and long-extended uncertainty of success. The segregation and the integrated group life of the 'public' school or grammar school should help to clarify the mobile person's social ties. (One investigator failed to discover clique formation along lines of social class in a sociometric study of a number of grammar schools.[34]) The problem of a system of

[32] Cf. Lipset and Bendix, op. cit., pp. 250 ff.

[33] See, e.g., August B. Hollingshead and Frederick C. Redlich, Social Class and Mental Illness, New York: Wiley, 1958; W. Lloyd Warner and James C. Abegglen, Big Business Leaders in America, New York: Harper, 1955; Warner et al., Who Shall Be Educated?, op. cit.; Peter M. Blau, 'Social Mobility and Interpersonal Relations,' American Sociological Review, 21 (June, 1956), pp. 290–300.

[34] A. N. Oppenheim, 'Social Status and Clique Formation among Grammar

values may be largely met when the elite recruit is taken from his parents and peers to be placed in a boarding school, though it may be less well clarified for the grammar school boy who returns each evening to his working-class family. Undoubtedly this latter limitation has something to do with the observed failure of working-class boys to continue through the last years of grammar school and into the universities.[35] In general, then, the factors stressed as affecting personality formation among the upwardly mobile probably are rather specific to the contest system, or to the incompletely functioning sponsorship system.

It is often taken for granted that there is convincing evidence to show that mobility-oriented students in American secondary schools suffer from the tendency for cliques to form along lines predetermined by family background. These tendencies are statistically quite moderate, however, leaving much room for individual exceptions. Furthermore, mobility-oriented students usually have not been studied separately to discover whether or not they are incorporated into higher-level cliques in contrast to the general rule. Nor is it adequately demonstrated that the purported working-class value system, at odds with middle-class values, is as pervasive and constraining throughout the working class as it is conspicuous in many delinquent gangs. The model of contest mobility suggests, then, that there is more serious and continuing strain over the uncertainty of attaining mobility, more explicit and continued preoccupation with the problem of changing friendships, and more contradictory learning to inhibit the acquisition of a value system appropriate to the class of aspiration than under sponsored mobility. But the extent and implications of these differences require fuller understanding of the American class system. A search for personality-forming experiences specific to a sponsorship system, such as the British, has yet to be made.

CONCLUSION: SUGGESTIONS FOR RESEARCH

The foregoing discussion is broadly impressionistic and speculative, reflecting more the general impression of an observer of both countries than a systematic exploration of data. Relevant data of a variety of sorts are cited above, but their use is more illustrative than demonstrative. However, several lines of research are suggested

School Boys,' *British Journal of Sociology*, 6 (September, 1955), pp. 228–245. Oppenheim's findings may be compared with A. B. Hollingshead, *Elmtown's Youth*, New York: Wiley, 1949, pp. 204–242. See also Joseph A. Kahl, *The American Class Structure*, New York: Rinehart, 1957, pp. 129–138.

[35] Floud *et al., op. cit.,* pp. 115 ff.

by this tentative analysis. One of these is an exploration of different channels of mobility in both England and the United States in an attempt to discover the extent to which mobility corresponds to the mobility types. Recruitment to the Catholic priesthood, for example, probably strictly follows a sponsorship norm regardless of the dominant contest norm in the United States.

The effect of changes in the major avenues of upward mobility upon the dominant norms requires investigation. The increasing importance of promotion through corporation hierarchies and the declining importance of the entrepreneurial path of upward mobility undoubtedly compromise the ideal pattern of contest mobility. The growing insistence that higher education is a prerequisite to more and more occupations is a similar modification. Yet, there is little evidence of a tendency to follow the logic of sponsorship beyond the bureaucratic selection process. The prospect of a surplus of college-educated persons in relation to jobs requiring college education may tend to restore the contest situation at a higher level, and the further possibility that completion of higher education may be more determined by motivational factors than by capacity suggests that the contest pattern continues within the school.

In England, on the other hand, two developments may weaken the sponsorship system. One is positive response to popular demand to allow more children to secure the grammar school type of training, particularly by including such a program in the secondary modern schools. The other is introduction of the comprehensive secondary school, relatively uncommon at present but a major plank in the Labour Party's education platform. It remains to be determined whether the comprehensive school in England will take a distinctive form and serve a distinctive function, which preserves the pattern of sponsorship, or will approximate the present American system.

Finally, the assertion that these types of mobility are embedded in genuine folk norms requires specific investigation. Here, a combination of direct study of popular attitudes and content analysis of popular responses to crucial issues would be useful. Perhaps the most significant search would be for evidence showing what courses of action require no special justification or explanation because they are altogether 'natural' and 'right,' and what courses of action, whether approved or not, require special justification and explanation. Such evidence, appropriately used, would show the extent to which the patterns described are genuine folk norms rather than mere by-products of particular structural factors. It would also permit determination of the extent to which acceptance of the folk norms is diffused among the different segments of the populations.

5

A TYPOLOGY FOR THE CLASSIFICATION OF

EDUCATIONAL SYSTEMS*

Earl Hopper

Many sociologists agree that the most useful typology for the classification of educational systems is the one developed implicitly by Ralph H. Turner in 'Contest and Sponsored Mobility and the School System'.[1,2]† A brief summary of his typology may be useful. Turner assumes that educational systems in industrial societies are the main 'modes of upward social mobility', and he argues that the distinguishing characteristics of these modes are based on folk-norms which are pervasive throughout a given host society or type of host society. He distinguishes between a mode of 'sponsorship mobility' based on 'sponsorship folk-norms' and a mode of 'contest mobility' based on 'contest folk-norms'. The former is defined as one in which

. . . elite recruits are chosen by the established elite or their agents, and elite status is given on the basis of some criterion of supposed merit and cannot be *taken* by any amount of effort or strategy. Upward mobility is like entry into a private club, where each candidate must be sponsored by one or more members. Ultimately, the members grant or deny upward mobility on the basis of whether they judge the candidate to have the qualities they wish to see in fellow members.

The latter, 'contest mobility', is defined as

. . . a system in which elite status is the prize in an open contest by some rules of fair play, the contestants having wide latitude in the strategies they may employ. Since the 'prize' of successful upward mobility is not in the hands of the established elite to give out, the latter are not in a position to determine who shall attain it and who shall not.

* First printed in *Sociology*, January, 1968, pp. 29–44.
† [Reprinted as Reading 4 in the present volume. E.H.]

Since the folk-norms of mobility are said to '. . . shape the (educational system directly through (their) effects on the values that implement social control . . .' of selection, a system based on a mode of sponsorship mobility is called a 'sponsorship system' of education, and one based on a mode of contest mobility, a 'contest system' of education.

Turner was primarily concerned with distinguishing between the educational systems of England and the United States, the former approximating to a sponsorship system and the latter to a contest system. But from his analysis an inference may erroneously be made that educational systems are likely to cluster around either the English or American pattern. Although some educational systems can be distinguished in this way, a large number of them cannot meaningfully be classified in terms of a 'sponsorship-contest' dichotomy. For example, it does not allow one to distinguish between the systems of the U.S.S.R. and Sweden, France and England, Australia and the U.S.A. or Canada, Sweden and France, India and the U.S.A., etc. Although the dichotomy is sensitive to many of the ways in which the American and English educational systems differ, it also tends to over-emphasize these differences, at least in comparison with other societies. However, by separating analytically the various dimensions which underlie this dichotomy it is possible to construct an expanded version of Turner's typology, and in this way to take account of the 'deviant' systems. It is also possible to show that just as England and the United States represent only two special cases of a larger variety of societal types, so their educational systems represent only two special cases in an expanded typology.

The Expanded Typology

As societies industrialize they develop specialized and differentiated systems of education. Such systems have three primary manifest functions: the *selection* of children with different types and levels of ability; the provision of the appropriate type of *instruction* for the various categories of children created by the selection process; and the eventual *allocation* of trained personnel either directly to occupational roles or to agencies which specialize in occupational recruitment. Because the last two functions are closely linked to the first, the structure of educational systems, especially those within industrial societies, can be understood primarily in terms of the structure of their selection processes.

Four questions may be asked about the selection process: *How* does educational selection occur? *When* are pupils initially selected? *Who* should be selected? and *Why* should they be selected? Four structural properties of an educational system are reflected in the answers to these questions. To a large extent, at least in the short run, these properties are independent with respect to one another. Consequently, with respect to these properties, one may conceptualize four dimensions along which educational systems may vary. A given educational system may be located at some point on each dimension. It may also be classified according to its simultaneous positions on all four dimensions.

(i) *The First Dimension: How does educational selection occur?*

Two aspects of the answer to this question may be singled out for special attention: the degree to which an educational system has a centrally administered selection procedure; and the degree to which the provision of education, especially up to the point of initial selection, is standardized for the population as a whole. Although these two aspects of the total selection process are closely related, some systems have a centrally administered selection procedure and an unstandardized educational programme, and vice versa. Given centralized administration, however, standardization of the educational programme is likely to occur. It is reasonable, therefore, to think of two polar types: one in which the total selection process is centrally administered and standardized; and the other—its opposite—in which the total selection process is decentralized and unstandardized.

The position of an educational system on the continuum ranging between these two polar types is an indication of the degree to which the system in question is characterized by a combination of the following more specific properties: a specialized department within a national civil service or its equivalent which is concerned exclusively with problems of education; the inclusion of the entire population, or in the case of fairly rapid social change an entire cohort, within a nationally organized educational programme; and the absence of regional and local variations in the application of this programme, i.e., with respect to educational facilities, equality of instruction, stringency of selection procedures, and proportional opportunities for further training despite variations in population density and/or demand for further training. Again, each of these specific properties is closely interrelated. But it should be stressed that a given system at a given time may be more centralized and standardized in some respects than in others.

Educational systems also vary with respect to the content of their 'ideologies of implementation' concerning how selection *should* occur.[3] In this connection, at least two types of ideologies of implementation can be distinguished: a 'sponsorship' ideology and a 'contest' ideology. A sponsorship ideology specifies: that selection via sponsorship is necessary in order for the 'best' people to be selected; that the sponsors are qualified 'by right' for the task; and that they will exercise good judgement in making selections. A contest ideology specifies: that selection should not be determined through a centrally administered procedure but through the 'natural laws' of a 'free market', e.g., 'survival of the fittest' and 'supply and demand'; and that the only task of central administration is to keep the market 'free'.

Societies with a centralized and standardized selection process tend to have sponsorship ideologies, e.g., the U.S.S.R., and those with a decentralized and unstandardized selection process tend to have contest ideologies, e.g., the U.S.A.[4] At a given period of time, however, contest ideologies are found in societies with a relatively centralized and standardized selection process, as well as in those with a relatively decentralized and unstandardized process; similarly, sponsorship ideologies are found in societies of both types.[5] Although the evidence suggests that systems characterized by incongruence between their ideology and their patterns of organization are not rare, they tend to occur primarily during times of rapid social change. And when a 'reasonably' long-term time perspective is taken, such systems can be seen to develop a congruent association between their ideologies and their patterns of organization.[6]

When the likely association between the ideology concerning how selection should occur and the organizational pattern of how it does occur is taken into account, the two polar types of systems, as outlined above, may be likened (for purposes of illustration) to different types of games. A system with a centralized and standardized selection process reinforced by a sponsorship ideology is similar to a 'Talent Show' in which participants display their talent to a panel of judges who are assumed to have good judgement. A system with a decentralized and unstandardized selection process reinforced by a contest ideology is similar to a 'Military Initiative Test' in which soldiers are expected to traverse a certain distance within a limited period of time by using only those means which they can acquire after the test begins. Both types of systems are designed to select winners and both demand that the contestants be motivated to win. But in the former the winners are likely to be selected formally, and relatively less importance is likely to be attached to their motivation; in the latter, a process analogous to natural selection is likely to occur, and a premium is likely to be attached to their motivation.

In sum, with respect to this first dimension, an approximate and tentative classification of a few educational systems is set out in the following table[7]:

Table I

Dimension of the System	Degree	Classification*
Centralization and Standardization of the Total Selection Process	High	France Sweden U.S.S.R.
	Medium	W. Germany Australia England
	Low	U.S.A. Canada

* Intra-cell classifications may not be ranked.

Educational systems which are similar in the degree to which their total selection processes are centralized and standardized may, however, be different in other ways. Therefore a second classicatory dimension must be introduced.

(ii) *The Second Dimension: When are pupils initially selected?*

Two aspects of the answer to this question may also be singled out for special attention: the degree to which an educational system is formally differentiated into specialized routes through which children are selected, trained, and guided to their future occupational roles; and the degree to which initial selection occurs early in the educational career.[8] Since people entering different types of occupations require, in part, different types of skills, and since educational systems are expected to play an important role in the development of such skills, almost all educational systems are likely to be characterized by some degree of internal differentiation and specialization, at least in those phases immediately prior to entry into the labour market. The crucial distinction is how long before the completion of education have children been formally segregated into specialized routes. In other words, only one variable need be considered: the degree to which an educational system is characterized by early formal differentiation and specialization of routes. And it is again reasonable to think of two polar types: one characterized by a high degree of early formal differentiation and specialization; and the other—its opposite—by a low degree.

The higher the degree of early formal differentiation and specialization, the greater the probability that a 'suitable' person will be
rejected because the selection procedures which have been used are
too 'stringent'; the lower the degree, the greater the probability
that an 'unsuitable' person will be accepted because the selection
procedures which have been used are too 'lenient'. Since the
probability of the former type of error is inversely related to the
probability of the latter type of error, no system can be structured in
order to minimize both—at least not in the short run, and not with
the conventional methods of teaching and class-room organization.[9]
Of course this statement is based on two sets of related assumptions:
that 'suitability' is not fixed at birth and is subject to the constraints
of experience; and that even if 'suitability' were fixed at birth, the
screening devices used at the initial selection would be imperfect,
and the earlier they are used, the greater their imperfection.

Industrial societies and even those attempting to industrialize
are quite similar with respect to the official versions of a second
component of their ideologies of educational implementation, i.e.,
that concerning when initial selection *should* occur. In general, the
official version is that within the confines of available economic and
other resources, all people should have as much education as is
possible.[10] Ordinarily, therefore, it is to be expected that the greater
a society's available resources, the more is it likely that a society
will have an educational system designed to minimize the probability
of rejecting a 'suitable' person, i.e., one characterized by a low
degree of early formal differentiation and specialization of routes.[11]
However, the evidence suggests three sets of exceptions to this general
expectation: societies with approximately equal Gross National
Products or, more importantly, *per capita* incomes vary with respect
to the percentage of their available resources which they spend on
education; even if the problem of investment priorities in government expenditure is disregarded, those societies which spend an
approximately equal percentage of their resources on education
vary in their degree of formal differentiation and specialization; and
the degree to which societies have either increased or decreased the
amount of differentiation and specialization in their educational
systems is not strongly related to changes in either their *per capita*
incomes or their expenditures on education.[12] It follows that variation in the organization of recruitment processes cannot be
explained only or primarily in terms of available economic resources,
and that many societies are characterized by incongruence between
the official versions of their ideologies concerning when selection
should occur and the actual organization of their recruitment

processes. These cases are too numerous and have persisted for too long a time to be attributed to the effects of rapid social change. At least one additional variable must be considered.[13]

Although industrial societies are similar with respect to the official versions of their ideologies concerning when initial selection should occur, they vary with respect to the less official and more informal versions. With respect to the latter it is possible to distinguish at least two types of ideologies of implementation: an 'elitist' ideology and an 'egalitarian' ideology. An elitist ideology specifies, for example: that the maximum amount of education for each citizen should depend on his future ability to contribute to economic productivity; that 'intelligence' and 'educability' are determined primarily by hereditary factors so that some people could not possibly benefit from education above a given minimum; and that those who appear to be bound for elite positions should be separated at an early age from those who appear to be bound for lower positions so that the former gain in their confidence to lead and the latter in their willingness to follow. This ideology supports the view that initial section should occur as early as possible, and that a relatively large number of routes should exist. An egalitarian ideology specifies, for example: that the maximum amount of education is the right of every citizen regardless of his future ability to contribute to economic productivity; that 'intelligence' and 'educability' are determined primarily by environmental factors so that with proper instruction all people could benefit from a maximum of education; and that those who appear to be bound for elite positions should work and play as long as possible with those who appear to be bound for lower positions so that the former will not lose touch with the 'common man' and the latter will not become overly subordinate and lacking in initiative. This ideology supports the view that selection should occur as late as possible, and that a relatively small number of routes should exist.

Egalitarian ideologies are found in societies with relatively high *per capita* incomes, e.g., Sweden and the U.S.A., and in societies with relatively low ones, e.g., the U.S.S.R. prior to its more recent periods of rapid economic growth; similarly, elitist ideologies are found in societies of both types, e.g. England, France, Brazil, and Italy.[14] Because the content of such ideologies is buttressed by cultural folk norms, it changes very slowly, and industrialization processes do not have an overriding effect.[15] Although it is difficult to assign weights to each factor, it follows that the degree to which an educational system is characterized by early formal differentiation and specialization of routes is a function of both available resources and a less official but more pervasive version of its ideology concerning when educational selection should occur. Consequently, at least with respect to this aspect of the recruitment process, close congruence between the ideology of an educational system and its actual pattern of organization is not to be expected.

In sum, with respect to this dimension, an approximate and tentative classification of a few educational systems is set out in the following table:

Table 2 [16]

Dimension of the System	Degree	Classification*
Early Formal Differentiation and Specialization of Educational Routes	High	France W. Germany England
	Medium	U.S.S.R.[17] Australia
	Low	U.S.A. Canada Sweden

* Intra-cell classifications are not ranked.

Again, educational sytems which are similar in the degree to which they are characterized by early formal differentiation and specialization of routes may be different, not only in the degree to which their total selection processes are administratively centralized and standardized, but in other important respects as well. Therefore, additional classificatory dimensions must be introduced.

(iii) *The Third and Fourth Dimensions: Who should be selected? and Why should they be selected?*

Stratified societies face, among others, the following three interrelated systemic problems: people in all positions in the various hierarchies of power must strive to justify their positions both to themselves and to others; in order to 'rule' effectively and efficiently, the elite must strive to maintain at least a minimal semblance of allegiance and cooperation from less powerful groups; and, in order to prevent a successful challenge to their power, the elite must be flexible enough to assimilate potentially able leaders from subordinate and competing groups. Hence, competition over the distribution of power is inherent in stratified societies, and tension and conflict are inherent in competition for power. Neither the dilemmas themselves nor the resulting tension and conflict are ever handled by a society with complete success.

One way in which most stratified societies have attempted to cope with such dilemmas is to develop fairly explicit ideologies which define the types of people whom the society values most highly and which justify why more power is given to them than to others. These may be called 'ideologies of legitimization'. Since educational systems in stratified industrial societies are mechanisms of selection and allocation, such societies are likely to have explicit ideologies of legitimization concerning educational selection. These ideologies translate questions concerning the distribution of power into questions concerning the distribution of educational suitability. They define who should be selected for higher training and explain why some people should be rejected when others are selected.[18]

One way in which educational systems may be classified, therefore, is according to their ideologies of legitimization concerning educational selection. Two properties of these ideologies warrant special attention. In answer to the question 'Who should be selected?' one can conceptualize a continuum ranging between two polar properties: the first representing a quality of complete *universalism*; and the second—its opposite—representing a quality of complete *particularism*. In answer to the question 'Why should they be selected?', one can also conceptualize a continuum ranging between two polar types: the first representing a quality of complete *collectivism*; and the second—its opposite—representing a quality of complete *individualism*. Educational systems may be classified on each continuum.

The two continua can be combined, however, to produce four ideal types of ideologies of legitimization concerning educational selection: 'aristocratic', 'paternalistic', 'meritocratic', and 'communistic'. Each ideal type may be defined as follows:

1. Particularistic

To the extent that pupils should be selected primarily on the basis of their diffuse skills and only secondarily on the basis of their technical skills, so that those with the most of the former need have least of the latter, the ideology has a 'particularistic' quality. This assumes that the society has a system of ascribed statuses on the basis of which certain diffuse skills and ascribed characteristics are likely to become unequally distributed. It also assumes that the opportunity for learning such skills is strictly limited to particular groups and that substitutes for ascribed characteristics are unacceptable.[19]

(a) *Aristocratic Ideology: an individualistic form of particularism*

When particularistic selections are justified to the population in terms of the right of those selected to privilege on the basis of their diffuse skills and ascribed characteristics one may refer to the 'aristocratic' quality of the ideology.

(b) *Paternalistic Ideology: a collectivistic form of particularism*

When particularistic selections are justified to the population in terms of the society's 'need' for people with diffuse skills and certain ascribed characteristics in order that the society may be led by the most 'suitable' people, one may refer to the 'paternalistic' quality of the ideology.

2. Universalistic

To the extent that pupils should be selected primarily on the basis of their technical skills and only secondarily on the basis of their diffuse skills, so that those with the most of the former need have least of the latter, the ideology has a 'universalistic' quality.[20] This assumes that the society does not have a system of ascribed statuses on the basis of which certain diffuse skills and ascribed characteristics are likely to become unequally distributed. It also assumes that maximum opportunity is available for such skills to be learned.[21]

(c) *Meritocratic Ideology: an individualistic form of universalism*[22]

When universalistic selections are justified to the population in terms of the right of the selected to privilege as a reward for their talents, ambition, and technical skills, one may refer to the 'meritocratic' quality of the ideology.

(d) *Communistic Ideology: a collectivistic form of universalism*

When universalistic selections are justified to the population in terms of the society's need for the most talented, ambitious, and technically qualified men to be guided to positions of leadership and responsibility, and for those less qualified in these respects to be guided to appropriately subordinate positions, one may refer to the 'communistic' quality of the ideology.

Most industrial societies contain several groups of elites with competing ideologies of legitimization of educational selection. Consequently, in order to represent the ideology of a given society as accurately as possible, the following technique was used: first, a paradigm was constructed by considering simultaneously the dimensions of universalism–particularism and individualism–collectivism, thereby producing four cells, indicating each of the four ideal types of ideologies; second, this paradigm was taken to be a 'grid' on which the ideology of a given society could be located by means of a 'topographical profile'; and, third, the cell of the paradigm containing the largest area of a profile was used to represent the dominant ideology of a given society. On this basis, an approximate and tentative classification of a few educational systems is set out in Figure 1.[23]

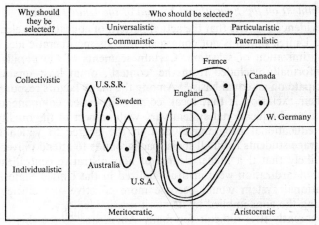

Fig. 1

The societies classified as similar with respect to their ideologies of legitimization of educational selection are clearly different in many important respects, even aside from those already conceptualized as classifying dimensions. But these differences will not be considered here.

(iv) *Summary*

It is not necessary to integrate the four dimensions in terms of a table or figure in order to show that a general typology of educational systems can be constructed. By considering each of the dimensions simultaneously, it can be seen quite clearly that educational systems which are similar with respect to any one dimension may be different with respect to the other three; and those which are similar with respect to any two or even three dimensions may still be different with respect to the fourth. It should also be stressed that the educational system of the United States, what Turner called a 'contest system', has been classified here as having a low degree of administrative centralization and standardization in its total selection process, a low degree of early formal differentiation and specialization of routes, and a 'meritocratic' ideology of legitimization of selection; and the educational system of England, what Turner called a 'sponsorship system', has been classified as having a medium degree of centralization and standardization, a high degree of differentiation and specialization, and primarily a 'paternalistic' ideology. These two systems represent two special cases in the expanded typology outlined above.

A Comment on the Educational System of the United States

The evidence suggests that the actual pattern of educational selection in the United States is not congruent with its meritocratic ideology of legitimization of selection. Certain segments of the population are informally excluded from the 'contest', or at least unable to participate on an equal basis.[24] Among the many factors responsible for their exclusion is that local, community-based components of the national educational system vary with respect to the quality of their educational programme, and in the degree to which they encourage students from all social backgrounds to attend university. It is likely that if a higher degree of administrative centralization and standardization were institutionalized in the United States, the educational system would become more effective and efficient in reaching the aims implied by its meritocratic ideology.[25]

Apparently it is difficult for many Americans to see this point. One reason for their difficulty may be that in the United States the ideological support for decentralization and grass roots control is based on folk-norms which define all centralized power as detrimental to freedom and universalistic practices.[26] In other words, the contest ideology in the United States (but not necessarily elsewhere) is associated with various cultural themes which are explicit in their disapproval of particularism in selection. And partly due to the constraints of a contest ideology in conjunction with these additional themes, Americans are led to emphasize only those aspects of their system which in fact do foster meritocratic selection patterns, e.g., 'open-gate' colleges and universities, delayed career decisions, transfer to more advantageous routes as late as graduate school, etc., but to ignore those aspects which hinder such patterns, e.g., variations among locally based schools with respect to the quality of their educational programmes and the degree to which they encourage all students to aspire to higher education.

Of course this is not a static situation. One of the inherent contradictions of a contest ideology within an industrial society is that in order to maintain the desired 'free market' for talent, a society is compelled to become more centralized in the administration of its total selection process. For example, it may have to accept the fact that in order to provide 'equal educational opportunity for all' it must insure that the family environments of certain children do not retard their educability, or that those children whose educability has been retarded prior to their entering formal education will receive 'positive discrimination'. Since locally based administrations are unlikely to have the funds and the skills for such activities, the task tends to fall to the central agencies. In addition, the gradual emergence of a national elite in the United States favours the development of a sponsorship ideology of implementation. But some of the current patterns of conflict between local and national elites, and the current debates concerning Federal *vs.* State control, suggest that these processes are neither rapid nor inevitable.[27]

Some Possible Applications of the Expanded Typology

It may be possible to demonstrate that by classifying educational systems in the four-dimensional typology one thereby acquires greater analytical power with respect to the understanding of how these systems work and of how they relate to their host societies. It is beyond the scope of this article to consider this task in detail. But several possible applications may be mentioned.

The comparative study of education has consisted, for the most part, of making detailed descriptions of educational systems in society after society. Although it is now clear that considerable variation exists in the structure of educational systems, even among societies at similar levels of industrial development, it is quite easy to become overwhelmed by this glut of 'facts'. This is especially so when a researcher begins to study a system for which there is abundant documentation. By highlighting some of the more important structural dimensions along which educational systems may vary, and, thereby, drawing attention to their more important similarities and differences, a typology for the classification of educational systems is a useful aid for the organization and interpretation of the wealth of available data.[28]

Secondly, it is often illuminating to analyse societies as though they were social systems, to conceptualize certain of their institutions as though they were sub-systems, and to treat these sub-systems as variables within the constructed social system. This enables a researcher to formulate propositions concerning relationships among the variables, e.g., the effects of variation in the structure of an economic sub-system on variation in the structure of an educational sub-system, with reference both to one society over time and to many societies at a given point in time or over time. This approach also draws attention to the fact that a society may not have a national educational system except in the most nominal sense, and that it may have several educational systems in a more concrete sense. To conceptualize educational institutions as a sub-system, however, demands that its defining dimensions be specified and, if at all possible, calibrated. Such a task is facilitated by thinking of educational systems in terms of their location in the above typology.[29]

Thirdly, the dimensions of the typology might be taken as guidelines for the study of the ways in which an educational system changes. Further, the dimensions can be treated as patterns towards which systems may be likely to converge as a result of industrialization processes. For example, a question which might be asked in this connection is 'What is the relationship between the level and trajectory of industrial development and the degree of centralization and standardization of educational selection, or the content of ideologies of legitimization?[30]

Fourthly, it would be of interest to study the effects of variations in the structure of educational systems on the structure of their educational routes. It would be helpful to know the pattern of interpersonal experiences and situations which are characteristic of each route within a given system, and how the structure of the system affects this pattern. For example, two questions which might be asked in this connection are as follows: 'Are educational systems which share a given location in the typology similar with respect to the ways in which they cope with the problem of making ambition commensurate with assessed achievement potential?' and 'How do educational systems use their formal routes to regulate the anticipatory socialization of different categories of students?'[31]*

Finally, studies could be made of the effects of variation in the structure of educational systems and of the routes within any given system on a range of personality characteristics. For example, it is possible to reformulate for a wider variety of systems Turner's hypothesis that upward mobility through the English educational system has a lower propensity for creating anxiety among the upwardly mobile than does upward mobility through the American educational system.[32] A further question which might be asked in this connection is 'What is the relationship between the educational

* [See Appendix II for a theoretical discussion of these questions. E.H.]

route taken by parents and the level of ambition of their children, within various types of educational systems?'

In conclusion, a proviso must be entered. If more detailed knowledge indicates that the educational systems considered here have been classified incorrectly, then they should be reclassified. Indeed, classification as such is not the main point of this article. Rather, the typology has been presented as a heuristic device, and as a preliminary step to more narrowly focused research. If the typology fails to generate such research, then it should be altered or discarded.

Notes

1. For their comments on earlier drafts of this article, I am indebted to: Eric G. Dunning (Department of Sociology, University of Leicester), John MacDonald (Department of Manpower, Canadian Government), R. L. Rowland (Peterhouse, Cambridge) and F. Birtek (St. Catherine's, Cambridge).

2. This article first appeared in *Amer. Sociol. R.,* 1960, 855–867; some of its themes were later developed in *The Social Context of Ambition*, San Francisco Chandler Press, 1964. For an example of an overly simple typology, see Louis V. Bone, 'Sociological Framework for a Comparative Study of Education Systems', *Education Review*, 1960, 121–126; for a lengthy list of imaginative questions and topics concerning education in any society, see Jules Henry, 'Cross-cultural Outline of Education', *Current Anthropology*, 1960, 267–305.

3. This is only one component of an educational system's ideology of implementation. A second component will be considered in due course. Other researchers have preferred the term 'method-ideology', e.g., see John W. Thomson, 'Method Ideology and Educational Ideologies', *Educational Theory*, 1962, 110–117.

4. For evidence concerning these two examples, see the Unesco Series 'The Development of Higher Education', especially *Access to Higher Education*, vol. II, 1965. See also I. N. Thut and Don Adams, *Educational Patterns in Contemporary Societies*, London, McGraw-Hill, 1964, especially the bibliographical references in the appropriate chapters.

5. Thut and Adams, *ibid.* They do not discuss this relationship, but they provide sufficient data to justify the inference. Further, and this is often overlooked by students of comparative education, contest ideologies are found in societies with a high degree of status rigidity in their stratification systems, e.g., possibly India, and in societies where stratification systems show a relatively low degree, e.g., the U.S.A.; similarly, sponsorship ideologies are found in societies of both types, e.g., France and the U.S.S.R. See W. D. Halls, *Society, Schools and Progress in France*, London, Pergamon Press, 1965, and Brian Holmes, *Problems in Education: A Comparative Approach*, Routledge and Kegan Paul, 1965.

6. This relationship reflects two constraints: the degree to which a society's total selection process is centralized and standardized, and the content of a society's ideology concerning how educational selection should occur are likely to be mutually reinforcing; and both properties are likely to be influenced in a mutually consistent way by industrialization processes, especially with respect to political and economic centralization. It is impossible to treat here the problems of why a system has a given degree of centralization and standardization and a given type of ideology. For a brief discussion of the effects of industrialization on

each of these properties and on the association between them, see E. G. Dunning and E. I. Hopper, 'Industrialization and the Problem of Convergence: A Critical Note', *Sociological Review*, 1966, 163–186.

7. It is impossible to provide here a complete bibliography of the material used to make these and later classifications. A cursory glance at any recent textbook in the comparative study of education will provide a useful starting point into the literature; especially useful in this connection is I. N. Thut and Don Adams, *Educational Patterns in Contemporary Societies, op. cit.* I have also found useful the bibliographical and statistical information on education provided by the London embassies of various countries. In addition, see Jean Floud and A. H. Halsey, 'The Sociology of Education', *Current Sociology*, 7, 1958, Burton R. Clark, 'The Sociology of Education', pp. 734–769, in R. E. L. Faris (ed.), *Handbook of Modern Sociology*, Chicago, Rand McNally and Co., 1964; A. H. Halsey, Jean Floud, and C. Arnold Anderson (eds.), *Education, Economy and Society* New York, The Free Press of Glencoe, 1961; E. A. G. Robinson and J. E. Vaizey (eds.), *The Economics of Education*, London, Macmillan, 1966; and the Unesco Series, 'The Development of Higher Education', 1965.

8. Educational routes are in fact likely to be ranked by prestige in terms of two criteria: the subsequent economic status and positions of those who use them; and the economic and status positions of the teachers and administrators associated with them. Because students are indeterminate with respect to stratification, it does not seem appropriate to speak of vertically ranked educational routes. Furthermore, since there is not a perfect association either between educational routes and subsequent adult statuses or between parental statuses and the child's educational route, it is misleading to think of educational routes as themselves being a vertical dimension of stratification. Of course some aspects of the routes may be considered in terms of their prestige connotations after a person takes his adult statuses, e.g., graduation from Cambridge rather than from London or Sheffield, and graduation from Harvard rather than from Missouri. For a slightly contrary view, see G. Elder, Jr., 'Life Opportunities and Personality: Some Consequences of Stratified Secondary Education in Great Britain', *Sociology of Education*, 1965, 173–202.

9. It has often been suggested that, in part, so long as selection decisions are not completely determinate, this problem does not arise. However, in most societies where initial selection occurs formally at an early age, but where theoretically a person may switch at a later date from a less promising route to a more promising one, and vice versa, the evidence shows that although many initial selection errors are made, extremely few moves actually occur. This is one reason why the formality of differentiation and specialization of routes is so important, i.e., when the routes are informally structured, movement is more likely to occur. However, in the conceptualization of this dimension, there are insufficient data to determine the relative weight which should be given to 'formality'. For a discussion of some aspects of this problem with special reference to England, see J. W. B. Douglas, *The Home and the School*, London, MacGibbon and Kee, 1964.

10. For evidence to this effect see, for example, the Unesco Series, 'The Development of Higher Education', 1965.

11. Many researchers have tried to explain the amount of differentiation and specialization of a given system in terms of the wealth of the host society. (For example, see Richard F. Tomasson, 'From Elitism to Egalitarianism in Swedish education', *Sociology of Education*, 1965, 203–223.) Two sociologists have even drawn an analogy to the decision which a researcher must make in the selection of a probability level in order to test an hypothesis. In statistics, the rejection of a

'true' hypothesis is called a Type I Error; and the acceptance of a 'false' hypothesis, a Type II Error. The probability of making a Type I Error is inversely related to the probability of making a Type II Error. A researcher selects his probability level on the basis of the relative costs of making one type of error rather than the other. Similarly, an educational system may be classified in terms of the probability that it will make a Type I Error with respect to selection—rejecting a 'suitable' person by using overly 'stringent' selection procedures—or that it will make a Type II Error with respect to selection—accepting an 'unsuitable' person by using overly 'lenient' selection procedures. The degree to to which an educational system is characterized by early formal differentiation and specialization of routes reflects, in part, a society's decision on the relative costs of wasting 'natural talent' and saving current resources as opposed to saving 'natural talent' and wasting current resources. (See A. W. Cicourel and J. I. Kitsuse, *The Educational Decision Makers,* Indianapolis, Bobbs-Merrill, 1963.) Of course, in addition to the argument set out in the text of this article, it should be stressed that the evidence does not fully support their analogy. A low degree of early formal differentiation and specialization may be as effective and efficient as a high degree in so far as those initially rejected are likely to be depreciated in value to the economy, and those initially selected may not be sufficiently appreciated to offset the loss.

12. John Vaizey, *The Economics of Education,* London, Faber and Faber, 1962; Vaizey and Robinson, *op. cit.*; and the Committee on Higher Education, *Higher Education,* Appendix Five, *Higher Education in Other Countries,* London, H.M.S.O., 1965. See also Thut and Adams, *op. cit.*

13. As mentioned previously, this article is not the place for a discussion of why any given system has a given set of properties. But blatant incongruence between ideology and pattern of organization is so interesting that it warrants a brief comment.

14. Of course the evidence concerning these points is not what one would wish. But reasonable inferences can be made from the following sources or from bibliographical material to which they refer. With respect to England and the United States, see: Douglas Pidgeon 'Education and the Concept of Intelligence', unpub. manuscript available from the National Foundation for Educational Research in England and Wales, 1966; Turner, *op. cit.*; J. Stuart Maclure (ed.), *Educational Documents: England and Wales 1816–1963,* London, Chapman and Hall, 1965; and Robert O. Hahn and David B. Bidna (eds.), *Secondary Education, Origins and Directions,* London, Collier-MacMillan, 1965. With respect to other countries which, by way of illustration, have been classified in the text, see: Tomasson, *op. cit.*; Marvin Farber (ed.), *The Philosophy of Education in France and the United States,* Buffalo, University of Buffalo Press; Halls, *op cit.*; Grace Richards Conant, 'West German Education in Transition; German Textbooks and the Nazi Past', *Saturday Review,* 20 July, 1963, 52–53; Richard Plant, 'West German Education in Transition', *Saturday Review,* 20 July 1963, 49–51 and 62–63; E. J. King, (ed.) *Communist Education,* Indianapolis, Bobbs-Merrill, 1963; *Bringing Soviet Schools Still Closer to Life,* London, Soviet Booklets, 1958; James S. Coleman (ed.), *Education and Political Development,* Princeton University Press, 1965; John Porter, *The Vertical Mosaic: An analysis of Social Class and Power in Canada,* Toronto, University of Toronto Press, 1965; Peter Coleman, (ed.) Australian Civilization, Melbourne, F. W. Cheshire, 1962; and Vernon Mallinson, *An Introduction to the Study of Comparative Education,* London, Heinemann Educational Books, Ltd., 1961.

15. For a discussion of folk-norms, see Turner, *op. cit.*

16. For evidence in support of these classifications, see references 5, 7, and 14,

especially with respect to the bibliographies contained in the books and articles mentioned.

17. A difficult problem is illustrated by classifying the U.S.S.R. as 'Medium' and, for example, England as 'High'. On the one hand, England is less differentiated and specialized than the U.S.S.R., but, on the other, the U.S.S.R. is thoroughly comprehensive up to the age of 15+. What are the relative weights to be assigned to the degree of formal differentiation and specialization of routes as opposed to the age at which these routes begin? In this case more weight has been assigned to age, but this should not be taken as a rule.

18. The greater the degree of status rigidity in the stratification system of a given society, the more is it likely that these systemic problems will be severe, and the society will have an *explicit* ideology with respect to the distribution of power; similarly, the more is it likely that the educational system in such a society will have an explicit ideology of legitimization of educational selection. However, it should be stressed that even though a society with a decentralized and unstandardized selection process is likely to have an ideology which specifies that selection should not be centrally administered, it still must define the types of people it values most highly and explain why these people are selected when others are rejected. Of course, it should also be stressed that the greater the status rigidity, the more likely that a society's ideology will have 'paternalistic' and/or 'aristocratic' qualities.

19. 'Technical and diffuse skills' are discussed by D. Lockwood, 'Social Mobility', pp. 501–502, in A. J. Welford, Michael Argyle, D. V. Glass, and J. N. Morris (eds.), *Society: Problems and Methods of Study*, London, Routledge and Kegan Paul Ltd., 1962. Although for some occupations a diffuse skill may actually be the main task requirement, e.g., salesmanship, and although most diffuse skills can be learned if the opportunity were available, e.g., table manners, the main point is that diffuse skills tend to be unequally distributed through the stratification system. To the extent they have to be learned intentionally, for example, while on the job or after childhood has passed, the task becomes time consuming and arduous, and seldom completely successful.

20. Selection processes within complex educational systems are likely to have a partially informal character, no matter how centralized their administration. Particularism of sort is likely to be associated with informality. For example, when there are 'ties' for a limited number of places in higher levels of training, those responsible for selection must often rely on such informal and particularistic devices as personal knowledge of a candidate's preparatory institution, his teachers, his family background, the amount of emotional support his family are likely to provide for higher education, etc. In addition such factors as intelligence, motivation, and technical skills are never likely to be sufficient criteria for selection in any bureaucratically organized system. One must have the qualities of, for example, 'psychological stability' and 'good citizenship'. Such qualities are difficult to assess, and they are impossible to assess in a value-free manner. Particularism in terms of middle class culture is almost certain to characterize such assessments. But these forms of particularism are likely to exist *even* in a society with meritocratic or communistic ideologies of selection. They should not be confused with the explicit ideology of particularistic selection, as defined in the text.

21. For example, although, compared with England, the United States has a less distinctive system of ascribed characteristics and a more equal distribution of diffuse skills, nonetheless, opportunities for acquiring such skills at a relatively early age, prior to initial selection, are being instituted in the United States, i.e., programmes for Negroes to learn to speak 'middle class English'; programmes to

teach working class boys various skills in order to free them from 'production oriented' jobs; courses in 'etiquette' and ballroom dancing in the schools, etc. Such programmes are also becoming available to adults (division of Adults and Vocational Research of the United States Office of Education, which administers the Vocational Education Act of 1963).

22. For a more detailed discussion of various aspects of meritocratic ideology, see Michael Young, *The Rise of the Meritocracy*, Penguin, Harmondsworth, 1961.

23. Two problems in the identification of an ideology of legitimization of educational selection (as well as of the ideologies of implementation discussed above) demand arbitary solutions: how to determine the content of the ideology, and how to determine the dominant ideology. Because there are no studies directly concerned with this type of ideology, one must depend on various kinds of public and official statements. Although they do not always indicate the ideologies of the majority, they are a reasonable indication of the ideologies of those with power. Some of the most useful statements are official legislation pertaining to education, speeches by government and civil service officials, government sponsored reports, the public statements by officials of such institutions as universities or well known secondary schools, statements by local interest groups, such as 'Adults for ...', and newspapers editorials. When there is no *a priori* evidence for the existence of competing ideologies, the ideology of the dominant group is taken as the dominant ideology; when, as is usually the case, competing ideologies do exist, the ideology of the dominant group is again taken as dominant; but when there are competing ideologies within the dominant group itself, it is necessary to construct some sort of profile which represents the proportions of the group holding different ideologies and the relative distribution of power among the competing factions. Obviously, this is very difficult problem, for which there is very little evidence. Therefore, I have attempted to construct very approximate profiles on the basis of the kind of information mentioned above. These are admittedly preliminary and, in part, arbitrary. For further material concerning ideologies of legitimization of educational selection, see the literature listed in reference 14. For a general discussion of testing for 'ability' and of ideology, see David A. Goslin, *The Search for Ability: Standardised Testing in Social Perspective*, New York, John Wiley and Sons; 1963; see also Thompson, *op. cit.*

24. For example, with respect to the Lower Social Class as opposed to the Middle Social Class, Negroes as opposed to Whites, the South as opposed to the North, and Rural areas as opposed to Urban areas, see Seymour Martin Lipset and Reinhard Bendix, *Social Mobility in Industrial Society*, London, William Heinemann, Ltd., 1959, and James B. Conant, *The American High School Today*, New York, McGraw-Hill, 1959 and *Slum and Suburbs*, New York, McGraw-Hill, 1964.

25. A similar point has been made by Cicourel and Kitsuse, *op. cit.*

26. This contrasts, for example, with the German philosophical traditions which define centralization as a possible, indeed as a likely, source of freedom for individuals against the whims of minority groups. Of course it is the structural dilemma of maintaining both freedom and equality which is at the root of these differences. And it is this dilemma which Turner overlooks when he implicitly equates a centralized and standardized selection process with a 'paternalistic' ideology of legitimization, an 'elitist' ideology of implementation, and a reduction of equality of educational opportunity; and a decentralized and unstandardized selection process with a 'meritocratic' ideology of legitimization, an 'egalitarian' ideology of implementation, and a maximization of equality of opportunity.

27. Dunning and Hopper, *op. cit.*

28. This point was made recently by A. Tropp. 'The Social Functions of Educational Systems', *Social and Economic Studies*, 1966, 1–7, see also the remarks about 'butterfly-collecting' in Edmund Leach, *Rethinking Anthropology*, London, London School of Economics Monographs on Social Anthropology, 1961.

29. For a further discussion of this approach, see E. I. Hopper and E. G. Dunning, 'Some Preliminary Methodological and Conceptual Notes on Industrialization and the Problem of Convergence', unpub. manuscript, prepared for the Study Group on Economy and Sociology, 6th World Congress of Sociology, Evian, 1966.

30. See Dunning and Hopper, *op. cit.*, and Hopper and Dunning, *ibid.* With special reference to Japan see Herbert Passin, *Society and Education in Japan*, Bureau of Publications, Teachers College and East Asian Institute, Columbia University, 1965; and Marius B. Jansen and Lawrence Stone, 'Education and Modernization in Japan and England', *Comparative Studies in Society and History*, 1957, No 2.

31. This problem is implied by Elder, *op. cit.,* See also Burton R. Clark, 'The "Cooling-out" Function in Higher Education', *Amer. Journ. of Sociol.* 1960, 569–76.

32. Turner, *op. cit.*

6

THE MANAGEMENT OF KNOWLEDGE:

A CRITIQUE OF THE USE OF TYPOLOGIES

IN EDUCATIONAL SOCIOLOGY*

Ioan Davies

I

One of the curiosities of work in the social sciences, as in science, is that the focus of research tends to concentrate on partial areas of immediate concern which in turn come to be defined as the entire field. The study of education is no exception. For many years sociologists have developed research on the relationship between social inequality and educational opportunity (with a few studies on educational institutions included as complements). That there is other research which has a direct bearing on the 'field' is often ignored. The sociology of education *is* the study of educational opportunity while such topics as the development of scientific research and the diffusion of ideas are relegated to other sub-areas of the discipline—the sociology of science or of knowledge. In recent years so widespread has been this practice that when a field of research and theory is developed which is clearly concerned with education, but which seriously challenges the whole framework of sociological research in education, it is immediately 're-written' and absorbed into the conventional wisdom. The reception of Bernstein's work on sociolinguistics is a case in point: so long as he seemed to be talking about stratification everyone assumed that he understood what the research was about. Here was simply a further demonstration of the inequalities in the educational system. The fact that he was using entirely different concepts ('symbolic orders', 'restricted and elaborated codes') to discuss relationships, learning processes and power structures was conveniently ignored.[1]

It is the argument of this paper that the current emphasis is disastrous for the development of a sociology of education which is

* An earlier version of this Reading appeared in *Sociology*, January 1970.

concerned with both the societal parameters of education and its system properties. (This procedure is, incidentally, also disastrous for educational sociology which sees stratification as an important indicator of educational competence. Without a theory of knowledge it is difficult to see what the stratification debate is about.) It is also an argument that the sociology of education—like any other branch of the social sciences—cannot begin to develop theory until it is conscious of the importance of comparison in establishing similarities, differences and pecularities in various systems. For this reason I have chosen to begin the discussion by examining an essay which has both of these concerns, but which demonstrates the distorting effect of assuming that the most important questions in the sociology of education are to do with social stratification and educational opportunity.

II

In a recent essay[2] Earl Hopper provided a typology for the classification of educational systems.* This is a welcome development in the sociology of education which has to date tended to range between unsystematic generalizations, detailed case-studies and untheoretical statistical comparisons. But however welcome the attempt, there are difficulties in accepting Hopper's framework as a basis for research. The heuristic value of a typology must be, as he says, 'a preliminary step to more narrowly-focused research'. It must also be capable of providing the basis for effective explanations of differences between systems and of accounting for major processes in particular systems. It can be demonstrated that Hopper's typology poses problems in relation to both of these objectives, but because the exercise is of crucial importance if a viable educational sociology is to develop, I intend to begin with a discussion of the logical properties of the essay and move from there to an alternative formulation.

The first, and most striking, thing about Hopper's essay is the assumption of what an educational system is for. As he puts it, 'the structure of educational systems, especially those within industrial societies, can be understood primarily in terms of their selection process'.[3] As this selection process is related directly to the demands of the labour market, education is seen by Hopper largely in terms of its economic functions and so might be expected to be treated as an extension of economic sociology. Oddly enough, however, it is not discussed in this context at all. For Hopper the educational system

* [Reprinted as Reading 5 in the present volume. E.H.]

inherits from the economic system certain values which in turn control certain processes of occupational training and selection: the whole point of educational research is how the system does this. ('How does educational selection occur? When are pupils initially selected? Who should be selected? Why should they be selected'?) The exercise of analysing selection processes is, of course, extremely important in educational research, and Hopper's method of posing the question allows for more flexible research on this set of problems than more economics-based or stratification-based frameworks. But as he formulates it the typology is open to two major objections.

1. If education is primarily about the structuring of selection this can surely only be done within a more comprehensive model of economics and stratification systems. Hopper's essay is primarily concerned with industrial societies, yet there is no attempt to adequately distinguish between the different characteristics of those societies in terms of both their relative technology and unit sizes and the selection by industry and commerce of its personnel. Further there is an implicit assumption that there is a one-to-one relationship between the selection process in schools and the requirements of the economy. As the economics literature more than amply demonstrates[4] this is just not true (although politicians in all countries may want to make it come true). It may be conceded that he does classify degrees of standardization of selection procedures but this is only from the point of view of the schools; there is no suspicion of whether economic selection might use educational criteria in non-standard ways. Even within the U.S.S.R. (with remarkable educational standardization) there are a large number of entry points to occupational posts which do not appear to depend on educational selection.[5] Within a more diversified educational system the independence of sectors of the economy from educational selection is even greater.[6] As I shall show later this is not simply a question of using economic and organizational variables to 'explain' educational variations, it is more centrally a question of the actual classifications to be used initially.

A similar objection can be raised against Hopper's assumptions on stratification. The basis of his stratification analysis rests on the 'ideologies of legitimation' and the convergence between stratification and ideology.[7] Although there is some evidence to support convergence, it is doubtful if its assumption helps much in the analysis of education. After all, education is as much about the *creation* of ideologies as it is about anything else. All Hopper is able to say about stratification is in relation to ruling groups who must legitimize their positions, be flexible enough to absorb potentially able leaders from the lower order, and obtain some cooperation from the less powerful groups. This Paretan definition does nothing to provide the basis for analyzing different forms of stratification: variations are reduced dramatically to elite competence. It is therefore relatively easy to demonstrate 'convergence' when the only focus of analysis is the ruling culture. Indeed in this sense the definition is tautological: elites have ideologies which are either centralized or diffused according to whether the elites are centralized or diffused. This tells us little about either the nature of the ideologies or the diffusion.

2. Unfortunately Hopper never discusses whether selection is only a part of the study of education. He seems to confuse systemic goals with extrasystemic ones, and hardly begins to analyze the relationship of goals to culture, organization, or the economy.[8] In part this is derived from the initial confusion over the function of education. Hopper plumps for the 'manifest function' of selection, which presumably implies that such issues as research, styles of pedagogy and the different organizational and cultural goals of places of education must be classified as latent or else encapsulated into the manifest function. This is very curious. In the Soviet Union, for example, a manifest function of education must as much be the education of students into the dominant nationalist-communist ideology as to select them according to criteria derived from that ideology or from other social/economic pressures. This is more than amply demonstrated by the literature,[9] which emphasizes the nationalist-communist philosophy all the way from curricula to regular indoctrination through such organizations as the Young Pioneers. In the United States a manifest function of education must surely be the integration of disparate groups into a common value-system. Both of these functions may contribute to the legitimation of the selection process, but they must be kept analytically separate if we are to make any sense of education as part of national culture. But even this overemphasizes the common framework of educational values. The *gemeinschaft-gesellschaft* dichotomy is plainly inadequate as a basis for analyzing values. The goals of a differentiated system must also be related to stratification discontinuities and to what Etzioni refers to as the 'culture goals' which 'institutionalize conditions needed for the creation and preservation of symbolic objects, their application, and the creation or reinforcement of commitment to such objects'.[10] Hopper's typology ascribes single culture-goals to all educational institutions, but surely even within his framework of selection the actual emphasis placed on selection varies enormously within regions and between different schools or institutions: this is as true of the U.S.S.R. as of Britain. In part this may be because of the goals set by the organizations themselves and

because of local culture pressures which operate quite distinctly from the ideologies of the center. Indeed the center-periphery framework used by political sociologists[11] would seem to have more relevance to the discussion of national ideologies than a simple framework based on the pattern variables, though in industrial societies the 'periphery' would have to be carefully re-formulated in relation to class structures and cultures.[12] In addition to this we have the existence within ruling elites (in all countries) of quite distinct value-systems which are in continual competition for the control of the educational system. This may be for the reasons demonstrated by Gramsci: 'every "essential" social class emerging into history from the preceding economic structure, and as an expression of one of the developments of this structure, has found, at least in all history up to now, intellectual categories which were pre-existing and which, moreover, appeared as representatives of an historical continuity uninterrupted even by the most complicated and radical changes in social and political forms'.[13] Thus if change take place in ideologies they take place in the context of this struggle which is at once a cultural and a structural one. Hopper is in danger of identifying ruling ideologies with the residual traditions. The distinction between goals and legitimation is a necessary one. What is more important is to identify the competing sectors (in the U.S.S.R. as in Britain) and assess their relative importance. This can only be a dynamic historical/structural study, whose object is to establish how the particular constellations of ideologies come to hold the influence they do and under what legitimizing symbols changes take place.[14] This is particularly true in societies which are apparently communistic-collectivistic, or, as in Britain, where the national attitudes become increasingly collectivistic-meritocratic while competing with residual particularism-individualism. On the first type of society Hopper seems to be reading Marion Levy when he should be reading Franz Schurmann, and on the second he reads vintage Shils when Raymond Williams or even Bantock would be more useful.[15] The problem arises partly from discussing only 'various public and official statements'[16] rather than focusing on the conflicts between national policy goals, symbols of legitimation and sectoral goals.

If we take the case of France where Hopper's criteria for selection is paternalist-collectivist, it is clear that these values relate more to the domination of a particular kind of social elite (the archtypical bourgeoisie) and the structured nature of its conflict with rural society and the working class than to any abstract concept of polity or culture: why not therefore start with the historical structuring of class culture and leave the values to be explained? The problem with the pattern variable approach is that it leaves very little room for the analysis of culture because the cultural variables which form the basis for the classification can in turn only lead to explanations in terms of social stratification. This is why Parsons inexplicably becomes a 'Marxist' when he talks about class,[17] but of course it is a class analysis from which culture has already been removed. In certain situations (e.g. in comparing economic and political development) this procedure is capable of producing important insights, but it is doubtful if it helps much in the study of such cultural areas as education. Hence we need to analyze precisely what constitutes a culture. This is bound to involve an analysis of the interrelationships between the organizations themselves, the characteristics of the economy and the political power structure, and communications systems (including language, mass media, and folk mores). It is impossible to see a way of including these in any research derived from Hopper's typology without doing serious injustice to the facts and without trivializing the cultural content of education.

But however weak Hopper's conceptual framework, it does have a number of distinct advantages for the comparatist. Too often comparative educational monographs simply list cases side by side or use crude measurements of inputs or outputs. As Hopper demonstrates, there *are* theoretical interconnections between system elements which are capable of being studied *as interconnections*. Further than this he does use the value-system as an important part of this exercise. My major complaint is not this—for Hopper comes very close to seeing education as a cultural-political process—but to the methodological confusion that is bound to arise in treating values in the way he does. Having said that it is now necessary to spell out what the alternatives might be.

III

Sociologists tend to approach education from one of three perspectives: that which stresses educational outputs in terms of wider societal demands (the approach favoured by Hopper): that which sees education as an encapsulated system and therefore most usefully approached from the perspective of organizational theory (the work of Turner, Conant, Lambert and others);[18] and the conventional British approach which sees education in terms of inputs. All approaches present great problems. The first masquerades as a general theory though its basic concern is more specific; but at the same time it is incapable of covering the range of problems necessary to answer the specific question because of its over-emphasis on education. The second has two major defects. Although educational organizations *may* be studied as enclosed systems for the sake of research convenience, this can provide theoretical importance only if the findings of the research are related to wider societal parameters and if the comparative relevance is established. Of course this is rarely, if ever, done. Either, as with research following from Etzioni (and indeed the whole macro-organizational perspective), educational organizations are studied as case studies within the typology bringing little of wider societal factors to bear on particular situations (except as inputs and outputs) or else, as in the Goffman tradition, they are simply internal interactional situations without the benefit of a comparative or societal context of any description. This latter seems to be the main defect of the work of Royston Lambert in this country.[19] Boarding schools are more or less total institutions with lesser or greater flexibility. If they are to be made less total then they have to be made more flexible. This leaves untouched the relationship of these schools to total cultural milieu, though Lambert's proposals would have a considerable effect on that milieu.

The third (British) perspective is primarily concerned with who gets into the system.[20] It stresses class factors, income factors and other elements of stratification. The system is examined—and conclusions drawn—largely from this perspective: if input suggests an unbalanced selection, then either the selection procedure must be changed (abolish 11 +) or else the institutions must be enlarged or made more 'open' (as with comprehensives). Some other questions do follow in the wake of this kind of analysis (such as extra-school socialization,[21] teaching methods[22] and the relationships between different levels of schools) but the emphasis is basically on input. In many respects this type of research has been very important for collecting data, but again one may wonder whether it has done much more than improve our knowledge of social stratification and raise uncomfortable questions about the consequences of political policy.

There is a fourth perspective, more favoured by psychologists than sociologists: the socialization of the child. As most of this is totally psychologistic, it need not concern us here. There are, however, two sociological variations which require comment. The interactional institutional study obviously poses some important questions about socialization, but it is important to stress that this is primarily an exercise in the study of a particular institution on the development of children. It is neither a comparative study of socialization (the data is much too fragmentary for that) nor is it a direct contribution to the sociology of education (the relationship of this particular institutional context to the wider process of education never being made explicit). Secondly, systemic theories which pose questions about compliance structures and multiple goals normally introduce the concept of strain to explain problems in organization. This, too, involves an indirect approach to socialization, but even less satisfactorily, for we are never given the opportunity to assess the nature of the strain except in terms of the organizations: because people break down, mobs go on the rampage, or students revolt this must be because the system is not flexible enough (or tough enough). This may well be true, but it may be equally due to the prior socialization of the people involved in the strain or their concomitant socialization. What a particular institution can do about this may be very minimal indeed, unless it can see itself as part of the total socializing process. Current changes in British secondary education may be based on false premises because they fail to realise this.[23] It is too easy to see changes in access to institutions as a solution to major cultural and social cleavages.

The problem of the sociology of education is thus centrally one of what it is that is being explained. Unfortunately what is often taken to be the sociology of education is not primarily about education at all—but about selection and stratification, socialization and organizations. All of these are obviously contributory factors in the study of education, and it is perhaps useful to indicate how two of them can make their contribution before moving on to the main concern of this paper. (The issue of socialization will be dealt with at greater length in a forthcoming book elaborating on the theme of this paper.)

1. *Stratification and Educational Selection*

Let us take the selection issue first. In Hopper's essay the value-orientations are the basic categories for classification. I have suggested that this poses a major problem if it is the value-system that we are actually trying to investigate: but it also poses a problem if we are attempting to account for shifts in social stratification. Hopper argues that most industrial societies are not rapidly changing: but of course in stratification they are changing rapidly enough for the argument to be suspect. And the British and French educational systems are currently in upheaval: pattern-variable classifications provide only marginal use in dealing with these changes. If we were to employ Hopper's strategy in order to explain these changes we would doubtlessly find ourselves in the circular situation of Almond and Verba where 'cultural' differences are 'explained' by reference back to historical factors which are in themselves unexplained.[24] It becomes impossible to analyze processes of change because a time-culture dimension is absent. If the object of investigation is to specify how selection takes place, then we clearly have a number of specific parameters: stratification factors (the actual distribution of populations according to the usual indices), the rates of movement between different levels (including the appearance of new occupations and the disappearance of old ones), the rate of technological/economic development (including size of units, ratios of differential skills), methods of recruitment to jobs (including public education and professional or industrial training and internal promotion), and intervening socio-psychological variables (family size, social communities, income and security differentials of parents, and so on). If we do all this it is important to note that education becomes a secondary factor in the analysis. The basic issue is to analyze the total selection process in a society (or segment of it): educational selection may be of lesser or greater importance. It might be found, for example, that although the educational system is highly centralized and stratified, the selection of people depends also on internal recruitment and in-service training. Conversely, although education may be deliberately selective and related to manpower requirements, many of the trainees may find themselves without jobs or with jobs at variance with their qualifications because of mobility features within industry and commerce. Considerable evidence exists for this in the Soviet, Polish, and Hungarian literature.[25] With this in mind, and the very extensive evidence for Britain, Scandinavia, France, and the U.S.A., it is inconceivable that educational selection should be studied independently of the total selection process. The most important basis for classification would then be rates of mobility, technological-economic structures and community-ecological features, these being the items most easily derived from cross-national data and in most cases the most reliable. The object of the research should be to find explanations for variations and for this purpose certain intervening variables become important: the educational selection process, patterns of socialization, political structures, and so on. Ultimately this means that we are seeking to establish (at a low level) how structures provide personnel for a given set of occupational positions; (at an intermediate level) to analyze discontinuities between selection processes, socialization patterns and system of stratification; and (at the macro level) to locate mobility as part of a cultural complex which may vary according to the combinations of structural features.[26] From the point of view of educational sociology this analysis is important for three reasons (but they are important enough): it establishes part of the wider economic and political parameters within which educational institutions have to operate; it provides a large amount of subsidiary data on the working of particular sectors of the educational system; and it allows us to isolate those attributes which individuals bring into education and distinguish them both from those they acquire during the educational experience, and those they acquire elsewhere during the educational period.

2. Schools and Colleges as Complex and Simple Organizations

A further criticism of Hopper's typology was that it attributed societal goals to the educational system without adequately distinguishing between systemic and extra-systemic goals. A possible alternative would be to use Etzioni's model of complex organizations and distinguish between goals which are derived from power and structural situations extrinsic to the organization itself and those which derive directly from the organization's own norms, traditions, and values. It may be one of the outcomes of this research that in collective-communistic societies the educational goals are more directly derived from extra-systemic ones, while in other societies they are not, but this is surely a subject for research, not an *a priori* assumption. In fact one of the major issues in the organizational study of education must be the power structure, and the power structure at all levels. There are two major areas for studying power in education: at the national, policy-making level (involving such organizations, in Britain as the Department of Education and Science, the Treasury, the LEAs, the Headmasters' Conference, the UGC and so on) where the focus must be on the resolution of competing interests, and at the lower institutional level where a distilled version of policy (though not necessarily fully resolved) is implemented in schools and colleges against their own culture, order and social goals. The main considerations for this second kind of study have, of course, already been established in the U.S.A.[27] The Harvard Studies on educational decision-making are far superior to anything existing in this country where the emphasis on who gets there has inhibited discussion on how the schools are organized. As Neal Gross[28] has shown, the locus of power in American schools is very much with the parents through the local boards of education. On all existing evidence it is clear in British schools that it is very much with the teachers, but we don't really have the comparative data, in spite of Asher Tropp's pioneering study of the NUT.[29] In some respects we need a good old-fashioned study of pressure group politics, but we also need a study of professionalism in relation to the school political situation on lines similar to Eckstein's Study of the BMA[30] or an analysis of career structures which has learned something from Michel Crozier.[31] A comparative analysis of decision-making processes, and of professionalism in its organizational context, would immeasurably add to our knowledge of how any one system worked and incidentally improve the quality of sociological theory. These considerations would seem *prima facie* to have validity in all educational systems, though some would be rather more difficult to conduct research into because of political constraints. (A Soviet '*Who Runs the Schools*' is probably further in the future than its British equivalent, though one can never be sure.) But there is no reason to assume complete uniformity in an educational system merely because we are not able to carry out research there.

But the question of the power structure is only part of an organizational study. The issue of goals in education also raises the important issue of the multiplicity of societal-culture goals, even if we were to accept that these derived directly from the value-orientations of the elite. Even for *them* education is not only about occupational selection but also about moral values, research, and the transmission of knowledge (of which more anon): it would be rash indeed to argue that all of these can ultimately be reduced to selection. The composite goals of the makers of education policy may be interpreted very differently by the educationalist: and even if they agree in general about what these goals are, they may still differ considerably on the priorities allocated to aspects of them. Thus although the political elites have goals which they try to impose on the educational system these policies have to be transmitted through the educational elites and the teachers and lecturers. The extent to which education is able to counter the political elite's policies will depend in part on its own economic independence, in part on patterns of socialization which are strong enough to resist the norms of the system, and in part on the persistence of centres of local political power which are able to back alternative schemes. This is not simply a question of centralist versus pluralist societies as implied by Hopper. If we examine Eastern Europe, the centralization of goals has very different consequences for different regions and social groups, producing outputs quite distinct from the objectives of the goals. In part this is because in certain organizational contexts the balance of priorities in implementing the official goals varies because of the exigencies of those contexts. Urban schools in Poland may stress the achievement orientations of the official ideology while rural schools may stress moral and integrative values.[32] This must in part be because of the predominant socialization patterns: urban middle class and skilled working class parents want their children to get on (even if they dislike the political context in which they will do this) while rural parents hold back because of resistance as much to the values of the industrial society as to those of communism. In the one case the goals are complemented by the school system (the integrative aspects being either irrelevant or ignored) while in the other the dominant integrative aspects of the social system are used to correct possible deviance while not noticeably increasing the achievement-orientations. This has little to do with official priorities as Hopper suggests, but with the mediation of policies through local structures. On the other hand, as the sad history of the various Academies of Sciences in Eastern Europe suggests, official organizations may consciously be granted relative autonomy from the formal societal goals. Their failure may depend on foreign political pressures (Czechoslovakia, 1968), internal political upheaval (Poland, 1968) and their success on the distance from political centres (Novosibirsk). They are not killed off because their goals are different from societal goals but because they look like challenging them. This is as true in the U.S.A. as in the U.S.S.R.: the main difference is the devolution of power.

For any systematic classification it is therefore necessary to note the degree of compliance in relation to both political and economic policy goals and to subcultural norms and values. Within particular educational systems it is important to be able to categorize the types and variations of schools and colleges on two dimensions—according to both the compliance with policy and the degree of reliance on particular cultural sets.[33] The scale of differentiation within one educational system might be quite wide and the relative degree of goal emphasis may vary not only in relation to different areas but also according to the age-levels of education: primary schools may be more 'open' (in goals and in relation to culture sets) than secondary schools, which in turn are more restrictive and dominated by occupational selection of subjects than universities. The 'open' and 'closed' nature of educational institutions is thus related to the two dimensions but the explanations of variations can only be established by comparison.

This poses some problems. For comparative analysis the usual method of classification is to average out the data, so that in this case societies would range from those with centralized control mechanisms and relatively complete domination of pedagogy and research to those with multiple structures and complex control mechanisms.[34] Of course this has to be done, but one of the drawbacks is that averaging out prevents us from investigating what is precisely of greatest theoretical importance: the relationships of particular kinds of institutions to the wider social structure and to their immediate socio-cultural environment. If we produce a typology based on national profiles and on organization types as Etzioni suggests the problem of interpretation of particular situations is reduced to ringing changes on the intervening variables. Again we have to ask what it is that we are trying to explain. The problem of a general typology which includes developmental stages is that a large number of issues have to be subjected to the same developmental process. For the study of educational institutions this is most unsatisfactory. The typology must be simple enough to be capable of elaboration according to particular situations and features of change. The use of comparison must primarily be to demonstrate both how general particular findings are, and also to check on the reliability of the particular hypothesis generated. For example, in *The Management of Innovation* Burns and Stalker use a simple typology of mechanistic and organic management-systems in their attempt to provide a 'description and explanation of what happens when new and unfamiliar tasks are put upon industrial concerns organized for relatively stable conditions'.[35] The typology is expanded by providing a taxonomy of intermediate types and subsequently the adoption of one type or another is discussed in relation to the technological and change processes of society and to the 'purposes and commitments of managers'. Why particular institutions accept technological change but do not alter their management system is discussed in the context of this flexible model. The essential point for our concern here is that the organizational comparisons are made in relation to a specific set of problems; taxonomies are of little use unless they are leading up to something, and they have little purpose unless they can be related to levels of interaction.

In education the problem of organizational *change* is of fundamental importance and comparison can be valuable in indicating how different kinds of institutions respond to changes in public policy and changes in knowledge. Burns' organic and mechanistic types approximate in some measure to the open and closed dichotomies instanced above,[36] but the importance of comparison at this level is that the research method must be clear about its cultural controls. Random cross-cultural research has little value unless the particular changes being considered have some comparability. The need for concomitant variation studies is suggested in the next section of this paper, but for organizational analysis the cultural 'inputs' must be similar (policy directives and types of knowledge-change) or else (as checks) the organizational system must be similar. This kind of analysis is crucial if anything is to be made of current changes in Britain in comprehensive schools, public schools, and grammar schools as well as the universities and technical colleges. Similarly there is little point in indicating that some of these changes have taken place elsewhere unless we are clear what the other social parameters are. The 'success' of comprehensive schools in Sweden is no guarantee of their 'success' in Britain. If we have evidence on the organizational dynamics of Swedish schools and of British, then we have the necessary groundwork for comparison. This task has hardly begun. But even if it were more advanced the problem still remains of the core content of the sociology of education.

3. Culture and the Management of Knowledge

The problem with organizational studies is that, although they are superior to what normally passes for the sociology of education, they tend to overemphasize the mechanics of the institutions without necessarily contributing to a sociology of knowledge. In particular, studies based on organizational criteria tend to stress the power aspects on the one hand and control-communications mechanisms on the other, without having much to say about the sources of the values and knowledge being transmitted. As one of the main exponents of the study of organizations puts it, the only way out of the organization miasma is 'by perceiving behaviour as a medium of the constant interplay and mutual re-definition of individual entities and social institutions'.[37] Because the study of education is so much concerned with actually moulding the reality-images of young people, it has remained conscious of this process all along and has never been in danger of completely falling into structural arthritis. But if it is to develop, it is important to stress that the study of education as culture is not peripheral to the subject but central. Selecting people for jobs is one of education's latent functions: its *manifest* function is the management of knowledge. Any comparative study which ignores this is in danger of trivializing the entire subject.

What issues are relevant for this study? Initially they must be concerned with three conceptual distinct entities: values, norms, and knowledge, each considered from its internal and external aspects. Although the three aspects have to be kept conceptually separate (because they seem to relate to different things) we cannot conclude that they are not interdependent. One of the major purposes of comparative research is to establish the conditions under which particular degrees of interdependence occur. This is not to assume—as the structural-differentiation thesis often implies—that increased differentiation in structures implies increasing differentiation between norms, values, and knowledge. Again this is a matter for research.

Unfortunately there is no major sociological analysis which directs itself to the management of knowledge. Some of the most suggestive literature is found in other fields of sociology,[38] while the most impressive educational literature is often not by sociologists at all.[39] It is one of the curiosities of sociology as a discipline that although early sociologists were concerned with the control and transmission of knowledge, their successors have been primarily interested in the selection process, socialization, and organization in ways that tell us little about the business of education. Some suggestive material appears on scientific issues[40] and in some few anthropological studies.[41] But most of this is not concerned with educational processes covering entire systems, but with isolated segments.

The problem is best stated by example. The anthropological literature on 'transitional' societies abounds with studies of syncretic religious organizations—millennialism, messianism, and so on.[42] The importance of the study is that it focuses on the breakdown of, or dramatic change in, one or all of these. Because of changed information the existing symbols do not make sense and have to be reformulated: what does this mean in terms of values and normative conduct? Alternatively new values arise to legitimize changed inter-action regulations; or, dual value systems are held, the one to legitimize order, the other to explain 'facts'. And so on. Crucially most studies stress the importance of changed knowledge and changed patterns of structure on the value-systems. These studies provide us with the nearest thing to closed laboratory-tests of theories in the sociology of culture.

A further instance occurs in the wider study of development. In his remarkable study, *The Labyrinth of Solitude*, the Mexican poet Octavio Paz is essentially concerned with the same problem. Mexico has acquired industry, through its revolution has modernized its social institutions, with its increased education has radically en-larged the area of Mexican knowledge. And yet, for all that, the values have not changed. 'The religious feelings of my people are very deep—like their misery and helplessness—but their fervour has done nothing but return again and again to a well that has been empty for centuries . . . (I cannot) believe in the fertility of a society based on the imposition of certain modern principles.'[43] If correct, this analysis presents us with a more curious case. The social structure changes, the knowledge changes, but the values remain unchanged. This seems unlikely on the face of it but at least it offers a challenge to the idea that there is a one-to-many relationship between values and norms as Neil Smelser seems to imply.[44] The central assumption in Smelser's thesis is that the values of a society involve a composite legitimation of *all* normative situations. He thus sees it possible to have campaigns against particular normative structures without challenging values, but that protests against values necessarily involve protests against all norms. This is clearly not true for all millennial or revolutionary movements and still less is it true for education. Education involves both the creation and transmission of values and might be reflected in a variety of normative structures which represent different values. The values of working-class education may be different from middle-class education—note the case of Risinghill Comprehensive School[45] where the Headmaster, Michael Duane, decided to run the school according to working-class values rather than middle-class ones: hence the conflict with authority and with middle-class parents and teachers. If he was head of a secondary modern school, there would have been fewer problems. Duane had put his finger on the dilemma of comprehensive education, one which has already been faced in the U.S.A.[46] Education is important both for transmitting values and establishing norms or reinforcing them. Under what conditions does it act? Is it a mediator or an actor? What part does it play in the creation of social consciousness? This is the crux of the management of education.

Unlike primitive or 'transitional' societies, modern industrial ones involve very complex relationships between values, norms, and knowledge. Two examples should make the point. Catholic secondary schools in England tend to be drawn from the children of manual and lower-paid white-collar workers. The normative aspects of education depend in part on the rules adopted by the schools themselves and in part derive from rules operating elsewhere in Britain. Some of these rules may derive from Catholic values (presumably those relating to worship) but most do not. The values of the school are presumably Catholic, and therefore different from those operating in the rest of the country but mediated through the school structure which is hardly specifically Catholic. The attempt will be made, however, to legitimize the rules by reference to Catholic values. On the other hand much of the knowledge transmitted will again be independent of Catholic values: curricula, exams, and even teaching syllabuses are set by central secular bodies. But even if the content is intended to be independent of Catholic values it is again mediated through a Catholic system. What does the value system do to the knowledge? In some measure this must be related to the social backgrounds of pupils and also to the ways that Catholic teachers resolve their role-conflicts. If the school is drawn from the children of manual workers, the ascriptive communal aspects of Catholicism may be stressed in preference to the individualistic aspects inherent in the examination selection process. On the other hand if the school is predominantly middle-class, one might expect that knowledge might be stressed as a Catholic value. The basic questions for research are therefore the extent to which the Catholic values are adapted to meet particular social exigencies, the extent to which these values intrude in the transmission of knowledge, and the degree to which the normative situation in the school takes precedence over them both. In all of this, the relationship of the school both to the immediate social catchment area and to the dual pressures of Church hierarchies and state educational authorities must be seen as a set of interactive levels influencing the school's 'behaviour'. It is only within this framework that the 'common sense knowledge of social structures' of both the teachers and the pupils can be studied usefully.[47]

If this example is over-simple (because the Catholic element introduces a simplified form of values), there are many more which illustrate the argument. A challengingly complex one is offered by Jules Henry.[48] 'Rome High School' has two orientations: fun and scholarship, but both are subsumed in the common-value-system which demands integration into the adult society. Thus the stress on games and early marriage is partly a response to the competitive nature of the system: games are a form of integration into the school subsystem but also a way of contracting out of the pressing values of the social system. The crucial thing about this school's social milieu is the general upward mobility of nearly all pupils. Thus if the formal values of the wider social system demand academic achievement, the dominating subcultural ones demand integration in the face of competition (which is manifested in the 'hedonistic mindlessness' of games and sex). But for both boys and girls the overriding values are symbolized by 'scholarship': 'Rome High' has emphasized scholarship so successfully, and it has come to have so much meaning in this community that is upwardly mobile, that it is possible, veritably in the teeth of fun, to get high grades and not be looked upon with disdain.[49] The interpersonal relationships of the school are not, however, based on 'scholarship' but on the normative structures of the 'slovenly morality' of gamesmanship and the sexual and group norms which dominate their day-to-day relationships. Thus if the values of the system lead students to compete to enter the adult world, the group norms (or the subculture) make them resist the world, though the conflicts, paradoxically, propel them into getting married and entering it earlier than they would otherwise do. The encouragement of 'knowledge' in this case can only be done by stressing its importance for achievement. What this implies is that the study of schools as organizations and as cultural units requires a distinction between the values attached to education both by the managers of institutions and by the pupils, the structuring of knowledge according to the hierarchical-organizational patterns and the regimentation of curriculum[50] and the relationship of these processes to wider societal demands and the ultimate life-chances of the pupils. Most studies of internal school organization in Britain, where they have been concerned with the structure of relationships at all, have ignored curriculum and the relationship between it and authority-patterns. As Bernstein has tried to show, the relationship between hierarchical school structures and failure to innovate in the curriculum and keep knowledge open may be a direct one.[51] In this sense students who campaign for academic freedom and reforms in the teaching, examination, and discipline structure of universities are putting their fingers on the one vital area of knowledge-management, but it is one which immediately leads to the wider question of the institutionalization of national culture.

To be effective such an approach must operate on two levels: the development of national intellectual styles, and the transmission of these styles through educational policies. The first is an extremely difficult thing to do but essential if the societal parameters of culture and especially education are to be established. The exercise is partly historical: how do particular styles of learning come to have the importance they do? What relationship have these styles in a particular culture? How are changes in knowledge elsewhere absorbed into the national styles? Attempts to do this for Britain are scarce, though recently a few brief attempts have been made.[52] Elsewhere there is rather more material, though little of it systematic enough to produce adequate comparative theory.[53] What is important is that the intellectual styles are related to particular kinds of social structure and also to the particular choices made because of surviving historical conditions. In a recent study[54] Etzioni has made the important point that choices (and decisions about educational policy can be represented as choices) are determined by three factors: functional prerequisites of situations, historical contingencies, and self-conscious choice. This is helpful, but the problem for comparative analysis must surely be to diminish between varieties of functional prerequisites and varieties of historical factors. Management training may be considered a prerequisite of a certain level of industrial development: but how are we to distinguish between Soviet management and American management? Both countries have managers, but what is central and what is peripheral to their training? Russian managers *may* be given certain kinds of training and be expected to do certain kinds of jobs which are due to cumulative historical features of the Soviet situation but which a western management consultant may consider extraneous to the actual industrial situation. An American may do the same job in a very different way, but be less successful because these extraneous factors are actually vital to good Soviet management.

One of the 'historical' situations is, of course, the educational system itself. The institutionalization of knowledge not only ensures the rapid transmission of intellectual styles, it also inhibits them by making old styles rigid. The study of educational systems must be focused on the ways that the educational power-structure and the institutions act as selective filters for different levels of praxis and consciousness. All knowledge is shrouded in ideology: the study of educational systems allows us to see what is ideological, to judge how new information is distorted by the combined historical-structural conditions which determine how it is absorbed or rejected by the ideology of the system. Thus the study of national cultural styles and the study of educational institutions are interrelated. For the development of educational sociology this interrelationship is a crucial and as yet unexplored territory. In Scotland two books have produced something like documentary models of what might be done[55] though neither with the detailed organizational study that I have called for. Elsewhere, the major comparative attempts are in the study of science, though the models are closer to a natural-history description than concrete theory.[56]

With this kind of research, the qualitative nature of the institutional process attains greater significance. Schools must be studied because they are recipients of this national cultural complex and because praxis for them is at once determined by commonsense knowledge of social structures and by the formal structural contours of the sub-systems themselves. The basic problem is the way that values are transmitted through normative situations and the way that knowledge contributes to the symbolic order of the participants. Returning to organizational studies this involves in part an analysis of types of educational structure (organic-mechanistic with intervening taxo-nomies), a framework for the study of professionalism (notably the recruitment, training, career structure of teachers and their power-position in relation to the educational structures), and in a large part a consideration of curricula in relation to organizational patterns. But it is difficult to see this being successfully done unless there is also some consideration of the subcultural inputs as emphasized by some British and American research. Even the most flexible, open system is doing something to people against their experience of prior socialization.

But I have so far not attempted to define 'knowledge' for the

purpose of the development of a sociology of education. In part this
is deliberate. Ultimately the definition that sociologists must accept
as a basis for research is Berger and Luckman's: 'knowledge' is
anything that 'makes sense' to people in society.[57] But this is so wide-
sweeping a definition that it requires some further clarification before
it can be put to use. In the sociology of education we are dealing
with the problem in at least three different contexts: in the academic
disciplines themselves we are treating knowledge as making sense of
behaviour and matter in specialized, often abstract symbolizations;
at the level of the individual and of social groups in educational
institutions and outside we are primarily concerned with devices
for constructing indexical frameworks for 'commonsense knowledge'
of social relationships; at the institutional level we are interested
primarily in the ways that configurations of structures generate
definitions of social reality which the individuals or groups have to
take account of in their assessment of knowledge-relevance, and
which provide the cultural context in which knowledge-as-discipline is transmitted. Thus the term 'management of knowledge'
has three meanings: it refers to the social structures and procedures
which generate knowledge-as-discipline; it further refers to the ways
that educational institutions control the discipline-knowledge imparted and the world views of the members of institutions; and it
finally refers to the ways in which individuals and collectivities
manage the tensions which arise out of the conflict between their
own world-view and the discipline-institutional conceptions of
knowledge. In other words for the practical purposes of examining
the relationships between 'knowledge' in the formal, academic sense
and in the informal Schutz sense we have the central task of exploring
the mediations in the educational institutions.

Comparative research on these lines raises fundamental problems,
some of which have already been referred to in the critique of Hopper
above. Basically they relate to the culture-structure dichotomy
which has troubled sociology and anthropology from early in the
nineteenth century. The simplest solution is to assume that the
definitions of 'knowledge' arise out of particular structural configurations; in other words by defining socio-educational networks
and power structures we pose the essential framework for indexing
reality-constructs. Although this looks like an obvious procedure,
it must be rejected as the sole method of operation suggested above:
culture is almost as much an independent variable as is structure.
In the analysis of discipline-knowledge, even if we keep to social
structure as a basic unit, much of the accumulated knowledge
derives from 'dead' structures which bear little resemblance to

contemporary research and teaching structures. In discussing the Protestant ethic Max Weber saw this problem very clearly: if once there had been a connection between the rise of capitalism and certain religious beliefs, they no longer held by the nineteenth century. But the historical 'memory' was still there: 'Victorious capitalism, since it rests on mechanical foundations, needs its support no longer. The rosy blush of its laughing heir, the Enlightenment, seems also to be irretrievably fading, and the idea of duty to one's calling prowls about in our lives like the ghost of dead religious beliefs.'[58] Structural change certainly implies changes in knowledge, but it does so with more than a nod in the direction of dying cultures. The problem is how to assess this transmission of traditional culture. Paradoxically the only answer to this is a social structural one.

If we return to the general question of national cultural styles, it is clear that two aspects are normally involved in common-sense interpretations of differences—'cultural' differences ('French anthropology is logical and metaphysical; British is empirical') and structural ones ('the University of Paris is a central university system dominating the entire French educational system; Britain has no educational centre, but many different institutions'). Whether such observations are 'true' or not is not the issue in question at this point: what *is* obvious is that both culture and structure are invoked in national comparisons. The solution to the problem can be arrived at both by content analysis of what the symbolizations are and by historico-political structural analysis of how cultural symbols are transmitted in changing social situations. In other words by teasing out the relationships between transmission and gestation in both cultural and structural terms we may arrive at something like a solution. But this solution must, to a very large extent, be concerned with the structures. A good example is furnished by Sheldon Rothblatt in his study of nineteenth-century Cambridge.[59] In the critical debates in the second half of the century on the future of the university, central issues in curriculum change hinged on the relevance of specific subjects to the 'needs' of society. Many dons and non-resident M.A.s 'decided the worth of an academic subject by its usefulness to commerce and industry. In their view almost no subject which could be turned to the benefit of business deserved university recognition.'[60] Even the introduction of German and French was contested on the grounds that they were useful in inter-national trade. There are several issues of importance here for our analysis. (i) Resistance to change was not purely cultural: structures existed which gave the conservatives a power-base for organization. (ii) In few cases was the resistance completely effective: Cambridge got its French, German and Mathematics, but (iii) the terms on which the changes were admitted were within a framework that insisted that all subjects must be liberal and non-utilitarian. It is, of course, quite irrelevant to point out that objection to professional demands ill-suited a university that had commenced as a training centre for priests. But it _is_ relevant to observe that the existing structures were symbolized in terms of a knowledge that to a large extent reflected 'dead' structures. The changes introduced involved both a strengthening of those conceptions of knowledge (in that they were transmitted to living structures) and ameliorations in those conceptions (because German and French are not Latin and Greek). The major problem in determining the dominant traits of the subsequent culture is in assessing the extent to which configurations of old and new are actually part of the consciousness of the actors concerned. But this involves a development of my argument which cannot be presented here. What must be stressed as the basis for comparative analysis is that 'national culture' requires the specifying of the following characteristics: (a) Origins of innovations in knowledge-discipline and in institutional patterns of symbolization; (b) Pre-innovative knowledge constructs and their structural bases; (c) Discipline and institutional adaptations to innovations; (d) The commonsense constructs of knowledge by the individuals and groups involved. Put in simpler language we want to know (a) which political, social and academic groups want changes and how they see or imply these changes in terms of world-views; (b) what are the world-views of the people and institutions they want to change; (c) how are these conflicts resolved; (d) in what ways are these changes apprehended by all the people involved in the process (and also, incidentally, by people not directly involved)? In doing this we are constantly asking questions from different vantage points: the meanings of knowledge-constructs are only evident if we examine them in the round and in the context of interrelationships. 'Meaning is not to be conceived, fundamentally, as a state of consciousness or as a set of organized relations existing or subsisting mentally outside the field of experience into which they enter; on the contrary, it should be conceived objectively, as having its existence entirely within this field itself. The response of one organism to the gesture of another in any given social act is the meaning of that gesture and also is in a sense responsible for the appearance or coming into being of the new object—or of the new content of an old object.'[61] The exercise suggested here as the basis for investigating the sociology of education in many ways simply takes the Mead analysis a stage further than he probably intended. 'The field itself' involves a set of

interlocking interaction situations: innovation in discipline-knowledge and educational institutional decision-making on curricula and
pedagogy, which in turn interact with students, research workers,
industry and back again.

'Look what they've done to my brain, ma.' Ultimately that is what
the sociology of education is all about. Until we can specify exactly
what was done and why, we cannot seriously claim to be sociologists
concerned with education.

IV

The main point of comparative research is to lead to substantive
theory. It is used in sociology because it is the nearest substitute for
the scientist's laboratory. But if it is used, it is also necessary to have
hunches about what is significant and purposeful. I have argued here
that there are four major areas affecting sociological research on
education: problems affecting the stratification-selection process;
problems affecting the dynamics of organizations; the entire
question of socialization; and the management of knowledge. It is
clear that I accept this last as being the central concern of the
sociology of education. Until it is treated as such then such topics
(which concern pupils, parents, and teachers alike) as the curricula,
the values of education and the relationship of education to wider
social processes will never be given their proper consideration.
Hopper's essay has provided a valuable attempt at reviewing the
problems inherent in a comparative approach. But in the last analysis
comparative method and theory has little point unless it is directed at
specific societal contours. Although there is some advantage in
creating comparative models which investigate a number of issues
cross-nationally, the ultimate advantage of comparison is that it
should generate a dialectic between the particular and the general.
Part of the task of explaining processes in British society is to
investigate comparable issues elsewhere. But the comparative
exercise is not an end in itself. In this case the ultimate problem
remains: an explanation of British society. Because of the wealth of
research available, education is a useful area with which to begin.
But also for more intrinsically theoretical reasons: it is perhaps the
only area of research in industrial societies where all the major
problems in sociological theory and methodology are focused.

Notes

1. For a recent example see P. Worsley and others, *Introducing Sociology*, Penguin Books, 1970, Chapter 4. For a psychological misreading see the Plowden report on Primary Education.

2. Earl Hopper, 'A Typology for the Classification of Educational Systems', *Sociology*, 2, 1968, 29–46.

3. *Ibid*, p. 30.

4. For examples, see the essays in Part Four of Mark Blaug (ed.), *The Economics of Education*, Harmondsworth: Penguin Books, 1968.

5. For the best account, Z. Katz, 'Hereditary Elements in Education, Occupations, Social Structure', unpublished paper.

6. There are three issues here: (i) the extent to which organizational and technical changes require categories of workers who are not being produced through the formal educational system; (ii) the extent to which selection into certain occupations has traditionally been structured in such a way that parts of the educational system are bypassed (e.g. accountancy, law, as well as many forms of apprenticeship); (iii) the extent to which particular kinds of education do not enhance entry to certain occupations because the education is not recognized by the industrial or commercial selection processes as being relevant.

7. This argument is further elaborated by Hopper and E. G. Dunning, 'Industrialization and the Problem of Convergence: a critical note', *Sociol. R.*, 1966, 14 : 163–186.

8. For a simplified analysis see Amitai Etzioni, *A Comparative Analysis of Complex Organizations*, New York: Free Press, 1961, 71–88.

9. For surveys see: Edmund J. King (ed.), *Communist Education*, London: Methuen, 1963: Helen B. Redl (ed.), *Soviet Educators on Soviet Education*, New York: Free Press, 1964.

10. Etzioni, op. cit. 73.

11. For a brief outline see Daniel Lerner, 'Some Comments on Centre-Periphery Relations', in Richard L. Merritt and Stein Rokkan (eds), *Comparing Nations*, New Haven: Yale University Press, 1966, 259–265.

12. Preliminary attempts are contained in Josephine Klein, *Samples From English Cultures*, London: Routledge and Kegan Paul, 1963; Perry Anderson, 'Origins of the Present Crisis', in Anderson and Robin Blackburn (eds.), *Towards Socialism*, London: Collins, 1965, 11–52; and Basil Bernstein, 'Social Class and Linguistic Development: A Theory of Social Learning', in A. H. Halsey, Jean Floud and C. Arnold Anderson (ed.), *Education, Economy and Society*, New York: Free Press, 1961, 288–314. But of course most of educational literature *assumes* two levels of centre-periphery dichotomies: the educational system is itself seen in these terms with public schools/grammar schools/Oxbridge at the centre and the rest on the periphery, while mobility studies assume individual progression from the periphery to the centre.

13. Antonio Gramsci, *The Modern Prince*, London: Lawrence and Wishart, 1957, 119.

14. See footnotes 47 and 48 for some examples.

15. The most important Levy reference in this context is *Modernization and the Structure of Society*, New York: Free Press, 1966, and Schurmann's classic study of China is *Ideology and Organization in Communist China*, Berkeley: University of California Press, 1966. Edward Shils has produced several studies on British society, although the only one in book form is *The Torment of Secrecy*, London: Heinemann 1956, which provides exactly the right period flavour. Both Raymond

Williams and Bantock owe something to that remarkable British literary critical tradition that reached its apogee in F. R. Leavis and *Scrutiny*. But whereas Williams has absorbed this into a Marxisant critique of culture (see in particular *The Long Revolution*, London: Chatto and Windus, 1961), Bantock has retained the high academic *trahison des clercs* tone of the master: witness G. H. Bantock, *Freedom and Authority in Education*, London: Faber and Faber, 1952.

16. Hopper, *op. cit*, note 23, 44.

17. See essays 14 and 19 in *Essays in Sociological Theory*, New York: Free Press, 1954.

18. Ralph H. Turner, *The Social Context of Ambition*, San Francisco: Chandler Press, 1964; James B. Conant, *The American High School Today*, New York, McGraw-Hill, 1959; Royston Lambert, unpublished mss on English Public and Boarding Schools.

19. Royston Lambert, 'The Public Schools: a sociological introduction', in Graham Kalton, *The Public Schools*, Longmans, 1966, xi–xxxii.

20. The tradition here is too lengthy to cite, but a convenient point is C. V. Glass (ed.), *Social Mobility in Britain*, London: Routledge and Kegan Paul, 1954. Representative summaries of sources are cited in Olive Banks, *The Sociology of Education*, London: Batsford, 1968, and a sample of the earlier contributions are included in A. H. Halsey, Jean Floud and C. Arnold Anderson, *Education, Economy and Society*, New York: Free Press, 1961.

21. Recent examples include, J. W. B. Douglas, *The Home and the School*, London: MacGibbon and Kee, 1964.

22. There are several non-sociological attempts, but an American book, Vincent Rogers, *The Social Studies in English Education*, London: Heinemann, 1968, is one of the more successful attempts at looking at one type of curriculum problem in the schools, Michael Young's *Innovation and Research in Education*, London: Routledge, 1966, is an excellent indication of where the reforms might take place.

23. For an example of research suggesting this see Julienne Ford, 'Comprehensive Schools as Social Dividers', *New Society*, 315, 10 October 1968, 515–517, and the correspondence in the next two issues.

24. Gabriel Almond and Sydney Verba, *The Civic Culture*, Princeton: Princeton U.P., 1963.

25. See Katz, *op. cit.*, and *Social Stratification in Hungary*, Budapest: Hungarian Central Statistical Office, 1967, especially section V, 'Social Mobility and the Open and Closed Character of the Strata', 111–128.

26. Some of the most coherent explorations of such a framework are found in Neil J. Smelser and Seymour Martin Lipset, *Social Structure and Mobility in Economic Development*, London: Routledge and Kegan Paul, 1966. See especially essays by Wilensky, Duncan, Romsoy and Germani.

27. Representative samples include: Neal Gross and others, *Explorations in Role Analysis*, New York: Wiley, 1958; Neal Gross and R. E. Herriott, *Staff Leadership in Public Schools*, New York: Wiley, 1965; Lavern L. Cunningham and Roderick F. McPhee, *The Organization and Control of American Schools*, Ohio: Charles E. Merrill Books, 1963; and Neal Gross, *Who Runs Our Schools?*, New York: Wiley, 1958. A Summary of some of the literature is included in Cole S. Brembeck, *Social Foundations of Education*, New York, Wiley, 1966, Chapters 17 and 18.

28. Neal Gross, *Who Runs Our Schools?*, *op cit*.

29. Asher Tropp, *The School Teachers*, London, Heinemann, 1957.

30. Harry H. Eckstein, *Pressure Group Politics: A Study of the BMA*, London: MacGibbon and Kee, 1963.

31. Michel Crozier, *The Bureaucratic Phenomenon*, London: Tavistock, 1965.

32. Maria Paschalaska, *Education in Poland*, Warsaw: Polonia Publishing House, 1962: S. M. Rosen, *Higher Education in Poland*, Washington, U.S. Dept. of Education, Health and Welfare, 1964; and private communication from Z. Baumann.

33. 'Cultural set' is used in the sense that Bernstein talks about the 'mode of established relationships' in his theory of social learning (Bernstein, *op. cit.*, pp. 295–296).

34. The literature based on this form of comparison is becoming increasingly influential though most of it refers to political comparisons. For examples and debates on the various forms of comparison see Richard L. Merritt and Stein Rokkan, *op cit.*, Stein Rokkan (ed.), *Comparative Research across Cultures and Nations*, Paris: Mouton, 1967, and for an attempt at 'averaging out' see Bruce M. Russett and others: *World Handbook of Social and Political Indicators*, New Haven, Yale, U.P. 1964.

35. Tom Burns and G. M. Stalker, *The Management of Innovation*, London, Tavistock Publications 1966, edition, vii. The typology is, of course, derived from Durkheim's mechanistic and organic solidarities, developed in *The Division of Labour in Society*, New York, Free Press, 1947.

36. See essay by Basil Bernstein 'Open Schools, Open Society?', *New Society*, 259, 14th Sept., 1967, 351–353. This very important statement which argues on lines similar to that developed here poses a number of specific problems of theory which comparative research should be directed towards clearing up. In particular these relate to the congruence between wider societal 'openness' and educational openness. Bernstein's basic concern is with the curriculum—which any study of the management of knowledge would have to examine centrally. What he is not clear about is whether structural openness necessarily leads to curriculum flexibility: the Swedish example would suggest not and this may have to do with a continuing professionalism carrying through from earlier days. An 'open' entrance system may still be compatible with an educational order controlled by the teachers (contrasted with the U.S.A., where 'citizens' have more control). There are thus a number of variations on the open-closed theme which could only be demonstrated by comparative analysis. But what Bernstein does do is to place educational sociology firmly as a study of culture. As he rightly stresses, Durkheim is still the most important starting-point for this, and *Moral Education* (New York: Free Press 1961) the most neglected classic. The clearest concise statement of Durkheim's general theories (with a persuasive critique) has been recently published by Percy S. Cohen, *Modern Social Theory*, London: Heinemann, 1968, esp. 224–234.

37. Burns and Stalker, *op. cit.*, xvi.

38. For example, the literature on innovations of which Burns and Stalker (*op cit.*); G. M. Rodgers, *The Diffusion of Innovations*, New York: Free Press, 1962, are fair examples; the literature on economic institutions, e.g. R. Blau, *Exchange and Power in Everyday Life*, New York: Wiley,1964; Georges Freidman, *Industrial Society*, New York, Free Press, 1955; Alvin W. Goulder, *Patterns of Industrial Bureaucracy*, New York: Free Press, 1954; and the vast amount of anthropological literature, e.g. Claude Levi-Strauss, *The Savage Mind*, London: Weidenfeld and Nicolson, 1965; Mary Douglas, *Purity and Danger*, London: Routledge, 1966; John Middleton (ed.), *Myth and Cosmos*, Garden City, N.Y.: Natural History Press, 1967; and Clifford Geertz, 'Ideology as a Cultural System', in David Apter (ed.), *Ideology and Discontent*, New York: Free Press, 1961.

39. There are two distinct traditions: that stemming from the literary critical tradition noted in footnote 14, and the philosophical *belles-lettres* tradition of

which Jacques Barzun, *The House of Intellect*, London: Secker and Warburg, 1959; C. P. Snow, *The Two Cultures and the Scientific Revolution*, Cambridge: C.U.P., 1964, are among the best known. Richard Hoggart's *The Uses of Literacy*, London, Chatto 1959, has not generated the research on the Management of Knowledge that it might have. It has merely provided an occasion for further studies of selection and some on public responses to the mass media. There is also the seminal literary-anthropological effort on communications: Jack Goody and Ian Watt, 'The Consequences of Literacy', in J.Goody (ed.), *Literacy in Traditional Societies*, Cambridge: C.U.P., 1969.

40. For example: A. de Grazia, *The Velkovsky Affair*, Chapman and Hall 1965; F. A. von Hayek, *The Counter-Revolution of Science*, Free Press, 1964; H. Kaplan (ed.), *Science and Society*, Chicago-Rand McNally, 1966. Oddly enough, however, there is no sociological literature on the teaching of science.

41. See especially: Jules Henry, *Culture Against Man*, London, Tavistock, 1966, and Theodore Brameld, *The Remaking of a Culture: Life and Education in Puerto Rico*, New York: Wiley, 1959; George T. Spindler (ed.), *Education and Culture: Anthropological Approaches*, New York: Holt, Rinehart and Winston, 1963.

42. For representative introductions and summaries see: Y. Talmon, 'The Pursuit of the Millennium', *Eur. Journal of Sociology*, 1963; Peter Worsley, introduction to *The Trumpet Shall Sound*, London: MacGibbon and Kee, 1968 edition; Anthony F. Wallace, 'Revitilization Movements' in S. M. Lipset and Neil J. Smelser, *Sociology—The Progress of a Decade*, Englewood Cliffs: Prentice Hall, 1961, 205–219.

43. Octavio Paz, *The Labyrinth of Solitude*, London: Allen Lane, 1967, 16.

44. See Neil J. Smelser, *The Theory of Collective Behaviour*, London: Routledge and Kegan Paul, 1962, chapters 5 and 10. For suggestions for a counter formulation see Alasdair McIntyre, *Secularization and Moral Change*, London: O.U.P., 1967. But my formulation of the problem owes much to an unpublished critique of Smelser by Herminio Martins, Essex University.

45. For an impressionistic account see Leila Berg, *Risinghill: Death of a Comprehensive School*, Harmondsworth: Pelican, 1968.

46. See: G. T. Keach, R. Fulton and W. E. Gardner, *Education and Social Crisis: Perspectives on Teaching Disadvantaged Youth*, New York: John Wiley, 1967. But for Britain see also R. S. Peters (ed.), *Perspectives on Plowden*, London: Routledge and Kegan Paul, 1969.

47. The reference is, of course, to the work of Albert Schutz, in particular Volume I of the Collected Papers, *The Problems of Social Reality*, The Hague: Martinus Nijhoff, 1967. But see also Harold Garfinkel, *Studies in Ethnomethodology*, Englewood Cliffs: Prentice-Hall, 1967, and Peter L. Berger and Thomas Luckman, *The Social Construction of Reality*, London: Allen Lane, 1967. The most convincing sociological research based on this approach is probably Alfred Willener, *Interpretation de l'organization dans l'industrie*, Paris: Mouton, 1967.

48. *Op. cit.*, note 40, 182–282.

49. *Ibid.*, 282.

50. For French examples see Jean-Claude Passeron and M. de Saint Martin, *Rapport Pedagogique et Communication*, Paris, Mouton, 1965; Pierre Bourdieu, 'Système d'enseignement et système de pensée', Proceedings of 6th World Congress of Sociology;* Pierre Bourdieu and Jean-Claude Passeron, 'L'examen d'une illusion', *R. Fran. de Soc.*, IX, Special Number, 1968, 227–253.

* [A revised version of this paper is reprinted as Reading 8 in the present volume.]

51. Private Communication. But see also Basil Bernstein, 'Open Schools, Open Society?', *op. cit.*, for an early formulation.

52. Perry Anderson, 'Components of the National Culture', *New Left Review*, 50, July–August 1968, 3–57; earlier, Alasdair MacIntyre, 'Breaking the Chains of Reason', in E. P. Thompson (ed.), *Out of Apathy*, London: Stevans and Son, 1960, 195–240. The first essay is challenging about the constituent parts of British national intellectual styles, but does not really answer the following questions: (a) why these particular styles? (b) what relation do they have to the institutions? (c) how profound and deep-rooted are alternative (sub-elite) styles? (d) how does one compare with other national cultural styles? It does, however, make some interesting suggestions about the conditions under which culture is transmitted and how a dying culture is kept alive by transfusion. MacIntyre's essay, though very suggestive about the relationship between intellectual styles and social action, is not really specific enough about the British situation.

53. Of a wide spectrum two samples are offered: the work of Richard Hofstadter in the U.S.A. and Michel Crozier's 'The Cultural Revolution: Notes on the Changes in the Intellectual Climate of France', *Daedalus*, 3, i, Winter 1964, 514–542.

54. Amitai Etzioni, *The Active Society*, New York: Free Press, 1968, especially Part One.

55. G. S. Osborne, *Change in Scottish Education*, London: Longmans, 1968, provides a general account of the current situation, while George Elder Davies, *The Democratic Intellect*, Edinburgh; Edinburgh University Press, 1961, is perhaps the finest example of intellectual history that exists in these islands. It has recently been joined by Sheldon Rothblatt, *The Revolution of the Dons*, London: Faber and Faber, 1968.

56. This is particularly true of Thomas S. Kuhn, *The Structure of Scientific Revolutions*, Chicago: University of Chicago Press 1960, which, although it offers a stimulating general perspective says little about *national* developments.

57. See especially Berger and Luckman, op. cit., 15, but for a more theoretical account, A. Schutz, *op. cit.*, 3–96.

58. Max Weber, *The Protestant Ethic and the Spirit of Capitalism*, London: Allen and Unwin, 1930, 182.

59. S. Rothblatt, *The Revolution of the Dons*, London: Faber and Faber, 1968.

60. Rothblatt, *op. cit.*, 257.

61. *G H. Mead on Social Psychology*, ed. Anselm Strauss, University of Chicago Press, 1965, 165.

7

SELECTION AND KNOWLEDGE MANAGEMENT IN EDUCATION SYSTEMS

Dennis Smith

In a recent article,[1]* Ioan Davies set out a framework for examining education systems in terms of the 'management of knowledge'. By way of a prologue, he elaborated a fairly detailed critique of Earl Hopper's typology of education systems[2]† which classifies such systems in terms of the structure of their selection processes. Davies attempted to demonstrate that a number of assumptions underlying the typology were invalid and that a 'central' aspect of education—the cultural dimension—has been ignored with damaging results. A consequence of these failings, he argued, was that 'research derived from Hopper's typology' would do 'serious injustice to the facts' by trivialising 'the cultural content of education'.[3] In the present paper, a number of propositions will be argued. First, that Davies misinterpreted Hopper's assumptions. Second, that Davies failed to recognise the significance of selection processes for the management of knowledge. Third, that despite Davies' assertions to the contrary, Hopper and himself are each concerned with similar aspects of the education system, though their emphases differ. Fourth, that the strengths of each formulation complement the weaknesses of the other in a striking fashion. Finally, it will be shown that although Hopper's typology makes a valuable contribution to the sociology of education he has overestimated its applicability.

I

Hopper's basic assumption is that selection for education routes, instruction within the education system, and subsequent allocation to

* [Reprinted as Reading 6 in the present volume E.H.].
† [Reprinted as Reading 5 in the present volume. E.H.]

positions within the occupational structure are three 'closely linked' processes or functions. 'Because the last two functions are closely linked to the first, the structure of educational systems, especially those within industrial societies, can be understood primarily in terms of their selection processes.'[4] On this basis, he claims that the following are 'some of the more important structural dimensions along which educational systems may vary':

The First Dimension: How does educational selection occur? The degree to which an education system has a centrally administered selection procedure; and the degree to which provision of education, especially up to the point of initial selection, is standardized for the population as a whole.

The Second Dimension: When are pupils initially selected? The degree to which an education system is characterized by early formal differentiation and specialization of routes.

The Third Dimension: Who should be selected? The extent to which pupils should be selected primarily on the basis of their diffuse skills or primarily on the basis of their technical skills (a continuum ranging between complete Particularism and complete Universalism).

The Fourth Dimension: Why should they be selected? The extent to which selection is justified in terms of society's need for a certain kind of skill or in terms of the right of the selected to privilege on the basis of their skills (a continuum ranging from complete Collectivism to complete Individualism).

The Third and Fourth Dimensions are combined to produce four ideal types of ideologies of legitimization: 'aristocratic', 'paternalistic', 'meritocratic' and 'communistic'.

Hopper asserts that these dimensions are 'a useful aid for the organization and interpretation of the wealth of available data'. The educational 'sub-system'—defined by these dimensions—may be treated as a variable within 'the constructed social system'. A number of research projects then become possible. For example, the dimensions could be used 'as guidelines for the study of the ways in which an education system changes . . . as a result of industrialization processes'.[5]

A typology such as the one presented by Hopper may be examined according to a number of criteria. For example, are the assumptions upon which it is based logically satisfying and empirically demonstrable? Does it direct attention to relationships and processes whose variations are of strategic importance to the institutional sector being studied? Does it yield a set of analytical dimensions which are sensitive to significant variations in the data yet not so complex that they are unmanageable as a research tool?

Davies finds Hopper's assumptions unacceptable, his concentration on selection misguided and his dimensions clumsy. Briefly summarized, his criticisms are as follows. Hopper analyses education systems in terms of the structure of their selection processes but the contribution of education systems to 'the total selection process' may be seen to differ in form and extent when different industrial societies are compared. Hopper is unable to mount an adequate discussion of this because he lacks a 'more comprehensive model of economic and stratification systems'. In the absence of such a model, he seems to make the inaccurate assumption that 'there is a one-to-one relationship between the selection process in the schools and the requirements of the economy' and is reduced to analysing different forms of stratification in terms of a crude Paretan model in which the crucial variable is the degree of elite competence.[6]

He points out that Hopper fails to distinguish the various—often conflicting—goals espoused by groups within ruling elites and in various sectors within a differentiated education system.[7] Both the plurality and the conflicting nature of goals are, he suggests, related to discontinuities in stratification and culture. According to Davies, Hopper is unable to take account of, or explain, such variations within single systems for three related reasons: first, he assumes that selection is the 'manifest function' of education systems—the primary concern of participants and the most significant process occurring within such systems; second, his initial classification of selection procedures is partly in terms of single 'dominant' ideologies —so that significant local variations and alternative ideologies fostered by competing groups are ignored;[8] and, third, his classification of these 'dominant' ideologies leaves 'very little room for the analysis of culture' and poses problems 'if we are attempting to account for shifts in social stratification'.[9]

The criticism that Hopper fails to solve the problem of incorporating both central tendency and peripheral variations in his ideological dimensions is a fair one. It should, however, be noted that Hopper discusses this problem at some length and attempts to cope with it by constructing 'some sort of profile which represents the proportions of the (dominant) group holding different ideologies and the relative distribution of power among the competing factions'.[10] Elsewhere, Davies acknowledges that 'Hopper's essay has provided a valuable attempt at reviewing the problems inherent in a comparative approach'.[11] There is no basis for the conclusion that 'Hopper's typology ascribes single-culture goals to all educational institutions'.[12] Faced with the need to avoid merely 'averaging out the data', each adopts a different solution. Davies follows his own discussion of the difficulties of concomitant variation studies by concluding that 'the ultimate problem' must be the explanation of particular societies,[13] the use of comparison being primarily 'to demonstrate both how general particular findings are, and also to check the reliability of the particular hypotheses generated'.[14] Both articles leave the basic problem unsolved.

The other criticisms made by Davies seem to arise partly out of a misunderstanding of the methodological intention of the paper and partly out of a series of ambiguities in the concept of 'selection'.

One of Hopper's stated objectives in specifying the dimensions of the educational sub-system was that of enabling research to be carried out on the circumstances in which the state of these dimensions might vary. An example he cites is the possibility of research on 'the effects of variation in the structure of an economic sub-system on variation in the structure of an educational sub-system'.[15] There is no basis for the assumption that a 'one-to-one' relationship with the economic system is assumed, either in terms of this system's 'requirements'[16] or in terms of the level of economic resources available. At one point he states that 'variations in the organisation of recruitment cannot be explained only or primarily in terms of available economic resources'.[17] Nor does Hopper even attempt to delineate or explain variations in patterns of stratification. What he does is to indicate a problem common to all industrial societies, the need for 'people in all positions in the various hierarchies of power' to 'justify their position to themselves and others'.[18] Legitimizing ideologies contribute to the attempted solution of this problem by defining those characteristics which are appropriate for the occupants of the various positions in the occupational structure.[19] The consequences of particular ideologies are manifest in the criteria of educational selection, possibly in a tendency to favour certain personality types, and, with more certainty—although Hopper does not stress this point—in the character of the transmission process itself.[20] Differences of this kind may explain the predominance of nationalist-communist philosophy in Soviet education and the emphasis on indoctrinating a particular life style in American schools.[21] The relatedness of such ideological variations to differences in the content and boundaries of certain occupational roles in these two societies may account for, say, different styles of management training.[22] The content of such ideologies may vary independently of the pattern of stratification within a society (although a fairly close relationship may exist). In view of these considerations, while it is perhaps unreasonable to expect Hopper to have put forward a 'more comprehensive model' which he did not set out to provide, the typology could be the first step to the development of such a model.

The debate has, perhaps, been obfuscated by the fact that the term 'selection' has been used in a number of ways in the two articles. The following distinctions might be made:

(i) *Selection* as allocation of children to routes in the education system;

(ii) *Selection* as (i) above plus *instruction* leading to the award of qualifications which have a specific value in the job market;[23]

(iii) *Selection* as (ii) above plus *recruitment to an occupation* with rewards of a specific kind and level.

Davies rightly points out the difference between 'selection' at level (iii) above and 'the total selection process in a society (or a segment of it)'.[24] To demonstrate this he sketches the outlines of a classificatory scheme which would be sensitive to the numerous parameters which determine the processes whereby individuals from families of diverse size, dissimilar in income and security, and located in social groups with different positions in the stratification system (whose contours may vary) move through—and undergo socialization experiences of various kinds within—a number of structures (including educational institutions) and are recruited by varous methods (including in-service training and internal promotion) to positions within an occupational structure which may be changing in different ways at varying rates. He demonstrates the complexity of these processes with great success.[25] The burden of Davies' argument at this point is that, considered in the context of all these parameters affecting the 'total selection process in a society', the particular effect of educational selection (at the first two levels) may be a relatively minor one. This is undeniable. In fact Hopper nowhere asserts that allocation to educational routes occurs in a social vacuum, that occupational recruitment is determined by formal education alone, or that a particular kind of education guarantees a specific job. Davies points out that there may be 'a large number of entry points to occupational posts which do not . . . depend on educational selection'. Examples may also be found, as he suggests, where the skills required at certain points in the occupational structure are not produced within the education system, where induction into certain occupations bypasses parts of the education system, and where particular kinds of education do not enhance entry into certain occupations.[26] Clearly, perfect co-ordination between the education system and the 'requirements' of the economy does not exist in any industrial society. This does not invalidate the two assumptions that certification is the main mechanism of occupational recruitment and that the education system is the principal avenue through which qualifications are achieved.

However, it is fair to say that Hopper confuses the issue. He does not specify clearly the different levels of selection and he neglects to discuss certification (i.e. the awarding of formal educational qualifications) in an explicit way. For example, Hopper's statement that 'selection . . . instruction . . . and the eventual allocation of trained personnel either directly to occupational roles or to agencies which specialize in occupational recruitment . . . are closely linked' could be interpreted in a number of ways. The most plausible interpretation is that educational certification is highly salient to occupational recruitment in industrial societies. As others have pointed out, certification of a specific kind is, in such societies, strongly associated with aspiration for and expectation of entry into the occupational structure at the corresponding level;[26a] and even where such expectations are frustrated (perhaps due to an over-production of qualified people) this does not diminish—in the medium term, at least—either the feeling that such certification *should* lead to appropriate occupations or the consequences of this feeling (and the associated expectations and aspirations) for processes occurring within the education system.*

The following assumptions then are implicit in Hopper's article:

first, that in an industrial society the main mechanism of recruitment to the occupational structure is certification obtained in the formal education system;

second, that initial allocation to education routes (selection at level (i)) has the character of a monitoring process whereby children with different kinds and levels of skill are formerly identified and classified;

third, that decisions taken at levels (i) and (ii) are, in each case, a major determinant of decisions taken at the next level (so that, for example, there is a strong—not perfect—relationship between allocation to a particular institution, receipt of instruction leading to certification of a specific type, and admission to the occupational structure at a certain level);

fourth, that most participants in the educational process are aware of these relationships (so that there is a need for ideologies which 'explain why some people should be rejected when others are selected');[27]

fifth, that the norms prevailing at the second and third level will in each case, directly or indirectly, have a determining effect upon

* [See 'Social Selection in the Welfare State', reprinted as Reading 2 in the present volume. E.H.]

processes occurring at the level below (so that, for example, the requirements for entry to and adequate performance in occupational roles and the social networks with which they are associated will have an effect upon patterns of transmission and criteria of initial allocation to educational routes);

and, *sixth*, that some of the constraints referred to above will be mediated through ideologies of legitimization and implementation with respect to the organization of initial allocation and subsequent transmission processes.

This discussion of Davies' criticisms should have established two points. First, that the assumptions underlying the Hopper typology have not been seriously challenged on logical or empirical grounds. Second, that far from diverting attention to concerns which are peripheral to an understanding of the educational process, Hopper's dimensions focus attention upon the character of the transmission process itself, suggesting how differences mentioned by Davies— for example, between Russian and American schooling—might be accounted for. Further contributions which Hopper's perspective might make to Davies' problems will be indicated when the latter's framework has been examined.

II

Davies asserts that 'the study of education as culture . . . is central; . . . its *manifest* function is the management of knowledge'.[28] He argues that within a society changing structural conditions contribute to the development of a national cultural or intellectual style which manifests itself in a social consciousness.[29] The development of the education system both conditions this process and is conditioned by it. The 'crux of the management of knowledge' is: 'what part does (education) play in the creation of social consciousness?'[30] The components of the social consciousness are values, norms and knowledge which have a complex and dynamic relationship in industrial societies. A central concern of the sociology of education must be to study 'the way that values are transmitted through normative situations and the way that knowledge contributes to the symbolic order of the participants'.[31] Learning experiences in educational institutions are conditioned by the hierarchical-organizational patterns within which they occur; at a societal level the management of knowledge takes place in the context of a national and local power structure within which a variety of goals are pursued by different groups. The study of these processes requires the investigation of decision-making processes, analysis of professionalism in its organizational context, inquiry into the values attached to education by various participants, 'the relationship of particular kinds of institutions to the wider social structure and their immediate environment' and the nature of 'subcultural inputs'.[32]

This summary suggests that there is a considerable amount of tacit agreement between Hopper and Davies concerning which aspects of the education system are problematic. Each seeks to explain how the values fostered and goals pursued within education systems are determined. Both are attempting to account for the organization of the educational process, that is, the process whereby different categories of students are directed through a number of educational routes and subjected to a variety of learning experiences. Both Hopper and Davies assume that to answer these questions attention must be directed at the mode of articulation of the education system with other social structures. Each professes a concern to account for processes of change in all the above respects.

The strengths and weaknesses of each approach derive from two sources: the manner in which the education process has been conceptualized; and the way in which the variety of constraints operating upon this process have been described.

Davies rightly asserts that in his exposition Hopper fails to emphasize the content which is transmitted through the education system—although, as has been shown, the assumptions underlying the typology hardly preclude a consideration of content. Just as serious, it will be argued, is Davies' neglect of the role of selection—in all the senses discussed—in the management of knowledge. Davies tells us that study of the management of knowledge entails looking at the ways in which 'social consciousness' is defined and transmitted. His evocation of the struggle to control the processes of definition and transmission is clear and convincing. Unfortunately, his analysis is lopsided. He concentrates on 'the ways that the educational power-structure and the institutions act as selective filters for different levels of praxis and consciousness'.[33] He completely omits to discuss the other problem, equally central to the management of knowledge: on what basis are different kinds of consciousness—or, to use an economic analogy, different types of cultural resources—distributed among the recipient population? In plainer language: who is taught what? The education system acts not only as a 'selective filter' but also as a 'selective distributor' of those cultural styles whose internal complexity Davies demonstrates. The reason for Davies' curious neglect of this central question is not difficult to see. It is a consequence of his dismissal of selection as peripheral to the education process. In fact it is central and the management of knowledge cannot be usefully discussed without taking it into account.

For example, initial allocation to educational routes—selection at level (i)—and subsequent instruction are merely two stages of the same overall process whereby different kinds of knowledge and values are transmitted in varying normative contexts to distinct categories of students. Each stage implies the other. Furthermore, the transmission process is affected by the knowledge of all participants that the life chances of the pupils—selection at levels (ii) and (iii)—are at issue. This awareness patterns the response of students to instruction and may influence the content of the values and norms which are transmitted; they may be specifically designed to prepare the student for the network of social relationships in which he is likely to find himself after his educational career. Davies refers in passing to the relationship between 'the structuring of knowledge' and 'the ultimate life-chances of the pupils'.[34] However, he fails to develop this insight.

The complementarity of selection and instruction is nicely described by Dahrendorf in the following passage:

The individual must somehow take into himself the prescriptions of society and make them the basis of his behaviour; it is by this means that the individual and society are mediated and man is reborn as 'homo socio-logicus'. Position allocation and role internalization are complementary, and it is no accident that industrial societies have assigned primary responsibility for both processes to a single institutional order—the education system.[35]

Turner makes a similar point when he stresses that recruitment to the occupational structure entails induction into the appropriate cultural niche.[35a]* Indeed at several points the conceptualization developed by Davies recalls Turner's formulation. The latter shows that the structure of an education system is affected by the pattern of stratification and by the 'internal equilibrium' of a culture.[36] He suggests that specific patterns of culture and stratification tend to co-exist with particular folk norms whose persistence has a number of consequences for school systems. When education systems in different societies are compared, differences in folk norms help to explain not only variations in selection strategies, route patterns and policies of resource allocation, but also 'different emphases regarding educational content' and 'the value placed upon education itself', for example, whether 'schooling is valued for its cultivation of . . . culture' or 'as a means of getting ahead'. It seems that Davies and

* [Reprinted as Reading 4 in the present volume. E.H.]

Hopper have each taken up and developed further some of the themes implicit in Turner's article while neglecting others.

Despite the close relationship between the two elements of the selection-transmission process, each writer emphasizes one element only, referring only obliquely to the other and tending to underestimate its importance. Davies seems to assume that experiences within the education system are largely responsible for the formation of those orientations and patterns of perception which contribute to the development or maintenance of a 'national cultural style'. It is not clear to what extent the contribution of formal education to this 'moulding' process is limited by the fact that—as he persuasively argues earlier—young people pass through a number of institutional settings in which socialization occurs—the family, local community, training schemes—before assuming their adult occupational roles. By comparison, Hopper neglects to consider the capacity of an education system to produce changes in the individual at the level of symbolic order and values. For the entering student, he implies, the world of reality is fixed; what is at issue is his own position within it. An education system, according to this view, merely provides opportunities for students with favoured social backgrounds, abilities and personality types to capture the prizes held before them. Each student is placed in the appropriate category. He is then provided with ideological equipment which allows him to reconcile his performance, aspirations and expectations.

In their extreme formulations—that education 'creates' reality for the student, that education is merely a process during which the 'best fitted' are identified—neither view is entirely plausible. However, both have their applications. Post-revolutionary efforts to create a 'new society' and attempts to carry out a 'cultural revolution' (for example, in Stalin's Russia and Mao's China) through intensive indoctrination of the young within the education system could be analysed in the terms suggested by Davies. The education of the 'labouring classes' in mid-nineteenth century England and the schooling of second-generation American immigrants are both promising areas for this approach. For the analysis of more recent developments in the English and American education systems, Hopper's model might be more appropriate.

Each of the two writers has adopted a different strategy to describe the constraints operating upon the organization of the selection-transmission process. Both, for example, are interested in the relationship between changes in the organization of this process and alterations in the structure of administrative control. Davies cites Bernstein and the organic-mechanistic typology of Burns and

Stalker. He also quotes illuminating evidence from Eastern Europe to exemplify the mediating effect of local power structures.[37] However, he is able to offer no equivalent of Hopper's systematic demonstration of independent variation in the structure of administrative control (degree of centralization) and the organization of certain aspects of the education process (criteria of selection, pattern of routes) across a broad range of societies.

Both are concerned with the general societal constraints upon education systems: Hopper indirectly through his assumptions with respect to the relationship of educational to occupational selection, Davies more directly through a discussion of cultural and stratification discontinuities. Again, the different approaches are demonstrated. Davies deploys a series of well-chosen examples to show the range of variations which may be found. Hopper's limited methodological goals preclude a direct discussion of these parameters, but his typology has two technical advantages. First, since it directs attention to the occupational structure-developments in which are closely linked not only to economic shifts but also to changes in stratification and status systems—it makes provision for a sharply focused analysis of the relationship between changes in these areas and in the education system. Second, the typology directs attention to the two tasks of allocating each new generation to the available occupational positions and reconciling them to the roles they are given. Education systems make a significant contribution to the attempted solution of these 'structural dilemmas' in all industrial societies. As a consequence, the Hopper typology is, potentially, a useful tool of comparative analysis.

III

In this final section, some of the merits of Hopper's typology which Davies did not mention will be noted. Some limitations overlooked by Davies will also be indicated.

Hopper has developed a typology which is an improvement on the one implicit in Turner's work in at least two ways. He has added a dimension referring to the administrative structure, thus confronting directly the Kantian dilemma of 'maintaining both freedom and equality' concealed in Turner's article.[38] Hopper also draws attention to two important distinctions. He distinguishes between ideologies (of legitimization) which *justify* institutional patterns by reference to goals, values and legitimizing symbols (which may be extremely vague and general) and ideologies (of implementation) which *specify* the principles of organization which 'should' be manifest in institutions. He also distinguishes between those principles which are *believed* or *intended* to be manifest in institutions and those embodied *in practice*. Within an education system, variation at any one level may occur independently of variation at other levels.[39] As a consequence, he is able to compare many more societies over a wider range of characteristics than Turner.

However, despite its value as a tool of comparative analysis, attempts to apply it to the description of change in the education system of a single society, say England, encounter considerable difficulty. In achieving a high degree of parsimony, Hopper has tolerated ambiguity, allowed single dimensions to describe possibilities of change which occur along a number of dimensions, and left unresolved some serious empirical problems. These drawbacks need not invalidate the original typology. As Davies point out, it is useful to have a typology which is both simple and 'capable of elaboration, according to particular situations and features of change'. In the rest of this section, some of the difficulties referred to above will be specified more precisely.

Much of the ambiguity is a consequence of failure to state the source or sources of the ideological definitions whose effects are manifest in the education system. This problem has already been mentioned but some of the practical consequences can now be shown. For example, in his discussion of 'dominant' ideologies, Hopper ignores a number of possibilities. The first is that an ideology may be 'dominant' merely in the sense that it consists of a set of 'core values' to which all groups adhere. Where such consensus exists, variations in the distribution of power over the education system among these groups will have no effect upon the 'dominance' of the ideology. However, such groups may be in conflict for a number of reasons. Agreement on a set of 'core values' in one sphere does not preclude fundamental disagreement in other spheres. In nineteenth century England, the Voluntary Societies and the Government agreed that a major objective of educating the Poor was to maintain social control and preserve the social hierarchy. However, the National Society competed desperately with the British and Foreign Society to capture the new urban poor for the Church and save them from the soul-shivering clasp of Non-conformity. Both Societies were united in resisting State control of education. The practice of identifying 'dominant' ideologies has little heuristic value if one is examining processes of change. It would conceal rather than illuminate changes in the spheres of influence of various non-'dominant' ideologies: for example, the progressive introduction of competitive examinations into the English system as a vehicle of new 'meritocratic' values; or, more recently, the gradually widening acceptance of the notion of some form of comprehensive education. Nor would one be able to trace significant changes of emphasis within a fairly stable matrix of values: the shift from 'paternalism' as a means of keeping the lower orders in their place to 'paternalism' as a strategy for sponsoring the admission of humble but talented aspirants into the elite; the shift from 'equality' of opportunity to 'equality' of provision. Hopper makes no provision for independent variation in the distribution of power over the education system and the relative influence of different values and goals. This is why the existence of a 'nationally organized education programme' is such a poor indicator of centralization. An education programme based upon a set of principles may be administered throughout an education system even in cases where, as in the United States, approximately 40,000 School Districts have extensive powers to formulate local education policy. The typology should be supplemented with dimensions which are sensitive to the consequences for the organization of the selection-transmission process of various patterns of internal differentiation with respect to power and ideology.[40]

Other difficulties arise from Hopper's references to the degree of 'early formal differentiation and specialisation of (educational) routes'.[41] One difficulty is that parents, students, administrators and employers may make 'informal' distinctions—such as that between 'Oxbridge' and 'Redbrick'—which reflect significant differences in both the prestige of institutions in these routes and the career prospects with which each is associated. Another difficulty is the question of whether 'streams'—for example, within comprehensive schools—count as 'routes'. Allocation to one stream rather than another might have profound effects upon the range of occupations for which a student eventually becomes eligible. Also, the implications of the term 'specialisation of routes' should be clarified. When comparison is made of institutions belonging to different routes —formally differentiated (e.g. grammar and public schools) and informally differentiated (e.g. 'Oxbridge' and 'Redbrick')—it may be found that there is considerable overlap in the content of formal curricula and in the range of technical abilities which students and teachers bring to the transmission process. In the above cases, the specialization may consist in differences in position within prestige hierarchies and variations in terms of the 'diffuse'—rather than 'technical'—skills which the institution sets out to foster.*

* [Several aspects of these problems are examined further by Earl Hopper in Appendix II of the present volume. E.H.]

Another problem is concealed multidimensionality. 'Degree of *early* . . . differentiation and specialisation of routes' is not clearly distinguished from 'degree of . . . *differentiation and specialisation* of routes'. Variations in the length of routes after the point of segregation may occur independently of variation in the extent to which the route pattern is differentiated or specialized. Change in the initial *point* of segregation does not determine change in the subsequent *pattern* of segregation (or vice versa). The multi-dimensionality in 'degree of centralisation' may be demonstrated by reference to changes in the administrative structure of the English education system. Hopper's indices for this dimension include the existence of 'a specialised department within the national civil service or its equivalent which is concerned exclusively with problems of education'.[42] Such a department—the Committee of Privy Council—existed in 1839. Although it did not have 'exclusive control' over the English education system it was 'concerned exclusively' with that system. The present Department of Education and Science does not have exclusive control; nor—as its title suggests—is it 'concerned exclusively' with education. During the intervening period, a number of administrative agencies have controlled the English education system. Their organization has been centralized, in different cases, to a great and small extent. They have exercised relative decision-making freedom with respect to each other, in different cases, to a great and a small extent. In the 1890s, for example, three central government bodies had administrative control over substantial parts of the system: the Education Department at Whitehall, the Charity Commission, and the Department of Science and Art. They were relatively autonomous with respect to each other and co-existed with a host of ad hoc local bodies, over some of which they exercised control. The local bodies included School Boards, School Attendance Committees, Voluntary Aid Associations, Technical Instruction Committees, the governing bodies of grammar schools, and others. In 1895, the Royal Commission on Secondary Education reported: 'The Charity Commissioners have had little or nothing to do with the Education Department and still less to do with the Science and Art Department. Even the Borough councils have, to a large extent, acted independently of the school boards, and have, in some instances, made their technical assistance grants with too little regard for the parallel grants which were being made by the Science and Art Department. . . .'[43] The single dimension of 'degree of centralisation' is unable to cope with variations of this kind. Additional dimensions are needed which are capable of describing the administration of education systems in terms of their structural complexity, the internal distribution of power and the relationships which exist between the various agencies. (See Reading 11.)

Finally, there is a set of serious empirical difficulties. With respect to his Second Dimension, Hopper states: 'the crucial distinction is how long before the completion of education have children been formally segregated into specialised routes'.[44] From the First Dimension, it may be deduced that 'formal segregation' is a consequence of an 'administered selection procedure' undergone after a period of schooling during which students are not formally differentiated.[45] Measurement of the 'crucial distinction' involves specifying the age at which selection procedures are initially administered to allocate students to routes and the age at which students complete their educational careers. The difficulties of applying the Second Dimension can be illustrated by reference, again, to the English education system. First, before the Hadow Reorganization,[46] which began in the mid-twenties, the use of 'administered selection procedures' to determine allocation to routes affected directly only a minority of children. For the majority of children, allocation to the appropriate route occurred on entry to the system—not as a result of special tests—and they stayed in these routes throughout their educational career. Not until 1931 was the Consultative Committee on the Primary School able to note in its Report: 'During the last few years general examinations of children in public elementary schools at the age of about eleven have increasingly been used, not only for the award of free places, but for the admission of fee-paying pupils to grammar schools and of entrants to modern schools. In more than half of the 75 administrative areas included in the inquiry which is summarised in the Board (of Education)'s "Memorandum on Free Place Examinations" (1928), the examination was compulsory, i.e. all children in public elementary schools under the conditions prescribed in each case were expected to take it.'[47] Described above is an education system in transition between two modes of using selection examinations. In the old system, specialized assessment procedures had been competitions, voluntarily entered by a small minority, which enabled a few to shift from one route to another. Under the new system, specialized assessment would be a monitoring device, compulsorily applied to all in the state system, in order to allocate each student to the appropriate route. A second difficulty is that the length of routes differs considerably (compare the secondary modern school leaver of 15 with the graduate student of 25). A possible solution is to measure the length of time students spend in compulsory segregated schooling. Such a measurement would indicate that segregation was occurring earlier in the school career of students in 1926 than in 1880.[48] If the length of time between initial selection and minimum school leaving age is examined, it is clear that initial selection is occurring earlier in the school career of students in 1970 than in 1926.[49] However, a third difficulty is that before 1880 there were no compulsory starting and leaving dates and there was substantial variation between different institutions in the ages of entry and leaving. It is practically impossible—as it stands— to apply the Second Dimension to the English education system before 1880. The First Dimension can only be applied with any rigour after 1926. In this case, the Hopper typology only becomes useful at a late stage in the development of the 'specialised and differentiated' education system, after the economic 'menopause' of the late nineteenth century. This is a serious drawback in a typology intended to be of use in 'the study of the ways in which an educational system changes . . . as the result of industrialisation processes'.

These difficulties do not invalidate Hopper's typology—but they suggest that the assumptions it embodies restrict its applicability. Hopper's reference to a 'point of selection'—a single point in the education system where all children are monitored and formally classified—suggests that he is envisaging a form of selection which was adopted fairly late in the development of some industrial societies. Selection—in the sense of allocation to educational routes— is a characteristic of all education systems. However, the application of a formal monitoring procedure to all children at a single point suggests, first, that the different kinds and levels of skills being measured may be found at any point within the cohort, and second, that —as a consequence—classification of students on the basis of these attributes will to a significant extent cut across classification in terms of the prevailing status hierarchy.[50] No formal monitoring procedures of this kind are required when allocation to educational routes is directly on the basis of status category, so that, for example, different institutions are designated as being 'for the Poor', 'for the industrial classes', 'for Mechanics', 'for men with considerable incomes independent of their own exertions', and so on. Furthermore, if selection does not offer the possibility of changing one's social position, if it is simply a means of expressing that position, allocation procedures are no longer problematic—either for the education system or for the student. Selection is regulated by a general consensus regarding the type of education institution which is appropriate for each of the social orders.[51] For the greater part of the nineteenth century, to send the son or daughter of a labourer to a grammar school was almost literally 'unthinkable'. A consequence of this was that failure to attend such a school was not regarded as 'rejection' and ideologies to 'explain why some people should be rejected when others are selected' had no place.[52] It is clear that the limits of applicability of Hopper's typology can only be determined by an analysis of the changing relationships of the education system to the status hierarchy and to the occupational structure. Such an analysis directs attention to changes at many levels: the saliency of formal qualifications for occupational recruitment, the extent to which control over certification is vested in the education system,[53] the criteria employed in initial allocation to routes, popular conceptions of what an education system is for, and the reciprocal influence exercised by the life styles of status groups and the cultural resources distributed through the education system upon each other.[54] Not the least of the merits of Hopper's article is that it has, indirectly, drawn attention to these issues.

Notes

I am grateful to Earl Hopper, Professor Ilya Neustadt and Dr. Olive Banks for their comments on earlier drafts of this paper.

1. Ioan Davies, The Management of Knowledge: A Critique of the use of Typologies in Educational Sociology, *Sociology*, 4, 1970, 1–22.

2. Earl I. Hopper, for the Classification of Educational Systems, Sociology, 2, 1968, 29–46. Hopper presents his typology as an expanded version of that developed implicitly by Ralph H. Turner in his article 'Contest and Sponsored Mobility and the School System', *American Sociological Review*, 1960, 855–867. References in the present paper to Turner's article refer to the version printed in *Education, Economy and Society*, Halsey, Floud and Anderson (eds), pp. 121–39.

3. Davies, op. cit., p. 4.

4. Hopper, op. cit., p. 30.

5. ibid., pp. 40–41.

6. Davies, op. cit., p. 2.

7. ibid., pp. 3–4, 7–11.

8. ibid., p. 3.

9. ibid., p. 4.

10. Hopper, op. cit., n. 23, pp. 44–45.

11. Davies, op. cit., p. 17.

12. ibid., p. 3.

13. ibid., p. 17.

14. ibid., p. 10.

15. Hopper, op. cit., p. 40.

16. Societies whose economic systems are broadly similar and in which similar proportions of the work force are employed at various levels in the industrial, agricultural and service sectors may be characterized by significant differences in the boundaries and contents of specific roles in the occupational structure. The 'requirements' of economic systems—insofar as they are mediated through the occupational structure—may vary in this way.

17. Hopper, op. cit., pp. 33–34.

18. ibid., p. 35.

19. Although both Turner and Hopper refer to 'elites', it is likely that both would accept the proviso of the former that 'the generalisations presented are . . . intended to apply throughout the stratification continuum' (Turner, op. cit., n. 4, p. 137). Both are concerned with the problems associated with recruitment not only to elites but to all social positions. Within his ideologies of legitimization, Hopper encapsulates ideologies of implementation which define the characteristics appropriate to the occupants of the various social positions. Whether or not such ideologies have been promoted by existing elites is a separate question, and ignored by Hopper. Quoting Gramsci, Davies suggests that emergent classes (and new elites) encounter 'intellectual categories which were pre-existing and which, moreover, (appear) as representatives of an historical continuity uninterrupted even by the most complicated and radical changes in social and political forms'. Ideologies of implementation are, as Hopper puts it, 'buttressed by cultural folk norms' which derive to a great extent from such systems of 'intellectual categories'. Turner makes a point similar to Davies' when he writes: 'Students of cultural change note that patterns imported into an established culture tend to be reshaped into coherence with the established culture as they are assimilated' (op. cit., p. 125).

20. On these last two points, Turner is more explicit than Hopper. For example, he states that 'many writers have noted that different kinds of society facilitate the rise of different kinds of personalities, either in the status hierarchy or in other ways' (ibid. n. 8, p. 38).

21. Davies, op. cit., p. 3.

22. ibid., p. 15.

23. Hopper uses the term selection at level (i) when writing of a 'centrally administered selection procedure', p. 30, 'initial selection', p. 32, and the 'stringency' of selection procedures, p. 33. Selection at level (ii) is implied when writing of the 'two aspects of the total selection process', p. 30, the indicators of standardization, p. 31, the two components of the Second Dimension, p. 32, and the contents of 'elitist' and 'egalitarian' ideologies, p. 34.

24. Davies, op. cit., p. 7.

25. ibid., pp. 6–7.

26. Davies, op. cit., p. 2 and n. 5, pp. 17–18.

26a. T. H. Marshall, 'Social Selection and the Welfare State', pp. 236–255, in *Class, Citizenship and Social Development*, Garden City, New York; Doubleday and Co. Inc., 1964.

27. Hopper, op. cit., p. 36.

28. Davies, op. cit., p. 11.

29. ibid., p. 15.

30. ibid., p. 13.

31. ibid., p. 16.

32. ibid., pp. 14–16.

33. ibid., p. 15.

34. ibid., p. 14.

35. R. Dahrendorf, 'Homo Sociologicus' in *Essays in the Theory of Society*, p. 56.

35a. Turner, op. cit.

36. 'A system of sponsored mobility develops most readily in a society with but a single elite or with a recognised elite hierarchy. When multiple elites compete among themselves, the mobility process tends to take the contest pattern, since no group is able to command control of recruitment. Sponsored mobility further depends upon a societal structure fostering monopoly of elite credentials.

Lack of such monopoly undercuts sponsorship and control of the recruitment process. Monopoly of elite credentials is in turn typically a product of a society with a well-entrenched traditional aristocracy employing such intrinsically monopolisable credentials as family line and bestowable title, or of a society organised along large-scale bureaucratic lines, permitting centralised control of movement up the hierarchy of success' (Turner, op. cit., p. 125). 'Under the contest system, society at large establishes and interprets the criteria of elite status. If one wishes to have his high status recognised he must display certain credentials that identify his class to those about him. The credentials must be highly visible and require no special skill for their assessment, since credentials are presented to the masses. . . . The nature of sponsored mobility precludes this type of operation, but assigns to credentials instead the function of identifying the elite to one another' (ibid., p. 124).

37. Davies, op. cit., pp. 9–10.

38. Hopper, op. cit., n. 26, p. 45.

39. Hopper's distinction between ideologies of legitimization and implementation—and his assumption that each may vary independently of the other—is akin to Davies' distinction between values and norms which may vary in a similar way.

40. See Hopper, op. cit., p. 31, for his discussion of these points. See also Reading 11 in the present volume where I develop my own position.

41. ibid., pp. 32–33.

42. ibid., p. 31.

43. Report of the Royal Commission on Secondary Education (The Bryce Report), 1895. Quoted in J. Stuart Maclure, Educational Documents, England and Wales, 1816–1967, p. 143.

44. Hopper, op. cit., p. 33.

45. '. . . the degree to which an educational system has a centrally administered selection procedure, and the degree to which the provision of education, *especially up to the point of initial selection*, is standardised for the population as a whole', Hopper, op. cit., p. 30 (my italics—D.S.).

46. The Hadow Report on the Education of the Adolescent (1926) recommended a clear distinction between Junior (7–11) and Senior (over 11) departments, the organization of 'post-primary' education into Grammar Schools, Central Schools (selective and non-selective) and Junior Technical Schools, and the holding of an examination at 11+ to discover the type of school 'most suitable to the child's abilities and interests' (p. 175 and p. 178).

47. The Report of the Consultative Committee on the Primary School, 1931, p. 124.

48. School Boards could enact bye-laws requiring school attendance from the age of five years (1870 Act). In 1880, Parliament enacted that attendance was to be compulsory. The minimum leaving age was fixed at 10 in 1876, 11 in 1893 and 14 in 1918.

49. As a result of raising the school leaving age to 15 in 1947.

50. The term 'status hierarchy' refers to the definition and vertical ordering of status categories. These categories derive from criteria embedded in status norms and their vertical ordering tends to reflect patterns of super- and sub-ordination established among the status groups which they define.

51. To a significant extent, the use of fee-paying ability as a criterion of initial selection allows parents whose economic position ranks higher than their status position to buy upward social mobility for their children through the education system. Criteria based upon 'talent' or on 'aptitude' open the possibility of similar mobility to members of social groups with a low ranking on scales of both status and economic position.

52. The appearance of such ideologies may be associated with shifts in the extent to which differences in the kind and level of rewards associated with different occupational roles are defined as 'inequality' and in the degree of imbalance between the supply of various kinds of reward and the demand for them.

53. The relevance of variation in this respect is emphasized by Ben-David. He argues in the more developed countries of Western and Northern Europe, because of the existence of 'a strong and articulate middle-class prior to the rise of modern universities in the nineteenth century . . . higher education attracted only the exceptionally talented and/or motivated few, and, in addition, those who deliberately and for good economic reasons chose a professional career. It never became the only, nor even the main, channel of mobility through which one could rise from the "masses" to the "classes". . . . . Britain, in addition to such a long-established middle class, also possessed a non-academic type of education for the professions. Until the end of the last century and well into the present one, British universities had played only a modest role in the education for professions. . . . (Although) British universities were not less open to members of the middle and lower class than European ones—as a matter of fact they were relatively more open—they did not become very important channels of mobility even for the professions prior to World War II.' Joseph Ben-David, 'The Growth of the Professions and the Class System', in R. Bendix and S. M. Lipset, *Class, Status and Power*, pp. 470–1. Excerpt reprinted from *Current Sociology*, vol. 12, 1963–4, pp. 256–77.

54. The substitution of criteria of initial allocation based upon 'talent' or 'aptitude' does not necessarily entail a reorganization of the pattern of routes through an education system or a reconstruction of the content transmitted. There may be a disjunction between allocation criteria based upon these new principles and a transmission process whose organization is still derived from the status hierarchy, reflecting it in terms of the pattern of routes, the cultural resources transmitted to students passing through the routes and the social relationships which are established between these different categories of students.

8

SYSTEMS OF EDUCATION AND
SYSTEMS OF THOUGHT*

Pierre Bourdieu

Speaking of the course of his intellectual development in *A World on the Wane,* Claude Lévi-Strauss describes the techniques and rites of philosophy teaching in France:

'It was then that I began to learn how any problem, whether grave or trivial, can be resolved. The method never varies. First you establish the traditional "two views" of the question. You then put forward a commonsense justification of the one, only to refute it by the other. Finally you send them both packing by the use of a third interpretation, in which both the others are shown to be equally unsatisfactory. Certain verbal manœuvres enable you, that is, to line up the traditional "antithesis" as complementary aspects of a single reality: form and substance, content and container, appearance and reality, essence and existence, continuity and discontinuity and so on. Before long the exercise becomes the merest verbalizing, reflection gives place to a kind of superior punning, and the "accomplished philosopher" may be recognized by the ingenuity with which he makes ever-bolder play with assonance, ambiguity and the use of those words which sound alike and yet bear quite different meanings'.

'Five years at the Sorbonne taught me little but this form of mental gymnastics. Its dangers are, of course, self-evident: the mechanism is so simple, for one thing, that there is no such thing as a problem which cannot be tackled. When we were working for our examinations and, above all, for that supreme ordeal, the *leçon* (in which the candidate draws a subject by lot, and is given only six hours to prepare a comprehensive survey of it), we used to set one

---

* Paper presented to the Sixth World Conference of Sociology, Evian, 1966 and published in the *International Social Science Journal,* 19(3), 1967.

another the bizarrest imaginable themes. . . . The method, universal in its application, encouraged the student to overlook the many possible forms and variants of thought, devoting himself to one particular unchanging instrument. Certain elementary adjustments were all that he needed. . . .'[1]

This admirable ethnological description of the intellectual and linguistic patterns transmitted—implicitly rather than explicitly—by French education, has its counterpart in the description of the patterns that direct the thinking and behaviour of the Bororo Indians when they build their villages to a plan every bit as formal and fictitious as the dualistic organization of the *agrégation* exercises, patterns whose necessity or, to put it another way, whose function is recognized in this case by the ethnologist, probably because he is, at once, more detached and more intimately involved: '. . . The wise men of the tribe have evolved a grandiose cosmology which is writ large in the lay-out of their villages and distribution of their homes. When they met with contradictions, those contradictions were cut across again and again. Every opposition was rebutted in favour of another. Groups were divided and re-divided, both vertically and horizontally, until their lives, both spiritual and temporal, became an escutcheon in which symmetry and asymmetry were in equilibrium. . . .'[2]

As a social individual, the ethnologist is on terms of intimacy with his culture and therefore finds it difficult to think objectively about the patterns governing his own thought; the more completely those patterns have been mastered and have become a part of his make-up —and therefore coextensive and consubstantial with his consciousness—the more impossible is it for him to apply conscious thought to them. He may also be reluctant to admit that, even though acquired through the systematically organized learning processes of the school, and therefore generally explicit and explicitly taught, the patterns which shape the thinking of educated men in 'school-going' societies may fulfil the same function as the unconscious patterns he discovers, by analysing such cultural creations as rites or myths, among individuals belonging to societies with no educational institutions, or as those 'primitive forms of classification' which are not, and cannot be, the subject of conscious awareness and explicit methodical transmission. Do the patterns of thought and language transmitted by the school, e.g., those which treatises or rhetoric used to call figures of speech and figures of thought, actually fulfil, at any rate among members of the educated classes, the function of the

1. C. Lévi-Strauss, *A World on the Wane,* Hutchinson, 1961, pp. 54–5.
2. ibid., p. 230.

unconscious patterns which govern the thinking and the productions of people belonging to traditional societies, or do they, because of the conditions in which they are transmitted and acquired, operate only at the most superficial level of consciousness? If it be true that the specificity of societies possessing a scholarly, cumulative, accumulated-culture lies, from the point of view that concerns us here, in the fact that they have special institutions to transmit, explicitly or implicitly, explicit or implicit forms of thought that operate at different levels of consciousness—from the most obvious which may be apprehended by irony or by pedagogical thinking to the most deeply buried forms which find expression in acts of cultural creation or interpretation, without being thought about specifically—the question then arises whether the sociology of the institutionalized transmission of culture is not, at any rate in one of its aspects, one of the paths, and not the least important, to the sociology of knowledge.

The school and cultural integration

To appreciate how unusual this approach is, we need only note that Durkheim and, after him, most of the authors who have dealt with the sociology of education from an anthropological standpoint emphasize the school's 'moral' integration function, relegating to second place or passing over in silence what might be called the cultural (or logical) integration function of the educational institution. Is it not paradoxical that, in his writings on education, the author of *Formes primitives de classification* and *Formes élémentaires de la vie religieuse* should have failed to realize that, like religion in primitive societies, the culture that comes from schooling provides individuals with a common body of thought categories which make communication possible? It is perhaps less paradoxical that Durkheim, in his sociology of knowledge, should try to establish the social origin of logical categories without mentioning the role of education, since he is concerned in the above-mentioned works with societies in which the transmission of these logical categories is not generally entrusted to an institution specially designed for the purpose, but it is none the less surprising that he should regard schooling as one of the most effective means of securing the 'moral' integration of differentiated societies and yet not realize that the school is tending, more and more completely and exclusively as knowledge advances, to assume a logical integration function. 'Programmed' individuals—endowed with a homogenous programme of perception, thought and action—are the most specific product of an educational system. Those trained in a certain discipline or a certain school have in common a certain 'mentality': as the 'arts' or 'science' mentality or, in France, the *normalien* or *polytechnicien* mentality. Minds thus patterned in the same way are predisposed to immediate communication and understanding among themselves. As Henri-Irénée Marrou points out, this applies to individuals trained in the humanistic tradition; the traditional form of education makes sure that there is, 'among all minds, those of a given generation and those of a whole period of history, a fundamental homogeneity which makes communication and communion easier. . . . Within a classical culture, all men share the same treasury of admiration, patterns, rules and, above all, of examples, metaphors, images, words, a common idiom.'[1] The aphorisms, maxims and apologues of Graeco-Latin culture, like the metaphors and parallels inspired by Greek or Roman history, play a part comparable in all respects with that which traditional societies allot to proverbs, sayings and gnomic poems. If it be accepted that culture and, in the case in point, scholarly or academic culture, is a common code enabling all those possessing that code to attach the same meaning to the same words, the same types of behaviour and the same works and, conversely, to express the same meaningful intention through the same words, the same behaviour patterns and the same works, it is clear that the school, which is responsible for handing on that culture, is the fundamental factor in the cultural consensus in as far as it represents the sharing of a common sense which is the prerequisite for communication. Individuals owe to their schooling, first and foremost, a whole collection of commonplaces, covering not only common speech and language but also areas of encounter and agreement, common problems and common methods of approaching those common problems: educated people of a given period may disagree on the questions they discuss but are at any rate in agreement about discussing certain questions. A thinker is linked to his period, and identified in space and time, primarily by the conditioning background of the problem approach in which he thinks. Just as linguists have recourse to the criterion of inter-comprehension for determining linguistic areas, so intellectual and cultural areas and generations could be determined by identifying the sets of dominant conditioning questions which define the cultural field of a period. To conclude in all cases, on the basis of the manifest divergences which separate the intellectuals of a given period on what are sometimes known as the 'major problems of the day', that there is a deficiency of logical integration would be to allow ourselves to be misled by appearances; disagreement presupposes

1. H. I. Marrou, *Histoire de l'éducation dans l'antiquité*, sixth edition revised and enlarged, Paris, Seuil, 1965, p. 333.

agreement on the areas of disagreement, and the manifest conflicts between trends and doctrines conceal from the people concerned in those conflicts the implied basic concurrence which strikes the observer alien to the system. The consensus in dissensus, which constitutes the objective unity of the intellectual field of a given period, i.e, participation in the intellectual background of the day— which is not to be confused with submission to fashion—is rooted in the academic tradition. Authors having nothing else at all in common are yet contemporary in the accepted questions on which they are opposed and by reference to which at least one aspect of their thought is organized: like the fossils that enable us to date prehistoric eras, the subjects of discussion—crystallized remains of the great debates of the day—indicate, though probably with certain shifts in time, the questions which directed and governed the thinking of an age. We might, for instance, in the recent history of philosophic thought in France, distinguish a period of dissertation on judgement and concept, a period of dissertation on essence and existence (or fear and anxiety), and finally a period of dissertation on language and speech (or nature and culture). A comparative study of the commonest subjects of academic essays or treatises and of lectures in different countries at different periods would make an important contribution to the sociology of knowledge by defining the necessary frame of problematic reasoning, which is one of the most fundamental dimensions of the intellectual programming of a society and a period. This was what Renan foreshadowed when he wrote: 'Will it be believed that, at ceremonies similar to our prize-givings, when in our country oratory is essential, the Germans merely read out grammatical treatises of the most austere type, studded with Latin words? Can we conceive of formal public meetings taken up with readings of the following: On the nature of the conjunction; On the German period; On the Greek mathematicians; On the topography of the battle of Marathon; On the plain of Crissa; On the centuries of Servius Tullius; On the vines of Attica; Classification of prepositions; Clarification of difficult words in Homer; Commentary on the portrait of Thersites in Homer, etc.? This implies that our neighbours have a wonderful taste for serious things and perhaps, too, a certain capacity for facing up bravely to boredom when circumstances require.'[1]

There may be coexisting in the thought of a given author, and *a fortiori* of a given period, elements which belong to quite different scholastic periods;[2] the cultural field is transformed by successive

1. E. Renan, *L'avenir de la science*, Paris, Calmann Lévy, 1890, pp. 116–17.
2. Because of its own inertia, the school carries along categories and patterns of thought belonging to different ages. In the observance of the rules of the

restructurations rather than by radical revolutions, with certain themes being brought to the fore while others are set to one side without being completely eliminated, so that continuity of communication between intellectual generations remains possible. In all cases, however, the patterns informing the thought of a given period can be fully understood only by reference to the schools system which is alone capable of establishing them and developing them, through practice, as the habits of thought common to a whole generation.

Culture is not merely a common code or even a common catalogue of answers to recurring problems; it is a common set of previously assimilated master patterns from which, by an 'art of invention' similar to that involved in the writing of music, an infinite number of individual patterns directly applicable to specific situations are generated. The *topoi* are not only commonplace but also patterns of invention and supports for improvisation: these *topoi*—which include such particularly productive contrasting pairs as thought and action, essence and existence, continuity and discontinuity, etc.— provide bases and starting points for developments (mainly improvised), just as the rules of harmony and counterpoint sustain what seems to be the most inspired and the freest musical 'invention'. These patterns of invention may also serve to make up for deficiency of invention, in the usual sense of the term, so that the formalism and verbalism criticized by Lévi-Strauss are merely the pathological limit of the normal use of any method of thought. Mention may be made, in this context, of what Henri Wallon wrote about the function of thinking by pairs in children; 'contrasts of images or of speech result from such a natural and spontaneous association that they may sometimes override intuition and the sense of reality. They are part of the equipment constantly available to thought in the process of self-formulation and they may prevail over thinking. They come under the head of that "verbal knowledge" whose findings, already formulated, are often merely noted, without any exercise of reflective intelligence and whose workings often outlast those of thought in certain states of mental debilitation, confusion or distraction.'[1]

Verbal reflexes and thinking habits should serve to sustain thought but they may also, in moments of intellectual 'low tension', take the

dissertation in three points, for example, French schoolchildren are still contemporaries of Saint Thomas. The feeling of the 'unity of European culture' is probably due to the fact that the school brings together and reconciles—as it must for the purposes of teaching—types of thought belonging to very different periods.

1. H. Wallon, *Les origines de la pensée chez l'enfant*, Paris, Presses Universitaires de France, 1945, Vol. I, p. 63.

place of thought; they should help in mastering reality with the minimum effort, but they may also encourage those who rely on them not to bother to refer to reality. For every period, besides a collection of common themes, a particular constellation of dominant patterns could probably be determined, with as many epistomological profiles (taking this in a slightly different sense from that given to it by Gaston Bachelard) as there are schools of thought. It may be assumed that every individual owes to the type of schooling he has received a set of basic, deeply interiorized master-patterns on the basis of which he subsequently acquires other patterns, so that the system of patterns by which his thought is organized owes its specific character not only to the nature of the patterns constituting it but also the frequency with which these are used and to the level of consciousness at which they operate, these properties being probably connected with the circumstances in which the most fundamental intellectual patterns were acquired.

The essential point is probably that the patterns which have become second nature are generally apprehended only through a reflexive turning-back—which is always difficult—over the operations already carried out; it follows that they may govern and regulate mental processes without being consciously apprehended and controlled. It is primarily through the cultural unconscious which he owes to his intellectual training and more particularly to his scholastic training, that a thinker belongs to his society and age—schools of thought may, more often than is immediately apparent, represent the union of thinkers similarly schooled.

An exemplary confirmation of this hypothesis is to be found in the famous analysis by Erwin Panofsky of the relationship between Gothic art and Scholasticism. What the architects of the Gothic cathedrals unwittingly borrowed from the schoolmen was a *principium importans ordinem ad actum* or a *modus operandi*, i.e., a 'peculiar method of procedure which must have been the first thing to impress itself upon the mind of the layman whenever it came in touch with that of the schoolman'.[1] Thus, for example, the principle of clarification (*manifestatio*), a scheme of literary presentation discovered by Scholasticism, which requires the author to make plain and explicit (*manifestare*) the arrangement and logic of argument—we should say his plan—also governs the action of the architect and the sculptor, as we can see by comparing the Last Judgement on the tympanum of Autun Cathedral with the treatment of the same theme at Paris and Amiens where, despite a greater wealth of motifs, consummate clarity also prevails through the effect of symmetry and

1. E. Panofsky, *Gothic Architecture and Scholasticism*, New York, 1957, p. 28.

correspondence.[1] If this is so, it is because the cathedral-builders were subject to the constant influence—to the habit-forming force—of Scholasticism, which, from about 1130–40 to about 1270, 'held a veritable monopoly of education' over an area of roughly 100 miles around Paris. 'It is not very probable that the builders of Gothic structures read Gilbert de la Porrée or Thomas Aquinas in the original. But they were exposed to the Scholastic point of view in innumerable other ways, quite apart from the fact that their own work automatically brought them into a working association with those who devised the liturgical and iconographic programs. They had gone to school; they listened to sermons; they could attend the public *disputationes de quolibet* which, dealing as they did with all imaginable questions of the day, had developed into social events not unlike our operas, concerts or public lectures; and they could come into profitable contact with the learned on many other occasions.'[2] It follows, according to Panofsky, that the con-nexion between Gothic art and Scholasticism is 'more concrete than a mere "parallelism" and yet more general than those individual (and very important) "influences" which are inevitably exerted on painters, sculptors or architects by erudite advisors'. This connexion is 'a genuine cause-and-effect relation' which 'comes about by the spreading of what may be called, for want of a better term, a mental habit—reducing this overworked cliché to its precise Scholastic sense as "a principle that regulates the act", *principium importans ordinem ad actum*'.[3] As a habit-forming force, the school provides those who have been subjected directly or indirectly to its influence not so much with particular and particularized patterns of thought as with that general disposition, generating particular patterns that can be applied in different areas of thought and action, which may be termed cultured *habitus*.

Thus, in accounting for the structural homologies that he finds between such different areas of intellectual activity as architecture and philosophical thought, Erwin Panofsky does not rest content with references to a 'unitarian vision of the world' or a 'spirit of the times'—which would come down to naming what has to be explained or, worse still, to claiming to advance as an explanation the very thing that has to be explained; he suggests what seems to be the most naïve yet probably the most convincing explanation. This is that, in a society where the handing on of culture is monopolized by a school, the hidden affinities uniting the works of man (and, at the

1. ibid., p. 40.
2. ibid., p. 23.
3. ibid., pp. 20–1.

same time, modes of conduct and thought) derive from the institution of the school, whose function is consciously (and also, in part, unconsciously) to transmit the unconscious or, to be more precise, to produce individuals equipped with the system of unconscious (or deeply buried) master-patterns that constitute their culture. It would no doubt be an over-simplification to end our efforts at explanation at this point, as though the school were an empire within an empire, as though culture had there its absolute beginning; but it would be just as naïve to disregard the fact that, through the very logic of its functioning, the school modifies the content and the spirit of the culture it transmits and, above all, that its express function is to transform the collective heritage into a common individual unconscious. To relate the works of a period to the practices of the school therefore gives us a means of explaining not only what these works consciously set forth but also what they unconsciously reveal in as much as they partake of the symbolism of a period or of a society.

Schools of thought and class cultures

Apart from collective representations, such as the representation of man as the outcome of a long process of evolution, or the representation of the world as governed by necessary and immutable laws instead of by an arbitrary and capricious fate or by a providential will, every individual unconsciously brings to bear general tendencies such as those by which we recognize the 'style' of a period (whether it be the style of its architecture and furniture, or its style of life) and patterns of thought which organize reality by directing and organizing thinking about reality and make what he thinks thinkable for him as such and in the particular form in which it is thought. As Kurt Lewin remarks, 'Experiments dealing with memory and group pressure on the individual show that what exists as "reality" for the individual is, to a high degree, determined by what is socially accepted as reality. . . . "Reality", therefore, is not an absolute. It differs with the group to which the individual belongs.'[1] Similarly, what is a 'topical question' largely depends on what is socially considered as such; there is, at every period in every society, a hierarchy of legitimate objects for study, all the more compelling for there being no need to define it explicitly, since it is, as it were, lodged in the instruments of thought that individuals receive during their intellectual training. What is usually known as the Sapir-

1. K. Lewin, *Resolving Social Conflicts*, New York, Harper & Brothers, 1948, p. 57.

Whorf hypothesis is perhaps never so satisfactorily applicable as to intellectual life; words, and especially the figures of speech and figures of thought that are characteristic of a school of thought, mould thought as much as they express it. Linguistic and intellectual patterns are all the more important in determining what individuals take as worthy of being thought and what they think of it in that they operate outside all critical awareness. 'Thinking . . . follows a network of tracks laid down in the given language, an organization which may concentrate systematically upon certain phases of reality, certain aspects of intelligence, and may systematically discard others featured by other languages. The individual is utterly unaware of this organization and is constrained completely within its unbreakable bounds.'[1]

Academic language and thought effect this organization by giving prominence to certain aspects of reality: thinking by 'schools' and types (designated by so many concepts ending in 'ism') which is a specific product of the school, makes it possible to organize things pertaining to the school, i.e. the universe of philosophical, literary, visual and musical works and, beyond or through them, the whole experience of reality and all reality. To use the terms of Greek tradition, the natural world becomes meaningful only when it has been subject to *diacrisis*—an act of separation introducing the 'limit' (*peras*) into indeterminate chaos (*apeiron*). The school provides the principle for such organization and teaches the art of effecting it. Basically, is taste anything other than the art of differentiating— differentiating between what is cooked and what is raw, what is insipid and what has savour, but also between the classical style and the baroque style or the major mode and the minor mode? Without this principle of separation and the art of applying it that the school teaches, the cultural world is merely an indeterminate, undifferentiated chaos; museum visitors not equipped with this basic stock of words and categories by which differences can be named and, thereby, apprehended—proper names of famous painters which serve as generic categories, concepts designating a school, an age, a 'period' or a style and rendering possible comparisons ('parallels') or contrasts—are condemned to the monotonous diversity of meaningless sensations. In the words of a workman from Dreux: 'When you don't know anything about it, it's difficult to get the hang of it. . . . Everything seems the same to me . . . beautiful pictures, beautiful paintings, but it's difficult to make out one thing from another.' And another workman, from Lille this time, comments: 'It's difficult for

1. Whorf, 'Language, Mind and Reality', in *Language, Thought and Reality*, p. 256.

someone who wants to take an interest in it. All you can see are
paintings and dates. To see the differences, you need a guide, otherwise everything looks the same.'[1] As the systems of typical pre-
knowledge that individuals owe to the school grow richer (in other
words, as the standard of education rises), familiarity with the
organized universe of works becomes closer and more intense. The
school does not merely provide reference marks: it also maps out
itineraries, that is to say methods (in the etymological sense) or
programmes of thought. The intellectual and linguistic master-
patterns organize a marked-out area covered with compulsory
turnings and one-way streets, avenues and blind alleys; within this
area, thought can unfurl with the impression of freedom and improvisation because the marked-out itineraries that it is bound to
follow are the very ones that it has covered many a time in the
course of schooling. The order of exposition that the school imposes
on the culture transmitted—which, most of the time, owes at least
as much to school routines as to educational requirements—tends
to gain acceptance, as being absolutely necessary, from those acquiring the culture through that order. By its orderly treatment of the
works of culture the school hands on, at one and the same time, the
rules establishing the orthodox manner of approaching works
(according to their position in an established hierarchy) and the
principles on which that hierarchy is founded. Because the order
of acquisition tends to appear indissolubly associated with the
culture acquired and because each individual's relationship with his
culture bears the stamp of the conditions in which he acquired it,
a self-taught man can be distinguished straightaway from a school-
trained man. Having no established itineraries to rely on, the auto-
didact in Sartre's *La Nausée* sets about reading, in alphabetical order,
every author possible. It is perhaps only in its decisive rigidity that
this programme seems more arbitrary than the usual syllabus
sanctioned by the school and based on a chronological order which,
though apparently natural and inevitable, is in fact equally alien to
considerations of logic and teaching; nevertheless, in the eyes of
people who have gone through the ordered sequence of the *cursus*,
a culture acquired by such a curious process would always contrast
as sharply with an academic culture as a tangled forest with a formal
garden.

Being responsible for instilling these principles of organization, the
school must itself be organized to carry out this function. If it is to

1. Cf. P. Bourdieu and A. Darbel, with D. Schnapper, *L'amour de l'art, les
musées et leur public,* Paris, Éditions de Minuit, 1966, pp. 69–76. (Coll. 'Le sens
commun').

hand on this programme of thought known as culture, it must subject the culture it transmits to a process of programming that will make it easier to hand on methodically. Whenever literature becomes a school subject—as among the Sophists or in the Middle Ages—we find emerging the desire to classify, usually by genre and by author, and also to establish hierarchies, to pick out from the mass of works the 'classics' worthy of being preserved through the medium of the school. Collections of excerpts and textbooks are typical of such works designed to serve the school's allotted function of ordering and emphasizing. Having to prepare their pupils to answer academic questions, teachers tend to plan their teaching in accordance with the system of organization that their pupils will have to follow in answering those questions; in the extreme case, we have those prose composition manuals providing ready-made essays on particular subjects. In the organization of his teaching and sometimes of his whole work every teacher is obliged to make some concessions to the requirements of the educational system and of his own function. Gorgias's *Encomium of Helen* is perhaps the first historic example of a demonstration of professorial skill combined with something like a 'crib'; and surely many of Alain's essays are but consummate examples of what French students in *rhétorique supérieure* (the classical upper sixth), whom he taught for the best part of his life, call *topos*, i.e., lectures or demonstrations closely tailored to the letter and spirit of the syllabus and meeting perfectly, in themes, sources, style and even spirit, the examination requirements for admission to the École Normale Supérieure. The programme of thought and action that it is the school's function to impart thus owes a substantial number of its practical characteristics to the institutional conditions in which it is transmitted and to specifically academic requirements. We therefore cannot hope fully to understand each 'school of thought', defined by its subjection to one or other of these programmes, unless we relate it to the specific logic governing the operation of the school from which it derives.

It follows that the gradual rationalization of a system of teaching geared more and more exclusively to preparation for an increasing variety of occupational activities could threaten the cultural integration of the educated class if, so far as that class is concerned, education, and more particularly what is known as general culture, were not at least as much a matter for the family as for the school, for the family in the sense of parents and their progeny and also in that of the fields of knowledge (many scientists are married to women with an arts background) and if all types of training did not allot a place, always a fairly important one, to classical, liberal education. The sharing of a common culture, whether this involves verbal patterns or artistic experience and objects of admiration, is probably one of the surest foundations of the deep underlying fellow-feeling that unites the members of the governing classes, despite differences of occupation and economic circumstances. It is understandable that T. S. Eliot should regard culture as the key instrument in the integration of the elite: 'A society is in danger of disintegration when there is a lack of contract between people of different areas of activity —between the political, the scientific, the artistic, the philosophical and the religious minds. The separation cannot be repaired merely by public organization. It is not a question of assembling into committees representatives of different types of knowledge and experience, of calling in everybody to advise everybody else. The elite should be something different, something much more organically composed, than a panel of bonzes, caciques and tycoons. Men who meet only for definite serious purposes and on official occasions do not wholly meet. They may have some common concern very much at heart, they may, in the course of repeated contacts, come to share a vocabulary and an idiom which appear to communicate every shade of meaning necessary for their common purpose; but they will continue to retire from these encounters each to his private social world as well as to his solitary world. Everyone has observed that the possibilities of contented silence, of a mutual happy awareness when engaged upon a common task, or an underlying seriousness and significance in the enjoyment of a silly joke, are characteristics of any close personal intimacy; and the congeniality of any circle of friends depends upon a common social convention, a common ritual, and common pleasures of relaxation. These aids to intimacy are no less important for the communication of meaning in words than the possession of a common subject upon which the several parties are informed. It is unfortunate for a man when his friends and his business associates are two unrelated groups; it is also narrowing when they are one and the same group.'[1] Intimacy and fellow-feeling, congeniality, based on a common culture are rooted in the unconscious and give the traditional elites a social cohesion and continuity which would be lacking in elites united solely by links of professional interest: 'They will be united only by a part, and that the most conscious part, of their personalities; they will meet like committees.'[2] It would not be difficult to find, within the ruling class, social units

1. *Notes towards the Definition of Culture*, Faber & Faber, London, 1962, pp. 84–5.
2. ibid., p. 47.

based on the 'intimacy' created by the same intellectual 'program-ming'—affinities of schooling play an extremely important part once a body can be recruited by co-option.

Unlike the traditional type of education, setting out to hand on the integrated culture of an integrated society—all-round education producing people equipped for their various roles in society in general—specialized education, imparting specific types of knowledge and know-how, is liable to produce as many 'intellectual clans' as there are specialized schools. To take the most obvious and crudest example, the relations between arts people and science people are often governed, in present-day society, by the very laws to be seen in operation in the contacts between different cultures. Misunder-standings, borrowings removed from their context and reinterpreted, admiring imitation and disdainful aloofness—these are all signs familiar to specialists on the situations that arise when cultures meet. The debate between the upholders of literary humanism and the upholders of scientific or technological humanism is usually conduc-ted in relation to ultimate values—efficiency or disinterestedness, specialization or general liberal education—just because each type of schooling naturally tends to be shut into an autonomous and self-sufficient world of its own; and because any action for the handing on of a culture necessarily implies an affirmation of the value of the culture imparted (and, correlatively, an implicit or explicit depreciation of other possible cultures); in other words, any type of teaching must, to a large extent, produce a need for its own product and therefore set up as a value, or value of values, the culture that it is concerned with imparting, achieving this in and through the very act of imparting it.[1] It follows that individuals whose education condemns them to a kind of cultural hemiplegia, while at the same time encouraging them to identify their own worth with the worth of their culture, are inclined to feel uneasy in their contacts with people with an alien and sometimes rival culture; this uneasiness may be reflected in a compensatory enthusiasm serving as a means of exorcism (we need only think, for example, of the fetishism and

1. As disparagement of the rival culture is the most convenient and surest means of magnifying the culture being imparted and of reassuring the person imparting it of his own worth, the temptation to resort to this means is all the greater in France because of the teachers' leaning towards charismatic instruction (which leads them to feel that subjects and teachers are on competitive teams), towards the charismatic ideology that goes with it, which encourages them to regard intellectual careers as personal vocations based upon 'gifts' so obviously mutually exclusive that possession of one rules out possession of the other: to proclaim that you are no good at science is one of the easiest ways of assuring others and yourself that you are gifted on the literary side.

Shamanism to be seen among certain specialists in the sciences of man with regard to the formalization of their findings) as well as in rejection and scorn.

The primary causes of the opposition between 'intellectual clans', of which people in general are aware, are never all to be found in the content of the cultures transmitted and the mentality that goes with them. What distinguishes, for example, within the large 'arts' group, a graduate of the École Normale Supérieure from a graduate of the École Nationale de l'Administration or, within the 'science' group, a graduate of the École Polytechnique from a graduate of the École Centrale is perhaps, quite as much as the nature of the knowledge they have acquired, the way in which that knowledge has been acquired, i.e., the nature of the exercises they have had to do, of the examinations they have taken, the criteria by which they have been judged and by reference to which they have organized their studies. An individual's contact with his culture depends basically on the circumstances in which he has acquired it, among other things because the act whereby culture is communicated is, as such, the exemplary expression of a certain type of relation to the culture. The formal lecture, for instance, communicates something other, and something more, than its literal content: it furnishes an example of intellectual prowess and thereby indissociably defines the 'right' culture and the 'right' relation to that culture; vigour and brilliance, ease and elegance are qualities of style peculiar to the act of communication which mark the culture communicated and gain acceptance at the same time as the culture from those receiving it in this form.[1] It could be shown in the same way how all teaching practices implicitly furnish a model of the 'right' mode of intellectual activity; for example, the very nature of the tests set (ranging from the composition, based on the technique of 'development', which is the predominant form in most arts examinations, to the 'brief account' required in advanced science examinations), the type of rhetorical and linguistic qualities required and the value attached to these qualities, the relative importance given to written papers and oral examinations and the qualities required in both instances, tend to encourage a certain attitude towards the use of language—sparing or prodigal, casual or ceremonious, complacent or restrained. In this way the canons governing school work proper, in composition or exposition, may continue to govern writings apparently freed from

1. Although there is no necessary link between a given content and a given way of imparting it, people who have acquired them together tend to regard them as inseparable. Thus some people regard any attempt to rationalize teaching as threatening to desacralize culture.

the disciplines of the school—newspaper articles, public lectures, summary reports and works of scholarship.

Taking it to be the fact that educated people owe their culture—i.e. a programme of perception, thought and action—to the school, we can see that, just as the differentiation of schooling threatens the cultural integration of the educated class, so the *de facto* segregation which tends to reserve secondary education (especially in the classics) and higher education almost exclusively to the economically and, above all, culturally most favoured classes, tends to create a cultural rift. The separation of those who, around the age of 10 or 11, embark on a school career that will last many years, from those who are shot straight into adult life, probably follows class divisions much more closely than in past centuries. Under the *ancien régime*, as Philippe Ariès points out, 'schooling habits differed not so much according to rank as according to function. Consequently, attitudes to life, like many other features of everyday life, differed not much more', notwithstanding 'the rigidly diversified social hierarchy'.[1] On the other hand, 'since the eighteenth century, the single school system has been replaced by a dual educational system, each branch of which is matched not to an age group but to a social class—the *lycée* or the *collège* (secondary schooling) for the middle classes and the elementary (or primary) school for the common people'.[2] Since then, the distinct quality of education has been matched by a duality of culture. 'The whole complexion of life', to quote Philippe Ariès again, has been changed by the difference in schooling given to middle class children and working class children'.[3] Culture, whose function it was if not to unify at least to make communication possible, takes on a differentiating function. 'It is not quite true', writes Edmund Goblot, 'that the bourgeoisie exists only in the practice of society and not in law. The *lycée* makes it a legal institution. The *baccalauréat* is the real barrier, the official, State-guaranteed barrier, which holds back the invasion. True, you may join the bourgeoisie, but first you have to get the *baccalauréat*.'[4] The 'liberal' culture of the humanist traditions, with Latin its keystone and the social 'signum' *par excellence*, constitutes the difference while at the same time giving it the semblance of legitimacy. 'When, instead of thinking of his individual interests, he (a member of the

1. P, Ariès, *L'enfant et la vie familiale sous l'Ancien Régime,* Plon, Paris, 1960, p. 375.
2. ibid.
3. ibid., p. 376.
4. E. Goblot, *La barrière et le niveau, étude sociologique sur la bourgeoisie française,* Alcan, 1930, p. 126.

bourgeoisie) thinks of his class interests, he needs a culture that marks out an elite, a culture that is not purely utilitarian, a luxury culture. Otherwise, he would fast become indistinguishable from the section of the working classes that manages to gain an education by sheer hard work and intelligence and goes on to lay siege to the professions. The educational background of a middle class child who will not work, despite the educational resources of the *lycée*, will not bear comparison with that of a working class child who studies hard with nothing but the resources of the senior primary school. Even when schooling leads nowhere professionally, therefore, it is still useful in maintaining the barrier'.[1]

The school's function is not merely to sanction the *distinction*—in both senses of the word—of the educated classes. The culture that it imparts separates those receiving it from the rest of society by a whole series of systematic differences. Those whose 'culture' (in the ethnologists' sense) is the academic culture conveyed by the school have a system of categories of perception, language, thought and appreciation that sets them apart from those whose only training has been through their work and their social contacts with people of their own kind. Just as Basil Bernstein contrasts the 'public language' of the working classes, employing descriptive rather than analytical concepts, with a more complex 'formal language', more conducive to verbal elaboration and abstract thought, we might contrast an academic culture, confined to those who have been long subjected to the disciplines of the school, with a 'popular' culture, peculiar to those who have been excluded from it, were it not that, by using the same concept of culture in both cases, we should be in danger of concealing that these two systems of patterns of perception, language, thought, action and appreciation are separated by an essential difference. This is that only the system of patterns cultivated by the school, i.e., academic culture (in the subjective sense of personal cultivation or *Bildung* in German), is organized primarily by reference to a system of works embodying that culture, by which it is both supported and expressed. To speak of 'popular' culture suggests that the system of patterns that makes up the culture (in the subjective sense) of the working classes could or should, in circumstances that are never specified, constitute a culture (in the objective sense) by being embodied in 'popular' works, giving the populace expression in accordance with the patterns of language and thought that define its culture (in the subjective sense). This amounts to asking the populace to take over the intention and means of expression of academic culture (as the proletarian writers do,

1. E. Goblot, op. cit., pp. 125–6.

whether of middle class or working class extraction) to express experience structured by the patterns of a culture (in the subjective sense) to which that intention and those means are essentially alien. It is then quite obvious that 'popular' culture is, by definition, deprived of the objectification, and indeed of the intention of objectification, by which academic culture is defined.

Schooling and the intellectual make-up of a nation

Like a great many features by which 'schools of thought' and 'intellectual clans' in the same society may be recognized, many national characteristics of intellectual activity must be referred back to the traditions of educational systems which owe their specific character to national history and, more especially, to their specific history within that national history. In the absence of a comparative study of the specific history of different educational systems, a history of the intellectual patterns (or, to put it another way, of the patent and latent programmes of thinking), that each school transmits implicitly or explicitly in every age (history of curricula, of teaching methods and of the ecological conditions in which teaching is carried out, of the types and subjects of exercises, of treatises of rhetoric and stylistics, etc.), we are obliged to make do with a partial treatment bearing on the French educational system alone. To account for such traits as the fondness for abstraction or the cult of brilliance and distinguished performance that are commonly regarded as part of the 'intellectual make-up' of the French, we must surely relate them to the specific traditions of the French educational system. At the end of a study in which he shows the extent of the influence of Aristotle's thought on French seventeenth-century literature, Etienne Gilson concludes: 'Abstraction is, for Aristotle and the Schoolmen, the distinctive act of human thought and . . . if the essence of the classical spirit was the tendency to generalize and abstract the essence of things, it was perhaps because, for several centuries, young Frenchmen had been taught that the very essence of thought was to abstract and generalize.'[1] Similarly, instead of relating the professorial cult of verbal prowess to the national cult of artistic or military prowess, as J. R. Pitts does,[2] should we not rather look for the cause in teaching traditions? Ernest Renan does so: 'The French educational system has patterned itself too closely on the Jesuits, with their dull eloquence and Latin verse; it is

1. E. Gilson, 'La scolastique et l'esprit classique', in *Les idées et les lettres*, Paris, Vrin, 1955, p. 257.
2. J. R. Pitts, *A la recherche de la France*, Paris, Seuil, 1963, p. 273.

too reminiscent of the rhetoricians of the later Roman Empire. The weakness of the French, which is their urge to hold forth, their tendency to reduce everything to declamation, is encouraged by the persistence of part of the French educational system in overlooking the substances of knowledge and valuing only style and talent.'[1] Renan foreshadows what Durkheim was to say in his *Evolution Pédagogique en France*, where he sees in the 'pseudo-humanistic teaching' of the Jesuits and the 'literary-mindedness' that it encourages one of the basic ingredients of the French intellectual temperament. 'Protestant France in the first half of the seventeenth century was in process of doing what Protestant Germany did in the second half of the eighteenth century. All over the country there was, as a result, an admirable movement of discussion and investigation. It was the age of Casaubon, Scaliger and Saumaise. The revocation of the Edict of Nantes destroyed all this. It killed studies in historical criticism in France, Since the literary approach alone was encouraged, a certain frivolity resulted. Holland and Germany, in part thanks to our exiles, acquired a near-monopoly of learning. It was decided from then on that France should be above all a nation of wits, of good writers, brilliant conversationalists, but inferior in knowledge of things and liable to all the blunders that can be avoided only by breadth of learning and maturity of judgement.'[2] And Renan, like Durkheim after him, notes that 'the system of French education created after the Revolution under the name of *université* in fact derives far more from the Jesuits than from the old universities',[3] as can be seen from its handling of literary material. 'It (the university) uses a superabundance of classical material but without applying the literary spirit that would bring it to life; the ancient forms are in daily use, passing from hand to hand; but antiquity's sense of beauty is absolutely lacking . . .; never does the arid exercise of the intellect give place to a vital nourishment of the spiritual man. . . . All that is learnt is a remarkable skill in concealing from oneself and others that the dazzling shell of high-flown expression is empty of thought. A narrow, formalistic outlook is the characteristic feature of education in France.'[4] This is the very language used by Durkheim: 'The tremendous advantage of a scientific education is that it forces man to come out of himself and brings him into touch with things; it thereby makes him aware of his dependence on the world about him. The "arts" man or the pure humanist on the

1. E. Renan, *Questions contemporaines*, Paris, Calmann-Lévy, n.d., p. 79.
2. E. Renan, op. cit. p. 80.
3. ibid., p. 81, No. 1.
4. ibid., p. 277.

other hand, never in his thinking comes up against anything resistant to which he can cling and with which he can feel at one: this opens wide the door to a more or less elegant dilettantism but leaves man to his own devices, without attaching him to any external reality, to any objective task.'[1] This literary teaching, based on the idea that human nature is 'eternal, immutable, independent of time and space, since it is unaffected by the diversity of circumstances and places', has, according to Durkheim, left its stamp on the intellectual temperament of the French, inspiring a 'constitutional cosmopolitanism', 'the habit of thinking of man in general terms' (of which 'the abstract individualism of the eighteenth century is an expression') and 'the inability to think in any other than abstract, general, simple terms'.[2]

Renan also points out how the institutional conditions in which teaching was given after the Revolution helped to strengthen the tendency towards literary showing-off.[3] 'Twice a week, for an hour at a stretch, the professor had to appear before an audience made up at random and often changing completely from one lecture to the next. He had to speak without any regard for the special needs of the students, without finding out what they knew or did not know. . . . Long scientific deductions, necessitating following a whole chain of reasoning, had to be ruled out. . . . Laplace, if he had taught in such establishments, would certainly not have had more than a dozen students. Open to all, having become the scene of a kind of rivalry inspired by the aim of drawing and holding the public, what kind of lectures were therefore given? Brilliant expositions, 'recitations' in the manner of the declamators of the later Roman Empire. . . . A German visitor attending such lectures is astounded. He arrives from his university, where he has been accustomed to treat his professor with the greatest respect. This professor is a *Hofrat* and some days he sees the Prince! He is an earnest man whose utterances are all worth attention, and takes himself extremely seriously. Here, everything is different. The swing-door which, throughout the lecture, is forever opening and closing, the perpetual coming and going, the casualness of the students, the lecturer's tone, which is hardly ever didactic though sometimes declamatory, his knack for finding the sonorous commonplace which, bringing nothing new, is unfail-

1. E. Durkheim, *L'évolution pédagogique en France,* Alcan, Vol. II, p. 55.
2. ibid., II, p. 128–32.
3. By making the formal lecture the type of teaching with the highest prestige, the French system of education encourages works of a certain kind and intellectual qualities of a certain kind, pre-eminent importance being attached to qualities of exposition. Consideration should be given to the question whether an institution such as the British lecture system is associated with other habits of thought and other values.

ingly greeted with acclaim by his audience—all this seems queer and outrageous.'[1] And we can only agree with Renan once more when, reviewing a book by a German observer, Ludwig Hahn,[2] he shows that such a procedure for selection as the competitive examination merely accentuates the weight and advantage given to qualities of form: 'It is most regrettable that the competitive examination is the only means of qualifying for a teaching post in secondary schools, and that practical skill allied to sufficient knowledge is not accepted for this purpose. The men with the most experience of education, those who bring to their difficult duties not brilliant gifts, but a sound intellect combined with a little slowness and diffidence, will always, in public examinations, come below the young men who can amuse their audience and their examiners but who, though very good at talking their way out of difficulties, have neither the patience nor the firmness to be good teachers.'[3] Renan finds everywhere signs of this tendency to prefer eloquence to truth, style to content. 'The institution to which France has committed the recruitment of its secondary and university teachers, the École Normale, has, on the arts side, been a school of style, not a school where things are learnt. It has produced delightful journalistic writers, engaging novelists, subtle intellects in the most varied lines—in short, everything but men possessing a sound knowledge of languages and literatures. On the pretext of keeping to general truths concerning ethics and taste, minds have been confined to the commonplace.'[4] It is indeed in the traditions of the school, and in the attitude to scholastic matters, that the school fosters, that the first cause of what Madame de Staël called 'le pédantisme de la légèreté' should be sought. To quote

1. E. Renan, op. cit. pp. 90–1.
2. L. Hahn, *Das Unterrichtswesen in Frankreich, mit einer Geschichte der Pariser Universität,* Breslau, 1848.
3. E. Renan, 'L'instruction publique en France jugée par les Allemands', *Questions Contemporaines,* Paris, Calmann-Lévy, n.d., p. 266. It would be easy to show how the values involved in the selection system govern the whole of intellectual life owing to the fact that, because they are deeply interiorized, they dominate the relationship of every creator with his work. This would explain, for example, the evolution of the thesis for the doctorate: individuals fashioned by a system requiring from each the unmatchable perfection that can give top place in competitive examinations are inclined to make steadily greater demands on themselves; thus, despite the ritual character of the actual ordeal of upholding the thesis, the authors of 'theses for the doctorate' set out, at it were, to outdo each other in intellectual ambition, erudition and lengthiness, devoting ten to fifteen years to producing their professional masterpiece.
4. E. Renan, op. cit. p. 94. It would be easy to show that there are affinities between the values directing educational activity and the values of the educated classes (cf. P. Bourdieu and J. C. Passeron, *Les héritiers, les étudiants et la culture,* Éditions de Minuit, Paris, 1964).

Renan again: 'The word pedantry, which, if not clearly defined, can be so misapplied and which, to superficial minds, is more or less synonymous with any serious scholarly research, has thus become a bogey to sensitive and discriminating people, who have often preferred to remain superficial rather than to lay themselves open to this most dreaded charge. This scruple has been taken to such a point that extremely distinguished critics have been known deliberately to leave what they are saying incomplete rather than use a word smacking of the schools, even though it is the appropriate one. Scholastic jargon, when there is no thought behind it or when it is merely used, by people of limited intelligence, to show off, is pointless and ludicrous. But to seek to proscribe the precise, technical style which alone can express certain fine or deep shades of thought is to fall into an equally unreasonable purism. Kant and Hegel, or even minds as independent of the schools as Herder, Schiller and Goethe, would certainly not, at this rate, escape our terrible accusation of pedantry. Let us congratulate our neighbours on their freedom from these shackles, which would nevertheless, it must be said, be less harmful to them than to us. In their country, the school and learning touch; in ours, any higher education which, in manner, still smacks of the secondary school is adjudged bad form and intolerable; it is thought to be intelligent to set oneself above anything reminiscent of the classroom. Everyone plumes himself a little on this score and thinks, in so doing, to prove that he is long past the school-teaching stage.'[1]

Because they always relate the 'intellectual make-up' of the French to the institutional conditions in which it is formed, Renan's and Durkheim's analyses represent a decisive contribution to the sociology of the intellectual make-up of a nation. Although the school is only one socializing institution among others, the whole complex of features forming the intellectual make-up of a society— or more exactly of the educated classes of that society—is constituted or reinforced by the educational system, which is deeply marked by its particular history and capable of moulding the minds of those who are taught and those who teach both through the content and spirit of the culture that it conveys and through the methods by which it conveys it. A good many of the differences dividing intellectual universes—differences in intellectual and linguistic patterns, like the techniques of composition and exposition, and more especially in the intellectual frame of reference (discernible, for example, through implicit or explicit, optional or inevitable quotations)— could be linked up with the academic traditions of the various

1. E. Renan, *L'avenir de la science*, Paris, Calmann-Lévy, 1890, p. 116.

nations and, more specifically, with the creative thinker's relationship with his national academic tradition, which depends, basically, on his educational background. Many of the distinguishing features of English 'positivism' or French 'rationalism' are surely nothing other than the tricks and mannerisms of the schools? Does not the ranking of intellectual activities (according to the degree of formalization, accessibility, abstraction and generality, or according to literary quality), which is implicitly and even explicitly conveyed and sanctioned by each scholastic tradition and finds concrete expression in the ranking of academic disciplines at any given point in time, govern intellectual productions just as much as the precepts of rhetoric inspired by the same values, which encourage or discourage, for instance, abstract treatment not based on examples, conceptual and syntactic esoterism, or stylistic elegance? Similarly, in each historical society, the ranking of questions worthy of interest determines a great many choices that are felt as 'vocations' and directs the keenest intellectual ambitions towards the subjects of study carrying most prestige. American sociologists regard the sociology of knowledge as 'a marginal speciality with a persistent European flavour'[1] because this branch of science is still dominated by an 'original constellation of problems', by a tradition perpetuated by education in Europe and still alive for European sociologists, who are more often inclined, because of their philosophical training, to state in sociological terms the traditional philosophical problem of the conditions in which objective knowledge is possible and the limits to such knowledge. The same logic should no doubt apply to many of the 'influences' that the historians of literature delight in detecting between authors, schools or periods, presupposing affinities at the level of thought patterns and problem approach and also, in some cases, a collective interest in groups of nations which are implicitly credited with legitimacy. The feeling of familiarity conveyed by certain works or certain intellectual themes, and conducive to their wide dissemination, is probably largely due to the fact that minds organized in accordance with the same programme have no difficulty in 'finding their bearings' with them. Would Heisenberg's

1. 'The sociology of knowledge remained of peripheral concern among sociologists at large, who did not share the particular problems that troubled German thinking in the 1920s. This was especially true of American sociologists who have in the main looked upon the discipline as a marginal speciality with a persistent European flavour. More importantly, however, the continuing linkage of the sociology of knowledge with its original constellation of problems has been a theoretical weakness even where there has been an interest in the discipline' (P. L. Berger and Thomas Luckmann, *The Social Construction of Reality,* New York, Doubleday and Co., 1966, p. 4).

Uncertainty Principle have had such a success in textbook literature if it had not landed, just at the right time, on a terrain already marked out between the determinism and the freedom of philosophy dissertations?[1]

'Because we were all children before reaching man's estate, and for a long time were governed by our appetites and our tutors, often at variance with one another, neither, perhaps, always giving us the best advice, it is almost impossible for our opinions to be as clear or as sound as they would have been had we had full use of our reason from the moment of our birth and had we never been guided by anything other than it.'[2] Descartes' utopia of innate culture, of natural culture, leads to the core of the contradiction defining the individual's relationship with his culture. As the light dove might imagine that it would fly better in a vacuum, the thinking individual likes to dream of thinking free from this unthought deposit that has formed within him, under the rod of his mentors, and which underlies all his thoughts.

'I received', says Husserl, 'the education of a German, not that of a Chinaman. But my education was also that of the inhabitant of a small town, with a home background, attending a school for children of the lower middle class, not that of a country landowner's son educated at a military college.'[3] Like Descartes, Husserl invites his readers to think about the paradoxes of finitude. The individual who attains an immediate, concrete understanding of the familiar world, of the native atmosphere in which and for which he has been brought up, is thereby deprived of the possibility of appropriating immediately and fully the world that lies outside. Access to culture can never be more than access to one culture—that of a class and of a nation. No doubt someone born outside who wishes to understand the universe of the Chinese or of the Junker class can start his education again from scratch on the Chinese or Junker model ('for example by trying', as Husserl says, 'to learn the content of the

1. However great the affinities, borrowings are always reinterpreted by reference to the structures into which they are incorporated, that is, in this instance, to the patterns of thought peculiar to each national tradition (we need only think, for example, of the changes undergone by Hegel's philosophy in France), even when, as in the case of the philosophical writings of phenomenological inspiration which flourished in France after 1945, the native forms of thought and indeed of language follow, even in their detail, the linguistic and verbal patterns of the imported philosophy, to such a point that they seem to be aping the labourious clumsiness of literal rather than literary translations.

2. R. Descartes, *Discours de la méthode*, Part II.

3. E. Husserl, A VII, 9, p. 15, quoted by R. Toulemont, *L'essence de la société selon Husserl*, Paris, Presses Universitaires de France, 1962, p. 191.

curriculum of the military college'), but such mediate, knowing acquisition will always differ from an immediate familiarity with the native culture, in the same way as the interiorized, subconscious culture of the native differs from the objectified culture reconstructed by the ethnologist.

9

ON THE CLASSIFICATION AND FRAMING OF
EDUCATIONAL KNOWLEDGE

Basil Bernstein

Introduction

How a society selects, classifies, distributes, transmits and evaluates
the educational knowledge it considers to be public, reflects both
the distribution of power and the principles of social control. From
this point of view, differences within and change in the organisation,
transmission and evaluation of educational knowledge should be a
major area of sociological interest. (Bernstein, B. 1966, 1967, Davies,
I. 1970,* 1971; Musgrove, 1968; Hoyle, 1969; Young, M. 1970.)
Indeed, such a study is a part of the larger question of the structure
and changes in the structure of cultural transmission. For various
reasons, British sociologists have fought shy of this question. As a
result, the sociology of education has been reduced to a series of
input-output problems; the school has been transformed into a
complex organisation or people-processing institution; the study of
socialisation has been trivialised.

Educational knowledge is a major regulator of the structure of
experience. From this point of view, one can ask 'How are forms of
experience, identity and relation evoked, maintained and changed by
the formal transmission of educational knowledge and sensitivities?'
Formal educational knowledge can be considered to be realised
through three message systems: curriculum, pedagogy and evaluation.
Curriculum defines what counts as valid knowledge, pedagogy
defines what counts as a valid transmission of knowledge, and
evaluation defines what counts as a valid realisation of this knowledge on the part of the taught. The term, educational knowledge
code, which will be introduced later, refers to the underlying princi-

* [Reprinted as Reading 6 in the present volume. E.H.]

ples which shape curriculum, pedagogy and evaluation. It will be argued that the form this code takes depends upon social principles which regulate the classification and framing of knowledge made public in educational institutions. Both Durkheim and Marx have shown us that the structure of society's classifications and frames reveals both the distribution of power and the principles of social control. I hope to show, *theoretically*, that educational codes provide excellent opportunities for the study of classification and frames through which experience is given a distinctive form. The paper is organised as follows:

(1) I shall first distinguish between two types of curricula: collection and integrated.

(2) I shall build upon the basis of this distinction in order to establish a more general set of concepts: classification and frame.

(3) A typology of educational codes will then be derived.

(4) Sociological aspects of two very different educational codes will then be explored.

(5) This will lead on to a discussion of educational codes and problems of social control.

(6) Finally there will be a brief discussion of the reasons for a weakening of one code and a strengthening of the movement of the other.

(1) *Two Types of Curricula*

Initially, I am going to talk about the curriculum in a very general way. In all educational institutions there is a formal punctuation of time into periods. These may vary from ten minutes to three hours or more. I am going to call each such formal period of time a 'unit'. I shall use the word 'content' to describe how the period of time is used. I shall define a curriculum initially in terms of the principle by which units of time and their contents are brought into a special relationship with each other. I now want to look more closely at the phrase 'special relationship'.

Firstly, we can examine relationships between contents in terms of the amount of time accorded to a given content. Immediately, we can see that more time is devoted to some contents rather than others. Secondly, some of the contents may, from the point of view of the pupils, be compulsory or optional. We can now take a very crude measure of the relative status of a content in terms of the number of units given over to it, and whether it is compulsory or optional. This raises immediately the question of the relative status of a given content and its significance in a given educational career.

We can, however, consider the relationship between contents from another, perhaps more important, perspective. We can ask about any given content whether the boundary between it and another content is clear cut or blurred. To what extent are the various contents well insulated from each other. If the various contents are well insulated from each other, I shall say that the contents stand in a *closed* relation to each other. If there is reduced insulation between contents, I shall say that the contents stand in an *open* relationship to each other. So far, then, I am suggesting that we can go into any educational institution and examine the organisation of time in terms of the relative status of contents, and whether the contents stand in an open-closed relationship to each other. I am deliberately using this very abstract language in order to emphasise that there is nothing intrinsic to the relative status of various contents, and there is nothing intrinsic to the relationships between contents. Irrespective of the question of the intrinsic logic of the various forms of public thought, the *forms* of their transmission, that is, their classification and framing, are social facts. There are a number of alternative means of access to the public forms of thought, and so to the various realities which they make possible. I am therefore emphasising the social nature of the system of alternatives from which emerges a constellation called a curriculum. From this point of view, any curriculum entails a principle or principles whereby of all the possible contents of time some contents are accorded differential status and enter into open or closed relation to each other.

I shall now distinguish between two broad types of curriculum. If contents stand in a closed relation to each other, that is, if the contents are clearly bounded and insulated from each other, I shall call such a curriculum a *collection* type. Here, the learner has to collect a group of favoured contents in order to satisfy some criteria of evaluation. There may of course be some underlying concept to a collection: the gentleman, the educated man, the skilled man, the non-vocational man.

Now I want to juxtapose against the collection type a curriculum where the various contents do not go their own separate ways, but where the contents stand in an open relation to each other. I shall call such a curriculum an integrated type. Now we can have various types of collection, and various degrees and types of integration.

(2) *Classification and Frame*

I shall now introduce the concepts, classification and frame which will be used to analyse the underlying structure of the three message systems, curriculum, pedagogy and evaluation, which are realisations of the educational knowledge code. The basic idea is embodied in the principle used to distinguish the two types of curricula: collection and integrated. Strong insulation between contents pointed to a collection type, whereas reduced insulation pointed to an integrated type. The principle here is the strength of the *boundary* between contents. This notion of boundary strength underlies the contents of classification and frame.

Classification and Frame

Classification, here, does not refer to *what* is classified, but to the *relationships* between contents. Classification refers to the nature of the differentiation between contents. Where classification is strong, contents are well insulated from each other by strong boundaries. Where classification is weak, there is reduced insulation between contents, for the boundaries between contents are weak or blurred. *Classification thus refers to the degree of boundary maintenance between contents.* Classification focusses our attention upon boundary strength as the critical distinguishing feature of the division of labour of educational knowledge. It gives us, as I hope to show, the basic structure of the message system, curriculum.

The concept, frame, is used to determine the structure of the message system, pedagogy. Frame refers to the form of the *context* in which knowledge is transmitted and received. Frame refers to the specific pedagogical relationship of teacher and taught. In the same way as classification does not refer to contents, so frame does not refer to the contents of the pedagogy. Frame refers to the strength of the boundary between what may be transmitted and what may not be transmitted, in the pedagogical relationship. Where framing is strong, there is a sharp boundary, where framing is weak, a blurred boundary, between what may and may not be transmitted. Frame refers us to the range of options available to teacher and taught in the *control* of what is transmitted and received in the context of the pedagogical relationship. Strong framing entails reduced options; weak framing entails a range of options. *This frame refers to the degree of control teacher and pupil possess over the selection, organization and pacing of the knowledge transmitted and received in the pedagogical relationship.**

There is another aspect of the boundary relationship between what may be taught and what may not be taught and, consequently, another aspect to framing. We can consider the relationship between

---

* It follows that frame strength for teacher and taught can be assessed at the different levels of selection, organisation and pacing of the knowledge.

the non-school everyday community knowledge of the teacher or taught, *and* the educational knowledge transmitted in the pedagogical relationship. We can raise the question of the strength of the boundary, the degree of insulation, between the everyday community knowledge of teacher and taught and educational knowledge. Thus, we can consider variations in the strength of frames as these refer to the strength of the boundary between educational knowledge and everyday community knowledge of teacher and taught.

From the perspective of this analysis, the basic structure of the message-system-curriculum is given by variations in the strength of classification, and the basic structure of the message-system-pedagogy is given by variations in the strength of frames. It will be shown later that the structure of the message system, evaluation, is a function of the strength of classification and frames. It is important to realise that the strength of classification and the strength of frames can vary independently of each other. For example, it is possible to have weak classification and exceptionally strong framing. Consider programmed learning. Here the boundary between educational contents may be blurred (weak classification) but there is little control by the pupil (except for pacing) over *what* is learned (strong framing). This example also shows that frames may be examined at a number of levels and the strength can vary as between the levels of selection, organisation, pacing and timing of the knowledge transmitted in the pedagogical relationship.

I should also like to bring out (this will be developed more fully later in the analysis) the power component of this analysis and what can be called the 'identity' component. Where classification is strong, the boundaries between the different contents are sharply drawn. If this is the case then it pre-supposes strong boundary maintainers. Strong classification also creates a strong sense of membership in a particular class and so a specific identity. Strong frames reduce the power of the pupil over what, when and how he receives knowledge and increases the teacher's power in the pedagogical relationship. However, strong *classification* reduces the power of the *teacher* over what he transmits as he may not over-step the boundary between contents *and* strong classification reduces the power of the teacher vis-à-vis the boundary maintainers.

It is now possible to make explicit the concept of educational knowledge codes. The code is fully given *at the most general level* by the relationship between classification and frame.

(3) *A Typology of Educational Knowledge Codes*

In the light of the conceptual framework we have developed, I shall use the distinction between collection and integrated curricula in order to realise a typology of types and sub-types of educational codes. The *formal* basis of the typology is the strength of classification and frames. However, the sub-types will be distinguished, initially, in terms of substantive differences.

Any organisation of educational knowledge which involves strong classification gives rise to what is here called a collection code. Any organisation of educational knowledge which involves a marked attempt to reduce the strength of classification is here called an integrated code. Collection codes may give rise to a series of sub-types, each varying in the relative strength of their classification and frames. Integrated codes can also vary in terms of the strength of frames, as these refer to the *teacher/pupil/student* control over the knowledge that is transmitted. The diagram in Fig. 1 on page 193 sets out general features of the typology.

Collection Codes
The first major distinction *within* collection codes is between specialised and non-specialised types. The extent of specialisation can be measured in terms of the number of closed contents publically examined at the end of the secondary educational stage. Thus in England, *although there is no formal limit*, the student usually sits for three 'A' level subjects, compared with the much greater range of subjects which make up the Arbitur in Germany, the Baccalaureate in France, or the Studente Exam in Sweden.

Within the English specialised type, we can distinguish two varieties: a pure and an impure variety. The pure variety exists where A level subjects are drawn from a common universe of knowledge, e.g. Chemistry, Physics, Mathematics. The impure variety exists where A level subjects are drawn from different universes of knowledge, e.g. Religion, Physics, Economics. The latter combination, although formally possible, very rarely substantively exists, for pupils are not encouraged to offer—neither does timetabling usually permit—such a combination. It is a matter of interest that until very recently the pure variety at the University level received the higher status of an honours degree, whereas the impure variety tended to lead to the lower status of the general degree.* One can detect the

---

* Consider the recent acrimonious debate over the attempt to obtain permission at Oxford to develop a degree in Anthropology, Sociology, Psychology & Biology—a relatively 'pure' combination.

beginnings of a shift in England from the pure to the impure variety which appears to be trying to work towards the non-specialised type of collection.

Within the non-specialised collection code, we can distinguish two varieties, according to whether a subject or course is the basic knowledge unit. Thus the standard European form of the collection code is non-specialised, *subject* based. The USA form of the collection is non-specialised, course based.

I have so far described sub-types and varieties of the collection code in simple descriptive terms; as a consequence it is not easy to see how their distinctive features can be translated into sociological concepts in order to realise a specific sociological problem. Clearly the conceptual language here developed has built into it a specific perspective: that of power and social control. In the process of translating the descriptive features into the language of classification and frames, the question must arise as to whether the hypotheses about their relative strength fits a particular case.

Here are the hypotheses, given for purposes of illustration:

1. I suggest that the European, non-specialised, subject based form of collection involves strong classification but *exceptionally* strong framing. That is, at levels *below* higher education there are relatively few options available to teacher, and especially taught, over the transmission of knowledge. Curricula and syllabus are very explicit.

2. The English version, I suggest, involves *exceptionally* strong classification, but relatively weaker framing than the European type. The fact that it is specialised determines what contents (subjects) may be put together. There is very strong insulation between the 'pure' and the 'applied' knowledge. Curricula are graded for particular ability groups. There can be high insulation between a subject and a class of pupils. 'D' stream secondary pupils will not have access to certain subjects, and 'A' stream students will also not have access to certain subjects. However, I suggest that framing, relative to Europe, is weaker. This can be seen particularly at the primary level. There is also, *relative* to Europe, less *central* control over what is transmitted, although, clearly, the various requirements of the University level exert a strong control over the secondary level.*

* The content of public examinations between the secondary and the tertiary level is controlled by the tertiary level directly or indirectly, through the control over the various syllabi. Thus, if there is to be any major shift in secondary schools syllabi and curricula, then this will require changes in the tertiary levels policy, as this affects the acceptance of students. Such a change in policy would involve changes in the selection, organisation, pacing and timing of knowledge at the tertiary level. Thus, the conditions for a major shift in the knowledge code at the secondary level is a major shift in the knowledge code

I suggest that, although again this is *relative*, there is a weaker frame in England between educational knowledge and the everyday community knowledge for certain classes of students: the so-called less able. Finally, relative to Europe, I suggest that there are more options available to the pupil within the pedagogical relationships. The frame as it refers to pupils is weaker. Thus I suggest that framing as it relates to teachers and pupils is relatively weaker, but that classification is relatively much stronger in the English than the European system. Scotland is nearer to the European version of the collection.

3. The course-based, non-specialised USA form of the collection, I suggest, has the weakest classification *and* framing of the collection code, especially at the secondary and university level. A far greater range of subjects can be taken at the secondary and University level, and are capable of combination: this indicates weak classification. The insulation between educational knowledge and everyday community knowledge is weaker, as can be evidenced by community control over school: this indicates weak frames. The range of options available to pupils within the pedagogical relationship is, I suggest, greater. I would guess, then, that classification and framing in the USA is the weakest part of the collection code.

Integrated Codes

It is important to be clear about the term 'integrated'. Because one subject uses the theories of another subject, this type of intellectual interrelationship does not constitute integration. Such intellectual interrelation may well be part of a collection code at some point in the history of the development of knowledge. Integration, as it is used here, refers minimally to the *subordination* of previously insulated subjects *or* courses to some *relational* idea, which blurs the boundaries between the subjects. We can distinguish two types. The first type is *teacher* based. Here the teacher as in the infant school has an extended block of time with often the same group of children. The teacher may operate with a collection code and keep the various subjects distinct and insulated, or he can blur the boundaries between the different subjects. This type of integrated code is easier to introduce than the second type, which is *teachers* based. Here, integration involves relationships with other teachers. In this way, we can have degrees of integration in terms of the number of teachers involved.

at the tertiary level. Changes in the knowledge code at the secondary level are likely to be of a somewhat limited nature without similar changes at the tertiary level. There clearly are other interests groups (industry) which may affect a given curriculum and syllabus.

We can further distinguish two varieties according to whether the integration refers to a group of teachers *within* a common subject, or the *extent* to which integration involves teachers of different subjects. Whilst integrated codes, by definition, have the weakest classification, they may vary as to framing. During the initiating period, the frames the teachers enter will be weak, but other factors will affect the final frame strength. It is also possible that the frames the *pupils* enter can vary in strength.

Thus integrated codes may be confined to one subject, or they can cross subjects. We can talk of code strength in terms of the range of different subjects co-ordinated by the code, or if this criterion cannot be applied, code strength can be measured in terms of the *number* of teachers co-ordinated through the code. Integrated codes can also vary as to frame strength as this is applied to teachers or pupils, or both.

Differences within, and between, educational knowledge codes from the perspective developed here, lie in variations in the strength and nature of the boundary maintaining procedures, as these are given by the classification and framing of the knowledge. It can be seen that the nature of classification and framing affects the authority/power structure which controls the dissemination of educational knowledge, and the *form* of the knowledge transmitted. In this way, principles of power and social control are realised through educational knowledge codes and through the codes enter into, and shape, consciousness. Thus variations within and change of knowledge codes should be of critical concern to sociologists. The following problems arise out of this analysis.

1. What are the antecedents of variations in the strength of classification and frames?

2. How does a given classification and framing structure perpetuate itself? What are the conditions of, and resistance to, change?

3. What are the different socialising experiences realised through variations in the strength of classifications and frames?

I shall limit the application of this analysis to the consideration of aspects of the last two questions. I feel I ought to apologise to the reader for this rather long and perhaps tedious conceptual journey, before he has been given any notion of the view to which it leads.

Application

I shall examine the patterns of social relationships and their socialising consequences which are realised through the European, particularly English, version of the collection code and those which are *expected* to arise out of the integrated codes, *particularly those which develop weak framing.* I shall suggest that there is some movement towards forms of this integrated code and I shall examine the nature of the resistance towards such a change. I shall suggest some reasons for this movement.

(4) *Classification and Framing of the European form of the Collection Code*

There will be some difficulty in this analysis, as I shall at times switch from secondary to university level. Although the English system has the distinguishing feature of specialisation, it does share certain features of the European system. This may lead to some blurring in the analysis. As this is the beginnings of a limited sociological theory which explores the social organisation and structuring of educational knowledge, it follows that all statements, including those which have the character of descriptive statements, are hypothetical. The descriptive statements have been selectively patterned according to their significance for the theory.

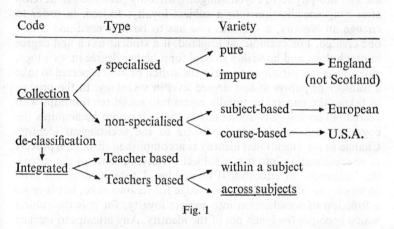

Fig. 1

One of the major differences between the European and English versions of the Collection Code is that, with the specialised English type, a membership category is established early in an educational career, in terms of an early choice between the pure and the applied, between the sciences and the arts, between having and not having a specific educational identity. A particular status in a given collection is made clear by streaming and/or a delicate system of grading. One nearly always knows the social significance of where one is and, in particular, *who* one is with each advance in the educational career.

(Initially, I am doing science, or arts, pure or applied; or I am not doing anything; later I am becoming a physicist, economist, chemist, etc.). *Subject loyalty* is then systematically developed in pupils and finally students, with each increase in the educational life and then transmitted by them as teachers and lecturers. The system is self-perpetuating through this form of socialisation. With the specialised form of the collection it is banal to say as you get older you learn more and more about less and less. Another, more sociological, way of putting this is to say as you get older, you become increasingly *different* from others. Clearly, this will happen at some point in any educational career, but with specialisation, thks happens much earlier. Therefore, specialisation very soon reveals *difference from* rather than communality with. It creates relatively quickly an educational identity which is clear-cut and bounded. The educational category or identity is *pure*. Specialised versions of the collection code tend to abhor mixed categories and blurred identities, for they represent a potential openness, an ambiguity, which makes the consequences of previous socialisation problematic. Mixed categories such as Bio-physicist, Psycho-linguist, are only permitted to develop after long socialisation into a subject loyalty. Indeed, in order to change an identity, a previous one has to be weakened and a new one created. For example, in England, if a student has a first degree in psychology and he wishes to read for a higher degree in sociology, either he is not permitted to make the switch or he is expected to take a number of papers at first degree level in sociology. In the process of taking the papers, he usually enters into social relationships with accredited sociologists and students through whom he acquires the cognitive and social style particular to the sociological identity. Change of an educational identity is accomplished through a process of re-socialisation into a *new* subject loyalty. A sense of the sacred, the 'otherness' of educational knowledge, I submit, does not arise so much out of an ethic of knowledge for its own sake, but is more a function of socialisation into subject loyalty: for it is the subject which becomes the lynch pin of the identity. Any attempt to weaken or *change* classification strength, (may be felt as a threat to one's identity and may be experienced as a pollution endangering the sacred. Here we have one source of the resistance to change of educational code.

The specialised version of the collection code will develop careful screening procedures to see who belongs and who does not belong, and once such screening has taken place, it is very difficult to change an educational identity. The various classes of knowledge are well insulated from each other. Selection and differentiation are early features of this particular code. Thus, the deep structure of the specialised type of collection code is *strong boundary maintenance creating control from within through the formation of specific identities.* An interesting aspect of the protestant spirit.

Strong boundary maintenance can be illustrated with reference to attempts to institutionalise new forms or attempts to change the strength of, classification, within either the European or English type of collection. Because of the exceptional strength of classification in England, such difficulties may be greater here. Changes in classification strength and the institutionalising of new forms of knowledge may become a matter of importance when there are changes in the structure of knowledge at the higher levels and/or changes in the economy. Critical problems arise with the question of new forms, as to their legitimacy, at what point they belong, when, where and by whom the form should be taught. I have referred to the 'sacred' in terms of an educational identity, but clearly there is the 'profane' aspect of knowledge. We can consider as the 'profane' the property aspect to knowledge. Any new form or weakening of classification clearly derives from past classifications. Such new forms or weakened classifications can be regarded as attempts to break or weaken existing monopolies. Knowledge under collection is private property with its own power structure and market situation. This affects the whole ambience surrounding the development and marketing of new knowledge. Children and pupils are early socialised into this concept of knowledge as private property. They are encouraged to work as isolated individuals with their arms around their work. This phenomena, until recently, could be observed in any grammar school. It can be most clearly observed in examination halls. Pupils and students, particularly in the arts, appear, from this point of view, to be a type of entrepreneur.

There are, then, strong inbuilt controls on the institutionalising of new knowledge forms, on the changing of strength of classification, on the production of new knowledge which derive from both 'sacred' and 'profane' sources.

So far, I have been considering the relationship between strong classification of knowledge, the concept of property and the creation of specific identities with particular reference to the specialised form of the collection code. I shall now move away from the classification of knowledge to its *framing* in the process of transmission.

Any collection code involves an hierarchical organisation of knowledge, so that the ultimate mystery of the subject is revealed very late in the educational life. By the ultimate mystery of the subject, I mean its potential for creating new realities. It is also the case, and this is important, that the ultimate mystery of the subject is not coherence, but incoherence; not order, but disorder; not the known, but the unknown. As the mystery, under collection codes, is revealed very late in the educational life—and then only to a select few who have shown the signs of successful socialisation—then only the few *experience* in their bones the notion that knowledge is permeable, that its orderings are provisional, that the dialectic of knowledge is closure and openness. For the many, socialisation into knowledge is socialisation into order, the existing order, into the experience that the world's educational knowledge is impermeable. Do we have here another version of alienation?

Now clearly any history of any form of educational knowledge shows precisely the power of such knowledge to create endlessly new realities. However, socialisation into the specific framing of knowledge in its transmission may make such a history experimentally meaningless. The key concept of the European collection code is discipline. This means learning to work *within* a received frame. It means, in particular, *learning* what questions can be put at any particular time. Because of the hierarchical ordering of the knowledge in *time,* certain questions raised may not enter into a particular frame.

This is soon learned by both teachers and pupils. Discipline then means accepting a given selection, organisation, pacing and timing of knowledge realised in the pedagogical frame. With increases in the educational life, there is a progressive weakening of the frame for both teacher and taught. Only the few who have shown the signs of successful socialisation have access to these relaxed frames. For the mass of the population the framing is tight. In a sense, the European form of the collection code makes knowledge safe through the process of socialisation into its frames. There is a tendency, which varies with the strength of specific frames, for the young to be socialised into assigned principles and routine operations and derivations. The evaluation system places an emphasis upon attaining *states* of knowledge rather than *ways* of knowing. A study of the examination questions and format, the symbolic structure of assessment, would be, from this point of view, a rewarding empirical study. Knowledge thus tends to be transmitted, particularly to elite pupils at the secondary level, through strong frames which control the selecting organisation pacing* and timing of the knowledge. The

---

* What is often overlooked is that the pacing of the knowledge (i.e. the rate of expected learning) is implicitly based upon the middle-class socialisation of the child. Middle-class family socialisation of the child is a hidden subsidy, in the sense that it provides both a physical and psychological environment which

receipt of the knowledge is not so much a right as something to be won or earned. The stronger the classification and the framing, the more the educational relationship tends to be hierarchical and ritualised, the educand seen as ignorant, with little status and few rights. These are things which one earns, rather like spurs, and are used for the purpose of encouraging and sustaining the motivation of pupils. Depending upon the strength of frames, knowledge is transmitted in a context where the teacher has maximal control or surveillance, as in hierarchical secondary school relationships.

We can look at the question of the framing of knowledge in the pedagogical relationship from another point of view. In a sense, educational knowledge is uncommonsense knowledge. It is knowledge freed from the particular, the local, through the various languages of the sciences or forms of reflexiveness of the arts which make possible either the creation or the discovery of new realities. Now this immediately raises the question of the relationship between the uncommonsense knowledge of the school and the *commonsense* knowledge, everyday community knowledge, of the pupil, his family and his peer group. This formulation invites us to ask how strong are the frames of educational knowledge in relation to experiential community based non-school knowledge? I suggest that the frames of the collection code, very early in the child's life, socialise him into knowledge frames which discourage connections with everyday realities, or that there is a highly selective screening of the connection. Through such socialisation, the pupil soon learns what of the outside may be brought into the pedagogical frame. Such framing also makes of educational knowledge something not ordinary or mundane, but something esoteric which gives a special significance to those who possess it. I suggest that when this frame is relaxed to include every-day realities, it is often, and sometimes validly, not simply for the transmission of educational knowledge, but for purposes of social control of forms of deviancy. The weakening of this frame occurs usually with the less 'able' children whom we have given up educating.

immensely facilitates, in diverse ways, school learning. The middle-class child is oriented to learning almost anything. Because of this hidden subsidy, there has been little incentive to change curriculum and pedagogy; for the middle-class child is geared to learn; he may not like, or indeed approve of, what he learns, but he learns. Where the school system is not subsidised by the home, the pupil often fails. In this way, even the *pacing* of educational knowledge is class based. It may well be that frame strength (as this refers to pacing) is a critical variable in the study of educability. It is possible that the weak frame strength (as this refers to *pacing*) of integrated codes indicates that integrated codes pre-suppose a longer average educational life. Middle-class children may have been potential pupils for progressive schools because of their longer educational life.

In general then, and depending upon the specific strength of classification and frames, the European form of the collection code is rigid differentiating and hierarchical in character; highly resistant to change particularly at the secondary level. With the English version, this resistance to change is assisted by the discretion which is available to headmasters and principals. In England, within the constraints of the public examination system, the heads of schools and colleges have a relatively wide range of discretion over the organisation and transmission of knowledge. Central control over the educational code is relatively weak in England, although clearly the schools are subject to inspection from both central and local government levels. However, the relationship between the inspectorate and the schools in England is very ambiguous. To produce widespread change in England would require the co-operation of hundreds of individual schools. Thus, rigidity in educational knowledge codes may arise out of highly centralised *or* weak central control over the knowledge codes. Weak central control does permit a series of changes which have, initially, limited consequences for the system as a whole. On the other hand, there is much stronger central control over the organisational style of the school. This can lead to a situation where there can be a change in the organisational style *without* there being *any* marked change in the educational knowledge code, particularly where the educational code, itself, creates specific identities. This raises the question, which cannot be developed here, of the relationships between organisational change and change of educational knowledge code, i.e. change in the strength of classification and framing.

In general, then, the European and English form of the collection code may provide for those who go beyond the novitiate stage: order, identity and commitment. For those who do not pass beyond this stage, it can sometimes be wounding and seen as meaningless. What Bourdieu calls 'la violence symbolique'.

Integrated and Collection Codes

I shall now examine a form of the integrated code which is realised through very weak classification and frames. I shall, during this analysis, bring out further aspects of collection codes.

There are a number of attempts to institutionalise forms of the integrated code at different strengths, above the level of the infant school child. Nuffield Science is an attempt to do this with the Physical Sciences, and the Chelsea Centre for Science Education, Chelsea College of Technology, University of London, is concerned almost wholly in training students in this approach. Mrs. Charity

James, at Goldsmiths College, University of London, is also producing training courses for forms of the integrated code. A number of comprehensive schools are experimenting with this approach at the middle school level. The S.D.S. in Germany, and various radical student groups, are exploring this type of code in order to use the means of the university against the meaning. However, it is probably true to say that the code at the moment exists at the level of ideology and theory, with only a relatively small number of schools and educational agencies attempting to institutionalise it with any seriousness.

Now, as we said in the beginning of the paper, with the integrated code we have a shift from content closure to content openness, from strong to markedly reduced classification. Immediately, we can see that this disturbance in classification of knowledge will lead to a disturbance of existing authority structures, existing specific educational identities and concepts of property.

Where we have integration, the various contents are subordinate to some idea which reduces their isolation from each other. Thus integration reduces the authority of the separate contents, and this has implications for existing authority structures. Where we have collection, it does permit in principle considerable differences in pedagogy and evaluation, because of the high insulation between the different contents. However, the autonomy of the content is the other side of an authority structure which exerts jealous and zealous supervision. I suggest that the integrated code will not permit the variations in pedagogy and evaluation which are possible within collection codes. On the contrary, I suggest there will be a pronounced movement towards a common pedagogy and tendency towards a common system of evaluation. In other words, integrated codes will, at the level of the teachers, probably create homogeneity in teaching practice. Thus, collection codes increase the discretion of teachers (within, always, the limits of the existing classification and frames) whilst integrated codes will reduce the discretion of the teacher in a direct relation to the strength of the integrated code (number of teachers co-ordinated by the code). On the other hand, it is argued that the increased discretion of the teachers within collection codes is paralleled by *reduced* discretion of the pupils, and that the reduced discretion of the teachers within integrated codes is paralleled by *increased* discretion of the pupils. In other words, there is a shift in the balance of power, in the pedagogical relationship between teacher and taught.

These points will now be developed. In order to accomplish any form of integration (as distinct from different subjects focussing upon a common problem, which gives rise to what could be called a *focussed* curriculum) there must be some relational idea, a supra-content concept, which focusses upon general principles at a high level of abstraction. For example, if the relationships between sociology and biology are to be opened, then the relational idea (amongst many) might be the issue of problems of order and change examined through the concepts of genetic and cultural codes. Whatever the relational concepts are, they will act selectively upon the knowledge within each subject which is to be transmitted. The particulars of each subject are likely to have reduced significance. This will focus attention upon the *deep* structure of each subject, rather than upon its surface structure. I suggest this will lead to an emphasis upon, and the exploration of, *general* principles and the concepts through which these principles are obtained. In turn, this is likely to affect the orientation of the pedagogy, which will be less concerned to emphasise *how* knowledge is created. In other words, the pedagogy of integrated codes is likely to emphasise various *ways* of knowing in the pedagogical relationships. With the collection code, the pedagogy tends to proceed from the surface structure of the knowledge to the deep structure; as we have seen, only the elite have access to the deep structure and therefore access to the realising of new realities or access to the experiential knowledge that new realities are possible. *With integrated codes, the pedagogy is likely to proceed from the deep structure to the surface structure.* We can see this already at work in the new primary school mathematics. Thus, I suggest that integrated codes will make available from the beginning of the pupils educational career, clearly in a way appropriate to a given age level, the deep structure of the knowledge, i.e., the principles for the generating of new knowledge. Such emphasis upon various *ways* of knowing, rather than upon the attaining of *states* of knowledge, is likely to affect, not only the emphasis of the pedagogy, but the underlying theory of learning. The underlying theory of learning of collection is likely to be didactic whilst the underlying theory of learning of integrated codes may well be more group- or self-regulated. This arises out of a different concept of what counts as having knowledge, which in turn leads to a different concept of how the knowledge is to be acquired. These changes in emphasis and orientation of the pedagogy are initially responsible for the relaxed frames which teacher and taught enter. Relaxed frames not only change the nature of the authority relationships by increasing the rights of the taught, they can also weaken or blur the boundary between what may or may not be taught, and so *more* of the teacher and taught is likely to enter this pedagogical frame. The inherent logic of the integrated code is likely to create a change in the structure of teaching groups which are likely to exhibit considerable flexibility. The concept of relatively weak boundary maintenance which is the core principle of integrated codes is realised both in the structuring of educational knowledge *and* in the organisation of the social relationships.

I shall now introduce some organisational consequences of collection and integrated codes which will make explicit the difference in the distribution of power and the principles of control which inhere in these educational codes.

Where knowledge is regulated through a collection code, the knowledge is organised and distributed through a series of well-insulated subject hierarchies. Such a structure points to oligarchic control of the institution, through formal and informal meetings of heads of department with the head or principal of the institution. Thus, senior staff will have strong horizontal work relationships (that is, with their peers in other subject hierarchies) and strong vertical work relationships within their own department. However, junior staff are likely to have only vertical (within the subject hierarchy) allegiances and work relationships. The allegiances of junior staff are vertical rather than horizontal for the following reasons. Firstly, staff have been socialised into strong subject loyalty and through this into specific identities. These specific identities are continuously strengthened through social interactions *within* the department *and* through the insulation between departments, Secondly, the departments are often in a competitive relationship for strategic resources. Thirdly, preferment within the subject hierarchy often rests with its expansion. Horizontal relationships of junior staff (particularly where there is no *effective* participatory administrative structure) are likely to be limited to *non-task* based contacts. There may well be discussion of control problems ('X of 3b is a —— How do you deal with him?' or 'I can't get X to write a paper'). Thus the collection code within the framework of oligarchic control creates for *senior* staff strong horizontal and vertical based relationships, whereas the work relationships of junior staff are likely to be vertical and the horizontal relationships limited to non-work based contacts. This is a type of organisational system which encourages gossip, intrigue and a conspiracy theory of the workings of the organisation for both the *administration* and the *acts of teaching* are *invisible* to the majority of staff.

Now the integrated code will require teachers of different subjects to enter into social relationships with each other which will arise not simply out of non-task areas, but out of a shared, co-operative educational task. The centre of gravity of the relationships between teachers will undergo a radical shift. Thus, instead of teachers and lecturers being divided and insulated by allegiances to subject hierarchies, the conditions for their unification exist through a common work situation. I suggest that this changed basis of the relationships, between teachers or between lecturers, may tend to weaken the separate hierarchies of collection. These new work-based horizontal relationships between teachers and between lecturers may alter both the structure and distribution of power regulated by the collection code. Further, the administration and specific acts of teaching are likely to shift from the relative invisibility to *visibility*.

We might expect similar developments at the level of students and even senior pupils. For pupils and students with each increase in their educational life are equally sub-divided and educationally insulated from each other. They are equally bound to subject hierarchies and for similar reasons to staff; their identities and their future are shaped by the department. Their vertical allegiances and work-based relationships are strong, whilst their horizontal relationships will tend to be limited to non-task areas (student/pupil societies and sport) or peripheral non-task based administration. Here again, we can see another example of the strength of boundary maintenance of collection codes; this time between task and non-task areas. Integrated codes may well provide the conditions for strong horizontal relationships and allegiances in students and pupils, based upon a common work task (the receiving and offering of knowledge).* In this situation, we might expect a weakening of the boundary between staff, especially junior staff, and students/pupils.

Thus, a move from collection to integrated codes may well bring about a disturbance in the structure and distribution of power, in property relationships and in existing educational identities. This change of educational code involves a fundamental change in the nature and strength of boundaries. It involves a change in what counts as having knowledge, in what counts as a valid transmission of knowledge, in what counts as a valid realisation of knowledge, *and* a change in the organisational context. At the cultural level, it involves a shift from the keeping of categories pure to the mixing of categories; whilst at the level of socialisation the outcomes of integrated codes *could* be less predictable than the outcomes of collection codes. This change of code involves fundamental changes in the classification and framing of knowledge and so changes in

* It is possible that the weak boundary maintaining procedures of integrated codes at the level of the organisational structure, knowledge structure and identity structure may increase the pupils/students informal age group affiliations as a source of identity, relation and organisation.

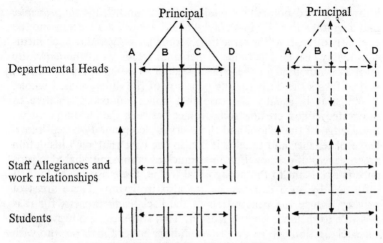

Fig. 2 Ideal Typical Organisational Structures

Key: Continuous lines represent strong boundaries. Continuous arrows represent direction of strong relationships. Dotted lines represent weak boundaries. Dotted line arrows represent direction of weak relationships.

Collection Code Type=Strong Classification: Strong Frames
Integrated Code Type=Weak Classification: Weak Frames

the structure and distribution of power and in principles of control. It is no wonder that deep-felt resistances are called out by the issue of change in educational codes.

Collection, Integrated Codes and Problems of Order

I shall now turn to aspects of the problem of order. Where knowledge is regulated by collection codes, social order arises out of the hierarchical nature of the authority relationships, out of the systematic ordering of the differentiated knowledge in time and space and out of an explicit, usually predictable, examining procedure. Order internal to the individual is created through the formation of specific identities. The institutional expression of strong classification and framing creates predictability in time and space. Because of strong classification, collection does allow a range of variations between subjects in the organisation, transmission and evaluation of knowledge. Because of strong classification, this code does permit *in principle* staff to hold (within limits) a range of ideologies because conflicts can be contained *within* its various insulated hierarchies. At levels below that of the university, the strong frames between educational knowledge and non-educationally relevant knowledge, *in principle*, may facilitate diversity in ideology held by staff because it cannot be explicitly offered. At the same time, strong framing makes such intrusion highly visible. The range of personal freedoms at the *university* level is symbolised in the ethical system of some collection codes and so forms the basis for the cohesion of the differentiated whole.

Whilst it is usually the case that collection codes, relative to integrated codes, create strong frames between the uncommonsense knowledge of the school and the everyday community-based knowledge of teacher and taught, it is also the case that such insulation creates areas of privacy. For, in as much as community-based experience is irrelevant to the pedagogical frame, these aspects of the self informed by such experiences are also irrelevant. These areas of privacy reduce the penetration of the socialising process, for it is possible to distance oneself from it. This still means, however, that the socialisation can be deeply wounding, either for those who wish for, but do not achieve, an identity, or for the majority for whom the pursuit of an identity is early made irrelevant.

Order created by integrated codes may well be problematic. I suggest that if four conditions are not satisfied, then the openness of learning under integration may produce a culture in which neither staff nor pupils have a sense of time, place or purpose. I shall comment briefly on these four conditions as I give them.

1. There must be consensus about the integrating idea and it must be very explicit. (It is ironic that the movement towards integration is going on in those countries where there is a low level of moral consensus.) It may be that integrated codes will only work* when there is a *high* level of ideological consensus among the staff. We have already seen that, in comparison with collection, integrated codes call for greater homogeneity in pedagogy and evaluation, and therefore reduce differences between teachers in the form of the transmission and assessment of knowledge. Whereas the teaching process under collection is likely to be invisible to other teachers, unless special conditions prevail, it is likely that the teaching process regulated through integrated codes may well become visible as a result of developments in the pedagogy in the direction of flexibility in the structure of teaching groups. It is also the case that the weak classification and relaxed frames of integrated codes permit greater expressions of differences between teachers, and possibly between pupils, in the selection of what is taught. The moral basis of educational choices is then likely to be explicit at the initial planning stage. Integrated codes also weaken specific identities. For the above reasons,

* In the sense of creating order.

integrated codes may require a high level of ideological consensus and this may affect the recruitment of staff. Integrated codes at the surface level create weak or blurred boundaries, but at bottom they may rest upon closed explicit ideologies. Where such ideologies are not shared, the consequences will become visible and threaten the whole at every point.

2. The nature of the linkage between the integrating idea and the knowledge to be co-ordinated must also be coherently spelled out. It is this linkage which will be the basic element in bringing teachers *and* pupils into their working relationship. *The development of such a co-ordinating framework will be the process of socialisation of teachers into the code. During this process, the teachers will internalise, as in all processes of socialisation, the interpretative procedures of the code so that these become implicit guides which regulate and co-ordinate the behaviour of the individual teachers in the relaxed frames and weakened classification.* This brings us to a major distinction between collection and integrated codes. With a collection code, the period of socialisation is facilitated by strong boundary maintenance both at the level of *role* and at the level of knowledge. Such socialisation is likely to be continuous with the teacher's own educational socialisation. With integrated codes both the role and the form of the knowledge have to be *achieved* in relation to a range of different others, and this may involve re-socialisation if the teacher's previous educational experience has been formed by the collection code. The collection code is capable of working when staffed by mediocre teachers, whereas integrated codes call for much greater powers of synthesis, analogy and for more ability to both tolerate and enjoy ambiguity at the level of knowledge *and* social relationships.

3. A committee system of staff may have to be set up to create a sensitive feed-back system and which will also provide a further agency of socialisation into the code. It is likely that evaluative criteria are likely to be relatively weak, in the sense that the criteria are less likely to be as explicit and measurable as in the case of collection. As a result, it may be necessary to develop committees for both teachers, students and, where appropriate, pupils, which will perform monitoring functions.

4. One of the major difficulties which inhere in integrated codes arises over what is to be assessed, and the form of assessment: also the place of specific competencies in such assessment. It is likely that integrated codes will give rise to multiple criteria of assessment compared with collection codes. In the case of collection codes, because the knowledge moves from the surface to the deep structure, then this progression creates ordered principles of evaluation in

time. The form of temporal cohesion of the knowledge regulated through the integrated code has yet to be determined, and made explicit. Without clear criteria of evaluation, neither teacher nor taught have any means to consider the significance of what is learned, nor any means to judge the pedagogy. In the case of collection codes evaluation at the secondary level often consists of the fit between a narrow range of specific competencies and states of knowledge, and previously established criteria (varying in explicitness) of what constitutes a right or appropriate or convincing answer. The previously established criteria together with the specific social context of assessment create a relatively objective procedure. I do not want to suggest that this necessarily gives rise to a form of assessment which entirely disregards distinctive and original features of the pupil's performance. In the case of the integrated code under discussion (weak frames for teacher and taught) then this form of assessment may well be inappropriate. The weak frames enable a greater range of the student's behaviour to be made public and they make possible considerable diversity (at least in principle) between students. It is possible that this might lead to a situation where assessment takes more into account 'inner' attributes of the student. Thus if he has the 'right' attitudes then this will result later in the attainment of various specific competencies. The 'right' attitude may be assessed in terms of the fit between the pupil's attitudes and the current ideology. It is possible then that the evaluative criteria of integrated codes with weak frames may be weak as these refer to specific cognitive attributes but strong as these refer to dispositional attributes. If this is so then a new range of pupil attributes become candidates for labels. It is also likely that the weakened classification and framing will encourage more of the pupil/student to be made public; more of his thoughts, feelings and values. In this way more of the pupil is available for control. As a result the socialisation could be more intensive and perhaps more penetrating. In the same way as pupils/students defend themselves against the wounds of collection or distance themselves from its overt code, so they may produce new defences against the potential intrusiveness of the integrated code and its open learning contexts.

We can summarise this question of the problem of order as follows. Collection codes have explicit and strong boundary maintaining features and they rest upon a tacit ideological basis. Integrated codes have implicit and weak boundary maintaining features and they rest upon an explicit and closed ideological basis. The ideological basis of the collection code is a condensed symbolic system communicated through its explicit boundary maintaining features. Its covert structure is that of mechanical solidarity. The ideological basis of integrated codes is *not* a condensed symbolic system; it is verbally elaborated and explicit. It is an *overt* realisation of organic solidarity and made substantive through weak forms of boundary maintenance (low insulations). Yet the covert structure of mechanical solidarity of collection codes creates through its specialised outputs *organic* solidarity. On the other hand the overt structure of organic solidarity of integrated codes creates through its *less* specialised outputs *mechanical* solidarity. And it will do this to the extent to which its ideology is explicit, elaborated and closed *and* effectively and *implicitly* transmitted through its low insulations. In as much as integrated codes do not accomplish this, then order is highly problematic at the level of social organisation and at the level of the person. In as much as integrated codes do accomplish such socialisation then we have the covert deep closure of mechanical solidarity. This is the fundamental paradox which has to be faced and explored.

(5) *Change of Educational Code*

I have tried to make explicit the relationships between educational codes and the structure of power and principles of social control. Attempts to change or modify educational codes will meet with resistance at a number of different levels irrespective of the intrinsic educational merit of a particular code. I shall now briefly discuss some reasons for a movement towards the institutionalising of integrated codes *of the weak classification and weak framing (teacher and taught) type* (see note 1), above the level of the primary school (see note 2).

1. The growing differentiation of knowledge at the higher levels of thought, together with the integration of previously discreet areas, may set up requirements for a form of socialisation appropriate to these changes in the structure of knowledge.

2. Changes in the division of labour are creating a different concept of skill. The in-built obsolescence of whole varieties of skills reduces the significance of context-tied operations and increases the significance of general principles from which a range of diverse operations may be derived. In crude terms, it could be said that the nineteenth century required submissive and inflexible man, whereas the twenty-first requires conforming but flexible man.

3. The less rigid social structure of the integrated code makes it a potential code for egalitarian education.

4. In advanced industrial societies which permit, within limits, a

range of legitimising beliefs and ideologies, there is a major problem of control. There is the problem of making sense of the differentiated weakly co-ordinated and changing symbolic systems and the problem of inner regulation of the person. Integrated codes, with their stress on the underlying unity of knowledge, through their emphasis upon analogy and synthesis, could be seen as a response to the first problem of 'making sense'. The *inter-personal* rather than *inter-positional* control of the integrated code may be set up as penetrating, intrusive forms of socialisation under conditions of ambiguity in the system of beliefs and the moral order.

If these reasons operate, we could consider the movement towards integrated codes as stemming from a technological source. However, it is possible that there is another and deeper source of the movement away from collection. I suggest that the movement away from collection to integrated codes symbolises that there is a crisis in society's basic classifications and frames, and therefore a crisis in its structures of power and principles of control. The movement from this point of view represents an attempt to de-classify and so alter power structures and principles of control; in so doing to unfreeze the structuring of knowledge and to change the boundaries of consciousness. From this point of view integrated codes are symptoms of a moral crisis rather than the terminal state of an educational system.

Conclusion

In this paper, I have tried to explore the concept of boundary in such a way that it is possible to see *both* the power and control components. The analysis focusses directly upon the structuring of transmitted educational knowledge.

Although the concept, 'classification' appears to operate on a single dimension, i.e., differences in degrees of insulation between content (subjects/courses etc.), it explicitly points to power and control components. In the same way, the concept, 'frame', appears to operate in a single dimension; what may or may not be taught in the pedagogical relationship. Yet the exploration of the concept again points to power and control components. Through defining educational codes in terms of the relationship between classification and framing, these two components are built into the analysis at all levels. It then becomes possible in one framework to derive a typology of educational codes, to show the inter-relationships between organisational and knowledge properties, to move from macro- to micro-levels of analysis, to relate the patterns internal to educational institutions to the external social antecedents of such patterns, and to consider questions of maintenance and change. At the same time, it is hoped that the analysis makes explicit tacit assumptions underlying various educational codes. It attempts to show at a *theoretical* level, the relationships between a particular symbolic order and the structuring of experience. I believe that it offers an approach which is well capable of exploration by diverse methods at the empirical level.

It should be quite clear that the specific application of the concept requires at every point empirical evidence. I have not attempted to bolster the argument with references, because in many cases the evidence which is required does not exist in a *form* which bears directly upon the chain of inferences and therefore would offer perhaps spurious support. We have, for example, little *first* hand knowledge which bears upon aspects of framing as this concept is used in the paper. We also have next to no *first* hand knowledge of the day by day encounters realised by various types of integrated codes.

I hope that the kinds of questions raised by this approach will encourage sociologists of education to explore both theoretically, and empirically, the structure of educational knowledge which I take to be the distinctive feature of this field.

Acknowledgements

I am most grateful to Professor Wolfgang Klafki, and particularly to Mr. Hubertus Huppauf of the University of Marburg, for many valuable suggestions and constructive criticism. I should also like to acknowledge many hours of discussion with my colleague Mr. Michael Young. I have also learned much from Mr. David Adelstein, graduate student in the Department of the Sociology of Education, University of London Institute of Education. I am particularly grateful to Mr. W. Brandis, research officer in the Department's Research Unit. I have also benefited from the stringent criticisms of Professor R. Peters, and Mr. Lionel Elvin, of the University of London Institute of Education. My greatest debt is to Professor Mary Douglas, University College, London.

I should like to thank the Director of the Chaucer Publishing Company, Mr. L. G. Grossman, for a small but vital grant.

Note 1

In the paper, I suggested that integrated codes rest upon a closed explicit ideology. It should then follow that this code would stand a better chance of successful institutionalisation in societies where (a) there were strong and effective constraints upon the development of a range of ideologies and (b) where the educational system was a major agency of political socialisation. Further, the weak boundary maintaining procedures of the integrated code would (a) increase the penetration of the socialisation as more of the self of the taught is made public through the relaxed frames and (b) deviancy would be more visible. On the other hand, integrated codes carry a potential for change in power structures and principles of control. I would therefore guess that in such societies, integrated codes would possess weak classifications, but the frames for teacher and taught would be strong.

Note 2

It is a matter of interest that, in England, it is only in the infant school that there is relatively wide-spread introduction of this form of integrated code. This raises the general question of how this level of the educational system was open to such change. Historically, the primary school developed distinct concepts of infant and junior stages, and distinct heads for these two stages. Given the relative autonomy over the transmission of knowledge which characterises the British system of education, it was in principle possible to have change. Although only a ceiling may separate infant from junior departments, two quite distinct and often incompatible educational codes can develop. We can regard this as a necessary, but not sufficient, condition for the emergence of integrated codes at the infant school level. It was also the case, until very recently, that the selection function started in the Junior department, because that department was the gateway to the grammar school. This left the infant school relatively free of control by levels higher than itself. The form of integration in the infant school, again until recently, was *teacher* based, and therefore did not set up the problems which arise out of *teacher* based integration. Finally, infant school teachers are not socialised into strong educational identities. Thus the English educational system, until recently, has two potential points of openness—the period between the ages of five to seven years, before selection began, and the period post eighteen years of age, when selection is virtually completed. The major control on the structuring of knowledge at the secondary level is the structuring of knowledge at the tertiary level, specifically the university. Only if there is a major change in the structuring of knowledge at this level can there be effective code change at lower levels.

Bibliography

Bernstein, B., Peters, R. and Elvin, L. (1966) 'Ritual in Education'. *Philosophical Transactions of the Royal Society of London*, Series B, Volume 251, No. 772.

Bernstein, B. (1967) 'Open Schools, Open Society?' *New Society*, September 14th.

Davies, D. I. (1970) 'The management of knowledge: a critique of the use of typologies in educational sociology', *Sociology 4*, No. 1.

Davies, D. I. (1970) 'Knowledge, education and power.' Paper presented to the British Sociological Association Annual Conference, Durham.

Douglas, M. (1966) *Purity and Danger*, Routledge & Kegan Paul.

Douglas, M. (1970) *Natural Symbols*, Barrie & Rockliff, The Cresset Press.

Durkheim, E. (1947) *On the Division of Labour in Society*, The Free Press. Glencoe, Illinois.

Durkheim, E. (1961) *Moral Education*, The Free Press, Glencoe, Illinois.

Durkheim, E. & Mauss, M. (1963) *Primitive Classification* (Translated by Needham, R.). Cohen & West.

Hoyle, E. (1969) How does the curriculum change? (1) A proposal for enquiries, (2) Systems and Strategies', *Journal of Curriculum Studies*, Vol. I, Nos. 2 and 3.

Jeffrey, G. B. (1950 'The Unity of Knowledge', *Reflections on the Universities of Cambridge and London*, Cambridge University Press.

Keddie, N. G. (1970) *The Social Basis of Classroom Knowledge*. M.A. Dissertation, University of London Institute of Education.

Musgrove, F. (1968) 'The contribution of sociology to the study of the curriculum' in *Changing the Curriculum* (ed)., Kerr, J. F., University of London Press.

Young, M. (in press) 'Curricula as socially organised knowledge' in *Knowledge and Control* (ed.) Young, M., Collier-MacMillan.

I O

THE POLITICAL FUNCTIONS OF

THE EDUCATIONAL SYSTEM*

Harmon Zeigler & Wayne Peak

V. O. Key, Jr. (1963:316) observed that 'all national educational systems indoctrinate the oncoming generation with the basic outlooks and values of the political order'. The conservative implications of this statement (and of others similar to it) are obvious to all who take time to reflect upon it. However, one cannot neglect the possibility that the conservative role of education in the socialization process is partially a consequence of the state of the development of the society in which it occurs. In 'developing' countries, for instance, Coleman (1965:3) suggested that the educational system is viewed as the key to rapid, if orderly, social change: 'Once regarded as an essentially conservative, culture-preserving, culture-transmitting institution, the educational system now tends to be viewed as the master determinant of all aspects of change.'

We suspect that Coleman's statement will be modified substantially when empirical research establishes what is expected of educational systems in developing nations. For instance, the goals of teachers in developing countries do not appear to be radically different from the goals of teachers in stable, industrial democracies. In both cases, the objectives are the conveying (or creation) of consensus values. Indeed, the *overt* instillation of consensus values probably is more characteristic of developing than established countries. In Kenya, Tanzania, and Uganda, the primary objective

* Revised version of a paper presented at the Western Political Science Association Meetings, Honolulu, Hawaii, April 1969. The authors wish to acknowledge the support of the Center for the Advanced Study of Educational Administration, University of Oregon, during a portion of the time that they devoted to the preparation of this paper. CASEA is a national research and development center which was established under the Cooperative Research Program of the U.S. Office of Education.

of the educational system is the teaching of good citizenship. In these areas, schools have the responsibility of establishing patterns of integration to replace the previously existing intra-social tensions and cleavages (Dawson and Prewitt, 1968:162). Therefore, one would suspect that the extent to which schools deliberately propagandize consensus values depends to some degree upon the extent to which societal integration has been achieved. Russia's relatively youthful regime undertakes overt indoctrination to a far greater extent than is true in the United States. English schools are less concerned than American ones with the inculcation of patriotism.

It is our intention to examine the extent to which the American educational system propagates consensus values in its citizens and to assess the degree of conservative bias thus injected into the political system. Such an undertaking necessarily must be concerned with the content of the values thus transmitted and with their compatibility with the fundamental precepts of the American political order. Therefore, before taking a closer look at education in the United States, we must present a brief analysis of consensus values and change within the context of political theory.

Conflict, Values and Social Change

E. E. Schattschneider (1960:13) has suggested that 'government in a democracy is a great engine for expanding the scale of conflict.' Implicit in this assertion is the assumption that men are in constant competition over a limited supply of values. Such competition, or conflict, is ubiquitous and exists on as many dimensions as there are objects of men's desires. It is precisely because conflict is endemic to social existence that the need for a political system arises, for it is through the political system that conflict is taken out of the private sector (where few if any checks exist on the virulence with which it is conducted) and placed in the public domain. The function of the political system is *not* that of stifling or smothering social conflict but rather that of providing an arena wherein it can be conducted within prescribed limits. In fact, it has been argued that societies which suppress conflict are inherently unstable.

Lewis Coser (1956), in expanding on earlier work by the German sociologist, Georg Simmel, has analyzed the social functions of conflict. His central thesis is that the expression of some minimal degree of conflict is necessary for any social group to survive. He discusses a number of major propositions relating to this thesis, For present purposes, however, these propositions can be grouped into two general categories, each of which pertains to a socially desirable function of conflict. In the first place, Coser indicates several ways in which conflict creates or strengthens social bonds:

(1) It creates and modifies common norms necessary for the readjustment of the [antagonistic] relationship.
(2) It leads each party to the conflict, given a certain equality of strength, to prefer that the other match the structure of his own organization so that fighting techniques are equalized.
(3) It makes possible a reassessment of relative power and thus serves as a balancing mechanism which helps to maintain and consolidate societies.
   And:
   Multiply group affiliations of individuals make for a multiplicity of conflicts criss-crossing society. Such segmental participation, then, can result in a kind of balancing mechanism, preventing deep cleavages along one axis. The interdependence of conflicting groups and the multiplicity of noncumulative conflicts provide one, though not, of course, the only check against basic consensual breakdown in an open society (Coser, 1956:79, 137).

With regard to this last point, Schattschneider (1960) has presented an illuminating analysis of what he calls 'the socialization of conflict' within the American political arena. He recognizes the inevitability of competing interests, and, like Coser, he points out the fact that widespread involvement in multiple conflicts reduces the likelihood that a society will become polarized along with any given battle line.

We should make it abundantly clear that the positive effects of increased conflict discussed by Coser and Schattschneider and implied by traditional theorists evolve from increases in the *scope* of conflict and not from increases in its *intensity*. The scope of conflict refers to the breadth of participation—the number of individuals party to it; intensity of conflict refers to the virulence with which it is conducted. It is precisely the recognition of such negative effects that underlies Coser's second category of the social functions of conflict.

After accepting the universality of conflicting values, Coser argues that societies which allow the relatively free expression of competition for values have less pent-up hostilities and, therefore, lower levels of conflict intensity than societies which inhibit such expression. Thus,

Realistic conflicts arise when men clash in the pursuit of claims based on frustration of demands and expectancies of gains.
Nonrealistic conflicts arise from deprivations and frustrations stemming from the socialization process and from later adult role obligations, or they result . . . from a conversion of originally realistic antagonism which was disallowed expression . . . [T]he second type [of conflict] consists of a release of tension in aggressive action directed against shifting objects . . . satisfaction is derived from the aggressive act itself (Coser, 1956:54–55).

An additional societal level function performed by conflict has to do with the ease with which social and, more specifically, political change is achieved. If one assumes that the environment within which a social system exists is in a state of constant flux (and we believe that it is safe to make such an assumption), then the relationship of social conflict to political change is straightforward. Individual values are developed partly in response to environmental conditions; thus, as changes in the latter are perceived, so are the individual value demands made upon the political system.

The survival of the political system is determined by the level of support which it receives, and support—particularly support in democratic polities—is a function of demand satisfaction and socialization (see Easton, 1957, 1965). Therefore, it follows that democratic political systems must respond to changes in value demands resulting from environmental change or suffer the consequences of decreased popular support. A political system which is open and admits the entry of new value demands is said to be in a state of dynamic equilibrium, or stable. The more unresponsive and rigid the political system is, the more it must rely on socialization to generate at least the minimal level of support necessary for its continued legitimation and, consequently, for its very existence.

Of course, coercion is an alternative source of support; however, any democratic political system which must rely principally upon negative outputs for its requisite support forfeits its claim to democracy and degenerates into totalitarianism.[1] But since socialization can never be totally effective, the fact remains that a rigid democratic political system has little or no chance of surviving. Moreover, when socialization is held constant, we can expect the level of support to vary directly with the amount of value satisfaction emanating in the form of policy outputs. Such outputs initially are dependent upon the free articulation of competing demands; consequently conflict is related directly to political change and, therefore, to the stability and health of the political system.

One undeniable fact emerges from our examination of conflict: regardless of the perspective from which it is approached, widespread social conflict is imperative for the vitality of democratic political systems. It is a necessary condition for the maximization of

---

[1] Concerning the use of coercion to generate support for a political system, Easton (1957:396) has stated that where policy outputs are negative: '. . . they threaten the members of the system with various kinds of sanctions ranging from a small monetary fine to physical detention, ostracism, or loss of life, as in our own system with regard to the case of legally defined treason. In every system support stems in part from fear of sanctions or compulsion; in autocratic systems the proportion of coerced support is at a maximum.'

individual values, for the maximization of support for the political regime, and for the maximization of social cohesion; it facilitates equilibrating political change; and it reduces the intensity with which inevitable social and political competition is conducted.

It is not our intention to imply that every petty quarrel should be injected into the political system, for surely no system could cope with the fantastic volume of demands thus transmitted to it (see Easton, 1965:57–69; 85–89). To guard against system overload developing from such a situation, some criteria must be established to screen conflicting value demands. However, our point is that the criteria so established must admit all demands which are so basic or widespread that failure to allow them expression would result in socially disruptive nonrealistic conflict outside of the political arena or the demise of the political system itself.

The importance of the screening function cannot be over-emphasized nor can the delicacy and difficulty involved in the establishment of screening criteria, for to err in the direction of leniency is to run the risk of overload, and to err in the opposite direction is to endanger the very existence of the political system. In one sense, the establishment of screening criteria can be considered a more important political act than the making of policy.

The delicacy to which we have alluded may become somewhat more apparent if we distinguish between two aspects of the problem. On the one hand there is the quantitative factor of the *volume* of demands which enter the system. With respect to considerations of volume, systematic requirements dictate the need for screening agents in order to avoid overload.

On the other hand, however, there are qualitative considerations of the *range* of demands. This aspect pertains to the extent of deviance from consensual norms that is tolerated. The more rigid and intolerant the screening agents, the greater is the likelihood that realistic demands will be disallowed entry to the political system. The dangers inherent in such a situation are apparent. The ideal balance to be struck is one which restricts the *volume* of demands while permitting entry of the full *range* of realistic demands.

The difficulty in arriving at such an ideal is complicated further by the fact that the realism of demands is a function of environmental characteristics, which are ever-changing. Thus, constant vigilance over screening criteria is required if they are to keep pace with the environmental change. A rigid, 'frozen' set of screening criteria can be expected to exclude more and more realistic demands the longer it remains unchanged. Coser's above-cited warning that 'nonrealistic conflicts arise . . . from a conversion of originally realistic antagonism that was disallowed expression' points out the undesirability of overly restricting the range of legitimate demands.

Limits on the range of acceptable demands largely are derived from the value consensus which obtains throughout society. In other words, tolerance of nonconformity is itself a social norm; the degree of tolerance directly affects the extent to which society will permit the expression of demands which depart from the existing consensus. Thus, to control the socialization process by which social norms are transmitted is also to control the screening criteria used to evaluate the acceptability of demands to the political system. Since the educational system is an important agent of socialization, it bears much responsibility for the establishment of tolerance, which makes realistic conflict and social change possible.

The Educational Experience

Students of socialization have made a strategic error in concerning themselves primarily with the manifest content of social studies programs. In advanced industrial societies, especially stable democracies, the important thing about socialization is not the explicit content of political education programs; *implicit* assumptions are more important. We need to address ourselves to the question of what is *not* told to American children as well as to what is told to them. At the outset, one could assert that the differences between the political education programs of developing and advanced societies are superficial at best.

In American schools, the emphasis clearly is upon orthodoxy. Hess and Torney, noting the repetitive emphasis upon symbolic indications of loyalty, such as singing patriotic songs and saluting the flag, are disturbed by what they view to be the excessive emphasis upon compliance with laws and authority and the underemphasis upon citizen rights. 'The school stresses the ideal norms and ignores the tougher, less pleasant facts of political life in the United States' (Hess and Torney, 1967:218). While Hess and Torney are concerned with elementary education, research by the senior author into high school teaching leads to the conclusion that there is less difference than we normally assume (Zeigler, 1967:116–119). What, then, is the difference between Tanzania, Russia, and the United States? The only appreciable difference is the extent to which indoctrination is explicit. Actually, the explicitness of the indoctrination might work to reduce its effectiveness, since the most persuasive communications usually are those with the least deliberately persuasive content. American schools actually might be doing a better job than Russia of grinding out loyal, compliant citizens.

What we are suggesting is that studies of socialization in the schools may be going about the problem in the wrong way. It is the manifest content of such programs which attracts most attention from political scientists, even though there probably is less of this content in American schools than in other educational systems. What is needed is a careful assessment of the latent consequences of the educational experience. While the effect of education upon political values and orientations has been examined, the extent to which values are shaped without any conscious attempt to do so has not been studied with any degree of care. There is, then, the process of 'schooling' whereby the older generation attempts to instruct the young through a set of institutions explicitly designed for that purpose, but there also is the process of *education* which may have more immediate effect than deliberate indoctrination. In directing our attention to this latter, less direct influence, we shall pay attention to two aspects of the education process: (1) aspects of political life not included in typical social studies courses, and (2) techniques of instruction.

Non-instruction

Concerning the first topic, the task is somewhat difficult and is not unlike the current dispute between the neo-elitists and pluralists in the study of community power. Pluralists have taken a hard-headed approach in insisting that the only legitimate datum is the *decision*. Neo-elitists have argued that the process of non-decision-making is more significant for the understanding of community power. Bachrach and Baratz have become the leading spokesmen for the neo-elitist position, and their remarks seem directly applicable to the argument herein advanced. By focusing entirely upon the process whereby highly contested decisions are reached, pluralists ignore both the more numerous routine decisions and the more mysterious 'non-decisions' which, Bachrach and Baratz (1962, 1963) assert, are of more impact upon the overall political style of a community than the more spectacular and tangible decisions. The process of non-decision-making allows only the relatively minor disputes— those well within the limits imposed by the consensus of the community—to become the subject of community conflict. The 'mobilization of bias'—by which Bachrach and Baratz mean the perpetuation of values tending to favor the maintenance of the *status quo*—sets the margins within which conflict can take place.

We are well aware of the ghostly quality of this type of argument,

and are bothered almost as much as Merelman (1968) by the con-
spiratorial 'they' who can *overtly* set the margins of debate. We find
it difficult to imagine a sort of community council of 'they' who
decide what can and cannot be subject to dispute. However, there are
some merits in this type of argument. Rather than talking about the
overt mobilization of bias by individuals, we are in a better empirical
shape if we inquire into the social institutions which might serve
the *covert* function of the mobilization of bias. We suggest that this
is the real function of schools.

Consensus has substantial value for political elites. If their positions of dominance and power are not challenged by opposing
value demands, elites are relatively free to conduct the affairs of
state with a minimum of difficulty. Dissensus clearly makes this
task of elites more difficult. In spite of what social scientists assert
about the functions of social conflict, most practicing politicians
do not appreciate its role. Social conflict tends to weaken the independence of elites by forcing them to resolve disputes not of their
choosing.

Schattschneider (1960:4) correctly has observed that a question
with importance at least equal to 'who gets what, when, and how'
is the question, 'What shall we argue about?' When a social system
erupts into conflict, it may indicate that a portion of the masses
normally excluded from routine political behaviour has become
dissatisfied. If the conflict continues and increases in intensity,
something will have to be done about a problem which did not
originate from within the elite. Even though the elite has to solve
the problem, it is not a problem which they would have chosen to
solve had they enjoyed the freedom of action which normally is theirs.

Conflict—which indicates the increasing imperfection of the
consensus—generates a more intense mobilization of bias. The
mobilization may shift from covert to overt. Pressures to cling to
accepted interpretations of reality increase, even though these
interpretations of reality appear to the more intense participants
in the conflict to be faulty. The educational system, under such
conditions, assumes part of the responsibility for the repudiation
of fundamental criticism—a task for which it is admirably suited,
partially because of the professional values which have achieved
a high degree of stability within the educational establishment. As
conflict reaches the level of challenge to the basic assumptions of a
society, the reaction of the educational system matches the challenge.
Etzioni (1968:117) speaks of a 'community of assumptions' which
characterize any social unit. In advanced societies a community
of assumptions, once established, can be maintained for long periods

of time without challenge. Individuals assume that the world really is as they see it; therefore, dissent is tolerated only within the margins set out in the community of assumptions. When dissent extends beyond these margins, the society has institutions to remove legitimacy from dissent and the screening agents of the political system deny entrance to demands thus branded as illegitimate. Thus, such 'margin-defending' institutions operate to limit the range of acceptable policy alternatives.

It might be argued that the extent to which margin-defending institutions—such as educational systems—engage in overt indoctrination is a function not of the degree of development of the political system, but rather of the extent of illegitimate conflict excluded from that system. In America of the 1960s, there is as much need to strengthen societal identifications as there is in Tanzania. If this assumption is correct, schools (which formerly avoided hard-line indoctrination) will begin to bear down upon those challenging the community of assumptions.

With regard to the performance of various societal institutions, it seems more helpful to avoid thinking about development as a linear process and to think of institutional reactions as cyclical. We are, then, currently going through a period in which the community of assumptions is being challenged and defended. Ours has been a fundamentally conservative society with popular opinion exercising a coercive and cohesive influence. Defensive institutions have enjoyed a more secure role within the society, and the education system is sensitive to the potentially dangerous consequences of the mistreatment of 'sacred objects' (children). Long before the advent of surveys, and indeed long before the industrialization and political development of America, de Toqueville (1835:263) observed the basic conservatism and coercive power of the American mass opinion. He concluded that only the 'presence of the black race on the soil of the United States' was capable of destroying the fundamental tranquility of the American policy. de Toqueville's insightful comment suffers only because of its failure to offer predictions of what sort of responses might be expected in the event that the 'presence of the black race' created tensions sufficient to shatter the consensus.

Whether one takes an alarmist position or not, the 1960s have produced a pattern of political behaviour not characteristic of the American political process. We are not speaking so much of the urban violence—the United States has always been a violent nation—but rather we are referring to the existence of a relatively large body of opinion willing to challenge a basic tenet of the community of assumptions. The protests about Vietnam should be understood against the coercive power of mass opinion to which de Toqueville referred. Even the crudest indicators of public opinion suggest that the masses have no patience with the Vietnam protestors, yet, the opposition increases in intensity. One can conclude that the agents of socialization charged with defensive operations have failed.

This assertion—that the socialization process is imperfect because we are undergoing fundamental criticism—does not resemble in any way the 'normal' interpretation of the educational function. Education is 'supposed' to make 'good citizens' of us all. Therefore, if some of us have become critical thinkers, the educational process should take credit. Many studies, of which the Almond-Verba (1963) study is merely the most recent, stress the role of formal education in the creation of efficacious, contented citizens: the more one is educated (at least in America) the more politically competent one becomes.

The main thrust of this type of argument is that education and commitment to the 'system' are linked closely. Without considering the implications of this finding, many political scientists became elitists. They argued that, since the educated minorities were those who really understood and appreciated the ongoing political process, extensive participation by the masses was dangerous. However, no distinction was made between secondary and higher education. Actually, if one examines the association between education and a variety of attitudes normally attributed to the political elite, it can be discovered that commitment to democratic decision-making becomes apparent only after substantial exposure to higher (as distinguished from secondary) education. At least through high school, learning how to be a good citizen does not include respect for the rights of minorities.

Making the usual assumption that racial progress and education were highly related in the South, Matthews and Prothro were surprised to learn that there was a substantial negative correlation between median school years completed by whites and Negro voting registration. As the average education of whites in a county increases, Negro voter registration decreases. Puzzled by this contradiction to one of the 'laws' of political behavior, Matthews and Prothro performed the usual controlling operations and found that the correlation withstood any assault. The authors clearly did not expect to find out that education was unrelated (indeed negatively related) to a worthwhile goal: 'These findings . . . are completely contrary to what we would have expected from earlier studies and 'common sense' interpretation (Matthews and Prothro, 1966: 129)

However, their explanation fits quite closely with the theory we are outlining for a social function of the secondary school. While it is true that the proportion of whites who are strict segregationists decreases with each increase in formal education, the combined number of moderates and integrationists does not exceed the number of segregationists within any educational level below college. Education decreases segregationist attitudes, but it takes extremely high doses of education to make much of an impact. For instance (Matthews and Prothro, 1966:343) the percentage of strict segregationists among high school graduates is 66 per cent, an improvement of 4 per cent when compared to those who did not complete high school.

One might suspect that schools—even if they had overtly confronted the biases of Southerners—would have failed to improve the racial climate in the South. However, the fact of the matter is that Southern schools were, with few exceptions, segregationist to the core. The administration and faculty of Southern schools were as much involved in encouraging resistance to the *Brown* decision as was the Klan and white Citizens Councils. Further, the minimum effect of education upon racial attitudes can be observed in non-Southern contexts. Campbell and Schuman's analysis (1968:35) of racial attitudes in 15 cities reaches the conclusion that:

The schools appear to have accepted without question the prevailing culture of race relations. Since World War II, those white students who have gone to college have evidently been exposed to influences which have moved their attitudes away from the traditional pattern. . . . We cannot say whether this resulted from specific instruction regarding questions of race or from a general atmosphere of opinion in the college community, but it is clear that a sizeable proportion of these postwar college students were affected. In contrast, the high schools which our respondents attended during the postwar years seem to have been little more involved in the nation's racial problems than they were in the prewar period. Or, to be more precise, their involvement has been so peripheral that it has had relatively little influence on the racial attitudes of their graduates.

The rather dismal conclusions reached by these scholars about the effects of high school education should come as no surprise to those familiar with the attitudes of professional educators and with the content of texts in high school civics courses. While one hardly can assert that the civics curriculum is directly and solely responsible for the unrealistic attitudes about race relations characteristic of American whites, it is clear that there is a missed opportunity for schools to inject some realism into the situation. The numerous studies of racial attitudes which have appeared since 1964 have been consistent in indicating that whites view America as a land of equal opportunity. To take one illustration, the Gallup Political Index of July, 1968, reported that a substantial majority believe that Negroes are treated the same as whites and only a minority agrees with the conclusions of the President's Commission on Civil Disorders that our nation is moving toward two societies. In Table 1, we can see that the only appreciable impact of education upon attitudes occurs after high schools. The relationship between education and realism is not necessarily positive; indeed, the high school experience, in many cases, seems to contribute to *less* realism.

TABLE 1

Attitudes of Various Educational Groups Toward Racial Problems
(Percentages)

	Grade School	High School	College
Agree with Kerner Commission	33	35	40
Believe Negroes are treated the same as whites	71	75	71
Believe Negroes are more to blame for present conditions than whites	56	58	42
Believe that businesses discriminate against Negroes in hiring	17	19	30
Believe that labor unions discriminate against Negroes in membership practices	13	18	30
Believe that looters should be shot on sight	54	55	46

Source: Gallup Political Index (July, 1968): 15–22.

Thus, the basic argument is that high school education is un-realistic; not because of what is said, but more because of what is *not* said. Among high school students who have taken courses in civics, the results are conflicting and inconclusive. In general, Langton and Jennings (1968) found there to be no association between being instructed formally in civics and any attitude (e.g., tolerance) which might be expected to result from such instruction. We can conclude that, with few exceptions, the formal education of youths makes no difference in regard to their image of the political world. Such courses are redundant; they are largely symbolic reinforcements of the 'democratic creed'—a liturgy heard by most students so many times that sheer boredom probably would allow for, at the most, slight increments of loyalty, patriotism, and other virtues presumed to be the goal of such courses.

An interesting exception is Langton and Jennings' (1968) discovery that the civics curriculum has a more impressive impact upon Negro children. Of particular interest is the effect of the civics curriculum upon the 'good citizen' role of Negroes and whites; 70 per cent of the whites and 63 per cent of the Negroes defined the 'good citizen' role either in terms of loyalty or participation. Among Negroes, the emphasis is upon loyalty while the opposite is true for whites. When the effect of civics courses is examined, we find that there is a very modest increase in participation emphasis and a decrease in loyalty emphasis among whites. However, among Negroes the opposite is true. The more courses taken, the greater becomes the emphasis upon loyalty, while the emphasis upon participation declines. The authors (Langton and Jennings, 1968:864) conclude that civics courses '. . . inculcate in Negroes the role expectation that a good citizen is above all a loyal citizen rather than an active one'. Presumably, loyalty and participation are emphasized in about the same degree. It is not likely that civics instructors overtly would discourage Negroes from seeking an active role in political society. However, Negroes (especially those with relatively high status) may be aware of the realities of discrimination and select from the curriculum those role characteristics which are congruent with their notions of their chances in life.

If we want to get an idea of the limitations of the civics curriculum, the best data would appear to be the responses of Negro youths. Since their prior exposure to the norms typically conveyed in such courses is significantly less than that of their white counterparts, their potential for absorbing them would appear to be uniformly greater. Thus, the selection of any particular norm for disproportionate acceptance by Negroes implies that a corresponding emphasis has been placed upon it in the classroom. It seems, then, that loyalty is the goal of the civics curriculum. Loyalty, perhaps admirable in the abstract, has become the catchword behind which a variety of parochial attitudes are hidden.

Given the natural clannishness of teenagers, it is not surprising that the experience of schooling does not decrease the ethnocentristic and chauvinistic propensities of this group. The early work by Remmers and Radler (1957) may have been unduly alarmist. The general conclusion of their work was that teenagers are an intensely patriotic group with little inclination to tolerate what they perceive to be disloyal conduct. For instance, a majority agreed that 'in these days, patriotism and loyalty to established American ways are the *most* important requirements of a good citizen', and that 'the average citizen does not show enough respect for the U.S. flag' (Horton, 1963:40). As students work their way through the curriculum, there is little evidence that their chauvinism changes. Seniors appear to be about the same as freshmen; those who have had civics courses are, if anything, worse—Remmers and Radler (1957:195) say they are 'more totalitarian'.

However, one gets the impression that the generation of teenagers studied by Remmers and Radler was characterized by a deterioration of once-held beliefs (in spite of the high correlation between the values of parents and children). Actually, we know that the attitudes reported by Remmers and Radler are not unique to any age group. Further, recent research by Jennings and Niemi (1968) indicates that high school students of the 1960s are somewhat more tolerant of diversity and less chauvinistic than those of the 1950s. On the other hand, in neither case was there much evidence of an unusually strong commitment to tolerance. On the slightly encouraging side, Jennings and Niemi found a *very slight* tendency for the pre-adults to take a more libertarian stance than their parents; however, the increments are not sufficiently impressive to justify a conclusion that 'things are getting better all of the time'.

Even if we assume that the educational process is primarily responsible for conveying a mythology to each generation and, therefore, do no expect that student values necessarily will change, we should not neglect the fact that some aspects of the mythology are organized more cogently than others. For instance, Pock (1967:134) found little comprehension of, or support for, 'several of the most fundamental tenets embodied in our heritage and expressed in the Bill of Rights'. Pock, rather than relying upon the use of items scales, presented high school seniors with a series of 18 cases, each raising a separate constitutional question. Most of the cases were based upon actual legal conflicts. Respondents were asked to agree or disagree with the specific action or decision involved in the case. He concluded (1967:134): 'Confronted by descriptions of situations in which both explicit and implicit civil rights has been violated, a preponderance of students responded approvingly to the use of improperly gathered evidence, secret trials, search without probable cause, setting of excessive bail, and to the use of anonymous witnesses.'

Here again we have evidence that the most significant aspect of civic education in American society is not the manifest content of the instructional program. It is very likely that students are presented with little more than the appropriate slogans, e.g., 'America is a land of freedom', without much effort to operationalize the concepts implicit in a slogan. It is possible that the same students who proved so discouraging to Pock would appear quite tolerant on an abstract

scale. Agreement with abstract ideals while disagreeing with application of these ideals to concrete situations is characteristic of the adult
population; presumably, such a characteristic is typical of high school
seniors also.

Techniques of Instruction

The inferences we can make about the nature of civic education
should be corroborated by direct observation of the classroom
situation. Failing this, we can learn something more about civic
education from examining the attitudes of social studies teachers and
the content of textbooks. In general, teachers are not inclined toward
using the classroom as a medium for the discussion of controversial
issues. While there are considerable variations in approach to the
classroom, teachers find their lives much less complicated if they
avoid controversy. We are referring here not only to the potential
for trouble within the community, but also to the potential for
trouble within the classroom. Classes are easier to manage if the
authority structure is not challenged. Engaging in controversy
presents a challenge to the authority structure and, therefore, is
avoided.

Avoidance of controversy is reinforced by the content of texts
which, for better or worse, establish the nature of the content of a
course of instruction. A brief survey of the quality of public school
texts in history, government, or civics indicates the Victorian attitude
toward politics which is typical of American education. The main
object of most texts apparently is to protect rather than to inform
the minds of youths.

In 1943, Hunt and Metcalf (1943:230) listed six closed areas in
social studies texts. They were:

1. Economics. Students and teachers could find little about possible
   shortcomings in the free enterprise system. They could certainly find
   nothing about the extent to which we actually have a free enterprise
   system.
2. Race and minority relations. There are virtually no realistic discussions of this problem.
3. Social class. In spite of obvious facts about the significance of
   social class in political behavior, the prevailing theme is that 'there
   are no social classes in America'.
4. Sex, courtship, and marriage. It should come as no surprise that
   this subject is treated in a wholly unreal fashion.
5. Religion and morality. Texts tactfully advised teachers to avoid
   this subject entirely.
6. Nationalism and patriotism. Nationalism as a destructive force
   is not mentioned. Patriotism is unquestionably accepted as an

over-arching goal, but the specific behaviors which are presumed to be patriotic are not discussed. Hence, saluting the flag is an unquestioned ritual.

From the available evidence, we conclude that Hunt and Metcalf's description is just about as valid today as it was in 1943. We cannot check each of the six closed areas as carefully as we should like, nor can we be assured that our survey is truly representative of the available texts. However, a few quotations from some widely used texts might prove helpful. Take, for example, the following statement about the American economic system:

One needs only to look at the great achievements and the standard of living of the American people to see the advantages of our economic system. . . . We believe that a well regulated capitalism—a free choice, individual incentives, private enterprise system—is the best guarantee of the better life for all mankind (McClenoghan, 1966:20 cited in Massialas, 1967:179).

There is no discussion of any alternatives to this economic system. not even in the 'some say—others say' style that characterizes some efforts to consider alternatives. Further, as Massialas (1967) notes, a picture accompanying this discussion shows people waiting in line in the rain to be treated in the English National Health Service.[1]

Race relations is regarded as a 'controversial social issue' and is treated with extreme caution. While there are some texts which are more realistic than others, the following quotation is typical:

In 1954, the United States Supreme Court made a decision stating that separate schools for Negro children were unconstitutional. This decision caused much controversy, but there has been general agreement, however, that some system must be developed to provide equal educational opportunity for all children—regardless of race, nationality, religion, or whether they live in cities or rural areas (cited in Krug, 1967:202).

Of course, this statement is patently false; but it also could allow support for the separate but equal doctrine. There is no discussion of the vigour with which Southern states resisted the order. Presumably, the students were given no explanation for the fact that race relations remain America's most divisive dilemma.

Concerning social class, sex, and religion, little can be said because the treatment of these topics is so sparse. Consider, for example, the following treatment of class (Cole and Montgomery, 1963:365 cited in Girault, 1967:227): '. . . classes in society are more

[1] Much of our analysis of texts is based upon material contained in this volume. Massialas' excellent article has been particularly useful, and citations from it have been of great help in the present undertaking.

or less inevitable . . . it is important to keep the social classes open.'
Warner, Hollingshead, the Lynds, and, in fact, most American
sociologists might never have written if this text is to be taken as
evidence of their impact below the college level. Sex usually is
discussed in psychology texts. Students are exposed to the arguments
for and against going steady. One of the most obvious advantages,
an advantage seized by the majority of those who 'go steady', is,
needless to say, ignored. In an age in which open cohabitation is
becoming an alternative to marriage, such discussions are absurd.
The treatment of religion, which occurs occasionally in sociology
texts, appears to be as far removed from the sociology of religion as
the treatment of sex is from the concerns of youth. Many texts assert
that reason alone cannot sustain man; faith is necessary. Usually
faith and Christianity are equated (Girault, 1967).

Patriotism, which is characteristic of the study of American
government in the public schools, maybe less jingoistic than it once
was. However, texts carefully intersperse discussions of government
structure (considered in purely legalistic terms) with appropriate
exhortations such as: 'No other country has more nearly approached
the goals of true democracy as has our United States. . . . No doubt
many of the early settlers were inspired men . . .' (Cole and Montgomery, 1963:341–342 cited in Girault, 1967:227); and 'Because the
nations of the world have not yet learned to live permanently at
peace, the United States today must maintain large defensive forces'
(Ludlum, et al., 1965 cited in Massialas, 1967:180).

The treatment of the American political process is totally unreal.
A single example selected from the abundance that exists should
serve to make the point. One text (Ludlum, et al., 1965) devotes an
entire chapter to the electoral process but fails to mention such
standard sources as *The American Voter*. As Massialas (1967:182)
observed: 'The five main ideas of the chapter on voting are: (1)
"voting is a process that makes possible peaceful change," (2)
"voting promotes citizen participation in government," (3) "voting
helps to promote equality," (4) "voting promotes obedience to
government," and (5) "voting promotes the self-respect of every
individual."'

The manner in which texts treat communism is even more
astonishing. In both the 'challenge of communism' courses which
have become quite popular recently and in the general civics courses,
communism is pictured as a total evil. Most state departments of
education primarily are concerned with demonstrating the fallacies
of communism rather than encouraging objective comparison. An
unswerving, ruthless conspiracy dominated by the Soviet Union

(texts have not yet discovered the shift toward China as the source of all evil) is the image which is presented, almost without exception. Texts warn students that they will be 'badly fooled' if they 'take the Russians at their word'; the 'errors' of Marx are listed (no communist sources are cited); and the contrast of good versus evil is made quite explicit. In the remote event that the student fails to get the message, end of chapter assignments, maps, and other visiual aids are equally biased (Brown and Pelthier, 1964:20–21, cited in Massialas, 1967:183). For instance, four projects accompanying one text are: (1) Write a short paper on agreements with other nations broken by the Soviet Union; (2) Draw a chart contrasting the way of life in a democracy and in totalitarian government; (3) Organize a panel to discuss United States Policy toward Cuba (preceded by the statement, 'The presence of a communist dictatorship in Cuba poses a threat to the peace of the Western Hemisphere'); (4) Compile a list of Marx's errors.

To provide a sense of geographical continuity, maps frequently are included in social studies texts. One such map divides the world into four camps: The United States, the communist bloc, the uncommitted nations, and the Free World—including Spain, Portugal, Formosa, and Haiti. (Presumably, 'free' is a synonym for degree of friendliness with the United States rather than a description of the internal politics of a country.) If, given the boredom which might be expected to accompany class discussions of such simplistic notions, the class still has not figured out how to get a good grade, the final assignment should reduce any remaining ambiguities: 'List as many criticisms of communism as you can' (McClenoghan, 1966, cited in Massialas, 1967:184).

Since most social studies teachers are not trained to distinguish facts from values and, in any case, probably find most of the anticommunism and ethnocentrism of the texts quite compatible with their own values, little contrary information filters into the classroom. Furthermore, since such unreal descriptions are reinforced by other sources of information (mass media and family), it is possible that our attention should be directed away from attitude change and toward attitude organization.

The notion of attitude organization, as developed by Jules Henry (1957), consists of grouping and focusing poorly articulated attitudes. Given the goals of the educational system, its success might be better measured in terms of providing order to attitudes and directing them toward larger social goals, such as the maintenance of positive attitudes toward national symbols. We suspect, however, that the crude indoctrination typical of texts is less effective in achieving organization than is the more subtle learning experiences manifested by means of teacher-student interaction and the norms of school organization. Furthermore, the consequences of the social studies curriculum might operate, in the long run, to increase cynicism rather than trust. Jennings and Niemi (1968:178) argue that the social studies curriculum—in postponing an encounter with the realities of political life—makes an increase in cynicism a natural consequence of the departure from high school. They find a 'rather sharp rise in the level of cynicism as high school seniors move ahead in a few years into the adult world'.

There is also the possibility that cynicism is latent in the high school population and, therefore, is released from constraint when adulthood is reached. Teachers in keeping with the general norms of public education, are overly concerned with authority. The style of teaching, emphasizing the authority of the teacher, may seem to some students to be in contrast with the democratic norms which comprise the official ideology. The available evidence, such as that presented in Table 2, strongly suggests that teachers are not capable of conducting an interaction with a student on an equal basis. Some of the data collected by Jennings and Zeigler is suggestive of the atmosphere of the class.

TABLE 2

Attitudes of Teachers Toward Authority

Item	Per Cent Agree	Per Cent Disagree
Children should be given greater freedom in expressing their natural impulses and desires, even if these impulses are frowned upon by people.	42	58
Schools should return to the practice of administering a good spanking when other methods fail.	59	41
A good teacher never lets students address him or her except as Mr., Miss, or Mrs.	75	25
What youth needs most is strict discipline, rugged determination, and the will to work and fight for family and country.	69	31
The main purpose of social studies courses is to teach students to be good citizens.	88	12
Obedience and respect for authority are the most important virtues children should learn.	60	40
Students today don't respect their teachers enough.	57	43

In Table 2, a few items which have yet to be analyzed systematically give some evidence of the concerns of teachers. While we do not know much about the actual behaviour of teachers, we might assume that such attitudes provide a strong propensity for creating a rigid classroom situation. Furthermore, in spite of the shibboleths of texts, to which teachers undoubtedly pay lip service, teachers appear to be as unclear about the application of democratic ideals to concrete situations as is the general population. A minority believe that police should not have the power to censor books and movies; a majority do not wish to provide First Amendment freedom to social or political nonconformists (Weiser and Hayes, 1966:477–478).

Since teachers are part of the educational grouping generally presumed to be the staunchest supporters of civil liberties, their attitudes are in conflict with what we have learned about the role of education in contributing to the open mind. However, teachers are part of an authoritarian system and develop appropriate occupational values (Jennings and Zeigler, 1969;77–79). This comment leads directly into our final section, but first there is the need to note the apparent contradiction between what we are saying and the evidence presented by Almond and Verba (1963:332–334). Forty per cent of their American adult respondents remembered participating in class discussions and debating political issues in school, in contrast with only 16 per cent of the British respondents and slightly fewer of the respondents in other countries. Two comments seem to be in order. First, a majority of adults do *not* recall participation, a fact which should be placed against the context of America's cultural emphases (as contrasted with those of England). Second, if the nature of the discussion resembled the study guides as set forth in texts, such discussions simply served to provide peer group reinforcement of prevailing ideologies.

The Controllers of Education

Why is the situation as it has been described? Three possible explanations come most readily to mind. First, and certainly the most popular, is the 'pressure group' argument. Schools are described as the victims of unrelenting pressure from extremist groups who keep a sharp lookout for deviations from the majoritarian ideology. Second, there is the assumption that schools mirror the dominant values of the society they serve and, therefore, can be expected to be replicas of the value structure of the society. Third, there is the argument that schools, because of the structure under which they are governed and because of patterns of occupational recruitment and socialization, are of necessity institutions that function to set limits to the legitimacy of policy alternatives. While each argument has some truth in it, we find the third more in keeping with the facts as we see them.

Pressure Groups

The pressure group argument collects information about cases in which teachers have become the focus of community controversy because of the manner in which they conduct their classes. However, a review of this literature does not tell one about the relative frequency of such attacks. When attacks occur, they are indeed spectacular. However, relative to the total amount of interaction between teachers, students, and the community, the activity of pressure groups seems to be relatively minor. This is not to suggest that pressure, when it is exerted, is not effective. One well publicized case may be enough to constrain many more teachers than those personally involved in the dispute. Nevertheless, there is virtually no evidence concerning the extent to which the demands of interest groups are communicated to administrators and teachers, and the extent to which demands can be linked to decisions regarding the values of the interest groups.

The principal author's own evidence indicates that teachers are not especially aware of—nor concerned about—the activities of interest groups (Zeigler, 1967:128–130). Administrators, on the other hand, are more sensitive to group demands. Therefore, it is possible that administrators, who have more immediate access to the weapons of sanction and who are viewed by teachers as a more potent threat, serve as transmission belts between interest groups and teachers. Such a possibility is given some credence because of the tendency of administrators to avoid conflict whenever possible. Thus they are likely to try to satisfy a group demand (by sanctioning the teacher) before it becomes public and places the school system within the context of a community conflict. Furthermore, both administrators and teachers might anticipate adverse response and, hence, modify their behaviour before a demand is made explicit.

Parents, perhaps, are a more potent source of external pressure. The potential for conflict between parent and teacher is substantial because of incompatible claims of each for authority over the child. Parents are likely to be hostile toward an educational system which threatens to socialize their children away from the values dominant within the family. The majority of a sample of Oregon residents voiced this concern. Corroborating the Oregon findings, Jennings (1966:18) reported that the substance of parental complaints lies in the domain of religion and politics. He suggests that, 'Instruction in the school—no matter how oblique—which threatens to undermine these orientations may be viewed very dimly by parents jealous of this prerogative. Even teaching about presumably objective facts, to say nothing of calling for tolerance of nonconformity or outright pitches for a point of view, may be enough to elicit a grievance. . . .' On the other hand, there was no clear direction to the complaints; parents about as frequently felt the content of a course was too conservative as too liberal.

Thus, parental pressure cannot be used to explain the status quo orientation of the social studies curriculum. Furthermore, many of the parents who were disturbed did nothing about it. Only 19 per cent of those parents who were upset by what a child was taught contacted the school in order to seek a redress of grievances. Again, one genuine hell-raising parent can have an influence beyond what is indicated by this percentage. The point is that in the normal, day-to-day operation of the schools, external demands are a less important source of constraint than are internal (especially administrative) expectations, Even when action against the school is initiated, it is rare that the strategy of influence will be an organizational effort. Organizational participation, probably signifying that a particular grievance has surfaced into a public issue, occurs in about 10 per cent of the cases of attempted influence that Jennings discovered.

Schools as Mirror Images

The idea of the school as the mirror image of the society certainly is compatible with the argument of this paper. Lacking values in conflict with those dominant in the community, schools can hardly be expected to act as agents of change. Yet the evidence for this conclusion is less than satisfying. Some sparse evidence, such as the work of Litt (1963) and Pock (1967), suggests that the values typical of a school's personnel seem to be comparable to values presumed to be typical of a particular type of community; for example, schools in upper income areas have teachers and students with more liberal values and offer more realistic social studies curricula than schools in other areas.

The basic problem with this argument is that no explanation has been offered for the fact that the personnel within a school do not necessarily have social class characteristics similar to those dominant in the community. Moreover, such arguments assume that social classes have clearly discernible values which are more or less automatically translated into an educational philosophy. The fact that most of the early work in school-community relations was done by sociologists probably contributed to the conclusion that classes and values could be roughly equated. However, this line of research neglected the role of occupational socialization in the organization of attitudes. While it certainly is true that teachers and administrators are 'middle class', they are products of a unique recruitment process which makes it likely that they will exaggerate, rather than merely reflect, a stereotypic middle class set of values. The role of the community, however this role is made manifest, is to set margins within which the educational task is to be performed. It is only upon the relatively rare occasions when the margins are breached that conflict between the school and community erupts. As Charters (1953:282) notes:

It is possible that something which we shall call a 'margin of tolerance' describes the school-community relationship. Citizens of each community may delegate to school personnel the freedom to educate youth according to their professional consciences—but freedom within certain well defined (or ill-defined) bounds. The boundary is composed of values dear to the particular community. If school personnel over-step the boundary, crisis ensues and community values enter the determination of school affairs.

Internal Structure

According to the above interpretation, we should look more closely at the internal structure of the school system to find out why it operates in defense of the status quo. If, as we can probably assume, administrators would prefer to keep community values out of the determination of school affairs, they must make certain that the margin of tolerance is not approached. In order to do this, they need to recruit teachers whose conduct is likely to cause little trouble. In short, the key to understanding why education is so admirably suited for its task is the recruitment process. The recruitment process in public education should be understood within the context of the educational 'establishment'. The word 'establishment', which has been ridiculed when applied to the general political system, seems quite apt when considering the educational sub-system. Teacher training programs, through which teachers must pass in order to be certified, provide the manpower. Schools of education are more closely coordinated than are most academic departments. They have become part of a stable pattern of interactions with accrediting associations, state departments of education, professional associations of teachers, and administrative associations. Certainly the most powerful force within the establishment is the school of education; but this power is reinforced by the support of the other components of the establishment. The crucial determinant of the existence, or lack thereof, of an establishment is a value consensus. Without having the evidence which would make such an assertion beyond question, it seems to us that there is substantial agreement among professional educators concerning the appropriate role of controversy in the classroom and the expected behaviour of teachers. The point may be disputed, but the low level of tolerance within the establishment seems to operate in the direction of driving out the dissenters.

Schools of education are very poor. Academically, the faculty of education schools ranks near the bottom. Attitudinally, the faculty of education schools appears more conservative and authoritarian than the faculties of other academic disciplines. Consequently, students attracted to education generally are the least capable on the college campus; they tend to be somewhat more conservative than the norm. Given the quality of education and the type of student recruited, it is not surprising that the products of schools of education do not view the classroom as an opportunity to develop creative thinking on the part of students. For instance, Jennings and Zeigler (1970), using an index of expressivism, found that 19 per cent of the social studies teachers with education majors in college as compared with 55 per cent of those with majors in social sciences were highly expressive.

Occupational socialization operates to reinforce the biases introduced in teacher training (Guba, et al., 1959; 274–275). The longer one teaches, the less likely the possibility of engaging in risk-taking behaviour; the longer one teaches, the more custodial becomes one's approach to the classroom. The goals of education gradually become dominated by concern with control of behaviour, creation of respect for authority, and establishment of orderly behaviour. Recently we have seen, in the current determination of schools to establish dress regulations for students, the extent to which such concerns are significant. Teachers, in insisting upon their authority over students, readily acquiesce to administrators' power over them. Corwin, for instance, noted that teachers accept the legitimacy of administrative decision-making even in the area of classroom performance. In the authority system of the schools there is a place for everybody; in order to succeed it is merely necessary that one avoid trying to move up. Thus Jennings and Zeigler (1969) found a strong association between administrator's approval and acquiescent teacher behaviour.

The recent disturbances in public education—teacher strikes and student unrest—can be understood as attempts to move up in the structure of authority. Consequently, administrators resist teacher demands and teachers resist student demands. In neither case has the making of demands escalated to the point of seriously threatening the established order. In both cases the responses to demands for restructuring have been repressive (see Rosenthal, 1969:96–109).

If we accept the argument that a conservative establishment is the major influence upon educational decision-making, then the participation of competitive units in the decision-making process becomes crucial. Generally, as we have argued, the school and the community interact only in cases of margin violation. In the normal decision-making process, the school board has a greater opportunity to compete with the administration for the control of educational policy. Generally it has been assumed that because school board members are recuited from the dominant class within a community, this body operates to reinforce commitment to the status quo. This assumption, however, is not supported by the available evidence.

Since all political bodies are dominated by those with the time and money to engage in politics, why should the school board— merely because it is typical of the political recruitment process— operate to maintain the status quo any more than other political institutions? Actually, the classes from which school board membership is drawn tend to be among the more liberal and tolerant within the community. Further, school board members have not endured the crippling *professional* socialization of the educational establishment.

Therefore, it is possible that school boards—to the extent that they can resist the strong pressure of cooptation from the administration—can serve as agents of change within the educational system. Such an assertion is supported by the recent research of Crain (1968). He found that school superintendents were likely to resist demands for desegregation but that, when the power to make decisions was taken from the superintendent by the school board, progress toward desegregation was more likely to occur. Likewise, Rosenthal (1969:143–153) reported that school boards in the cities he studied (with but one exception) tended to take the lead in establishing policies relating to integration.

The initiative that school boards have exhibited with respect to integration policies well may prove to be an issue-specific phenomenon rather than an indicator of a general trend. It may be the case that changes in school integration policies are inevitable and that board-inspired innovation merely is an example of short run marginal adjustment. Or, it may be that the nature of the integration issue is such that the school board—inasmuch as it is a lay institution which is roughly representative of non-professional values—is the only agent of the educational system which is competent to deal with it. Integration has much broader ramifications and attracts much wider attention than other issues confronting education. Perhaps it is 'too hot' or too political an issue for professional administrators (whose expertise and resources do not extend to such matters) to handle.

Wherever the truth of the matter lies, the fact remains that in this one issue area, lay boards *have* exerted themselves and they *have* established policy independent of the more conservative and 'professional' organs of the educational establishment. It remains to be seen whether the momentum thus generated will lead them into other areas of involvement in which professional resources are more apparent and, if so, whether they will be able to withstand the pressures imposed by their respective administrations. These pressures —to resist intrusion into technical matters—might be less irresistible if the scope of conflict is enlarged. In conditions of expanded conflict, the resources of non-professionals are potentially greater. Viewed from this perspective, the characteristic style of the educational establishment (the mimimization of conflict) is rational because there is a higher value placed upon technical resources. We would argue, however, that at this particular juncture in the development of the nation, the social consequences of technical expertise are too costly.

References

Almond, Gabriel, and Sidney Verba.
    1963   The Civic Culture. Princeton: Princeton University Press.
Bachrach, Peter, and Morton S. Baratz.
    1962   'The two faces of power.' American Political Science Review 56 (December): 947–952.
    1963   'Decisions and non-decisions: an analytical framework.' American Political Science Review 57 (September): 632–642.
Brown, Stuart Garry, and Charles L. Pelthier.
    1964   Government in Our Republic (revised edition). New York: Macmillan.
Campbell, Angus, and Howard Schumann.
    1968   'Racial attitudes in fifteen American cities.' pp. 1–215 in Supplemental Studies for the National Advisory Committee on Civil Disorders. Washington, D.C.: Government Printing Office.
Charters, W. W., Jr.
    1953   'Social class and the control of public education.' Harvard Educational Review 23 (Fall): 268–283.
Cole, William E., and Charles S. Montgomery.
    1963   High School Sociology. Boston: Allyn and Bacon.
Coleman, James S. (ed.)
    1965   Education and Political Development. Princeton: Princeton University Press.

Coser, Lewis
    1956   The Functions of Social Conflict. New York: The Free Press.
Crain, Robert L.
    1968   The Politics of School Desegregation. Chicago: Aldine.
Dawson, Richard E., and Kenneth Prewitt.
    1968   Political Socialization. Boston: Little, Brown and Company.
Easton, David.
    1957   'An approach to the analysis of political systems.' World Politics 9
                (April): 383–400.
    1965   A Systems Analysis of Political Life. New York: John Wiley and
                Sons.
Etzioni, Amitai.
    1968   The Active Society. New York: The Free Press.
Girault, Emily S.
    1967   'Psychology and sociology.' pp. 218–237 in C. Benjamin Cox and
                Byron G. Massialas (eds.), Social Studies in the United States. New
                York: Harcourt, Brace and World.
Guba, Egon G., Philip W. Jackson, and Charles E. Bidwell.
    1959   'Occupational choice and the teaching career.' Educational
                Research Bulletin 38:1–12. Reprinted in W. W. Charters and N. L.
                Gage (eds.), Readings in the Social Psychology of Education.
                Boston: Allyn and Bacon (1963).
Henry, Jules.
    1957   'Attitude organization in elementary school classrooms.' American
                Journal of Orthopsychiatry 27:117–133.
Hess, Robert D., and Judith V. Torney.
    1967   The Development of Political Attitudes in Children. Chicago:
                Aldine.
Horton, Roy E.
    1963   'American freedom and the values of youth.' pp. 18–60 in H. H.
                Remmers (ed.), Anti-Democratic Attitudes in American Schools.
                Evanston: Northwestern University Press.
Hunt, Maurice P., and Lawrence E. Metcalf.
    1943   Teaching High School Social Studies: Problems in Reflective
                Thinking and Social Understanding. New York: Harper and Row.
Jennings, M. Kent.
    1966   'Parental grievances and school politics.' Paper presented at the
                CASEA Conference on Politics and Education, University of
                Oregon, Eugene, Oregon.
Jennings, M. Kent, and Richard G. Niemi.
    1968   'The transmission of political values from parent to child.' Ameri-
                can Political Science Review 62 (March): 196–184.
Jennings, M. Kent, and L. Harmon Zeigler.
    1969   'The politics of teacher-administrator relations.' Education and
                Social Science 1:73–82.
    1970   'Political expressivism among high school teachers.' In Roberta
                Siegel (ed.), Learning About Politics: New York: Random House
                (forthcoming).
Key, V. O., Jr.
    1963   Public Opinion and American Democracy. New York: Alfred A.
                Knopf.
Krug, Mark N.
    1967   History and the Social Sciences. Waltham, Massachusetts: Blaisdell.

Langton, Kenneth P., and M. Kent Jennings.
    1968   'Political socialization and the high schoool civics curriculum.' American Political Science Review 62 (September): 852–867.

Litt, Edgar.
    1963   'Civic education, community norms, and political indoctrination.' American Sociological Review 28 (February):69–75)

Ludlum, Robert P., et al.
    1965   American Government. Boston: Houghton Mifflin.

Massialas, Byron G.
    1967   'American government: we are the greatest!' pp. 167–195 in C. Benjamin Cox and Byron G. Massialas (eds.), Social Studies in the United States. New York: Harcourt, Brace and World.

Matthews, Donald R., and James W. Prothro.
    1966   Negroes and the New Southern Politics. New York: Harcourt, Brace and World.

McClenoghan, William A.
    1966   Magruder's American Government. Boston: Allyn and Bacon.

Merelman, Richard M.
    1968   'On the neo-elitist critique of community power.' American Political Science Review 62 (June):451–460.

Pock, John C.
    1967   Attitudes Toward Civil Liberties Among High School Seniors. Washington, D.C.: U. S. Department of Health, Education, and Welfare. Cooperative Research Project No. 5–8167.

Remmers, H. H., and D. H. Radler.
    1957   The American Teenager. New York: Charter Books.

Rosenthal, Alan.
    1969   Pedagogues and Power: Teacher Groups in School Politics. Syracuse: Syracuse University Press.

Schattschneider, E. E.
    1960   The Semi-Sovereign People. New York: Holt, Rinehart, and Winston.

Tocqueville, Alexis de.
    1835   Democracy in America. Richard D. Heffner (ed.). New York: The New American Library (1956).

Weiser, John C., and James E. Hayes.
    1966   'Democratic attitudes of teachers and prospective teachers.' Phi Delta Kappa 47 (May):476–481.

Zeigler, L. Harmon.
    1967   The Political Life of American Teachers. Englewood Cliffs, N.J.: Prentice-Hall.

I I

POWER, IDEOLOGY, AND THE TRANSMISSION OF

KNOWLEDGE: AN EXPLORATORY ESSAY

Dennis Smith

This paper considers selected elements in a strategy for the analysis of education systems. In the first section, the strategy is outlined briefly. In the second, a number of dimensions are suggested for the analysis of the structure of administrative control. The third section discusses several aspects of legitimising ideologies.

I

The objective of this section is primarily a heuristic one. Three related foci for the analysis of education systems are specified. A number of questions are posed with respect to each, and some dimensions are tentatively suggested for the analysis of structural variations. The section concludes with a critical review of two recent works.

In an education system, groups of students are taught sets of facts and ideas by teachers. Participants in this process and all those groups who are able to exert some influence over it have some notions—implicit or explicit, vague or specific—about what should be taught, to whom, and why. Of particular importance, clearly, are the notions entertained by those groups whose control over the education process is most direct and persistent. Norms, values and goals defined by them will be embodied in the education process itself.

In other words, one may think of the education system in terms of a process of knowledge transmission[1] which takes place within a structure of power relationships through which constraints are operated on it. The way in which these constraints are applied is to a great extent determined by the ideational context in terms of which this transmission process is perceived by controlling groups. This characterisation of education systems suggests that three related foci of analysis may be identified. These are the power structure, the process of educational transmission, and the structure of meaning embodied in the transmission process itself and attempts to impose specific patterns upon it.

A number of questions arise. Some of these are suggested by the way each focus is related to the other two, and others derive from a more general concern with phenomena such as power and ideology. For example, the educational power structure may be examined in a number of ways. One may identify the agencies which control the transmission process. What is the sphere of control specific to each agency? (Divisions of control may account for discontinuities in the transmission process.) Which social groups exercise the control vested in the various agencies? (The interests and assumptions of controlling groups are likely to determine the structure of the transmission process.) What is the nature of the power relationships through which control is exercised by the agencies concerned? How do these agencies stand in relation to each other? (These last two questions underlie the dimensions developed in the second section of this paper.)

Another set of questions arises when considering the ideational context within which controlling groups seek to impose a structure on the process of transmission. How do these groups perceive their interests? Is it possible to identify a set of goals and values embodied —implicitly or explicitly—in the structure which they impose on the transmission process? Does this structure manifest a set of assumptions about the ordering of society and the organisation of knowledge?[2] How do the evaluations and conceptual ordering manifest in this structure compare with the more explicit ideological claims that are made? In answering these questions, the distinction set out by Earl Hopper between ideologies of implementation and ideologies of legitimisation[3] may usefully be employed. As Hopper implies, the norms, goals and values specified in such ideologies may not be embodied in practice.[4] However, the norms and values which *are* embodied in practice may be identified by a careful analysis of prevailing institutional arrangements such as patterns of streaming and the way in which curricula are organised.[5*]

The original distinction made by Hopper may be developed in at least two ways. First, ideologies of legitimisation have previously

* [See Readings 5, 6, and 7 in the present volume. E.H.]

been described in terms of the values they embodied (collectivism/ individualism).[6] An alternative approach—which will be followed in the final section—is to distinguish among them in terms of the goals which they enshrine. Second, ideologies of implementation have previously been specified for the mode of initial selection (sponsored/ contest) and the subsequent pattern of routes (elitist/egalitarian).[7] It is suggested that implementing ideologies with respect to the transmission process may be analysed in terms of another set of dimensions. These dimensions refer to the relationships between types of students and areas of knowledge which 'should' be manifest in the transmission process. These relationships may be considered to constitute two linked category systems—a categorisation of knowledge and a categorisation of student types. Such an ideology of implementation might be analysed in terms of: the content and boundaries of the two sets of categories; the relationships deemed appropriate between the two sets of categories; and the relationships within each set of categories deemed appropriate in terms of (a) patterns of segregation and combination, and (b) patterns of hierarchical ordering. A brief example may be given. The assumptions underlying the 'tripartite' system were: three types of knowledge—academic, technical and 'practical'— may be distinguished, each of which is appropriate for a corresponding psychological type of student; in each case, the transmission process should take place in a segregated institution (Grammar, Technical, and Modern schools); in theory, 'parity of esteem' should exist among the three categories of institutions.[8]

The third focus of enquiry is the structure of the transmission process itself. As has already been implied, attention may be directed to the pattern of knowledge distribution (who is taught what[9]), prevailing modes of segregating or combining students and knowledge areas in the process of teaching,[10] the relative prestige accorded different types of institutions, disciplines, students, and so on.*

However, it is likely that when all the educational institutions within a particular system are considered together a number of overlaps, inconsistencies, sometimes glaring contradictions, will become evident. In the English system, for example, students may take the same Ordinary level G.C.E. course at Grammar schools, Modern schools, Comprehensive schools, and Technical colleges. Theoretically incompatible modes of secondary school organisation —Tripartite, Comprehensive, Private—coexist within the same system. The division of labour among the various institutions of higher education is far from clear. Such a system seems to have the character not of coherence but of 'bricolage'. Fortunately, the

* [See Readings 7 and 9 in the present volume. E.H.]

distinctions developed so far in this section make it possible to suggest two of the factors which determine the occurrence of these discontinuities: the distribution of control over different aspects of the transmission process[11] and the pattern of consensus and disagreement among agencies with respect to the mode of implementing this process.[12]

These remarks on the analysis of education systems were in part stimulated by an attempt to interpret particular patterns of institutional change in the English education system. It is therefore interesting to note that a perspective in some ways similar to this has been adopted in a recent book[13] discussing the development of the Colleges of Advanced Technology from local technical colleges to universities. Two themes underlie the detailed documentation provided by Tyrrell Burgess and John Pratt. They demonstrate that a perilous and largely uncharted maze intervenes between public statements of policy in higher education and their implementation. Ministerial speeches on the need for more scientists, engineers and technicians have been made for over a hundred years. Such 'perorations' have less influence on the course of educational development within technical institutions than the assumptions, interests and objectives of those agencies which exercise day-by-day control: the education service, local authorities, college principals, academic boards, examination councils, and so on. Even building regulations embody a philosophy of education: '*Building Bulletin 5* is . . . an unself-conscious reflection of historical attitudes to further education. Its implied philosophy is simply that building for further education must accommodate a wide variety of institutions and a vast range of courses within them, that these must respond readily to outside demand, that building must be done as cheaply as possible, often by instalments, and that further education is to be thought of largely as an extension of secondary schooling.'[14] To use terms developed by Hopper,[15] Burgess and Pratt have shown how ideologies of legitimisation stating the goals and values which validate public policy may not be accompanied by detailed policies of implementation. Institutional change may be directed by a wide variety of interests located at many points within a complex administrative structure, possibly producing results quite different from those envisaged in the original statement of public policy.

Their second theme—which emerges naturally out of the first—concerns 'the effects of different forms of government and administration on the educational experience of staff and students'.[16] They argue, for example, that the reason for the spate of technical college building in the 1880s was 'the creation of competent local authorities with the power to raise money and to create colleges. In a similar fashion the educational innovation of the national certificate scheme depended upon the existence of an established, central, Board of Education.'[17] At another level, they describe in detail the consequences for curricular development in the CATs of the changing pattern of internal and external control associated with successive shifts from local authority to Direct Grant and finally to University status.[18]

The mode of analysis suggested so far in this paper bears a more superficial resemblance to another approach that has been applied to the interpretation of educational change, particularly in England. The reference is to P. W. Musgrave's model for the analysis of the English educational system.[19] Although the differences between the two approaches may be stated quite briefly, it is convenient to extend the discussion in order to make a number of points about the distribution of power in education systems and the role played by official definitions of their nature.

Musgrave argues that struggles among groups competing for control over an education system are punctuated by periods of bargaining ending in 'truce situations'. Sufficient consensus in values may exist to permit the specification of an agreed 'definition of situation' from which are derived the goals of the education system and the content of the roles which constitute it. When these decisions have been made, he says, men and materials are claimed and institutions developed to administer the system, socialise the actors engaged in it and ensure 'that its products, namely educated beings, meet the requirements laid upon it by the definition'. Change occurs partly as a consequence of 'autonomous development . . . within the system itself' (a 'socially permitted range of indeterminacy' existing in norms and roles), partly through shifts in power and ideology among controlling groups.[20]

Musgrave rightly stresses that change can be accounted for in part by examining the ideologies of controlling groups and the power relations existing among them. However, he assumes implicitly that there exists only a single point at which definition of the education process may be enforced within a system and that various interest groups sponsoring competing policies dispute control of this point. In fact, policy disagreements need not generate active conflict. Within a single system a large number of educational initiatives may be conducted by relatively autonomous groups each controlling resources which enable them to do this. There are many such examples of independent enterprise within the English system: the competitive building programmes of the Voluntary societies, the philanthropic Ragged School movement, the mushrooming of the Mechanics' Institutes, Quintin Hogg's sponsorship of the London Polytechnics, the establishment of the civic Universities in provincial towns, commercial ventures such as the 'proprietary' Public schools, and so on. The education system of the United States is to a great extent a product of local initiative of this kind. Congregationalist purists founded Harvard for their sons. Virginian planters preferred the Anglican William and Mary College. The Dutch Reformed Church (Rutgers), Presbyterians (Princeton), Baptists (Brown), Jews (Brandeis) and many other groups invested their zeal in bricks and mortar. Other 'special interests' followed the pattern. Nearly 300 independent colleges for women are scattered about the land. A host of private colleges for Negro students sprang up after the Civil War. In the words of a recent study, '. . . instead of a national system of higher education, America got a Balkanised pattern that made even the decentralised and polycentric German approach look orderly and monolithic'.[21] As these examples show, initiating potential may be quite widely diffused within the administration of an education system. Furthermore, active conflict may lead to a hiving off of groups and institutions rather than a 'truce'. This was an option being considered by some English Direct Grant schools following the issue of a Circular by the Labour Secretary of State for Education in 1965 requesting local authorities to submit schemes for a comprehensive reorganisation of secondary education.

The sequence of change assumed by Musgrave to be typical bears little relation to the actual pattern of educational development. The 'truce situations' of 1870, 1902 and 1944 within the English system were in fact stages in the progressive accretion of power to statutory authorities, increasing their importance both relative to other agencies and in terms of the sphere of education over which they exercised control. Such 'truces' were a consequence of overwhelming disparities in power, not of some happy meeting of minds. No such cosy myths have gathered around the history of the French education system. The laws of the Revolutionary government, the Falloux Law, the enactments of the Third Republic, and so on, back and forth, were temporary victories for either side in a prolonged and bitter struggle between Church and State for control over education.

Returning to the English case, the agreed 'definitions of the situation' which have emerged tend to be vague, general and frequently self-contradicting. They are hardly clear blueprints for the detailed specification of norms and values, certainly not suitable to be handed direct to some Parsonian quartermaster who will supply men and materials. Variations in values, goals and norms occur in a far more complex fashion than is assumed in this model. For the last hundred years the only common 'definition of the situation' acceptable to most interest groups in English education is that set out in the Report of the Royal Commission on Secondary Education (1895):

'We mean by "system" neither uniformity nor the control of a Central Department of government. Freedom, variety, elasticity are, and have been, the merits which go far to redeem the defects in English education, and they must all at hazards be preserved. The "system" which we desire to see introduced may rather be described as coherence, an organic relation between different kinds of schools which will enable each to work with due regard to the work to be done by the others, and will therefore avoid waste both of effort and of money.'[22] Devolution of power and a variety of forms: these are principles which raise inconsistency and parochial exclusiveness to the level of virtues. They embody a recognition that there are many interests seeking a wide range of goals through the education system. Similar themes persist even in the White Paper on Educational Reconstruction (1943) which foreshadowed the 1944 Education Act:

'The Government's purpose . . . is . . . to ensure a fuller measure of education and opportunity for young people and to provide means for all of developing the various talents with which they are endowed and so enriching the inheritance of the country whose citizens they are. The new educational opportunities must not, therefore, be of a single pattern. It is just as important to achieve diversity as it is to ensure equality of educational opportunity. But such diversity must not impair the social unity within the education system which will open the way to a more closely knit society and give us strength to face the tasks ahead.'[23]

The justification for diversity and inconsistency reappears in a new form, contradicting in the same breath the promise of equal opportunity with all that implies in the way of standardisation. Musgrave fails to recognise the role played by statements such as these in papering over the cracks and giving a superficial gloss of unity and purpose.

II

In this section, a set of dimensions is proposed for the analysis of the structure of administration control over education systems. An application of these dimensions suggests some significant differences among the administrative structures of education systems in England, France, and the United States.

The Structure of Administrative Control

The transmission of knowledge takes place in the context of a structure of power relationships through which varying constraints are exercised upon it. The power vested in agencies may derive from a direct appeal to some form of authority or from their ability to manipulate resources whose disposition is strategic to the implementation of the transmission process. The following distinctions may be made:

I. *Power derived from a direct appeal to Authority*

Three forms of authority may be distinguished:

(i) *legal* or authority based upon statutory or similar provisions, legitimately enacted, vesting specific powers in designated agencies.

(ii) *professional* or authority based upon a claim to have exclusive possession of specialised knowledge which gives the holders particular competence to make decisions in the relevant institutional spheres.

(iii) *diffuse*[24] or authority based upon a generalised claim to directive powers associated with occupancy of a position within a status hierarchy.

II. *Power derived from ability to manipulate strategic resources*

Two kinds of resources may be specified:

(i) *financial*—control over the amount of finance available and the mode of its application.

(ii) *certification*—control over the character and distribution of educational qualifications and the requirements which have to be satisfied before they are awarded.

Power derived from professional or diffuse authority or the control of certification or finance is typically used to 'colonise' areas of uncertainty within and outside the sphere covered by legal regulations. The power of a particular agency is likely to take more than one of the forms specified. Her Majesty's Inspectorate in the 1860s, for example, buttressed their legal authority with power derived from the diffuse authority associated with their status position (they were overwhelmingly Oxbridge men), a degree of professional authority, indirect control over the allocation of finance to the schools (through the application of the Revised Code), and control over curricula (especially in the training colleges) through their administration of certificate schemes.[25] A more extended example may also be given.

In 1830, control over the English education system was mainly in the hands of three groups: local ratepayers (who were land-owners, professional and business folk, and other 'men of means'), the clergy, and—in the Universities—academics. Statutory agencies did not exist for education. The control exercised by the middle orders derived from their ability to provide financially not only for the education of their own children (through private tutoring and school fees), but also for artisans (through the Mechanics' Institutes they sponsored), the indigent (through the Schools of Industry, later replaced by Workhouse Schools) and the worthy poor (through their subscriptions to the Voluntary Societies). Their involvement in these enterprises was a corollary of their diffuse authority over, and responsibility for, the welfare of the lower social orders (stimulated, no doubt, by a healthy concern for maintaining social control). No 'teaching profession' existed. A professional responsibility for the education of the people was being asserted by the Church of England clergy, some of whom cherished the ambition 'to plant a Church school in every parish in the land'.[26] The control exercised by the University academics ultimately rested upon their ability to admit candidates to degrees or debar them at pleasure—that is, it was control over certification.[27]

Turning to the configuration of relationships established among administrative agencies, it is clear that these are subject to a good deal of variation, both over time and cross-nationally. A comparison of the English system with either the Napoleonic 'University of France' or the pattern of the United States[28] suggests this immediately. In all three societies, administrative hierarchies have developed but they differ considerably in complexity and disposition. Some of the differences will be indicated below following the specification of three dimensions along which the structure of administrative control over the transmission process may vary.

The three dimensions are degree of Lateral Autonomy, degree of Vertical Integration, and degree of Centralisation:

(a) *Degree of Lateral Autonomy*

At the apex of administrative hierarchies may be found agencies which, although exercising control over various subordinate agencies, are themselves subject to no such continuing regulation. Vested with authority or directly controlling strategic resources (or both), such agencies have the capacity to make and enforce decisions with respect to the organisation of the transmission process in certain sectors of the education system without reference to other agencies. The degree of lateral autonomy within an education system is determined by the number of agencies able to make and enforce decisions in this way. Not all agencies of this kind are at the apex of administrative hierarchies; there are some, for example, whose activities are restricted to a single institution or locality. The term 'lateral' is used to distinguish the decision-enforcing capacity which is based upon direct control of resources from the decision-making responsibility which may be delegated from a superior to a subordinate agency within a vertically integrated hierarchy. This issue is complicated by the fact that an agency which has independent control over one function may be subject to regulation with respect to others. Furthermore, a network of informal consultation may be established among several 'laterally autonomous' agencies, sometimes formalised as in the Headmasters' Conference set up in 1869.

(b) *Degree of Vertical Integration*

Vertical Integration exists when, in the performance of one or more of its functions, an agency is subject to regulation by a superior agency. Total vertical integration—that is to say, when every agency, with respect to all its functions, belongs to a single hierarchical system of command—only occurs when the degree of lateral autonomy, is minimal. Hower, given a fixed state of lateral autonomy the degree of vertical integration is variable. This is because new agencies may be added to a chain of command and given delegated powers. An increase in vertical integration may, then, be the result of either the creation of new agencies or the imposition of regulation upon agencies which were previously free of such control. The sociological manifestations may be quite different in the two cases because of the strong resistance of residual traditions in the latter case.

(c) *Degree of Centralisation*

Superior agencies differ in the degree to which they delegate decision-making powers to subordinate agencies. A body such as the Department of Science and Art, for example, gave 'little or no room for local committees to exercise judgment on any issue of weight or significance'.[29] Degree of centralisation is a dimension referring to the extent to which delegation occurs within administrative hierarchies. It is a crude measure, since the distribution of initiative within a hierarchy may be extremely complex and may vary in several ways. For example, an agency located in the middle ranges may be given a great deal of decision-making freedom, which it may either reserve mainly for itself or delegate still further down the line.

The education systems of England, France and the United States may be compared in terms of the dimensions just specified.

Degree of Lateral Autonomy

In France, the Ministry of Education allows few rivals, the Church alone being worth a mention. The very low degree of lateral autonomy in this system may be compared with the very high degree in the United States, where approximately 40,000 School Boards have, for example, the power to raise and apply education taxes. England and Wales, with a fairly substantial 'Independent' sector and approximately 150 Local Education Authorities with some degree of independent control in certain areas, lie somewhere in the middle.

Degree of Vertical Integration

Although the recent 'mutations' in France have led to some administrative changes, before these occurred the Minister sat unchallenged at the apex of a complex and rigid hierarchy of control which included over twenty 'Académies' administered by Recteurs (higher and secondary education) and, the Inspectorate and Departmental Prefects (primary education). By contrast, a corrolary of the very high degree of lateral autonomy in the United States is a low degree of vertical integration. The English system may be placed rather nearer the French than the American on this dimension.

Degree of Centralisation

The French and American systems may be placed without difficulty at opposite ends of the scale. Traditionally, the French Education Minister has controlled not only all appointments in the system, but also curricula, timetables, syllabuses, examinations and pedagogy, delegating few matters. The American experience embodies the reverse tendency, which is that power over the education system should be vested in the local community, a tradition recently reasserted in some New York State school districts.[30] In England, where neither the Secretary of State nor the Parent-Teacher Associations are as strong as their counterparts in France and the United States respectively, much more real power is vested in the teaching profession itself.[31] A greater degree of initiative seems to be located in the middle ranges of administrative hierarchies within the English system.

The dimensions specified may be used, as above, to provide a preliminary orientation for cross cultural analysis. They may also be used to trace changes over time within a single system. It has already been suggested that in the early nineteenth century, the English system was characterised by a fairly high degree of lateral autonomy, financial control being buttressed by diffuse authority. Although a detailed analysis would outrun available space, the overall sequence of change since that date is fairly clear: an initial increase in lateral autonomy as the middle classes expanded their educational enterprise; the steady intrusion of the State through financial aid (later control) and the sponsorship of certificate schemes; a sharp decrease in lateral autonomy at the turn of the century with the merging of the three main government bodies into the Board of Education and the rationalisation of the local mosaic through the creation of Local Education Authorities; at the same time, an increase in vertical integration as the ties between local and national agencies were strengthened; since the beginning of the century a slow shift in the balance between local and national agencies in favour of the latter; and over the whole period a steady increase in the importance of legal authority and control through certification relative to other means.

Shifts along these dimensions are closely linked to other changes: for example, the expansion of the State, the increasing dominance of new business and professional groups, the gathering self-confidence and status of the academic profession itself. Light may be thrown back onto the comparison with France and the United States. To what extent, for example, may differences in administrative structures be related to variations in the relationships among the three interests mentioned—the State, the bourgeoisie and the academic profession? When questions such as these are asked, one is at the threshold of a wider, though intimately related, analysis which directs attention beyond the boundaries of the education system itself.

III

It is important to identify the groups controlling the transmission process for other reasons apart from that of explaining how shifts occur in the structure of administrative control. The education system contributes to the attempted resolution of various problems that have to be solved in all societies. The manner in which the education system contributes to these tasks is likely to be favourable to certain groups, particularly those with power over the system. For example, two related tasks are confronted in all societies. First, the inculcation of ways of perceiving and thinking about the world which are to a certain extent crystallised into sets of values, goals and norms. Second, the process of equipping people with the skills necessary to the adequate performance of the adult roles to which they are allocated, roles which are associated with characteristic networks of social relations, which carry distinctive privileges and penalties, and which locate the occupant in various relationships of power and subordination.

The groups who control the education system have decisive influence over the way in which these problems are faced. By defining the content to be transmitted through the system they may further a number of objectives—guaranteeing the survival and prestige of certain forms of knowledge, sustaining notions of authority which buttress their own power, facilitating the development of particular kinds of competence, and so on. In so far as educational certification is the chief mechanism of allocation to the occupational structure, they may also determine the distribution of opportunities for access to positions of power and privilege.

The following section attempts to illustrate the variety of goals which legitimise the education system, providing a rationale for the way in which it is organised. A necessary caveat is that the goals which legitimise a system may not be the goals which are fostered by it. For convenience, the following examples, which are taken from the development of the English education system, refer to legitimising ideologies enshrining goals actively pursued by the groups who articulate them. It is useful to distinguish among ideologies concerned with the following: the content which is to be transmitted through the education system, the pattern of its distribution among different groups, the consequences of the education process for mobility within an existing social structure, and the consequences of the education process for various aspects of the social structure itself.

Within any education system may be found 'traditionalist' groups who are determined that an established cultural tradition shall be maintained, that existing patterns of perceiving and thinking about the world should continue to predominate. Such groups may find themselves resisting change in many ways, refusing to recognise new academic disciplines, insisting on the 'old' wisdom, adhering to well-tried pedagogic techniques, and so on. Such resistance may be directed against the efforts of 'innovationist' opponents who seek to revitalise or replace an existing cultural tradition, perhaps to undertake a 'cultural revolution'. These goals may entail the establishment of new institutions (such as the 'Anti-Universities' of which University College, London, was an early nineteenth century example),[32] the creation of new disciplines (Sociology), the redefinition of old ones (Darwin), the propagation of new thoughts and ideas (Mao's 'little red book'), and so on.

However, the concern may be not only the character of the cultural resources transmitted through the system but also the pattern of their distribution among social groups. 'Preservationist' groups strive to prevent outsiders from learning the mysteries. In a pamphlet attacking Charity schools in the eighteenth century, one writer warned: 'If a horse knew as much as a man, I should not like to be his rider.'[33] A tacit alliance may be formed with the other social orders who likewise prefer to keep their place. A cautious edging beyond the limits—as was happening in English elementary schools in the 1850s—is brusquely stopped, in this case by the sharp provisions of the Revised Code (1862) which tethered these schools firmly to the teaching of basic literacy.[34] An alternative strategy is the re-making of a particular group's life style and consciousness. Arnold was engaged on just such an enterprise at Rugby, fashioning his students into Christian gentlemen. Sir Robert Morant—through his creation, the local authority Grammar school—attempted to spread the culture of the Public schools to the burgeoning white collar stratum. At the same time, the missionaries of University Extension were taking Virgil to the masses. 'Reconstruction' is perhaps the dominant ethos among the English teaching profession at present.

The maintenance or alteration of particular patterns of cultural distribution may not be an end in itself. These processes may be viewed instrumentally, either as a means of equipping people for mobility within an existing social structure or as a means of altering that structure. Alternatively, it may be a way of preventing both these possibilities.

The focus may be upon the instrumentality of education as an aid or barrier to mobility. Certain groups may seek to use the education system to prevent 'outsiders' gaining access to resources of power and privilege enjoyed by themselves. Such goals were served, for example, by the National Society's policy, which was: 'to communicate to the Poor generally . . . such knowledge and habits, as are suflcient to guide them through life, in their proper stations, especially to teach the doctrines of Religion, according to the discipline of the Established Church, and to train them in the performance of their duties by early discipline.'[35] Such a policy—the use of education to promote the maintenance of existing status positions from one generation to the next—was endorsed later by a head of the Education Department in the 1850s who told Parliament that ' . . . if they were to pass a law to compel poor parents to send their children to be made scholars of, they might just as well pass another law to compel the noble lord to send his children to a school where they would be educated for becoming ploughboys or artisans. The one law would be no more absurd and tyrannical than the other.'[36]

However, already by that time an alternative view of education's role—as a medium of status redistribution, a means whereby individuals could improve their station—was becoming popular. Sponsors of competitive examinations, such as Jowett of Balliol, admitted that 'a smile may be raised at the idea of subjecting excisemen and tide-waiters to a competing literary examination as there might have been thirty years ago at subjecting village schoolmasters to a similar test'. But such examinations would have a happy influence by 'acting on the surest of all motives: the desire that a man has of bettering himself'.[37]

The possibility of individual social mobility through the education system may serve other purposes also. As Joseph Lancaster, a successful propagandist for the monitorial system, had written earlier: 'I have ever found the surest way to cure a mischievous boy was to make him a monitor.'[38] Writ large, the lesson was that the promotion of potential malcontents was an effective strategy for the containment of the lower orders, a method of preventing a significant or sudden accretion of power and privilege to the labouring classes at the expense of their betters. The contrary message—that through mobilisation a new equilibrium of power and privilege might be established—was preached in Chartist halls.

Another goal pursued through the education system was that of revising the techniques used in training skills and recruiting to occupations in such a way that institutions might be 'reformed' and made to function more efficiently. This 'reformist' ideology lay behind, for example, the Northcote-Trevelyan reforms with respect to civil service entrance, the award of grants for technical studies by the Department of Science and Art,[39] and the establishment of Colleges of Advanced Technology. 'Education for efficiency'—a mild 'reformism'—has been an increasingly predominant ideology in England since the Second World War. The Crowther Report, for example, noted that one way of regarding education was 'as a means of increasing the efficiency of the whole community, and therefore as a form of national investment'.[40] 'Reformism' of this kind can be distinguished from a less clearly articulated 'ritualism' which may be characteristic of some forms of professional training.

Procedural reform and the pursuit of efficiency may be sharply distinguished from 'radical' attempts to re-define the goals of institutions through the education system or to instill a new set of values in students who will eventually move into such institutions. Notions such as these are unlikely to be transmitted formally through an education system controlled by groups whose interests are served by existing institutions; an 'orthodox' message is more likely. However, two examples of 'radical' enterprises are the training of cadres in a pre-revolutionary situation and, although not strictly comparable, the summer schools run within the British Labour Movement between the wars on, among other things, nationalisation.

By way of a conclusion, it may be pointed out that the mode of analysis suggested in the three sections of this paper opens a way to a rather broader discussion of the relation between social stratification and the education system than has been customary. It is conventional to argue that in performing its dual role as a distributor of life chances and cultural orientations the education system tends to discriminate against certain strata. At least two other promising lines of investigation may be briefly suggested, although lack of space and knowledge forbid a longer discussion.

First, in the course of the nineteenth and twentieth centuries, control over the English education system has shifted away from provincial elites, with diffuse authority and economic power which were aspects of their dominance in local status hierarchies, towards national agencies manned by groups whose power derives from their location in bureaucracies. An explanation of these changes must take into account, for example, the professionalisation of functions (particularly administrative) previously performed by local elites, shifts in the size and structure of provincial towns, the development of new forms of relationship among the various strata, an increased tendency to define status position in terms of occupational grouping rather than one's location within a local hierarchy, and so on. A careful study of these processes would help to account for shifts in the structure of administrative control (and the policies promoted through the structure).

A second sphere of investigation is the contribution made by the education system to the 'cultural definition' of the new strata which emerged in the course of social change. For example, the various forms of 'elementary' schooling designed for the new urban poor were in one respect an attempt to teach these groups, newly created in the furnace of industrial change, doctrines and habits of subordination known to their rural forefathers but under threat in the city. Another case is that of the Public schools whose success in defining the boundaries and orientations of a whole stratum is witnessed by the habit of using the type of school to refer to the stratum itself.

It might be argued that since the mid-nineteenth century, as educational background and then educational certification became increasingly important in occupational recruitment, the boundaries of social strata have increasingly tended to reflect the pattern of routes through the education system rather than vice versa. Instead of describing our educational institutions in terms of the strata from which they recruit ('the Poor', 'the industrial classes', 'Mechanics', 'the sons of gentlefolk', etc.) we now tend to think of various social strata in terms of the educational background of their members ('Public school', 'graduate', etc.). In so far as this is so, one might describe the shift in the structural relationship between the education system and the stratification system, in this respect, as being from 'derivative' to 'generative'. In other words, the education system not only largely determines the distribution of ex-students among the various social strata but also makes a significant contribution to the definition of the cultural boundaries between different strata.

The last serious attempt to determine the cultural orientations of a new stratum is embodied in the 1904 Regulations for Secondary schools which set out in detail the curricular organisation (largely borrowed from the Public schools) which should be followed in the new local authority Grammar schools created after 1902. Even when these detailed regulations were dropped it was still insisted that 'when two languages are taken, and Latin is not one of them, the Board (of Education) will require to be satisfied that the omission is for the advantage of the school'.[41] In the Elementary schools, the object was explicitly one of containment (or social control). Teachers were told that their task was to 'lay the foundations of conduct', inculcate 'a sense of discipline' and 'implant in the children habits of industry, self-control, and courageous perseverance in the face of difficulties'. In this way the children would be prepared 'practically as well as intellectually, for the work of life'.[42] In less than twenty-five years, explicit statements of that kind were well on the way to being anathema, quite unacceptable ideologically. Since that data also, many of the premises embodied in the 'liberal culture' imposed upon the Grammar schools by the Board have seriously been questioned. However, curricular forms validated by an ethos forged for an Imperial elite have only very recently begun to lose their dominance. The Secondary Modern school, the College of Advanced Technology and, perhaps, the Polytechnic are all monuments to the failure of repeated efforts to develop viable alternatives to the Grammar school and the University. In one respect, the development of English education since the early twentieth century may be interpreted as a long drawn out crisis. This crisis has occurred in a system whose response to the onset of universal secondary schooling and a greatly expanded tertiary sector has been to offer to an increasing number of students a rapidly ossifying tradition for which no convincing substitute has yet been found.[43]

Notes

I would like to thank Earl Hopper (L.S.E.), Professor I. Neustadt and Dr. Olive Banks (University of Leicester) for their comments on earlier drafts of this paper.

1. Not all institutions described as 'schools' have been primarily concerned with education in the sense of the transmission of knowledge. A distinction may be made between a transmission function and a custodial function (as exemplified by the Workhouse schools in mid-nineteenth century England). This latter may be closely linked with the manipulation of the custodial relationship in order to exploit the labour of those under tutelage (as in the early Spinning schools and Schools of Industry). In such cases, the transmission of knowledge may have a low priority in the institutions concerned. The original statement may be modified in another way. The process of knowledge transmission is often closely associated with the task of monitoring the student population in order to identify skills, apply criteria of categorisation, assess what has been learnt, and certify different kinds and levels of trained competence. In some respects, for example occupational recruitment, students may be more immediately and indirectly affected by the consequences of this monitoring process than by the content transmitted within the educational system. To summarise, the transmission function may be supplemented by a number of others.; the monitoring, the custodial, and, occasionally, the exploitative.

2. A significant factor is the presence of stratifying principles built into the organisation of knowledge within a particular society. For example, a number of dichotomies appear and re-appear within the English education system: between the academic and the vocational; theory and practice; humane and technical; generalist and specialist; amateur and professional; classical and modern: and so on. The persisting assumption has been that the type of knowledge characterised by the first term in each of these dichotomies is more worthy and prestigious than the type of knowledge characterised by the second term. Such dichotomies are relevant in other ways also. Not only do they provide criteria of stratification applicable to categories of knowledge and the institutions which embody them, but also they contain two other assumptions: first, that activities and disciplines which are academic, theoretical, humane, generalist, amateur and classical should be segregated from those which are vocational, practical, technical, specialist, professional and modern; second, that the higher the social group is located in the social order, the more likely it is to have access to the former kind of knowledge and the less likely it is to be acquainted with the latter—so that there is a tendency for lines of cultural and social stratification to run parallel. Where this situation pertains within an education system categories of students and curricular content are likely to be matched across by implicit reference to these parallel systems of stratification.

3. A distinction must be made between two types of ideology or two aspects of ideologies. An ideology has a *legitimising* function in so far as it justifies particular institutional patterns by reference to goals, values, and other legitimising symbols.

At another level, principles of organisation which 'should' be manifest in particular institutions may be specified by *ideologies of implementation*. This distinction between ideologies of legitimisation and ideologies of implementation must be supplemented by another, that between the principles of organisation which are believed or intended to be manifest in institutions and those which are embodied in practice. These distinctions are made by Earl Hopper in his article entitled 'A Typology for the Classification of Educational Systems', *Sociology*, 2, 1968, pp. 29–46.

4. The danger entailed in challenging dominant legitimising ideologies—however far divorced from reality they might be—is demonstated by the recent experience of Michael Huberman. In a brochure entitled *'Reflections on the Democratisation of Secondary and Higher Education'* (UNESCO. 1970), Huberman challenged the assumption that a significant contribution is made by education systems (as at present organised) to democratisation or economic growth. All but a few copies of his brochure were ordered to be destroyed by the UNESCO establishment. See, for example, *The Times Educational Supplement*, 21.8.70.

5. The ascription of goals to controlling groups is a diflcult task once the decision is taken not to treat explicit statements of goals at their face value. Tentative conclusions may emerge after careful analysis of specific policy decisions and their implementation, consideration of the location of the group within the social structure, and the study of evidence with respect to the group's perception of itself, its relationship to other social groups, and its interests in various spheres of social life, and so on.

6. Hopper, op. cit., p. 36.

7. op. cit., pp. 31 and 34.

8. See, for example, the Report of the Committee of the Secondary Schools Examination Council on Curriculum and Examinations in Secondary schools, 1943. The relevant extracts are quoted in J. Stuart Maclure, *Educational Documents, England and Wales, 1828–1967*, London, Chapman & Hall, 1965, pp. 201–3. The very lack of 'parity of esteem' awarded Modern schools in the years after the 1944 Education Act is a good example of the gap that may exist between an ideology of implementation and the actual situation. Another example of an ideology of implementation may be found in the Report of the Schools Inquiry of 1868, which distinguished between three 'gradations of society'. The first consisted of 'men with considerable incomes independent of their own exertions', professional men, and those less well-off, 'who, having received a cultivated education themselves, are anxious that their sons should not fall below them'. The second consisted of the 'larger shopkeepers, rising men of business, and the larger tenant farmers'. The third was 'distinctly lower in the scale' and included the 'smaller tenant farmers, the small tradesmen, the superior artisans'. Three grades of school were recommended, corresponding with each of the above. The first retained classics as the staple of the curriculum, adding some mathematics, modern languages and natural science. The second grade would concentrate upon 'those subjects which can be turned to practical use in business'. The third grade was to provide 'very good reading, very good writing, very good arithmetic'. Quoted in J. Stuart Maclure, op. cit., pp. 93–5.

9. For example, are 'classical' subjects restricted to students in certain status categories? Is it assumed that certain levels of intelligence are best fitted for training in 'practical' subjects? Are all categories of student given some training in common followed by later specialisation or is the degree of overlap minimal? Alternatively, are students distinguished from each other in terms of the degree of progress they make along a common path of learning (perhaps distinguished by the length of their educational routes or the intellectual pitch at which trans-

mission takes place) rather than by the different spheres of learning to which they have been introduced?

10. For example, are different elements of curricular content taught separately and at different times with no attempt to relate them to each other? Or is an attempt made systematically to relate them through 'inter-disciplinary studies', 'mixed curricula' and an absence of time-based segregation? To use terms developed by Bernstein, is the curriculum nearer to the 'collection' type—in which subject boundaries are clearly defined and perform an insulating function—or the 'integrated' type—in which subject boundaries are blurred and indistinct, their contents having an 'open' relationship to each other? Where there is segregation of elements of curricular content, does this extend to the development of separate educational institutions for different kinds of curricula (such as 'technical' subjects) or is it restricted to segregation within a comprehensive institution? Similar questions may be asked of the different categories of students. During the process of transmission are they physically segregated through 'streaming' or are there, for example, mixed ability groups catering for students in several intellectual categories? Where there is segregation of student categories, does this extend to the development of separate institutions for different sorts of students or is it, again, simply segregation within a comprehensive institution? (c.f. B. Bernstein, 'On the Classification and Framing of Educational Knowledge', Chapter 9, op. cit.).

11. A distinction may be made between cases where the division of control falls *between* educational institutions and cases where such division occurs with respect to complementary processes *within* a particular institution. In the latter case, one administrative agency may control selection procedures, another curricular organisation, yet another may be responsible for certification. Where these agencies enforce contradictory policies, a form of conflict is generated within the institution. (The selection process may divide students into academic and non-academic; a school assigned the task of teaching non-academic students may introduce an academic curriculum which it attempts to teach in a manner which is then frustrated by the demands of the examination system; and so on.) Where division of control falls between rather than within educational institutions, the consequences of contradictory modes of implementing the transmission process differ according to whether or not the institutions concerned transfer students to each other to a significant extent. When such transferences do take place on a wide scale between institutions belonging to the same route (e.g. Grammar schools and Universities) then the consequence may be a form of malintegration within the route. For example, Grammar school sixth forms may produce a high proportion of students with specialised knowledge in 'Arts' subjects, whereas Universities may have a high proportion of places for Science students with a 'good general knowledge'.

12. To the extent that consensus exists among agencies with respect to implementation, the education system as a whole is likely to manifest what the Bryce Commission described as 'organic . . . coherence' (see note 22). In societies whose early education development was characterised by a series of independent local initiatives, two kinds of change are likely to result from a decline in local autonomy. Education institutions which previously belonged to parallel routes may be placed 'end on' as different stages of the same route. Institutions which previously had a separate existence may be reorganised into new 'comprehensive' institutions. The English system yields clear examples of both processes. 'Elementary' and 'Secondary' schools were, until the 1920s, parallel routes through the education system. The Hadow Reorganisation re-defined this dichotomy as 'Primary' and 'Post-primary', two stages which the 1944 Act renamed 'Primary'

and 'Secondary'. One consequence of such changes was to increase the extent
to which the system was 'at risk' from malintegration. The second process has
had more dramatic results, transforming inconsistencies into sources of active
conflict. The Comprehensive reorganisation and the establishment of the new
Polytechnics have sown fertile seeds of discord. Many Comprehensive schools
are amalgrams of Modern and Grammar schools, bringing together staff socialised within the traditions peculiar to each. Similarly, Colleges of Technology,
Commerce, Art, Design and Education are some of the extremely diverse
building blocks from which the Polytechnics are being built. Powerful residual
traditions are being thrust together. Proponents of each are likely to make strong
efforts to preserve their vested interests. The early nineteen-seventies will witness
a continuing struggle among these groups to enforce their own difinitions of the
transmission process within these new institutions.

13. T. Burgess and J. Pratt, *Policy and Practice: The Colleges of Advanced
Technology*, London, Allen Lane, The Penguin Press, 1970.

14. op. cit., pp. 158–9.

15. See note 3.

16. Burgess & Pratt, op. cit., p. xiv.

17. op. cit., pp. 17–18.

18. op. cit., Chapter 8, passim.

19. P. W. Musgrave, 'A Model for the Analysis of the Development of the
English Educational System from 1860', *Transactions of the Sixth World Congress
of Sociology*, Vol. IV, pp. 65–82, 1970. Reprinted in P. W. Musgrave (ed.), *Sociology History and Education*, London, Methuen, 1970. Page references are to this
version.

20. Musgrave, op. cit., pp. 16–17.

21. C. Jencks & D. Riesman, *The Academic Revolution*, New York, Doubleday
& Co., 1968, p. 157. See chapters IV and VII–X.

22. Quoted in Maclure, op. cit., p. 147

23. op. cit. p. 206

24. Some term is necessary to refer to the power which derives from the way
in which 'social honour' is distributed within a society. Members of a status
hierarchy stand in relationships of superiority and inferiority towards each
other. In certain circumstances these may be translated into relationships of
superordination and subordination. In such cases, the authority relationship
is validated by reference to the status hierarchy. The term 'diffuse' was chosen
because the form of power being described derives from the fact that, as Hopper
states, '(a) society has a system of ascribed statuses on the basis of which certain
diffuse skills and ascribed characteristics are likely to become unequally distributed' (op. cit. p. 36). Occupants of certain status positions are able to exercise
authority because they are recognised to possess these 'diffuse skills' and 'ascribed
characteristics'. The term 'diffuse' also distinguishes this generalised form of
authority which is effective in a wide range of social situations from professional
authority which may only be exercised in a few highly specific spheres. Needless
to say, the term 'diffuse' does not imply a weak form of power.

25. On the Inspectorate, see E. L. Edmonds, *The School Inspector*, London,
Routledge 1962. After 1846, a substantial proportion of the entrants to teacher
training colleges were financed through Queen's Scholarships awarded on the
basis of an annual examination of pupil-teachers conducted by the Inspectorate.
The Inspectorate was also heavily involved in the organisation of examinations
at the end of the training courses.

26. T. J. Burgess, *Enterprise in Education*, Nat. Soc. & S.P.C.K., 1958.

27. See, for example, T. W. Bamford, *The Rise of the Public Schools*, London,

Nelson, 1967, F. J. C. Harrison, *Living and Learning*, London, Routledge, 1950, W. H. G. Armitage, *The Civic Universities*, London, Ernest Benn, 1955, Mary Sturt, *The Education of the People*, London, Routledge, 1967.

28. Basic information on the French and American systems has been culled from W. D. Halls, *Society, Schools and Progress in France*, Oxford, Pergamon, 1965. W. W. Brickman, *Education Systems in the United States,* New York, Centre for Applied Research in Education, 1964, Jencks & Riesman, op. cit., and W. R. Fraser, *Education and Society in Modern France*, London, Routledge, 1963.

29. P. H. J. H. Gosden, *The Development of Educational Administration in England and Wales*, Oxford, Blackwell, 1966, p. 55.

30. The issues raised by the Ocean Hill–Brownsville School controversy are discussed in M. Gittel & A. G. Helvesi (eds.), *The Politics of Urban Education*, New York, Praeger, 1969.

31. cf. George Baron & Asher Tropp, 'Teachers in England and America', in A. H. Halsey, J. Floud & C. A. Anderson, *Education, Economy and Society*, London, Collier-Macmillan, 1961, pp. 545–557.

32. The 'Godless institution in Gower Street' was founded in 1827 to break the Anglican monopoly over the English universities.

33. Quoted in Mary Sturt, op. cit., p. 2.

34. The guiding principles of the Revised Code were: a single capitation grant would be calculated on the basis of average attendance and each child's performance when examined by the Inspector in the three Rs. This would be the only grant. It would be paid direct to the managers who fixed the salary of the teacher themselves. 'If the schools are expensive, they will be efficient, and if they are not efficient they will be cheap.' (Robert Lowe, introducing the Revised Code in the House of Commons.)

35. *First Annual Report*, National Society, 1812, p. 19.

36. *Hansard*, CXLI, 804.

37. Quoted in R. J. Montgomery's *Examinations: an account of their evolution as administrative devices in England*, London, Longmans, 1965, p. 24.

38. Quoted in Mary Sturt, op. cit., p. 25.

39. Established in 1853, the object of the Department of Science and Art was 'to extend a system of encouragement to local institutions for Practical Science'. A 'payment by results' scheme of grant aid developed, grant awards being contingent upon examination successes. See Gosden, op. cit., Ch. 3.

40. The Crowther Report (*15 to 18*), London, H.M.S.O., 1959, p, 450.

41. Maclure, op. cit., p. 159.

42. op. cit., p. 159. cf. note 35.

43. The following description of the Secondary Modern school is a study in calculated vagueness: 'The majority will do best in a school which provides a good all-round education in an atmosphere which enables them to develop freely along their own lines. Such a school will give them a chance to sample a variety of "subjects" and skills and to pursue those which interest them most.' *The New Secondary Education*, London, H.M.S.O., 1947.

THEORETICAL ADVANCE AND

EMPIRICAL CHALLENGE

A. H. Halsey

This volume of readings represents the notable achievements of students of the sociology of education during the past decade. It can be 'placed' in the literature as the descendant of a similar compilation which appeared in 1961 under the title of *Education, Economy and Society*.[1] On that basis three things strike me; there has been impressive theoretical advance, an old definition has been sharpened and refreshed especially by Bernstein, and a programme of empirical validation is now the most urgent task. In this concluding essay I will try to illustrate and comment on these three main reactions to the foregoing chapters.

Section 1   Theoretical Advance

One direction of theoretical advance concerns the articulation of educational systems with the stratification systems of contemporary societies. It is perhaps a measure of the progress made that only two essays, those by T. H. Marshall and R. H. Turner, have survived from the earlier collection. It is also, perhaps, a measure of the tremendous recent preoccupation with the theoretical status of the subject that no empirical studies testing the theoretical prescriptions made by the authors are included. The essays are dominantly heuristic; field enquiries have yet to prove the value of the tools which have been fashioned by recent theorising. The two earlier essays have formed the basis for the cumulative refinement of a

1. A. H. Halsey, J. E. Floud and C. A. Anderson (Eds), *Education, Economy and Society*, Glencoe Free Press, 1961.

typology of educational systems which focuses primarily on the selective functions of education. The elaboration of the typology has been highly successful at the level of guiding comparative research between different societies. I shall want to argue, however, following Smith (Reading 7) that it needs further development as an instrument for analysing change in a given society. This I shall do in the third section of this chapter by going back to the empirical question of how the differentiated élites of Britain have been educationally and socially recruited in this century. At the same time it may be noted that the same typological theme pursued by Hopper, Davies and Smith is in effect an elaboration and illumination of the principal underlying theory of *Education, Economy and Society*, viz. the thesis of a tightening bond between education and occupation in advanced industrial societies. T. H. Marshall's essay formulates this thesis and ends by drawing attention to the conflict (which Hopper calls a dilemma) between the distributional principles of the Welfare state and the unifying principle implicit in the 'tightening bond' thesis. As Marshall puts it: 'Leadership and power are exercised from many stations in life, by politicians, judges, ecclesiastics, business men, trade unionists, intellectuals and others. If these were all selected in childhood and groomed in the same stable, we should have what Raymond Aron calls the characteristic feature of a totalitarian society—a unified *élite*.' I want to raise my empirical question in order to comment on the applicability of the Turner–Hopper typology to the 'tightening bond' thesis.

Meanwhile a second direction of theoretical advance in this volume consists in the attack by Davies (Reading 6) on the typology as a distraction from the central problems of the sociology of education. Davies caricatures the work of his predecessors as a tradition of *identifying* the sociology of education with the study of educational opportunity and as an intellectually restrictive rewriting of fundamentally new research by absorbing it into the conventional wisdom. Without for a moment denying the existence of such academic parochialism, I would claim that Davies is here over-emphasising the discontinuity of thought at the expense of its no less apparent continuity. His own example, Bernstein's work on the sociology of linguistics which began to appear at the end of the nineteen fifties, serves to show this double character of theoretical advance. Davies stresses that it was absorbed into established preoccupations by being interpreted as a contribution to research on stratification. But in fact the first and subsequent celebrated formulation by Bernstein[1] was

1. B. Bernstein, 'Some Sociological Determinants of Perception', *British Journal of Sociology*, 1956, vol. 9, pp. 159–174.

put forward explicitly as a contribution to understanding of the social determinants of educability. In other words, what was then termed a 'public language' was discussed with reference to its use by the unskilled and semi-skilled strata and as a barrier to ability through educational attainment. From the point of view of continuity in theoretical work it would be equally true to say that the fruitfulness of the ideas put forward at the time by Bernstein were such as to promote an integration between theories concerning the selective functions of education and the more general problems of the structure of cultural transmission.

Smith makes essentially the same point when he insists that both Hopper and Davies are concerned with the mode of articulation of the educational system with other social structures and that Davies' emphasis on what is taught (i.e. the content of cultural transmission) also raises the question of who is taught what. One must agree with Smith that 'the education system acts not only as a "selective filter" but also as a "selective distributor" of those cultural styles whose internal complexity Davies demonstrates'[1]. The reason, as Smith argues, 'for Davies' curious neglect of this central question is not difficult to see. It is a consequence of his dismissal of selection as peripheral to the education process. In fact it is central and the management of knowledge cannot be usefully discussed without taking it into account'.[2] Further advance depends on integrating theories as to how knowledge is defined with theories as to how it is socially distributed.

Section 2   Redefinition and Integration

A third and fundamental direction of theoretical advance which begins in Davies' critique of Hopper is illustrated by Bourdieu (Reading 8) and is carried furthest by the exciting exposition put forward by Bernstein (Reading 9). It is the insistence that the central substance of the sociology of education is the structure of cultural transmission. More particularly, 'how a society selects, classifies, transmits and evaluates the educational knowledge it considers public',[3] must be the central dependent variables and these, I would emphasise, are to be explained primarily in terms of the 'distribution of power and the principles of social control'.[4]

These chapters constitute an illuminating theoretical definition of

1. Smith, Reading 7.
2. ibid.
3. Bernstein, Reading 9.
4. ibid.

the essential scope and problems of the sociology of education and of its general articulation with the study of social change and social order. But again I want to argue that the apparent discontinuity of definition is not as sharp as the reader may have been led to suppose. The International Encyclopaedia of the Social Sciences tells us that 'educational systems have one universal characteristic: they transmit knowledge and belief. They consist, therefore, of a disciplined relation between teacher and taught, but they can and do vary according to what is to be taught, how, by whom, and to whom'.[1] Indeed the dissident and irreverent Victorian undergraduate who wrote

> I am the great Professor Jowett
> And what there is to know I know it.
> What I don't know isn't knowledge,
> And I am Master of this College.

can be said to have anticipated it. Moreover I shall want to argue presently that the conception of education involved, within the tradition of sociological writing, is at least as old as Max Weber.[2] Bernstein, like Davies, seems to me to overstate the case in asserting that previous British sociologists had reduced the sociology of education to a series of input and output problems and hence the study of socialisation had been 'trivialised'. There is nothing intrinsically trivial about input-output problems, and the essays by T. H. Marshall, Hopper and Smith on the selective functions of education show an impressive cumulation of theory which both owes much to an input-output or 'people-processing' approach and at the same time clarifies some of the problems relating the selection process to the power structure of industrial society.

However I would not, by labouring the point about continuity and discontinuity, wish to detract from the illuminating achievement of Bernstein's new contribution to the definition of the sociology of education. As he shows, in discussing the successful journey of an educand to the frontiers of knowledge through a specialised collection code, the frontiersman acquires a balanced identity which is conservative in its subject loyalty and yet at the same time rebellious in its awareness of the openness and permeability of knowledge. It is therefore not surprising that the style of presentation of an intel-

1. A. H. Halsey, 'Educational Organisation' in *International Encyclopaedia of the Social Sciences*, Macmillan and the Free Press, 1968, vol. 4, p. 526.
2. Consciousness of intellectual descent has perhaps been directed too much to Durkheim. He comes in for some characteristically adroit and adulatory castigation from Bourdieu (Reading 8).

lectual innovator tends to exaggerate the difference between his own and the received definitions of knowledge. Moreover, and this is the crucial point, it is sometimes necessary to rediscover what we know in order to re-invigorate it. This Bernstein has done in such a way as to give us new theoretical insight and a challenge to more fruitful empirical work. Thus, while it is true that the functions of education for economy and stratification through the selection process constitute a set of important problems for societies with a complex division of labour, it is also true that much of the literature has had little or no concern with either the content of curricula or with the pedagogical process as such. He has, with unprecedented clarity, reversed the emphasis and put what is taught at the centre of attention.

What is even more illuminating here is that the language of the educationist is translated into that of the sociologist in order to identify the social relations of education and so to lay bare the sociological problems involved in the study of the structure of cultural transmission. Curriculum, pedagogy and evaluation are thus made amenable to sociological study through the use of the concepts of classification and framing, referring respectively to the degree of boundary maintanance between the contents of the curriculum and to the degree of control exercised by teachers and pupils over the selection, organisation and pacing of the knowledge transmitted and received in pedagogical relationships. The concepts of classification and frame are of immediate relevance to a wide range of problems. Let me take a single example from the current discussion as to whether, in terms of content, mass higher education threatens standards of academic excellence. In a contribution to a recent symposium on this topic Richard Hoggart remarked 'I spent fifteen years in extra-mural work before I came to internal university teaching, and I am still surprised at the lack of respect for teaching inside. . . . Many university teachers simply disregard the problems of teaching, and assume anybody can do it just by nature.'[1] The reference, using Bernstein's concepts, is to two different types of frame where the first (extra-mural teaching) tips the balance of power in favour of the student and hence punishes poor teaching technique while the second (internal teaching) has the reverse tendency reinforced by the institutionalised career rewards of research.

Evaluation is then treated as a function of the strengths of the boundaries involved in classification and framing. Consideration of the way in which variation in the strength of classifications and

1. 'Concepts of Excellence—1969–1989', *Universities Quarterly*, 23, 3, Summer 1969, p. 275.

frames is determined then brings in the articulation of the educational system with the economic, political and social structure of society and, in particular, the distribution of power and the principles of social control. Returning to my example, it may be remarked that Bernstein's concept of evaluation enables us to translate 'excellence' into a sociological concept and thereby to explain its variations of definition in terms of the power structure into which curriculum and pedagogy are placed.

There are two points at which further theoretical development of Bernstein's scheme seems to be possible and desirable. First, the distinction between collection and integrated codes, though clearly fascinating and important in the illustration he gives it, is not so clear in its application to actual cases of curriculum. For example, in discussing the collection code he cites the example of the Oxford Human Sciences degree (in order to distinguish between a pure and an impure variety). But is not this new degree in fact an example of an integrated rather than a collection code, i.e. of a curriculum in which there is '*subordination* of previously insulated subjects or courses to some *relational* idea, which blurs the boundaries between the subjects'? And would it not be the case, again, that this new degree would illustrate the second of Bernstein's two types of inte-gration—the one which is *teachers*-based? More generally it may be asked whether the distinction between collection and integration is not too sharply drawn in the sense that the blurring of classifi-cation boundaries may proceed over time from one collection to another through intermediary phases of integration.

The other point refers to my remark about Weber. As I read Bernstein's chapter it occurred to me that, in a novel way, and with respect to a different set of problems than those tackled by Archer and Vaughan,[1] he was carrying on Weber's discussion of a typology of educational systems. Weber was applying the concepts of charisma and bureaucracy to the social roles of the Chinese literati. His principal reference was to the aims and functions of whole systems of education rather than to the differentiation of functions of parti-cular organisations within them. His attention was, moreover, largely confined to those forms of education aimed at producing members of the élite and thus, unlike Bernstein, he had little or nothing to say about modern mass education. What is common however between the two writers is a concern to relate the content of education to the power structure of society. From the point of view of élite recruitment Weber distinguished three broad types of social personality (the charismatic, that of the cultivated man, and

1. See above, Reading 3.

the expert) corresponding to three types of power and authority in society.[1] The first is that of the charismatic leader whose personal gift or mission is magically or divinely inspired. The second includes a wide range of forms of authority sanctioned by custom and tradition—for example, that of the Chinese mandarins, the minority leisure class of citizens in ancient Greece or Rome, or the gentlemanly strata of eighteenth-century Europe. The third type corresponds to the racial and bureaucratic forms of authority typical of advanced industrial societies, for example, that of the special expertise of scientists and professional men. In the total range of educational systems, the first and third of Weber's types are polar opposites, and the most numerous actual examples are found within the intermediate range. In reality there are no pure cases of these types, as Weber took care to emphasise.

Strictly speaking, the qualities necessary for charismatic leadership cannot be transmitted by a system of education in the sense that this would be understood in the modern world. By definition, charisma cannot be created by any kind of education code; it is a personal gift of grace that either exists in a person or infiltrates him through magical rebirth. In contrast, the cultivation of the pupil for the style of life of a secular or religious status group is in principle possible for anyone, and this is likewise true for the type of organisation that sets out to train experts for practical usefulness in a public authority, a business enterprise, or a scientic laboratory. Although entry to either the second system (that of 'education') or the third (that of 'training') is open in principle to individuals of any social origin, the goals will nevertheless vary—in the former case, according to the idea of cultivation held by the dominant stratum; in the latter, according to the internal requirements of the expertise. Thus, the second type of organisation includes a wide range of actual educational goals. The goal may be the production of a socially distinctive type of knight or courtier, as in the case of the Japanese samurai; it may be the education of a scribe or intellectual, where a priestly class is dominant; or it may be the amateur gentlemanly administrator, as in imperial Britain. Classification and framing would vary accordingly and be determined by different principles of social control in each case. Systems of education for membership in a cultivated status group have usually been under religious control. This is true of the Christian, Islamic, and Judaic traditions, but the Chinese literati and the Hellenic philosophers' schools are important exceptions. The education of the Chinese mandarin,

1. This and the following three paragraphs are taken from A. H. Halsey (1968), loc. cit., p. 527.

although based on sacred texts, consisted in laymen teaching laymen, and the Hellenic schools were completely secular and designed for the education of a leisured ruling class.

The characteristic mark of the type of education that aims at imparting specialised expert training is the standardised examination system. In Bernstein's terms it is distinguished by the mode and strength of its evaluation. This is not to say that examination systems are either indispensable to beaureaucratic forms of authority or unknown to prebureaucratic systems. For example, the special examination system came late to the French, English, and American bureaucracies whereas classical China for many centuries enjoyed a politically organised examination system for official careers. However, the Chinese system was not designed to examine special skills but rather to ensure that successful candidates were broadly equipped with the high culture of the literati. In the case of the modern bureaucracies, qualifications for entry are increasingly defined in terms of specialised scientific and technological training, at the expense of wide humanistic cultivation. As Weber put it: 'Behind all the present discussions of the foundations of the educational system, the struggle of the "specialist type of man" against the older type of "cultivated man" is hidden at some decisive point. This fight is determined by the irresistibly expanding bureaucratisation of all public and private relations of authority and by the ever-increasing importance of expert and specialised knowledge'.[1] The question raised by Bernstein's approach is whether this struggle is systematically related to classification and framing and particularly whether certain kinds of modern expertise require integrated instead of collection codes.

More generally it would be illuminating to have an integration between Bernstein's discussion of classification and frames and the process of formation of social personalities discussed by Weber. It may be for example that collection codes contribute to the maintenance of educational systems which aim at producing the cultivated man while integrated codes are increasingly called for in those societies where education is aimed on the one hand at non-vocational pedagogy for the masses and on the other hand at recruitment to professionalised sectors of the élite whose functions are to manage change and to pursue new knowlege or its applications through research.

However, whatever further developments of Bernstein's theoretical

1. Max Weber, from *Max Weber's Essays in Sociology*, translated and edited by Hans H. Gerth and C. Wright Mills, New York, Oxford University Press, 1946, p. 243. For an extension and application of Weber's approach see A. H. Halsey and Martin Trow, *The British Academics*, Faber, London, 1971.

scheme may be expected, his illustrative discussion of the English and European forms of the collection code make it clear that his theoretical approach shares with the education-stratification typology derived from Turner a capacity to guide the hitherto nebulous field of comparative education. Both approaches promise to formulate sharp hypotheses which would replace the commonsensical botanising comparisons of so-called comparative education with clear prescription of the relevant data to be collected in empirical enquiry.

Bernstein's theory also has a feature lacked by the Turner–Hopper typologies: it presents us with a paradigm for the analysis of particular educational organisations or micro-analysis whereas Turner and Hopper confine themselves to the macroscopic properties of societies and their educational systems.[1] The limitations of the Turner–Hopper theory from this point of view may be illustrated by considering the relation of particular types of school on the one hand to the function of mobility promotion and on the other hand to the function of status differentiation. Turner's theory has this macroscopic character. It begins with the proposition that the schools are partially moulded by organising norms of upward social mobility. The American system is characterised as approximating to a contest norm in which competition for social ascent is open and prolonged; the English system, by contrast, is described as approximating to a principle of sponsorship in which élite recruits (=upwardly mobile children) are selected early, segregated, 'freed from the strain of competitive struggle' . . . 'and long extended uncertainty of success'.[2]

Now, when these global characteristics are applied to the various types of schools in the two countries, the theory encounters three difficulties. First, the facts concerning the emphasis or intensity of competition do not distinguish clearly between the two countries. Thus the supposedly élite recruits of the English grammar school find themselves in a highly competitive atmosphere where every class has a rank order of pupils in every subject while the English secondary modern school is non-competitive and the American high

1. Earl Hopper has since addressed himself to this problem, particularly to the phenomenon of rejection after sponsorship (i.e. the grammar school as *also* a terminal course) in his 'Educational Systems and Selected Consequences of Patterns of Mobility and Non-mobility in Industrial Societies: a Theoretical Discussion', a paper delivered at the British Sociological Association conference of 1970, which was devoted to the sociology of education. [Reprinted as Appendix II in the present volume.]

2. R. H. Turner, 'Sponsored and Contest Mobility', *American Sociological Review*, vol. 25, no. 6.

school, like the emerging comprehensive secondary school in England, occupies an intermediate position in this respect.

The second difficulty is that the distinction between sponsorship and contest does not take account explicitly of the degree to which a given type of school discharges mobility functions as distinct from status differentiation functions. In this respect the American high school and the English grammar school stand together in contrast to the English public school and the secondary modern school.

Third, Turner insists[1] that all his statements about mobility are intended to apply to all upward mobility and not only to that which is strictly into élite groups. But in fact the higher the social destination the longer the schooling, which suggests the need to distinguish between élite and non-élite mobility through education. And this suggestion is strengthened by the further fact that the English system has traditionally been divided into two sets of schools, one (the preparatory and public schools) having little to do with mobility but much to do with élite status while the other (the state system) has much to do with mobility and little to do with the recruitment of élites, except for a tiny handful who achieve eminence in professional or public life after protracted competitive struggle through the universities and beyond. It is true of course, as Turner has noted,[2] that, since the facilitation of mobility is only one of several social functions of the school, and not the most important function in the societies in question, only a very partial account of the whole set of forces making for similarities and differences in the educational systems of the United States and England is possible. However, to overcome these difficulties and to be able to use the school as a unit of analysis, it is necessary to treat involvement with the mobility function as a separate variable. Using a dichotomy we can classify schools as follows.

Involvement with the mobility functions	Sponsorship	Contest
HIGH	GRAMMAR	AMERICAN HIGH ENGLISH COMPREHENSIVE
LOW	ENGLISH PUBLIC	SECONDARY MODERN

1. ibid., p. 856, fn. 3.
2. See his reply to my communication in the *American Sociological Review*, vol. 26, no. 3, June 1961, p. 455.

Thus it appears that both the sponsored and contest norms have two variants as reflected in school organisation. The English public school illustrates the nearest case to Turner's sponsorship in that it inducts into élite status with relatively little emphasis on competition. It emerges, however, that this is a special case occurring in those social strata where the status differentiating functions dominate over the mobility promoting functions of education. Similarly the secondary modern school performs the same function for the lower social strata. A different type of sponsorship occurs in high mobility societies in the form of the state grammar school which fits Turner's definition with regard to early selection, segregation etc. but contradicts them in exhibiting more intense and protracted competition than the American high school. Similarly, in the American high school where the folk-lore of mobility simultaneously stresses educational opportunity and the status equality of Americanisation, competition is muffled by such devices as 'cooling out' in junior colleges, as compared with the grammar school, but is more in evidence than in the English secondary modern school where the mobility contest is severely restricted to the non-élite ranges of the stratification system.

It may also be noticed that adding the variable of involvement with the mobility function enables us to distinguish between schools according to the range of statuses for which their graduates are destined. This distinction cuts across sponsorship and contest so as to group grammar with high school as preparatory institutions for a wide range of strata by contrast with public and modern schools which serve a narrow band of statuses.

This illustration must serve to show the complexity of a typology which would be adequate for microscopic as well as macroscopic analysis on a comparative basis and even then, as Smith has shown in his comments on the Hopper typology, there would still remain problems of the applicability of such a model to a wider range of societies than those in which a formal monitoring procedure is applied to all children at a single point. As Smith shows, further refinements would be needed to include societies in which the mobility promoting functions of education are of relatively minor importance (i.e. where the bond between education and occupation is a loose one) or where education serves to put a stamp on previously established status differences (i.e. where family status determines both occupation and education).

Section 3   Empirical Work

The main task now must be to set these advances in theory to work through a programme of empirical enquiry. By way of conclusion the tasks can be illustrated with reference to the explanation of the changing pattern of recruitment to élites in twentieth-century Britain. In part, of course, the collection of relevant data has to be deduced from the theory. We can however begin with some of the facts which are already available.[1]

T. H. Marshall concludes his essay with the assertion that 'the welfare state, more than most forms of democracy, cannot tolerate a governing class'.[2] W. L. Guttsman's book on the British political élite appeared in 1963 in which he concluded, after a detailed historical analysis, that 'there exists today in Britain a "ruling class", if we mean by it a group which provides the majority of those who occupy positions of power, and who, in their turn, can materially assist *their* sons to reach similar positions'.[3] Guttsman was concerned primarily with the political élite (members of the government, M.Ps and active peers in the House of Lords). As to cabinet ministers, of whom there were 408 between 1895 and 1966, about 14 per cent were of working class origin—a total of 55, 54 of whom were contributed by the Labour Party and one by the Liberals.

Using a wider definition of élite status to include all the professional and managerial sectors of the occupational structure, I have put together Table 1 in order to show the amount of upward movement into the Register General's social classes I and II, i.e. roughly the amount of upward mobility into the upper and upper middle classes. It emerges from this table that about a third of the members of the elevated strata are recruited from below, though with fairly marked differences between sectors.

Thus selective processes of some kind, and ones which are of considerable quantitative moment, are involved in the recruitment of modern élites. For example, in the mid-nineteen sixties 30 per cent of the members of the administrative class of the British Civil Service were promotees in the sense of having first joined a lower division in which graduate recruitment is not normal: and over half of these had been recruited initially into the clerical or sub-clerical classes. Marshall's question however was whether there was

1. I rely for the most part of what follows on data from A. H. Halsey and Ivor Crewe, *Social Survey of the Civil Service* (Evidence submitted to the committee under the chairmanship of Lord Fulton 1966–68, vol. 3(1)), HMSO, 1969.
2. See Reading 2, above.
3. W. L. Guttsman, *The British Political Elite*, Basic Books, 1963, p. 356.

Table 1[1]
Mobility into Elite Status in Britain

Class Origin	Business men		Administrative Civil Servants	Scientists (Civil Servants)	University teachers	British population in social class I & II
	Top Managers (1954–55)	Directors (1965)	(1966)	(1966)	(1966)	(1949)
Upper and middle (RG classes I & II)	72	50	79	54	60	67
Lower middle and working (RG classes III, IV and V)	28	50	21	46	40	33
Total	100	100	100	100	100	100
(N)	(182)	(2378)	(571)	(403)	(1401)	(91)

1 For sources see A. H. Halsey and Ivor Crewe, op. cit., Table 3. 22, p. 58

an increasing tendency for élites to be selected early and 'groomed in the same stable'—two factors which appear as dimensions of Hopper's typology. If therefore we look at trends we can also throw light on the adequacy of Hopper's characterisation of the English educational system as

(1) moderately centralised and standardised in its total selection process;

(2) marked by early formal differentiation and specialisation of educational roots;

(3) collectivistic in that the norms which are appealed to justify selection in terms of 'the society's "need" for people with diffuse skills and certain ascribed characteristics in order that the society may be led by the most "suitable" people';

(4) particularistic in that the relevant norms stress selection based 'primarily' on the possession of diffuse skills and only secondarily on the possession of technical skills, so that those with most of the former need have least of the latter.

(5) (combining 3 and 4) paternalistic, i.e. a collectivistic form of particularism.[1]

Trends in the recruitment of the political élite are clear enough. Among the Conservatives the proportion recruited from the public schools has risen from two-thirds at the beginning of the century to 80 per cent in 1966 and the proportion who received a university education has risen from just over a half to 67 per cent. What however is even more indicative of the unification of the political élite and its separation from the educational experience of the mass is that, whereas in 1906 no Labour members had attended either public schools or universities, by 1966 the figures were respectively 18 per cent and 51 per cent. Thus, in respect of this important section of the élite, it is clear that an increasingly common educational background has evolved during the course of the century; but it is also clear that the role of the public schools increased in the first half of the century in such a way as to lead us to expect that, on that evidence alone, the English educational system would be classified by Hopper as dominated by an aristocratic rather than a paternalistic ideology of legitimation (i.e. one 'where particularistic selections are justified to the population in terms of the right of those selected to privilege on the basis of their diffuse skills and ascribed characteristics'[2]).

Further comparisons of different sections of the élite strata from the point of view of their educational and non-educational routes

1. See Reading 5 above.
2. ibid.

into occupational positions suggest more and more strongly that typologies which treat each system as either homogeneous or dominated by a unique set of structural features and ideology are inadequate. The basic reason for this is precisely that the character of élites in advanced industrial countries tends increasingly towards differentiation in ways which reflect the struggles of transition referred to in Weber's original analysis and which can only be satisfactorily dealt with by the type of theory put forward by Bernstein which, as I noted earlier, makes it possible to distinguish between units within the system as a whole.

This argument can be illustrated by comparing the educational backgrounds of the administrative and non-administrative recruits to the Higher Civil Service, managers in industry and university teachers.[1] The administrative class is more exclusively educated than either the scientific officer class although less so than the legal class. Fifty-six per cent of the administrative class were educated in the private sector (i.e. direct grant, public and other fee-paying schools) compared with 36 per cent of the scientific officer class but as many as 67 per cent of the legal class. As far as university education is concerned the contrast between the administrative and legal classes on the one hand and the scientific officer class on the other is most striking. While two-thirds of graduates in the administrative class come from Oxford or Cambridge, only 17 per cent of the scientific officer class graduates are from these two universities. The great majority of the graduates in the scientific officer class (69 per cent) come from the universities of London, the English provinces, Wales and Scotland compared with only 26 per cent in the administrative class.

A comparison with university teaching staffs indicates that the administrative class is recruiting disproportionately from middle class graduates. Seventy-nine per cent of direct entrants to the administrative class were born into social classes I and II compared with 60 per cent of all university teachers and as against 59 per cent of students graduating in 1961–62. This comparison with university teachers is particularly worth emphasising since both the administrative class and the universities seek to attract those with high academic qualifications. Both, therefore, recruit from the same university undergraduate populations. Yet while university teachers (both in Arts and Social Science faculties and also as a whole) fairly precisely reflect the social and educational composition of the undergraduate body from which they are drawn, the administrative class is much

1. The figures refer to 1965–66. Details may be found in A. H. Halsey and I. Crewe, op. cit., Chs. 3 and 13.

more predominantly middle class. In this connection it is worth pointing out that there is *not* a similar contrast between university teachers in Science faculties and graduates directly recruited into the scientific officer class. In the scientific officer class the members very closely resemble in terms of social composition both ithe university teachers in science and also the undergraduate body from which they are drawn. Moreover, it may be added to this general contrast that there are only negligible differences in the social backgrounds of Arts and Science students in the universities.

The exclusive educational background of members of the administrative class (compared with the scientific officer class) is further underlined in comparison with British industry and the professions. Greater proportions of graduates in Local Education Authorities, the management of large industrial organisations and university teaching have been educated at LEA maintained schools than their administrative class counterparts. There is a similar contrast as far as university education is concerned. Large industrial concerns and university Arts and Social Science departments recruit a significantly larger proportion of graduates from London, the Welsh, Scottish and English provincial universities than does the administrative class.

The type of university curriculum followed by graduate recruits to the administrative class may also be compared with foreign experience and with the British business and professional groups referred to above. The great majority of graduates in the administrative class have taken their degrees in the Arts or Humanities (71 per cent), mainly in History or Classics; just over a quarter come from the Social Sciences; about one in ten studied a Natural Science and only a negligible proportion graduated in Applied Science. This is in sharp contrast with the United States and France. In the United States only a small proportion are Arts graduates—the rest come in from the Social Sciences and Natural Applied Science. In France, the counterparts of the administrative class are graduates of the Ecole Nationale d'Administration where they have had a general education in the Social Sciences (Economics, Law, Public Administration, Finance, Statistics, etc.) preceded by a two-year period in one of the Ecole Politiques. Again comparison with British industry and local government suggests that the top men in industry and important officials in local government, with whom members of the administrative class will probably deal, are more likely, if graduates, to have had some kind of social-scientific education.

This picture of social and educational routes into the administrative élite may also be traced over time. The main trend in the recruitment of direct entrants to the administrative class from before the war and up to the mid-sixties was contrary to what has sometimes been assumed: it was not towards recruiting from a steadily widening social background. Overall, it was static. For a number of years, indeed, in the nineteen fifties and early nineteen sixties the trend, against a background of educational democratisation and expansion in the system as a whole, was towards an increase in the proportion of direct entrants from the middle classes (i.e. social classes I and II) whereas, over the same period, there was a steady decrease in the proportion recruited to the scientific officer class and into university teaching.

The trends in educational recruitment have had similar tendencies. Considering the gradual rise in the number of children from LEA grammar schools going to universities, it is remarkable that there was no significant increase until 1966 in the proportion of recruits educated in the public sector among direct entrants to the administrative class. The proportion from LEA grammar schools entering between 1961 and 1966 (29 per cent) was the same as for the surviving members established before the war (28 per cent) and considerably less than among wartime direct entrants (46 per cent). In fact in the period 1961–66 the proportion of direct entrants from public and other fee-paying schools actually increased compared with the period 1951–60 (i.e. from 46 per cent to 50 per cent); and if we add those from the direct grant schools we find that the administrative class has throughout the nineteen fifties and the first half of the nineteen sixties been receiving a relatively high and stable proportion of direct entrants with a 'privileged' education. However, more recently and particularly in 1967 there has been a significant increase in the proportion of direct entrants recruited from the state sector (44 per cent in 1967 compared with 28 per cent in 1961–65).

At the university stage, too, the trend in recruitment has not matched the post-war pattern of graduate output. There was a slight fall in the proportion of Oxford and Cambridge graduates directly recruited to the class between the nineteen fifties and the period 1961–66, but the figure for the latter period (73 per cent) is nearly the same as that for the immediate post-war period and considerably higher than during the war. By contrast, the proportion of all students graduating from Oxford and Cambridge declined from 22 per cent in 1938–39 to 14 per cent in 1963–64. However, in 1966–67 Oxford and Cambridge direct entrants went down to 66 per cent compared with 85 per cent for the period 1957–63.

Moreover, the trend in the type of subjects studied by graduate recruits has also been surprising. Between 1940 and 1960 the proportionate recruitment of Arts graduates was increasing and of Natural and Applied Science students decreasing; in the nineteen fifties the proportion of the Social Science students also decreased. Though both these tendencies were reversed in the nineteen sixties, the fact remains that whereas the proportion of all undergraduates taking a Natural or Applied Science degree at British universities had increased considerably from just before the war to 1963–64 (26 per cent to 41 per cent) there was no change in the relative number of Natural and Applied Science graduates taken into the administrative class in the same period (13 per cent to 12 per cent).

These trends in the school and university background of direct recruits to the administrative class are in marked contrast to the post-war trends in the recruitment of university staff, graduates in local government and graduates in business. They are all the more remarkable when set against the corresponding patterns in direct recruitment of the scientific officer class. For the latter class the trends have been away from public and direct grant schools and from Oxford and Cambridge towards the State schools and the Scottish, Commonwealth and English provincial universities. Thus, for example, of graduates recruited directly to the scientific officer class before the war 31 per cent came from Oxford and Cambridge compared with 9 per cent during the nineteen fifties.

One further aspect of selection may be mentioned. Although over half the graduates in the administrative and scientific officer classes hold first or upper second class degrees there appears to have been in both classes a substantial post-war decline in the quality of their direct recruits as judged by class of degree. The proportion of firsts directly recruited to the administrative class in the period 1961–66 was about a fifth of that before the war (13 per cent compared with 3 per cent) and a substantial drop from the nineteen fifties when the proportion was 31 per cent. In the scientific officer class the decline appears to have been smaller. The proportion with firsts directly recruited to that class in the nineteen sixties is about two-thirds of that before the war (37 per cent compared with 59 per cent); and the figure of 37 per cent in the nineteen sixties represents virtually no change from the nineteen fifties when it was 36 per cent.

What can be said then about these trends in educational selection and routing into different sectors of the élite strata? The case of the administrative class seems to reveal a fundamental shift in the pattern of élite recruitment. There has been a fall in quality as judged by class of degree, a continuing predominance of Arts graduates and continuing near monopoly of Oxford and Cambridge even though the output of high quality graduates has not fallen while the proportion of Arts graduates and Oxbridge graduates has fallen markedly. Part of the answer presumably lies in the expansion of science and the attraction into university science courses of increasing numbers of talented young men and women. This raises the question of whether the traditional definition of the ideal recruit into the administrative class, reflecting an ideology of diffuse skills and ascriptive qualities (i.e. the Oxford graduate in Classics or History) has not forced the recruitment of this sector of the élite on to a narrower social base. It is perhaps not so much an explicit definition on the part of the Civil Service Commissioners of the need for 'the cultivated man' as a conception among students of their own suitability, their chances of succeeding in the competition and the expansion of other opportunities for graduates in the world of the 'expert' which reduced the potential number of applicants. The application rate to the administrative Civil Service outside the Arts, and more especially outside Oxford and Cambridge, is accordingly low. Moreover, this question raises not only the further question of what criteria enter into the evaluation of the educational background of candidates for the administrative class but also that of the relation between the administrative class and the other graduate classes, especially the scientific officer class.

Meanwhile, at least until the late nineteen sixties, recruitment to the administrative class continued to be dominated by Oxford and Cambridge and the schools from which they had traditionally recruited. The main bulk of applicants have been largely men who have read the traditional Arts subjects. Yet it is precisely among men reading the Arts that the relative decline in the arithmetic importance of Oxford and Cambridge has been least marked over the past twenty years; it may even have been reversed, at least in respect of the most able students. Thus, in very recent years particularly, Oxford and Cambridge have become more selective and have drawn students from a wider range of schools, increasingly including the maintained grammar schools. At the same time, there has been a relatively dwindling interest in classics among school leavers and the concentration in Oxford and Cambridge of those who have reached the requisite standard in Latin and Greek. The number of male honours students in Classics in the redbrick and new universities in England is tiny. Classics is admittedly the most extreme case: but for men somewhat similar trends may be observed in History, English and Modern Languages. Moreover, the restricted number of places for women in Oxford and Cambridge has tended to raise the relative number of women in these subjects in the modern universities.

The survey material on which I am relying here does not enable us to establish the validity of this interpretation which requires further research. But it seems likely that despite policy intentions in the opposite direction recruits in the administrative class have come increasingly from Oxford and Cambridge and from the middle classes. This is explained by the development of the graduate market on the one hand and the place of Oxford and Cambridge in an expanding system of higher education on the other; a high proportion of the most talented Arts men have been drawn into the older universities while growth in science and technology from which the administrative class does not draw its recruits has been relatively great outside Oxford and Cambridge. In this way the differentiation of the educational system in a changing society has created a crisis in recruitment to a section of the élite strata, seriously loosening its traditional grip on the flow of high talent from the educational system. In terms of Hopper's typology the traditional flow must presumably be characterised in terms of the persistence of an aristocratic or a paternalistic ideology while developments in the expanding educational system have tended to adapt themselves to the more meritocratic requirements of the scientific and academic sectors of the élite. In terms of Bernstein's theory it suggests that the function of evaluation and recruitment may be determinant of as well as interactive with, rather than dependent on, the strength of classification and framing.

Appendices

The sociological perspective concerning education in industrial societies is often limited to the study of either the selection and allocation of personnel or the moulding of consciousness and sensibility or, at best, to the study of both. The sociology of education has concentrated on social problems of the welfare state which might be ameliorated by manipulating the structure of the educational system, such as inequalities of opportunity or the retarded development of a qualified technical élite. More recently it has begun to consider those aspects of childhood and adolescent socialization which are best understood in terms of the formal and informal management of knowledge. There has been a shift in emphasis to problems concerning the relationships between the political system and the institutions of education, such as the interpersonal politics of instruction or the development of curricula. Thus far, however, few sociologists have seen the educational system either as a mirror of the society which reflects the most fundamental properties of its social organization and process, or as an arena within which competing groups try to resolve its basic structural dilemmas.

Appendix I is an extract from the late Professor Jules Henry's 'A Cross-Cultural Outline of Education'. The outline of topics and problems suggests the potential scope and depth of a mature sociology of education. It also indicates some neglected areas of inquiry which are crucial for the development of the discipline. Although the outline provides few answers, Professor Henry asks many questions which might be considered at various levels of analysis for societies at different degrees of complexity. Inherent in his anthropological perspective are the kinds of questions which are usually asked about societies other than our own.

Appendix II is a version of a paper presented to the British Sociological Association in April 1970. It offers some preliminary considerations of problems which must be faced by those interested in the comparative study of social mobility in industrial societies. Whereas Professor Henry shows that a study of educational institutions will lead to a more comprehensive understanding of the society, it is argued in Appendix II that a study of basic societal processes requires the prior knowledge of how a society attempts to solve its educational tasks. It also tries to demonstrate three principles of analysis: that a systems perspective is axiomatic to sociological inquiry; that the sociological perspective need not exclude a concern with properties of personality; and that in answer to specific sociological questions, holistic and action perspectives need not be antithetic.

E.H.

Appendix I

A CROSS-CULTURAL OUTLINE OF EDUCATION*

Jules Henry

I. On what does the educational
process focus?

    1. Environment (other than
        human)
        1. Flora
        2. Fauna
        3. Climate
        4. Geographical features
        5. Anthropomorphized flora
        6. Anthropomorphized
           fauna
        7. Anthropomorphized or
           zoomorphized
           machines
        8. Anthropomorphized or
           zoomorphized natural
           phenomena other
           than flora or fauna
           (winds, rivers,
           mountains, etc.)
        9. Space
      10. Time
      11. Motion
      12. Space-time-motion
      13. The world view of the
           culture
        1. Isolate-static
        2. Communicate-changing

        1. Engulfing
      3. Hostile or pacific
        1. Hostile
        2. Pacific
        3. Selectively hostile or
           pacific
      4. Geographical position
           of places studied
        1. Near: own town,
           state or pro-
           vince, village,
           tribe
        2. Near-distant: other
           states or pro-
           vinces, nation
           in general;
           other villages or
           tribes
        3. Distant: other lands
      5. Temporal position
        1. Immediate
        2. Contemporary
        3. Near past
        4. Distant past
        5. Mythological past
      14. Clothing
      15. Food
      16. Transportation and
           communication

* This Reading is an extract from an article first published in *Current Anthropology,* col.1, no.4, July 1960.

2a. Values
1. Good and bad: moral rules
2. Work, success, failure
3. Being on time
4. Culture
5. Proper dress
6. Strength, activity, power
7. Beating the game
8. Politeness, tact
9. Cooperation, helpfulness, togetherness
10. Patriotism
11. Cleanliness, orderliness
12. Thrift, saving, don't waste
13. Parents are good
14. Prettiness, beauty
15. Love
16. Mother, motherhood
17. Happiness
18. Competiveness
19. Equality
20. Novelty, excitement
21. Pride
22. Knowledge as value
23. The 'beautiful person'
24. Private property
25. Democracy
26. Family
27. Responsibility
28. Generosity, doing more than required, non-commercialism
29. The state
30. Deference
31. Enlightened self-interest
32. Independence, toughness
33. Physical intactness
34. Sense of emergency
35. Constancy
36. Solicitude for others, kindness
37. Composure under stress
38. Courage
39. Knowledge as means to an end
40. Compromise
41. Fun, relaxation
42. Friends, friendship, faithfulness
43. Fairness
44. Flattery, empty praise
45. Honor (integrity), personal autonomy
46. Self-restraint
47. Trying hard, don't give up
48. Fame, ambition
49. Honesty
50. Prestige
51. Niceness, likeableness
52. Respect for authority
53. Excitement
54. Gentleness, non-violence
55. Speed, alertness
56. Sacredness, etc., of parents
57. Flexibility
58. Modesty
59. Tolerance
60. Freedom
61. Peace
62. Progress
63. Wealth
64. U.S.A.
65. Loyalty
66. Money, greed, etc., are corrupting
67. Smartness, cleverness, thinking
68. Profit
69. Size

2b. Value conflict
3. Institutions
1. Social structure
2. Religion
3. Economic system
4. Technology, machines
5. Reading, writing and arithmetic
6. Social manipulation
1. Recognition-seeking behaviour
2. Manipulation of others
3. Manipulation of self
7. Responsibility
8. How to compete
9. How to take care of others
10. Use of the mind
1. How to think
2. Disjunction
1. When to disjoin
2. How to disjoin
3. From what to disjoin

3. Concentration
    1. Interest stimulation defining purpose; motivation
    2. Force
    3. Shutting out external stimuli
    4. Visualization
    5. Focused retention
    4. Preparation of the mind
    5. 'Mental discipline'
11. Body parts or functions
    1. The voice
    2. The sphincters
    3. Care of the body (like getting enough rest)
    4. Posture
    5. How to relax
    6. The mouth
12. Art
13. History
14. Some other facts about which information is communicated
    1. About systems of rewards and punishments
    2. About what the culture promises its members
    3. About permitted and forbidden activities
    4. About how to get pleasure and avoid pain
    5. About whom to love and whom to hate
    6. How to handle frustration
    7. The difference between the real and the manifest (this refers to situations in which an effort is deliberately made to enable the child to see 'behind' the obvious)
    8. About death
    9. About sex relations
    10. About race, class, or ethnic differences
15a. Instruction in identifiable adult tasks

15b. Teaching about adult tasks
16. Scientific abstractions
17. Science (general)
18. Routine procedures
19. Childish handiwork
20. Cultural stereotypes
21. Warfare and associated activities
22. Safety
23. Songs, music
24. Mythology
25. The object system
26. Games
27. Cultural fictions

II. How is the information communicated (teaching methods)?

1. By imitation
2. By setting an example
3. By instruction in schools, ceremonials, or other formal institutions
4. By use of punishments
5. By use of rewards
6. Problem-solving
7. Guided recall
8. Giving the child tasks to perform beyond his immediate capacity
    1. Jamming the machine
9. Mechanical devices
10. By kinesthetic association
11. By experiment
    1. By teacher
    2. By pupil
12. By doing
13. By symbolic association
14. By dramatization
15. By games or other play
16a. By threats
16b. By trials
17. By irrelevant association
18. By relevant association
19. Through art
    1. Graphic
    2. Music, general
    3. Songs
    4. Literature (stories, myths, tales, etc.)
20. By stating the opposite of the truth ('Water's a

solid, isn't it?'); writing antonyms

21. By holding up adult ideas
22. Acting in undifferentiated unison
23. Physical force
24. By positive or negative assertion
25. Repetition
26. By specifically relating information to the child's own body, bodily function, or experience
27a. Through ego-inflation
27b. Through ego-deflation
28. Through use of humor
29. By telling
30. By watching
31. By listening
32. Questions and answer
    1. Teacher question, pupil answer
    2. Pupil question, teacher answer
33. Holding up class, ethnic, national, or religious ideals
34. By doing something on his own
35a. By repeating the child's error to him
35b. By repeating the child's correct answer
36. By accusing
37. By following a model
    1. Human
    2. Non-human
38. By comparison
39. By filling in a missing part
40. By associative naming (e.g., a book mentions gingham as a material, and teacher asks students if they can name other materials)
41. By identifying an object (like going to the board and underlining 'a noun' in a sentence)
42a. By group discussion
42b. By class discussion
43. Physical manipulation

1. Bodily manipulation
2. Bodily mutilation and other physical stresses
44. Rote memory
45. By working together with a student (as when teacher and student work together to make a battery, or as when teacher and student go over reference books together)
46. Through special exhibits
47. By having children read substantive materials (e.g., reading the chemistry lesson in the reader)
48. By putting the child on his mettle ('Now let's see how well you can read.')
49. Through group projects
50. By giving procedural instructions
51. By demanding proof
52. Through reports by students
53. By pairing (e.g., one child gives a word and calls on another child to give a sentence with the word; one child gives the state and another gives the capital)
54. By asking for volunteers
55. Through isolating the subject

III. Who educates?

1. Males or females?
2. Relatives or others?
3. On which age group does the burden of education fall?
    1. Peers
        1. Boy
        2. Girl
    2. Older children
        1. Male
        2. Female
    3. Adolescents
        1. Male
        2. Female
    4. Adults

1. Male or female
2. Younger or older
3. Married or unmarried
5. Others
4. Is education by 'successful' people?
5. What rewards accrue to the educator?
    1. Enhanced status
    2. Material rewards
    3. Emotional satisfactions
6. Are there education specialists?
7. Does the educator wear distinctive dress or other insignia?
8. Is the educator of the same or of a different social group from that of the person being educated? (national, racial, class, etc.)

IV. How does the person being educated participate? (What is his attitude?)

1. Accepting
2. Rejecting, resistive
3. Bored, indifferent
4. Defiant
5. Inattentive
6. Social closeness of teacher and child
7. Social distance of teacher and child
8. Finds the process painful?
9. Finds the process gratifying?
10a. Competitively
10b. Cooperatively
11a. With inappropriate laughter
11b. Ridiculing peers
12. Laughter at humor of peers or teacher
13. Overt docility
14. Eagerly
    1. Facial expression
    2. Hand-raising
    3. Talking out
    4. Heightened bodily tonus
15. Through making independent decisions and suggestions

16. Asks for clarification, direction, etc.
17. Through spontaneous contributions or other demonstrations not precisely within the context of the lesson
18. Through spontaneous contributions within the context of the lesson
19. Attentively
20. Spontaneously humorous
21. Spontaneously expressive
22. Approaches teacher physically
23. Mobile—free
24. Immobile—constricted
25. Through performing special assigned tasks
26a. Hostile to peers
26b. Protective of peers
27. Diversion to peers
28. Anxiously
29. Disjoined hand-raising
30. By whispering to teacher
31. Laughs at peers
32. Corrects teacher
33a. Disruptively
33b. Critically
34. By carping criticism
35. By praising work of peers
36. Dishonesty, cheating, lying, etc.
37. Attempts to maintain order
38. Guiltily
39. With sense of inadequacy
40. With sense of adequacy
41. By copying from peers
42. Attempts to control the class
43. No response
44. Uses teacher's last name
45. Uses teacher's first name
46. Calls out to teacher
47. Uses kinship term
48. By public performance

V. How does the educator participate? (What is his attitude?)

1. Eagerly
    1. Facial expression
    2. Bodily movement

3. Tone of voice
4. Heightened bodily tonus
2. Bored, uninterested, etc.
3. Embarrassed
4a. Dominative
4b. Integrative
5. Insecure
6. Politely
7. Enjoys correct response
8. Resents incorrect response
9. Can't tell
10. Seeks physical contact with person being educated
11. Acceptance of blame
12. Putting decisions up to the children
13. Discouraging
14. Encouraging
15. Hostile, ridiculing, sarcastic, belittling
16. Relatively mobile
17. Relatively immobile
18. Personalizing
    1. Use of request sentence with name
    2. Use of name only
    3. Use of hand-name technique
    4. Use of equalizing, leveling term like 'comrade'
19. Depersonalizing
    1. Use of class seating plan for recitation in succession
    2. Use of 'next' or some such impersonal device
    3. Use of 'you' instead of name
    4. Pointing, nodding, looking
20. Irritable
21. Accepts approach
22. Repels approach
23. Accepting of child's spontaneous expressions
24. Rejecting of child's spontaneous expressions
25. Humorous
26. Handles anxiety, hostility, discomfort, etc.
27. Acts and/or talks as if child's self-image is fragile

28. Acts and/or talks as if child's self-image is irrelevant
29. Defends child against peers
30. Responds to non-verbal cue other than hand-raising
31. Excessively polite
32. Keeps word
33. Fails to keep word
34. Praises and rewards realistically
35. Praises and rewards indiscriminately
36. Critical (does not point out good things in student's work)
37. Does not reward correct answer or good performance
38. Does not punish incorrect answer or poor performance
39. Acknowledges own error
40. Uses affectional terms like 'honey' or 'dear'
41. Awakens anticipation ('Now we are going to get some nice new books.')
42. The inclusive plural

VI. Are some things taught to some and not to others?

1. Do different age groups learn different things?
2. Do the sexes learn different things?
3. Are different groups taught different things?

VII. Discontinuities in the educational process

1. Discontinuities between age-periods
   1. In regard to techniques
   2. In regard to values
2. How do all of these apply between the sexes?
   1. Are discontinuities different for boys and girls?
   2. The secrecy of initiation rites

VIII. What limits the quantity and quality of information a child receives from a teacher?

1. Methods of teaching
2. Available time
3. Quality of equipment
4. Distance from the object
5. Ignorance or error of teacher
6. Stereotyping of the object
7. Failure of teacher to correct pupil's mistakes
8. Failure of teacher to indicate whether the pupil's answers are right or wrong
9. Failure of teacher to respond to a question
10. General vagueness or fumbling of the teacher

IX. What forms of conduct control (discipline) are used?

1. Relaxed
2. Tight
3. Sense of propriety
4. Affectivity
5. Reprimand
   1. Direct
   2. Gentle
   3. Mixed ('We like for you to have an opinion but it is childish for you to shout out your numbers like that.')
   4. Impersonal ('Some of you are holding us up.')
6. Ridicule
7. Exhortation ('How can I teach you if you keep making so much noise?')
8. Command
9. Command question or request

10. 'We' technique
11. Instilling guilt
12. Cessation of activity
13. Group sanction
14. Threat
15. Putting the child on his mettle
16. Non-verbal signal
17. Reward
18. Promise of reward
19. Special strategems
20. Awakening fear
21. Using a higher power
    1. Human
    2. Non-human
22. Exclusion
23. Punishment
24. Encourages peer-group control

X. What is the relation between the intent and the results of education?

1. Relatively high correlation between intention and results
2. Relatively low correlation between intention and results

XI. What self-conceptions seem reinforced?

1. Ego-forming factors
   1. Syntonic: praise, support, status inflation
      1. Grandiose self-conception
   2. Dystonic: blame, shame, guilt, fright, exclusion, depersonalization

XII. How long does the process of formal education last?

Appendix II

EDUCATIONAL SYSTEMS AND SELECTED

CONSEQUENCES OF PATTERNS OF MOBILITY AND

NON-MOBILITY IN INDUSTRIAL SOCIETIES:

A THEORETICAL DISCUSSION

Earl Hopper

Introduction

In 1958 at the IVth World Congress of Sociology, Professor Ralph
H. Turner presented a paper on educational systems which was
published subsequently as 'Sponsored and Contest Mobility and
the School System'.[1]* His typology of 'contest' and 'sponsorship'
educational systems and mobility processes has helped us to understand variations in these phenomena in many societies.[2] In the
conclusion to his article, Turner suggested that the structure of a
sponsorship educational system would be less likely than that of a
contest educational system to increase the probability that the
upwardly mobile from the Lowest Social Class would encounter
conditions which tend to produce various types of anxiety. Insofar
as a sponsorship system obtained in England, and a contest system
in the United States, upward mobility was hypothesized to be less
pathogenic in England than in the United States.[3]

In 1966 at the VIth World Congress, I presented a paper on educational systems which was published subsequently as 'A Typology
for the Classification of Educational Systems.'[4]† It was shown in
this article that sponsorship and contest systems represented two
special cases in an extended typology. The two types of systems do
not constitute polarities, at least in terms of this typology, and they
are far from being empirically comprehensive. I concluded with the
cautious suggestion that one of the ways in which the utility of the
expanded typology might be demonstrated would be to take considerations which derived from it in order to revise and reformulate

* [Represented as Reading 4 in the present volume. E.H.]
† [Represented as Reading 5 in the present volumes. E.H.]

Turner's hypotheses concerning mobility and anxiety in England and the United States.

As one of the main concerns of the present paper, shortly before the VIIth World Congress, I intend to pursue these tasks. The paper is comprised of four sections: I, a statement of the problem which includes a summary of Turner's thesis followed by a brief, general critique; II, a discussion of several societal processes which affect educational systems; III, an analysis of some of the possible effects of variations in the structure of educational systems on the life experiences of the mobile and the non-mobile, at least during the student phases of their life cycles[5]; IV, a brief analysis of one of the determinants of variations in the structure of educational systems; and V, a set of propositions concerning the personal consequences of mobility and of non-mobility.

I   *Statement of the Problem*

(i)   *A Summary of Turner's Thesis*[6]

The author assumed that four conditions were likely to be pathogenic:[7]
1. a negative discrepancy between a level of normative expectations and a level of achievement;
2. competition for desirable occupations;
3. interpersonal isolation and loss of interpersonal support;
4. working out a personal value system.

Then, with respect to England, he argued that due to the effects of educational sponsorship, of subsequent segregation and systematic allocation of students to their eventual occupations, neither the non-mobile nor the upwardly mobile from the Lowest Social Class would be likely to encounter any of the four pathogenic conditions stipulated above. Implicit in his thesis is the assumption that children in England are not really ambitious until they pass the initial selection examination: if one passes the test, one becomes ambitious; if one fails, one develops a relatively low level of ambition. Those who fail are unlikely to become mobile or to want to become mobile; hence they are unlikely to encounter the pathogenic conditions. Those who pass are encouraged to desire mobility, are given skills and qualifications which enable them to become mobile, and, in general, are guided, insulated and protected; and, hence, they too are unlikely to encounter the pathogenic conditions.

The United States, he argued, presents a different situation. Due to the absence of systematic regulation of aspirations, training, and allocation to desirable occupations, both the non-mobile and the mobile from the Lowest Social Class in the United States are more likely to encounter the pathogenic conditions outlined above. Implicit in his thesis is the assumption that a generalized success ideology exists in the United States, and that all members of the society want to be successful despite the fact that both the opportunities for upward mobility and the number of people who are capable of becoming mobile are limited. Consequently, the non-mobile are likely to develop discrepancies between their levels of normative expectations and levels of achievement: and the mobile, despite their relative success, are likely to encounter one or a combination of the other pathogenic conditions. In sum, both the non-mobile and the mobile from the Lowest Social Class in the United States are more likely than their counterparts in England to develop certain types of anxiety as a consequence of their non-mobility or their upward mobility.

(ii) *A Brief Critique*

This thesis is plausible, and was supported by much of the evidence available in the late 1950s. It is also possible to interpret more recent findings as consistent with the thesis, at least in a very general way. However, it has several basic limitations:

1. Although it is perhaps most peripheral to Turner's main concerns, mobility is conceptualized simplistically. It is viewed as an attribute or nominal variable, i.e., people are either upwardly mobile from the Lowest Social Class or they are non-mobile. And it is seen as a monolithic process, i.e., there is only one route to the top and it involves the same consecutive steps for all. I am certain that Turner does not adhere to such a model of mobility processes. But both the logic of his original article and the clear implication that such a model would be consistent with his discussion of stratification and mobility make it appear as though he would. Consequently, although a fuller discussion of mobility processes is beyond the scope of the present paper, this point must be made here. However, one should keep in mind the notions of 'patterns of mobility and of non-mobility', as well as those of 'mobility route', 'educational route', 'life-cycle', 'occupational route', and 'career'. These refer to related but distinct social phenomena. Although they may be difficult to separate empirically, they must be distinguished analytically.*

2. Apart from its main concern with variations in the folk-norms of stratification, the thesis ignores the effects of variations in the structure of the stratification systems of England and the United States. In this connection, nothing is said of the effects of variations in status rigidity between social classes, between the core and

* [See Reading 1 in the present volumes. E.H.]

peripheral status groups within social classes, and between the economic and status hierarchies generally. Variations in status rigidity determine to a very great extent the nature of a mobility experience, as well as the formal and informal organization of educational experiences. These points will be developed at greater length later in the present paper.[8]

3. The thesis does not take sufficient account of the variety of educational experiences which are available to both the potentially mobile and the potentially non-mobile students. This is especially evident with respect to England. For example, it is possible that the educational experiences of some portions of the non-mobile population may be as, if not more, pathogenic than the experiences of some portions of the mobile population. Whereas the upwardly mobile through a given educational route may be more likely to encounter pathogenic conditions than are the non-mobile through the same route, the non-mobile through another educational route may be even more likely to encounter such conditions than are the mobile through the first route. In other words, it may be exceedingly difficult to distinguish an educational experience from a mobility experience, especially when there are a large number of routes in the educational system, and when these routes lead to different entry points into the labour market. In brief, evidence suggests that certain patterns of consecutive experiences are characteristic of particular educational routes. These patterns are influenced and organized through ideologies of legitimization and of implementation of educational selection. Such ideologies are properties of the educational system as a whole. And in order to understand the varieties of both educational and mobility experiences available to a population, it is necessary first to locate the educational system in its societal context, and in this connection to understand the various functions it attempts to perform. Although in its entirety such a topic is beyond the scope of this paper, some aspects of it are among my main concerns.[9]

II *Selected Aspects of Society and Educational Systems*

(i) *The Total Selection Process as a Societal Functional Problem*[10]

All societies, no matter how simple, strive to solve their various functional problems, both universal and organizationally specific. One such problem is the conduct and management of the 'total selection process'.[11] It is comprised of four sub-problems: training, selection, recruitment or allocation, and the regulation of ambition. Although all societies are confronted by these tasks, the social organizations which are concerned primarily with their solution are more readily apparent in societies with a complex system of social stratification, and especially in industrial societies. I am concerned with the attempted solutions of these tasks within Industrial Societies, and in this context I will discuss each component of the total selection process:

1. *Training*. All societies strive to provide their personnel with sufficient kinds and amounts of technical and diffuse skills so that the solution of still other problems can be attempted and, at least in large measure, be met. These skills pertain primarily to the fulfilment of roles associated with adult occupational positions. However, insofar as industrial societies are stratified with respect to status as well as economic and political power, adult occupational roles are embedded within a status hierarchy, and, more precisely, within relatively distinct status groups. Therefore, in addition to the technical and diffuse skills required for adult occupational and economic roles, such societies also strive to provide their personnel with those skills which facilitate their membership of and participation in adult status roles. Of course, these two sets of skills are interrelated: the fulfilment of occupational roles requires both technical and diffuse skills; and, insofar as occupations bestow both economic and status rewards, some technical skills will be required for the fulfilment of status roles, and some diffuse skills for economic ones.

A special case of the provision of skills for the fulfilment of status roles generally is that societies prepare their upwardly mobile members for their mobility experience, i.e., leaving a lower social class and becoming a member of a higher one. Were occupations not such an important source of status positions, such a task would not be so essential. That they do determine the status positions of the vast majority of the population in all industrial societies is beyond dispute. And, to put it bluntly, in all these societies the upwardly mobile are taught through both formal and informal means to speak 'properly', to use the 'correct' accent, to dress 'well', to make friends with the 'right' kinds of people, etc. They are taught to extricate themselves from friendship-networks containing people from their own initial economic and status positions, and to handle the cross-pressures inherent in both conflicting status norms and retentive and rejective normative orientations towards upward mobility (especially as manifest in their relationships with non-mobile kin).[12] It is also important that they learn to exercise authority over those below and to submit in the appropriate manner to authority from those above.[13]

2. *Selection*. All societies select their personnel for more special-

ized training, but vary with respect to the stringency of their procedures, the degree of specialization, and the phases of the life-cycle in which they do so. For various reasons, all societies also strive to make their selections as effectively and efficiently as possible. They are always constrained by limited resources, the diffuse norms of substantive rationality, and the ideologies of implementation.[14] Most important, however, is that the effectiveness and efficiency of the training process depend on the efficiency and effectiveness of a selection process. Indeed, the two are so interdependent as to be almost inseparable.

3. *Recruitment and/or Allocation*. All societies structure the process through which their personnel leave the training phases of their life-cycles and enter those phases in which they participate in a labour market and eventually take occupational roles. Such procedures of recruitment and/or allocation are the culmination of the total selection process. However, not everyone is either willing or able to fulfill the most demanding and rewarding occupational roles. Nor are all occupations equally demanding and rewarding.[15] In all societies some people will enter occupations which bestow essentially superordinate economic and status positions, and some will enter those which bestow essentially subordinate ones. Thus, some will be more likely than others to fulfil their expectations of economic and status goals, and to feel contented with their achievements. Similarly, feelings of discontent will also be generated. Such discontent is closely associated with various forms of personal tension and social conflict, both of which are at least to some extent endemic in any society with a clearly stratified distribution of power.[16]

4. *Regulation of Ambition*. The most difficult task in a society's total selection process is the regulation of the ambition of its personnel. This takes place at two different phases in the life-cycle. Firstly ambition must be regulated at early and subsequent selection and rejection steps in the training process. Secondly, it must be regulated during the final phases of recruitment to occupational roles. Each should be discussed further:

(1) Effective and efficient training demands effective and efficient selections. Consequently, a society must try to assess the distribution of abilities among its personnel as accurately as possible. But 'ability' is not only an inherited set of qualities. Environmental influences are determinant, there are various kinds of abilities, and people develop them at various rates. Further, all the methods available for the selection of the

more able from the less able are exceedingly imperfect, no matter how long their application is delayed.[17] Thus, to make accurate assessments a society must try to encourage its children to develop their abilities, and to display them in whatever is deemed the appropriate manner. This means that all societies must try to raise and maintain at a high level the ambition of a maximum number of people until they have been selected for their eventual occupational roles. Ideally this task must be attempted not only as early as possible, but also at every stage of the selection process. It will involve the management of what objects are cathected as goals, and what amounts of these goals are taken as levels of normative expectations. In effect, all industrial societies must strive to inculcate each of their successive cohorts with the desire to fill the most demanding and rewarding occupations, and to acquire the requisite skills.

(2) To recruit effectively and efficiently a society must try not only to guide its personnel into occupations the demands of which are commensurate with their abilities, but also to encourage the more able to have stronger and higher ambitions than the less able, at least in terms of the 'official' assessments. It must strive to minimize the personal discontents associated with the failure to reach one's level of normative expectations. However, if personal discontents were the only consequence of such discrepancies, most societies would not be concerned. Insofar as such feelings are also the foundation of social discontent, it is necessary to regulate them. In brief, in any stratified society the most powerful groups in various spheres of interest and activities will try to strengthen the established social orders and to minimize potential threats to it. Therefore, they will strive to reduce and to maintain at a low level the ambition of those personnel who fill essentially subordinate positions. They will also strive to sponsor and to maintain at a higher level the ambition of those who fill essentially superordinate ones.

In sum, the total selection process is a functional problem which consists of four separate but interdependent component tasks, and with which all societies, and especially highly stratified societies, must strive to cope. However, all societies do not meet this problem with the same degree of effectiveness and efficiency. Some are more successful with one component or combination of them than they are with another. Structural constraints inherent in the complexity of the problem make it difficult to cope equally well with all four. In fact, several structural contradictions are inherent in any attempted solution of the total selection process. This gives rise to a structural dilemma, one which no society can eliminate, yet one with which all societies must cope.

(ii) *The Structural Dilemma Inherent in the Total Selection Process*

The dilemma is easy to describe: the more effective is a society in raising and maintaining ambition at a high level initially, the more difficult is it to reduce and to suppress ambition at a relatively low level at a later phase. For example, it will usually be necessary to reduce the expectations of adults who as children or as younger men were encouraged to aim high. All the available evidence suggests that such a task is extremely difficult, if not impossible. Thus, the more effective is a society at an early phase of the total selection process in the motivation of its personnel to fill demanding occupations, to acquire the requisite skills, and to forego immediate economic rewards during extensive periods of training, the more is it likely to have to face two problems: the personal discontent and its personal manifestations among those of its personnel who eventually fill essentially subordinate positions and, hence, who fail to meet their ambitions; and the social discontent and its manifestations in social conflict between them and those people who eventually fill essentially superordinate positions, and, hence, who do succeed in their ambitions. In other words, there is an inverse relationship between the likelihood of success in the regulation of ambition at the early stages and the likelihood of success at the later ones.

The social organizations which any society develops to cope with the total selection process will be constrained by the conflicting pressures of this dilemma. Societies vary in the structural mechanisms through which they attempt to cope with it, and in the degree which they do so successfully. Especially important is that a system of social stratification not only contributes to the severity of the problem (indeed, it tends to define the dimensions), but also helps to resolve it. This is not the place to elaborate the view that stratification is both functional and dysfunctional with respect to the attempted solutions of a large number and variety of societal problems. But a few points are in order concerning the effects of variation in stratification systems on the total selection process.

With respect to the problems under consideration here, it is especially important to determine the degree to which a stratification system is characterized by status rigidity. This can be defined in terms of several aspects of stratification and mobility, but primarily in terms of the status hierarchy and its relationships to the stratification system of which it is a part, as follows:

1. the existence of distinct and mutually exclusive status groups which are arranged hierarchically according to status power;
2. the life styles associated with each status group are distinctive and extensive, so that they are difficult to shed as well as to acquire, especially after childhood;
3. it is difficult to legitimize a newly acquired economic position by entering with speed the core of the commensurate status group;
4. various occupations or sets of them are governed and regulated by certain status groups, with special reference to recruitment and promotion;[18]
5. there is great social distance between adjacent status groups, between any one echelon in the hierarchy and any other, and between the core and periphery of status groups in each echelon.

It is impossible to discuss this property of stratification in greater detail here.* But it is important to see that a system can be more rigid in some respects than in others. One part of a given system can be more rigid than other parts of the same system. Yet one system can be more or less rigid generally than another. For example, perhaps France is the most rigid Industrial Society in the West, and the United States the least. England would be more rigid than the United States, and perhaps almost as rigid as France. But it is quite possible to find segments of any one of these societies which are either more or less rigid than segments of the others.

The evidence from many industrial societies suggests that the greater the degree of status rigidity, the more is it likely that the lower a person's initial economic and status positions, the less is his:[19]

1. ambition to raise them as an adult;
2. willingness to acquire the skills requisite for raising them as an adult;
3. ability to acquire the requisite skills and to raise these positions.

For the sake of clarity, the converse of this threefold empirical generalization should also be stated. The greater the degree of status rigidity, the more is it likely that the higher a person's initial positions, the greater are his: ambition to perpetuate them and possibly to raise them; willingness to acquire the skills to enable him to do so; and ability to reach these positions, both in the sense of the acquisition of skill and in the sense of encouragement from, and the lack of inter-

*[See Reading 1 in the present volume. E.H.]

ference by, others. These relationships are verycomplex, but because they are axiomatic for the analysis which follows, at least a brief discussion is necessary.

Much of the variance in talent and ambition which exists prior to initial selections and rejections of personnel can be accounted for by variations in inherited qualities, social class background and its attendant attributes, as well as a number of aspects of family environment. All three factors are interrelated so that children from the lowest social class tend to have less ambition and 'measurable talent' than do the children from higher social classes.[20] The origins of achievement orientations are numerous and multi-dimensional. Although certain biological and psychological qualities are needed, the ease, frequency and patterns with which they are developed are determined by social experiences.[21] Similarly, the relationship between achievement orientations and mobility orientations is also problematic. However, the evidence suggests that the greater the mobility opportunities, the more likely are people to translate their general achievement orientations into more precise mobility orientations with respect to economic and status positions.[22]

Yet, mobility opportunities alone are not enough. Although they are essential in this respect, equally important is the degree to which people perceive the occupational structures as open to them, and are ready to utilize the means available for occupational achievements. In other words, it is necessary to consider the effects of variations in the degree of status rigidity. For example, the more mobility is visible to members of the lowest social classes, the more likely are they to learn of their opportunities and to act upon them. The greater the proportion of mobility which is accounted for by long range movements, the more is attention drawn to the possibilities of success. The more the acquisition of a new life style depends on the purchase of status symbols, and the less it depends on learning the subtleties of using them, the more obvious will be the rewards for the mobility efforts. The less the most prestigious and economically rewarding occupations (like those of doctor, barrister, corporation president) are maintained as the prerogatives of traditional and tightly knit higher status groups, the more likely are long range mobility and its rapid legitimization to be taken as realistic possible achievements.

To the extent that higher status groups make it difficult for the economically mobile to acquire a legitimate position in the status hierarchy, the currency of their economic achievement is devalued. Thus, when the effort to become upwardly mobile involves leaving a highly supportive status group and family, and is coupled with a low probability of becoming rapidly and easily reintegrated into a new and higher status group, occupational and economic success does not necessarily smell sweet. Moreover, when membership in a status community does not depend primarily on economic accomplishments, money loses its salience as a source of motivation. In other words, although to a potential candidate for upward mobility the greater the difficulty of status legitimization, the greater the value of a new and higher status, it is also the case that he will be less likely to become mobility oriented in the first place. When economic mobility demands occupational mobility, and when the latter removes a person from his original status group and kinship network, even mobility orientations towards economic positions are likely to be less frequent and less intense.

It follows from this discussion that variations in status rigidity will greatly affect the balance, emphasis, and elasticity of the dilemma inherent in the total selection process, as outlined above. The greater the degree of status rigidity, the more difficult is it for a society to motivate able people from low initial positions both to fill its most demanding and rewarding occupations and to acquire the requisite skills. Status rigidity will be functional with respect to the suppression of ambition of the less able from low initial positions who eventually enter low adult positions, and with respect to the maintenance of ambition of the more able from high initial positions who later perpetuate them. But status rigidity will also be dysfunctional in two respects: it will be difficult to raise and to maintain at a high level the ambition of the more able from low initial economic and status positions, and difficult to reduce and to suppress at a low level the ambition of the less able from high initial economic and status positions who eventually enter low adult positions. In sum, the greater the degree of status rigidity, the easier is it to cope with some aspects of the dilemma in question, and the more difficult to cope with others.

However, it is not the case that the lower the degree of status rigidity, the less thorny the dilemma. It is easier to cope with those aspects of the dilemma which are most troublesome under conditions of high status rigidity, and more difficult to cope with those which are least troublesome. The lower the degree of status rigidity, the easier is it for a society to motivate able people from low initial positions, and the more difficult to motivate able people from high initial positions. A low degree of status rigidity will be functional with respect to the development and maintenance of ambition of the more able from low initial positions, and with respect to the reduction and suppression of ambition of the less able from high initial positions who eventually enter low adult positions. However, it will also be dysfunctional in two respects: it will be difficult to develop and to maintain the ambition of the more able from high initial positions, and to reduce and to suppress the ambition of the less able from low initial positions.

These effects of variations in status rigidity on the relative ease and difficulty with which each component of the dilemma can be solved are illustrated in Matrix 1.

Matrix 1: Status Rigidity and the Dilemma of the Total Selection Process

Status Rigidity	Initial Economic and Status Positions	The Development and Maintenance of a High Level of Ambition	The Reduction and Suppression of a Low Level of Ambition
High	High	+	−
	Low	−	+
Low	High	−	+
	Low	+	−
Key: (+)=relative ease; (−)=relative difficulty			

This paradigm indicates that certain properties of the stratification system partly create the initial functional problem of the total selection process as well as the inherent dilemma. It also indicates that variations in status rigidity help to solve some aspects of the dilemma but to accentuate others. Clearly, then, a stratification system alone is not sufficient to cope with either the problem or the dilemma. To do so a society will have to develop additional structural mechanisms.

(iii) *Educational Systems in Industrial Societies*
Societies have in fact developed a very large number of functionally alternative social organizations through which they try to cope with the problem and dilemma in question. Further, although any given society is likely to utilize more than one social organization, some structural arrangements are likely to be more important than others. In Industrial Societies the most important mechanism is the educa-

tional system. It becomes responsible, both normatively and actually, for the training, selection, allocation, and regulation of personnel with respect to their adult occupational roles, and, hence, their economic and status positions.[23] Thus, it becomes responsible for the task of 'forward placement' in the stratification system.[24] Although this development is by no means inevitable, it is the case in each of the present Industrial Societies, and is rapidly becoming so in most societies now undergoing industrialization processes.[25] This pattern is part of the wider phenomenon of specialization, differentiation, coordination, and centralization which characterize these societies, largely in response to the emergence of an occupational system which is itself specialized and differentiated both internally and with respect to such institutions as the family and religion.[26] It is therefore understandable that the educational systems of these societies should all be characterized by at least a minimal degree of specialization and differentiation of routes and selection points, and of centralization, standardization, and coordination of the total selection process.

In industrial societies the functional problem of the total selection process and its attendant dilemma are translated into the terms of reference of their educational systems. With respect to training, the educational system will try to provide their student personnel with the technical and diffuse skills necessary for their subsequent allocation into occupational roles, and for their achievements of various amounts of economic and status rewards. 'Career-training' experiences will be provided with respect to occupational and economic goals, and will involve primarily the development of technical skills. 'Status-training' experiences will be provided with respect to status goals, and will involve primarily the development of diffuse skills. And as a special case of status-training, 'mobility-training' experiences will be provided with respect to the mobility goals of those of its student personnel who are likely to be upwardly mobile from the lower social classes. In fact, more detailed examination of the curricula and extra-curricula activities within educational organizations as well as within classrooms themselves would probably indicate that considerable time and effort are spent on status and mobility training relative to career-training.[27]

The provision of skills, however, is not enough. Because some candidates for 'higher-learning' are not sufficiently talented and/or the society has provided a smaller number of places in institutions of 'higher-learning' than it has eligible candidates, the educational system must also try to organize the selection of students at various phases of their educational experiences. And this means that the system must also try to organize the regulation of the ambition of its students, especially during the early phases of their formal education.

In this respect, the system is set four tasks:

1. In order to maximize the development and display of academic abilities, the ambition of *all* students must be sponsored and maintained at a high level prior to the initial selections.

2. In order to minimize social conflict and personal discontent, the ambition of those students who are rejected initially must then be reduced and maintained at a low level so that it is commensurate with their newly assessed achievement potentials.

3. In order to continue to select effectively and efficiently those who it deems worthy of still further promotion to still higher educational levels, the system must continue to maximize the development and display of academic abilities of those who are selected initially. Thus, the ambition of all those who are selected initially for advanced training must be sponsored further and maintained at as high a level as possible.

4. And in order to regulate social conflict, personal discontent, and social participation, the ambition of all those who are selected initially but rejected subsequently (at various levels and through various routes) must be reduced and maintained at lower levels so that it is commensurate with their reassessed achievement potentials.

In sum, at every level and through every route within its total selection process, an educational system must strive, on the one hand, to 'warm-up' some of its students, and, on the other, to 'cool-out' those who are rejected for further training.[28] Those who are warmed-up receive further and more specialized training, and those who are cooled-out are sent more or less directly into the labour market. Throughout the system, then, a need exists for the simultaneous provision of warming-up and cooling-out experiences.

The dual tasks of warming up and cooling out must be directed, moreover, towards the provision of career-training, status-training, and mobility-training experiences. In other words, students must be warmed-up and cooled-out more or less continuously, successively, and correctly with respect to their eventual occupational roles, and, hence, with respect to their eventual economic, status, and mobility goals. This means that they must also be warmed-up and cooled-out more immediately with respect to their contemporary educational goals which stand for each of these long term adult goals.

However, as outlined above, the more successful an educational system is in its warming-up processes at a given phase in the selection process, the more difficult it will be to manage and conduct its cooling-out processes at a subsequent phase. This is not to state that the effective and efficient provision of both sets of experiences is impossible, but to stress that the likelihood of success with one is inversely related to the likelihood of success with the other. Continual tension and conflict are likely to surround any system's attempts to resolve this structural dilemma. It is a contradiction which is likely to generate pressures for structural change, both within the educational system and in the relationships of the system to other institutions. But no matter what the substance and the direction of the structural changes which might occur, the essential nature of the dilemma remains constant, as do the pressures for further change.

Which horn of the dilemma is presented by a society as the longer and the sharper, will greatly affect the basic structure of its educational system. This horn represents the demands which the society makes on its educational system over and above the relatively small request for the provision of skills of various kinds and amounts. Thus, a key to the understanding of the basic structure of any educational system is how it attempts to solve its assignment; that is, how it copes with the dilemma implicated by the structure of its warming-up and cooling-out processes. And this, in turn, is a key to the understanding of the personal and interpersonal consequences of various patterns of mobility and of non-mobility.

(iv) Variations in the Structure of Educational Systems

Before turning to the effects and determinants of variations in the structure of educational systems, it would be useful first to consider some of the dimensions with respect to which they vary. An almost infinite number and variety of structural properties are involved. To understand these variations requires in the first instance an identification of what merits priority in one's attentions. This depends greatly on a researcher's interests as well as the concerns of traditional research problems. My expanded typology for the classification of educational systems was constructed on this basis.[29] It involves several dimensions of the social organization of educational systems which pertain to the kinds and patterns of experiences which are available to students as they progress through their life cycles.*

Educational systems vary according to each of these dimensions. Their positions on any one dimension are not necessarily related to their positions on any of the others. Although it is possible to observe 'strains towards consistency', a system's position on the organizational dimension of a given structural property does not necessarily correspond with its position on the ideological dimension

* [See Reading 5 in the present volume. E.H.]

of the same property. It was also shown that although a very approximate relationship might exist, a society's degree of status rigidity is a surprisingly poor indication of the positions of its educational system on any of these dimensions.

(v) *Variations in the Structure of Educational Systems and the Attempted Solution of the Warming-up : Cooling-out Dilemma*

It is possible to trace the hypothetical effects of variations in the structure of educational systems on the degree of success in its attempt to resolve the warming-up:cooling-out dilemma. It is also possible to trace the hypothetical effects of the structured emphasis in the dilemma (that is, the prominence of the warming-up problems relative to the cooling-out problems, and the relative flexibility of this balance) on variations in the structure of the educational system. However, these two sets of relationships are embedded in an intricate and complex set of social processes. To examine them further demands that they be abstracted from this context. Because it is not possible within the limits of the present paper to consider the very many interesting aspects of this context, it would be useful at least to locate them schematically, as shown in Fig. 1.

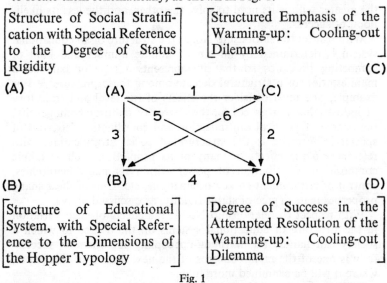

Fig. 1

With respect to relationship No. 1: the greater the degree of status rigidity in the stratification system, the harder is it to warm-up people rom the lower social classes and to cool-out people from the upper

f

social classes, and the easier is it to cool-out those from the lower social classes and to warm-up those from the upper social classes. The degree of status rigidity will greatly affect the need to provide mobility training experiences, as well as the difficulty of their provision. And the distribution of the population among a society's social classes will determine the extent to which warming-up will be either more or less essential than cooling-out especially during the early phases of the selection process.

With respect to relationship No. 2: the greater the degree of inflexibility and emphasis of one component relative to the other, the more difficult is it to resolve the dilemma successfully. The more intransigent the solution of one of the component sets of problems, the greater is the need for a large investment of resources of various kinds in its attempted solution. The greater this investment, the less the resources available for the other component set of problems. Usually, too much emphasis on one component gives rise to an organization which becomes too rigid to concentrate on the solution of the counter problem; and a successful solution of one component tends to eliminate the need for the organization in its contemporary form.[30] In any event, the greater the success of the system with one component, the greater will be its need to solve the other, and the less its likelihood of success.

With respect to relationship No. 3: the structure of an educational system is determined by an almost infinite number and kind of competing pressures so that it represents a type of balance, a manifestation of a structural détente among these pressures.[31] For example, one must consider the effects of the level and trajectory of industrialization processes, the degree of cultural homogeneity, the degree of political centralization and coordination, etc. But of special importance is the structure of social stratification, with reference to the effects of many of its properties, such as ethnic composition, distribution of power within its main hierarchies, control of recruitment to key occupations, etc. One of these many properties is its degree of status rigidity, as discussed above.

With respect to relationship No. 4: the effects of such variation in the structure of educational systems on the degree to which a society can handle the warming-up:cooling-out dilemma successfully is one of the main concerns of the next section of this paper, where it will be examined more fully.

With respect to relationship No. 5: variations in social stratification not only affect the structural emphasis of the dilemma (Relationship No. 1) and the structure of an educational system (Relationship No. 2) and, hence, *indirectly* affect the degree to which the system can resolve the dilemma successfully; but they also *directly* affect the degree to which the resolution is successful. It is important to stress in this connection that educational systems are not the only source of attempts to solve the dilemma inherent in the functional sub-problem of the regulation of ambition. They may be the most important source, but as was suggested above, systems of social stratification also provide their own structural mechanisms for the attempted resolution of this dilemma. The entire task is never assigned solely to an educational system. For example, the degree to which the dilemma can be resolved also depends on the number of mobility routes available, the number of evaluational criteria which underpin the status hierarchy, the number and variety of occupational situses available at a given echelon, etc. Thus, to trace the effects of variations in the structure of educational systems and in the structure of the warming-up:cooling-out dilemma on the likelihood that the dilemma will be resolved successfully may not be sufficient to explain a large portion of the total variance in successful resolution. It will be necessary always to examine the many direct effects of social stratification as well. But this is not to argue that the effects of any other property cannot be traced.

With respect to relationship No. 6: another of the main concerns of the next section of this paper is how the structure of educational systems is affected by the structural emphasis of the warming-up: cooling-out dilemma. It will be considered more fully there.[32]

Two subsidiary points should still be noted, and then eliminated from further consideration. Each variable in the preceding diagram is determined by many other variables in addition to the ones under consideration here. This is implicit in the discussion thus far. It should be made explicit, however, that this paper is not concerned with the explanation of the maximum amount of variance in any of these variables. It is concerned only with tracing the contributions which certain variables make to such explanations. Second, as is the case with almost all propositions in sociology, these relationships are likely to be reciprocal. Thus, they could be examined in terms of their feed-back and looping effects. For example, it is obvious that the degree to which a society resolves the warming-up:cooling-out dilemma successfully will affect the structure of its stratification system, which helped to generate and to define the dilemma in the first place. Such reciprocities are important, but they are beyond the scope of this paper.

III   *The Hypothetical Effects of Variations in the Structure of*
      Educational Systems on the Degree to which an Attempt to
      Resolve the Warming-up : Cooling-out Dilemma will be Successful

(i)   *The Effects of Variations in Selected Dimension of the Typology*
      of the Classification of Educational Systems

The effects of variations in selected properties of educational systems
on the relative ease and/or difficulty which a system is like to encounter in its attempts to resolve the warming-up: cooling-out dilemma
involve two sets of problems. One is that variation in a given dimension does not affect each component of the dilemma in the same
way. In fact, it is often likely to have opposite effects. Another is
that the way in which the lower social classes are affected is often
likely to differ from the way in which the upper social classes are
affected. What is effective for the lower social classes is likely to be
ineffective for the upper social classes, and vice versa, for most of
the dimensions in question. Thus, the degree to which variation
in a particular dimension or in a set of dimensions contributes to
a successful attempt to resolve the dilemma depends on the distribution of a society's population among its social classes and the
degree to which its stratification system is characterized by status
rigidity. Success is not a function only of the structure of the educational system. It follows, however, that the first task in the consideration of these processes is to trace the hypothetical effects of variations
in each dimension on both the lower and the upper social classes.
These are summarized in the table on p. 311.

I shall now discuss each of these effects. However, I should like
to stress in the strongest possible terms that this discussion constitutes
only a preliminary attempt to work out the variety of forces and
counter-forces which underpin a particular effect. Such a brief
treatment must, of necessity, be incomplete. It is intended as an
initial guideline for further research, including the formulation of
counter-hypotheses.

1. *Degree of Centralization and Standardization of the Educational*
Programme and its Administration. Two dimensions were conceptualized with respect to how educational selection occurs. Although
positions on the two dimensions are not necessarily interrelated,
the effects of variation in the standardization of the educational
programme are consistent with those of the centralization of its
coordination and administration. Therefore, to simplify the presentation of the argument, it is reasonable to combine them both into
one dimension, the degree of centralization and standardization of
the educational programme and its administration.

The Main Dimensions of an Educational System	Position of Index	The Components of the Dilemma			
		Warming-up		Cooling-out	
		Lower social classes	Upper social classes	Lower social classes	Upper social classes
1. Degree of Centralization and Standardization	High	= 1	= 1	+ 1	− 1
	Low	− 2	+ 2	= 2	= 2
2. Degree of Early Formal Specialization and Differentiation	High	− 2	+ 1	+ 1	− 2
	Low	= 1	= 2	− 2	+ 1
3. Ideologies of Implementation of Selection	Sponsorship/Elitist	− 2	+ 1	+ 1	− 2
	Contest/Egalitarian	= 1	= 2	= 2	= 1
4. Ideology of Legitimization of Selection	Communistic	+ 1	− 4	+ 1	− 1
	Paternalistic	− 3	+ 2	+ 2	− 3
	Meritocratic	+ 2	− 3	+ 4	− 2
	Aristocratic	− 4	+ 1	+ 3	− 4

Key: (+) = Relative Ease; (−) = Relative Difficulty
(=) = No Difference; equally easy or equally difficult
(1—4) = The higher the number, the greater the difficulty.

(1) In the first instance, the effects of variation in the composite dimension on attempts to resolve the warming-up: cooling-out dilemma are unduly obvious and easy to describe. Although too much centralization and standardization of an educational programme and its administration may be covered by the laws of diminishing returns, it is generally accepted in sociology that the greater the centralization and standardization of processes of these kinds, the more effectively and efficiently can any organization conduct its affairs, and progress towards its goals, whatever they are. This applies to an educational system,[33] and includes any attempts to resolve the dilemma in question. However, insofar as movements towards

either greater or lesser centralization and standardization generate new patterns of responsibility, autonomy, and interdependence for the roles within an educational bureaucracy, such variation is likely to generate tension and conflict both within the system and between it and other institutions. Although this may reduce the degree to which the system can resolve its dilemma, as its new structure becomes more stable, the full effects of its new position with respect to centralization and standardization are likely to ensue.

(2) A high degree of centralization and standardization is likely to be more effective in cooling-out the lower social classes than the upper social classes. Among the most important of the many reasons for this is that an official agency can be held responsible for the rejections. No matter how institutionalized the cooling-out process, the personnel who are ultimately responsible for rejections are likely to be members of the upper social classes or their agents. They are the targets for all projections of bitterness over the experience of failure. This offers the rejected student from the lower social classes a set of ready-made excuses for his failure, e.g., 'You can't break the system.' or 'I was up against the Establishment.' A rejected student from the upper social classes is denied this luxury. He cannot say that he was a victim of 'class-bias' when his own social class is responsible for his rejection. Moreover, for a student from the lower social classes to be rejected by a member of the upper social classes is consistent with the structure of interpersonal relationships which comprise the status hierarchy. It fits the general pattern of expectations concerning exchanges between status groups. The opposite is so with respect to a student from the upper social classes.

(3) A low degree of centralization and standardization is likely to be more effective in warming-up the upper social classes than the lower social classes. Among the many reasons for this is that children from the lower social classes are less motivated and less able to participate in the formal activities of an educational system at an early age then are children from the upper social classes.[34] Not only does it take them longer to develop to any given level their potential motivation and abilities, but also to utilize the materials and tools of learning, such as language skills, in a class room situation.[35] In brief, children from the upper social classes, by virtue of their family and peer group backgrounds, enter the formal

educational system with a sizeable head start. To the extent that the educational programme is not standardized for all social and geographical segments of the population, it is almost always the case that the programme will be richer for the upper social classes and poorer for the lower social classes. This augments the initial bias. However, children from the lower social classes are able to an appreciable extent to develop from their lower base line when exposed to compensatory teaching and curricula organization. But to the extent that the administration of the educational programme is not centralized and coordinated, it is difficult if not impossible to conduct such procedures.

2. *Degree of Early Formal Specialization and Differentiation of Routes.* Two dimensions were conceptualized with respect to when educational selection occurs. Although positions on the two dimensions are not necessarily interrelated, the effect of variation in the degree of lateral autonomy[36a] will serve only to reinforce those of variation in the degree of early formal specialization and differentiation of routes. Therefore, for present purposes, it is not necessary to consider the independent effects of the former property. However, the effects of variations in the degree of early formal specialization and differentiation of routes depend entirely on the social class of the group in question. Variations do not affect all social classes in the same way for either the warming-up process or the cooling-out process. Thus, the effects of variation for this dimension must be examined for each social class.

(1) The greater the degree of early formal specialization and differentiation of routes, the easier is it likely to be to warm-up the upper social classes and the more difficult the lower social classes. Among the most important of the many reasons for this is that the sooner initial selections are made, the easier will it be to reinforce the initial enthusiasms and abilities of children from the upper social classes, and the more difficult to overcome the initial retardation of children from the lower social classes. Furthermore, when children from the lower social classes mix with those from the upper social classes, the former are likely to acquire the qualities of the latter, and the latter the qualities of the former. With respect to the warming-up process, this benefits the lower social classes and impedes the upper social classes. Thus, the sooner initial selections are made, the less are children from the lower social classes liable to take advantage of this opportunity.

(2) In contradistinction, the greater the degree of early formal specialization and differentiation of routes, the easier is it likely to be to cool-out the lower social classes and the more difficult the upper social classes. Again there are many reasons for this. The most important is that to cool-out a member of the lower social classes is likely to involve his eventual non-mobility, whereas to cool-out a member of the upper social classes is likely to involve his eventual *downward mobility*. With respect to the lower social classes, the earlier the initial rejections, the less are they likely to have been warmed-up, and, thus, the more are they likely to experience their failure as self-confirming and appropriate. Further, the earlier the initial rejections, the longer the period within the system prior to entry into the labour market; thus, the longer the time during which those who will be non-mobile from the lower social classes can acquire and reinforce their collective identity as societal subordinates. With respect to the upper social classes, the earlier the initial rejections, the less are they likely to have anticipated their eventual downward mobility, and through a process of self-selection, to have begun a process of anticipatory socialization for the lower social classes. Further, the fewer will have been their opportunities to develop in a natural and spontaneous way friendships which cut across social class boundaries, and which might compensate for the ones they are liable to lose. Whereas a lengthy period between early initial rejections and entry into the labour market may assist the cooling-out process for the lower social classes, it is likely to have the opposite effect for the upper social classes. It highlights in formal terms the eventual status discontinuities of the family of orientation, and, in general, subjects the children to cross pressures between parents and peers.

(3) The less the degree of early formal specialization and differentiation of routes, the easier is it likely to be to cool-out the upper social classes, and the more difficult the lower social classes. This is the converse of the proposition examined above, but is also supported by independent factors. Although the converse of the proposition which concerned the warming-up process is not likely to hold, this one is.

The preceding discussion concerns the early phases of the selection process in which an attempt to resolve the warming-up: cooling-out dilemma depends on the differential effects of variations in the degree of early formal specialization and differentiation of routes upon the lower and the upper social classes. However, at later phases of the selection process, variations in this dimension present a further problem which does not involve social class differences. Ideally, the cooling-out process should be effective through all routes in the system, i.e. ambitions and achievement potentials should be commensurate at all levels.[36] Yet it is exceedingly difficult, if not impossible, to accomplish an effective cooling-out process through a certain range of routes. This range is distinguished by its origins in initial selections and its terminations in eventual rejections at various levels prior to final selection at the apex.[37] In these routes people will have experienced an initial sponsorship of their ambitions and an official selection for an eventual position in the upper social classes; but they will also experience a subsequent rejection for which they are unlikely to have been prepared. Such inconsistency does not make for an effective regulation of ambition. The greater the degree of early formal specialization and differentiation of routes within a system, the more is it likely to be characterized by these types of middle range routes.

All systems with a high degree of early formal specialization and differentiation of routes have a built-in bias towards the apex. In effect, whether for reasons of ideology or limited resources, they are concerned primarily with the creation of an élite. Those who are selected initially and continuously and who eventually enter the labour market through the apex receive careful grooming during the entire process. Those who are rejected initially in such a system often receive considerable attention prior to their entry into the labour market; they comprise a large segment of the population, and to cool them out is always essential. Both groups of people are likely to undergo effective cooling-out experiences. The first group will be cooled-out at a lower level of potential achievement, and the second at a high level. Both are likely to have ambitions which are commensurate with their achievement potentials, and, the evidence suggests, their eventual achievements.

In contrast, the middle range routes are likely to be neglected. These routes function primarily to generate the groups to be selected at the next stage of the process. They are a sieve through which the most highly motivated and highly trained élite will filter. They do not function primarily to train those who utilize them to enter the labour market. Those who do enter the labour market in this way are likely to have comparatively low achievement potentials. Their training will have consisted primarily of preparation for the next phase of formal education, and not for occupational roles which are available to them. In this respect they may be less well trained than if they had been rejected initially and received direct vocational instruction. In any case, they will enter the labour market with ambitions which were initially sponsored combined with comparatively low achievement potentials. Although they do experience a subsequent official rejection, it is a symbol that the system has defined their identities in inconsistent ways. First they are encouraged to identify themselves as potential members of an élite, and then they are rejected as unsuitable. If the system is felt to be in error, the problem arises whether the error was manifest in the initial selection or in the subsequent termination. In the event of the latter, they are left with a structured discrepancy between their expectations and achievement potentials, and, the evidence suggests, their eventual achievement. But in either case, they are left with ambiguous and ambivalent self-expectations, and without institutional support for their self-identifications.

Such ineffective cooling-out routes are also found at later phases in the selection process. They exist within the matrix of institutions of further and higher education, and are close to the élite apex itself. The apex of an educational system is usually represented by one or two universities which, even in very large complex societies, represent a maximum achievement potential with respect to both economic and status goals, as well as to a wide range of direct occupational goals. To graduate from the apex institutions is to receive very strong sponsorship with respect to a large number and variety of goals. Expectations and achievement potentials are likely to be high, and these potentials are likely to be realized subsequently. However, there are likely to be many other institutions of further and higher education. The achievement potentials which they provide are likely to be almost as high, if not as high, as those provided by the apex institutions, but not with respect to as large a number and variety of goals. From the point of view of the population generally, selection into any one of these institutions appears to represent a success; but the closer one gets to the apex, the more one is aware that the apex is unique. Especially important in this connection is that many of these institutions provide achievement potentials with respect to economic and occupational goals which are commensurate with those provided by the apex institutions. But they are seldom able at the same time to provide commensurate achievement potentials with respect to status goals. For example, graduates from both an apex university and another university are both able to become engineers, but the apex graduate is likely to be employed by the most prestigious firm and the other graduate is not. In other words, educational routes which culminate in graduation from institutions of further and higher education other than the apex institutions are likely to be effective in the cooling-out process with respect to some goals but ineffective with respect to others. They are especially likely to be ineffective with respect to status goals.

In sum, given the effects of initial social class positions, systems with a high degree of early formal specialization and differentiation of routes will be effective in the cooling-out process with respect to those who are rejected initially and with respect to those who are subsequently selected into an élite. But they are especially likely to be ineffective with respect to a particular segment of the population. This segment is likely to enter the labour market with a discrepancy between their levels of normative expectations and their levels of achievement potentials, and eventually to develop a discrepancy between their expectations and their actual achievements. It is likely to be more ineffectively cooled-out than any of those which might enter the labour market through a system which is characterized by a low degree of early formal specialization and differentiation of routes. It epitomizes and personifies the warming-up:cooling-out dilemma at its most severe.

3. *Ideologies of Implementation: Sponsorship or Contest, and Elitist or Egalitarian.* The analysis of the effects of variations in ideologies involves several problems.[38] One of the most important in terms of the present paper is that variations in ideologies are not necessarily consistent with variations in their analogous structural properties. This implies that variations in ideologies may have an effect on the attempted resolutions of the warming-up:cooling-out dilemma which is independent from an effect of variations in the analogous structural property. Such independent effects are likely to be either facilitating or impeding, and are not necessarily determinant. In either case, however, it is important to know their etiological contributions.

An important example of one aspect of this problem is that, for example, variations in an ideology of implementation concerning how educational selection *should* be organized are unlikely to have the same patterns of effects as variations in how it is *actually* organized. In other words, the effects of a Sponsorship ideology do not correspond with those of a high degree of centralization and standardization of the selection process, and the effects of Contest ideology with those of a low degree. Alternatively, the effects of variations in an ideology of implementation concerning when selections should occur are likely to correspond with those of when they actually do occur. In other words, the effects of an Elitist ideology correspond with those of a high degree of early formal specialization and differentiation of routes, and the effects of an Egalitarian ideology correspond with those of a low degree. The fact that the effects of variations in an ideology may not correspond with the effects of variations in its structural analogue does not raise new problems for this analysis. But it does highlight the need to consider all dimensions of the structure of educational systems before ranking them in terms of their ability to resolve the warming-up : cooling-out dilemma. Although the systemic referents of Sponsorship and Contest ideologies differ from those of Elitist and Egalitarian ideologies, I will argue that the effects of a Sponsorship ideology are the same as those of an Elitist ideology, and that the effects of a Contest ideology are the same as those of an Egalitarian one. Consequently, for purposes of presentation, these two dimensions can be combined into one: Sponsorship and Elitist ideologies, on the one hand, and Contest and Egalitarian ideologies on the other.[39]

The basic hypotheses are that whereas Sponsorship and Elitist ideologies are likely to facilitate the warming-up of students from the upper social classes and the cooling-out of those from the lower social classes, and to impede the warming-up of students from the lower social classes and the cooling-out of those from the upper social classes, Contest and Egalitarian ideologies are likely to have the opposite pattern of effects. Each component of the dilemma should be examined separately.

With respect to the *warming-up* component of the dilemma, one must first consider to what extent and intensity the general achievement orientations and mobility orientations of the young are dependent primarily upon their early educational experiences. In an educational system with Sponsorship and Elitist ideologies, the development of achievement and mobility orientations is more likely to follow than to precede some sign of educational success. Educational achievements, which are the first phase of mobility, are, therefore, more likely to create achievement orientations and mobility orientations than to be created by them. This is not to argue that variations in initial ambition are not important in determining initial educational achievements. But it is to stress that due to the constraints of Sponsorship and Elitist ideologies, ambition is not a totally legitimate personal quality until some sign of educational achievement has been recognized within the formal boundaries of the system and through an appropriate communication with some representative of its authority structure. In other words, mobility orientations must be sponsored in order that they be assessed as legitimate by the authorities, and in order that they be allowed to develop to their fullest strength and extent.

Some examples of how sponsored educational achievements and, subsequently, sponsored social mobility are likely to instigate mobility orientations may serve to illustrate this point.[40] Note a middle class school teacher who recognizes the abilities of a boy from the lowest social class, and then encourages him to work hard and to prepare for further and higher education—long before either he himself or his family were motivated in this direction, and were aware of the possibility. Or, at a much different level, consider the behaviour of students in their last year in University who might wish to work for a higher degree. They tend to wait for their tutors to suggest that they are able to handle the work before they themselves consider the matter. It is common for them to manifest an over-dependence on members of staff to handle the details of their applications to graduate schools.

In contrast, in an educational system with Contest and Egalitarian ideologies, the development of achievement and mobility orientations is more likely to precede than to follow an early educational success. These orientations are more likely to depend upon properties of family and neighbourhood than upon initial experience within one formal educational system. Ambition is legitimate prior to formal and appropriate signs of educational achievements. In fact, ambition is more likely to create than to be created by them. One example of how Contest and Egalitarian ideologies affect mobility orientation is the way in which ambitious students strive to bring themselves to the attention of their teachers by persistent extra reading assignments, etc. They are also likely to initiate their own admission to graduate school with relatively little encouragement and assistance from their teachers.

The evidence from all industrial societies suggests that in order to develop their achievement and mobility orientations, children from the lower social classes are more dependent upon a Sponsorship experience than are children from the upper social classes. In other words, with respect to the warming-up problem, the lower social classes are more difficult than are the upper social classes. The effects of status rigidity may intensify this difference, but they do not alter it. Hence, all industrial societies use some form of personal and institutional sponsorship for their mobility processes, and have some elements of a Sponsorship ideology. However, in a system *character-ized* by Sponsorship and Elitist ideologies both the mobility orientations and subsequently the mobility itself are more likely to await a relatively formal judgement from the educational authorities. In a system characterized by Sponsorship and Elitist ideologies both the mobility orientations and subsequently the mobility itself are more likely to await a relatively formal judgement from the educational authorities. In a system characterized by Contest and Egalitarian ideologies, although a potentially mobile student must struggle to acquire a sponsor and to convince him of his work, formal sponsorship is not required to foster his ambition as much as to help him find a means to satisfy it. Ambition is more likely to be the price of sponsorship than the purchase. However, it will be harder to warm-up the lower social classes than the upper social classes under either set of ideologies.

The hypotheses concerning the effects of ideologies of implementation, are as follows:

(1) A combination of Contest and Egalitarian ideologies is more likely than one of Sponsorship and Elitist ideologies to facilitate the warming-up of the lower social classes, but to impede that of the upper social classes. Among the most important reasons for this relationship is that a combination of Contest and Egalitarian ideologies is premised on the assumption that choices of one group by another are likely to be imperfect, biased, and inefficient and that they should be discouraged as legitimate procedure. In so far as the 'best' are regarded as those who 'make it' rather than those who should be chosen, a premium is placed on ambition from the very start. And when such personal qualities are highly regarded relative to ascribed characteristics, the lower social classes are normatively encouraged to develop mobility orientations from their earliest phases in the educational system. In contrast, under conditions of Sponsorship and Elitist ideologies it is less appropriate for the lower social classes than for the upper social classes to nourish their ambitions prior to formal assessments. In other words, the children of the upper social classes are permitted to behave in ways which are consistent with their location in the status hierarchy, whereas the children of the lower social classes are not.[41] This early fostering of ambition in family and peer group settings will favour the selection of children from the upper social classes as opposed to those from the lower social classes.

(2) It should also be stressed that whereas a combination of Sponsorship and Elitist ideologies is likely to be much more effective in warming-up the upper social classes than the lower social classes, a combination of Contest and Egalitarian

ideologies is likely to be about as effective in warming-up the one as the other. Although the children of the upper social classes may be more easily warmed-up than those of the lower social classes, Contest and Egalitarian ideologies are likely neither to offset nor to augment this difference.

With respect to the *cooling-out* component of the dilemma, one must first consider the extent to which a person's ambition, once it has been developed and fostered initially, can then be reduced and maintained at appropriately low levels. The evidence suggests that such a task is never easy, and may even be impossible.[42] However, the reduction of ambition might be manifest in a person's decathexis of occupational, economic, and status goals, and possibly a new cathexis of alternative goals, coupled with a neutralization of existing normative expectations. In addition, there is the problem that whereas the lower social classes are more difficult than the upper social classes with respect to the warming-up component of the dilemma, the reverse is true with respect to the cooling-out processes. As outlined above in the discussion of specialization and differentiation of routes, to cool-out a member of the upper social classes is likely to involve his eventual downward mobility, which is always a difficult process; but to cool-out a member of the lower social classes is likely to involve his eventual non-mobility, which, depending on the phase at which it occurs, is likely to be an unexceptional experience of maturation.

The problem remains whether such a process is likely to be more responsive to a combination of Sponsorship and Elitist ideologies than to one of Contest and Egalitarian ideologies. In other words, whether decathexis, recathexis, and neutralization of goals and expectations would be facilitated through an ideology which implies, for example, that the system should employ a more or less formal assessment by the authorities of a pupil's present merit and future potentials, or conversely, through one which implies, for example, that the system should employ a more or less informally organized and open competition by which a pupil might slowly come to assess himself relative to others.

(1) A combination of Contest and Egalitarian ideologies is more likely than one of Sponsorship and Elitist ideologies to facilitate the cooling-out of the upper social classes, and to impede that of the lower social classes.[43] Among the most important reasons for this relationship is that insofar as the combination of Sponsorship and Elitist ideologies is more likely than one of Contest and Egalitarian ideologies to

facilitate the warming-up of the upper social classes, and insofar as a more effective warming-up process implies a correspondingly more difficult cooling-out process, it follows that a combination of Sponsorship and Elitist ideologies is likely to be less effective than one of Contest and Egalitarian ideologies for cooling-out the upper social classes. Similarly, it follows that insofar as a combination of Contest and Egalitarian ideologies is more likely than one of Sponsorship and Elitist ideologies to facilitate the warming-up of the lower social classes, the former combination will be less effective than the latter with respect to the upper social classes. Another reason is that ideologies of implementation contain elements which pertain both to the warming-up process and to the cooling-out process. An ideology of implementation is more likely to facilitate either set of processes when its sets of elements are consistent with the other normative orientations of the people involved. As suggested in the above discussion of warming-up processes, the most important of these normative orientations concerns attitudes towards authority. With respect to the cooling-out process, elements of Sponsorship and Elitist ideologies are consistent with Receptive normative orientations towards authority, and elements of Contest and Egalitarian ideologies are consistent with Rejective normative orientations (although the reverse is true with respect to warming-up). The lower social classes are likely to have Receptive normative orientations towards authority and the upper social classes Rejective ones.[44] Thus, with respect to the cooling-out process, Sponsorship and Elitist ideologies are consistent with the normative orientations towards authority of the lower social classes, and Contest and Egalitarian ideologies are consistent with those of the upper social classes. It follows that in so far as this kind of consistency facilitates the cooling-out process, Sponsorship and Elitist ideologies will facilitate the cooling-out of the lower social classes, and impede that of the upper social classes. The opposite will be true for Contest and Egalitarian ideologies.

(2) In conclusion, it is noteworthy that whereas a combination of Sponsorship and Elitist ideologies is likely to be much more effective in cooling-out the lower social classes than the upper social classes, a combination of Contest and Egalitarian ideologies is likely to be about as effective in cooling-out the one as the other. Although the children of the lower social classes may be easier to cool-out than those of the upper social classes,

Contest and Egalitarian ideologies are likely neither to offset nor to augment this difference.

4. *Ideologies of Legitimization: Communistic, Paternalistic, Meritocratic, and Aristocratic.* In my earlier article on educational systems I suggested that one of the ways in which most stratified societies have attempted to cope with various functional problems inherent in their stratification '. . . is to develop fairly explicit ideologies which define the types of people whom the society values most highly and which justify why more power is given to them than to others. These may be called "ideologies of legitimization". Since educational systems in stratified industrial societies are mechanisms of selection and allocation, such societies are likely to have explicit ideologies of legitimization concerning educational selection. These ideologies translate questions concerning the distribution of power into questions concerning the distribution of educational suitability. They define who should be selected for higher training and explain why some people should be rejected when others are selected.'[45] Four ideologies which purport to answer these questions were conceptualized: Communistic, Paternalistic, Meritocratic, and Aristocratic.

As was the case with the previous two dimensions, the effects of variations in the ideologies of legitimization depend entirely on the social class of the groups in question. Variations do not affect all social classes in the same way for either component process of the dilemma. Thus, the effects of variations in ideologies of legitimization must be examined for each social class. It should be stressed, however, that many of the following hypotheses are almost self-evident. Insofar as the ideologies of legitimization of educational selection were developed *in order* to help cope with both components of the warming-up: cooling-out dilemma, their effects on the various social classes become clear by definition.

(1) With respect to warming-up the lower social classes, the ideologies of legitimization can be ranked in order of their likely effectiveness: Communistic, Meritocratic, Paternalistic, and Aristocratic. With respect to the upper social class, the converse ranking is likely to apply: Aristocratic, Paternalistic, Meritocratic and Communistic. The extreme differences are represented by Aristocratic and Communistic ideologies. Although the differences between Paternalistic and Meritocratic are marked, they are not as great.

It is equally clear, almost by definition, that an Aristocratic ideology is likely to help to warm-up the upper social classes and to impede the lower social classes. A Communistic ideology is likely to help to warm-up the lower social classes, and to impede the upper social classes. These differences are likely to be extreme. A Paternalistic ideology is likely to help to warm-up the upper social classes and to impede the lower social classes, but the difference is unlikely to be as great as in the cases of Communistic and Aristocratic ideologies. Although a Paternalistic ideology shares collectivistic elements with a Communistic ideology, when in combination with the particularism of the former as opposed to the universalism of the latter, collectivism is likely to discourage the ambitions of the lower social classes. Finally, a Meritocratic ideology is as likely to help to warm-up the lower social classes as it is the upper social classes.

In sum, although Communistic and Aristocratic ideologies are likely to have the most helpful effect on the lower and the upper social classes, respectively, their inherent polarities are likely to impede the warming-up of the population generally. Meritocratic and Paternalistic ideologies have less marked effects on either the lower or the upper social classes, but their balance is likely to reach a larger proportion of the population.

(2) With respect to the cooling-out of the lower social classes, the ideologies can be ranked in terms of their likely effectiveness: Communistic, Paternalistic, Aristocratic, and Meritocratic. A Meritocratic ideology is likely to be less effective than an Aristocratic ideology in this respect insofar as it offers no legitimate excuses for failure. At least an Aristocratic ideology contains elements of particularism which can be used to support a claim of 'bias'. A Meritocratic ideology not only denies an excuse for failure, but encourages an individual to accept full responsibility for it. With respect to the cooling-out of the upper social classes, the ideologies can be ranked as follows: Communistic, Meritocratic, Paternalistic and Aristocratic. I rank them in this order for two reasons. Insofar as Communistic and Meritocratic ideologies are less likely than Paternalistic and Aristocratic ones to warm-up the upper social classes effectively, they also make it easier to cool them out. The collectivistic elements of a Communistic ideology are more helpful than the individualism of an Aristocratic ideology, but the universalism of a Meritocratic, as opposed to the particularism of a Paternalistic, at least offers one an explanation of failure, no matter how painful. Each ideology is likely to help to cool-out a member of the lower social classes more effectively than a member of the upper social

classes. The possibility of downward mobility from the upper social classes always presents a problem, but no ideology of legitimization is designed to justify it. The ideologies are developed primarily to legitimize the continuity of the stratification system, and to explain upward social mobility in a way which helps to satisfy and to stabilize the non-mobile from the lower social classes. Due to the effects of economic growth in industrial societies and other changes in their occupational structures, downward mobility from the upper social classes has been both limited and inconspicuous. Consequently, as a rule, ideologies which justify downward mobility have not developed.

In sum, a Communistic ideology is likely to be most helpful with respect to the cooling-out of members of both social classes, but better with respect to the lower than to the upper. An Aristocratic ideology is likely to be the least helpful in the cooling-out of the upper and lower social classes, but it is decidedly better with respect to the lower than the upper. A Meritocratic ideology is the least helpful with respect to the lower social classes, and is so much worse than with the upper social classes that its inherent polarity is likely to make it the least helpful for the population generally.

5. *The Effects of Variations in Positions on Combinations of the Dimensions.* In terms of the typology for the classification of educational systems, as outlined above, it has been shown that a very large number of types of educational systems exist. When the dimensions of this typology are treated as interval or ordinal levels of measurement, an even larger number of systems can be specified. It has also been suggested that variation in each dimension has certain effects on the likelihood that an educational system will be able to resolve its warming-up:cooling-out dilemma successfully. It follows that when all dimensions are considered simultaneously, each system will have its own propensity towards the successful resolution of the warming-up:cooling-out dilemma. If each property of the system has the same kind of effect, it is relatively easy to predict this propensity.

It is more difficult when the properties of a system have inconsistent and even conflicting effects. For example, consider a system which is characterized by a high degree of early formal specialization and differentiation of routes as well as by a Communistic ideology of legitimization: the former is likely to be effective in warming-up the upper social classes and ineffective for the lower social classes; the latter is likely to be effective in warming-up the lower social classes, and ineffective for the upper social classes. Further in this connection, such a system would be likely to generate the middle-range routes which produce people who are notoriously difficult to cool-out at levels of achievement which are neither very low nor very high; but a Communistic ideology would be more likely than the other types to be helpful in cooling-out this segment.

The question arises whether the effects of the route structure are more or less determinant than those of the ideology of legitimization. The answer to such problems cannot be formulated on an *a priori* basis. It requires empirical research. But it can be stressed that the propensity of each educational system for the successful solution of the warming-up: cooling-out dilemma will depend on its full combination of structural properties, and will, therefore, have both consistent and inconsistent as well as conflicting and coordinated effects.

(ii) *The Contribution of Variations in the Structure of Educational Systems to the Successful Resolution of the Warming-up: Cooling-out Dilemma*

I have taken pains to stress that no society can ever resolve its warming-up: cooling-out dilemma with complete success. The way in which any society organizes its attempts to do so is a source of tension, conflict, and pressure for change. There will always be a weak link in the structure, a source of alternative perspectives and competing claims. It is, therefore, the attempt which counts, and how well it succeeds in balancing the competing demands of the society.

In the first instance one might think that the system's degree of success will be a simple function of matching the weaknesses of one dimension of educational structure with the strength of another. But this will not always have the desired effect. For example, it is likely that the inconsistent pressures will generate conflict and tension both within the system and between the system and other institutions. Competing interest groups both within and between are likely to align themselves along these axes of strain. Consider the Soviet Union under conditions of relatively recent economic and political stress. Economic resources press towards a high degree of early formal specialization and differentiation, whereas an Egalitarian ideology of implementation presses for a low degree. On the basis of a communistic ideology of legitimization, the society must try to warm-up those who are disadvantaged by the complex route structure, and to try to cool-out those who are rejected into the middle of the economic and status hierarchies. In such a system these pressures create continual strains toward deviation from and non-conformity to ideological demands. The legitimacy of the system is challenged. Apart from how such structural fragmentation generates latent conflicts among people in terms of personality differences (e.g. to be simplistic—radicals v.s. conservatives, idealists v.s. pragmatists), administrators and teachers and parents and civil servants are likely to be at odds. Clearly, this account is overdrawn, and might be applied to any society in recent years. But it is equally clear that to the extent that all the dimensions of the system are not considered simultaneously, it is extremely difficult to alter any one of them.

It follows that the degree to which the dilemma can be resolved successfully depends in large part on the matching of the structure of the educational system with the structure of the warming-up: cooling-out dilemma. Recall the hypotheses set out above: that when status rigidity is high, it is likely to be easier for a society to warm-up the upper social classes and to cool-out the lower social classes, and more difficult to warm-up the lower social classes and to cool-out the upper social classes; and that when status rigidity is low, the opposite is likely to obtain. In this respect, it is essential to know the distribution of the population among a society's social classes and its patterns and rates of social mobility and non-mobility, which are not always constant. Variation in such factors will then determine the balance and elasticity of the dilemma at a given time. Its successful resolution will depend on how well a society can design an educational system which can cope with these conflicting demands.

Because the structure of an educational system is not a function only of the structure of the warming-up : cooling-out dilemma, this becomes an extraordinarily difficult task. For example, the greater the status rigidity, the greater the power of the upper social classes relative to that of the lower social classes. This is nowhere more apparent than in patterns of parental control in educational systems, and can be observed too readily in too many areas to require documentation here. Hence, to design or to alter a system in order to make it more effective in its attempt to resolve the conflicting demands of the dilemma is likely to require that the upper social classes surrender their relative power, at least in the short run. For obvious reasons, this is not easily achieved, even if the national needs are paramount.

In conclusion, an ideal model can be suggested for conditions of high and low status rigidity in conjunction with a given and fixed distribution of the population among the society's social classes. The preceding argument suggests that: to the extent that status rigidity is *high,* the ideal system should tend towards:

1. high degree of centralization and standardization of the educational programme and its administration,

2. low degree of early formal specialization and differentiation of routes,
3. contest and egalitarian ideologies of implementation,
4. meritocratic ideology of legitimization;

and to the extent that status rigidity is *low,* the ideal system should tend towards:

1. high degree of centralization and standardization of the educational programme and its administration,
2. high degree of early formal specialization and differentiation of routes;
3. sponsorship and elitist ideologies of implementation,
4. paternalistic ideology of legitimization.

It should be stressed that these models are based on tendencies toward a particular pole of each dimension, and not on precise locations. In fact, extremes may encourage diminishing returns. In sum, to the extent that educational systems under conditions of high and low status rigidity deviate from these two models, respectively, they will tend to cope less successfully with the warming-up: cooling-out dilemma, in which case, the societies will experience the consequences of their system's lack of success. Whether additional organizations are developed to absorb the slack or whether change in the educational systems occurs depends on many other factors.

It is perhaps needless to add: the likelihood that such combinations of properties will be associated with high and low status rigidity, respectively, are slight.

IV   *Some Hypothetical Effects of Variations in the Structure of the Warming-up : Cooling-out Dilemma on the Structure of Educational Systems*

All else being equal, an educational system is likely to be structured in such a way as to maximise the degree to which the warming-up: cooling-out dilemma can be resolved successfully. Because the structure of an educational system is affected by so many additional factors, it is very hard to discern this relationship empirically. However, some aspects of it might be illustrated.

Consider the cases of England and the United States.[46] In the 1940's England could have been identified as a society with relatively high status rigidity, and with an educational system which manifested:

1. a moderate degree of centralization and standardization,
2. a high degree of early formal specialization and differentiation of routes,

3. sponsorship and elitist ideologies of implementation,
4. primarily a paternalistic ideology of legitimization.

At the same time the United States could have been identified as having a relatively low degree of status rigidity, and with an educational system which manifested:

1. a low degree of centralization and standardization,
2. a low degree of early formal specialization and differentiation of routes,
3. contest and egalitarian ideologies of implementation,
4. primarily a meritocratic ideology of legitimization.

Although the stratification systems of the two countries have changed in many ways, they have probably not altered in their respective degrees and patterns of status rigidity, at least not in dramatic or obvious ways. The basic structure of their warming-up : cooling-out dilemmas has remained more or less the same. Insofar as the preceding arguments have been correct, if the structure of the dilemmas has had an effect on the structures of the two respective systems, then in England the educational system should have developed towards:

1. *greater* centralization and standardization,
2. *less* early formal specialization and differentiation of routes,
3. contest and egalitarian ideologies of implementation,
4. meritocratic ideology of legitimization;

and in the United States, the educational system should have developed towards:

1. *greater* centralization and standardization,
2. *greater* early formal specialization and differentiation of routes,
3. sponsorship and elitist ideologies of implementation,
4. paternalistic ideology of legitimization.

It is my contention that such patterns of change can be seen with ease in both England and the United States. To document these patterns is beyond the scope of the present paper. To be sure, more careful and detailed study of the evidence is necessary. But it would seem that at least in these respects patterns of one-way and two-way partial convergence have occurred between the two countries.[47] For example, England is now developing the familiar American complex system of further and higher education combined with its more simple, comprehensive system of elementary and secondary schooling.[48] In this connection, as formal selection at an early age is reduced, England is beginning also to develop a system of professional counselling in the schools, which has been an established fixture of secondary schools in the United States since the early 1950s. In contrast, the United States is developing more selective secondary schooling, including private institutions as well as more elaborate techniques of streaming and setting. Vocational and technical training in secondary schools is also emerging as a serious alternative to non-selective pre-university comprehensive schools.

These highly speculative notes should be joined by several qualifications. I have not considered here the effects of industrialization on the patterns of status rigidity in any detail, and its attendant consequences for the structure of the dilemma. Nor have I mentioned the problem of the Blacks in the United States. The changing distributions of population among the social classes in each country has also been ignored. In sum, these patterns might well be traced to many other forces, and many counter-pressures have not been examined. But the patterns are consistent with the hypothesis that the structure of the warming-up: cooling-out dilemma is likely to influence in no small way the structure of an educational system.

V   Conclusion: A Set of Revised Hypotheses Concerning Some of the Personal and Interpersonal Consequences of Patterns of Mobility and Non-Mobility in England and the United States

I have considered the ways in which variation in the structure of educational systems is related to the success with which a society can resolve its warming-up: cooling-out dilemma. I suggested that warming-up and cooling-out processes pertain to career-training and status-training, as well as mobility-training. However, I have focussed the discussion primarily on the first two sets of experiences, and dealt with mobility-training only by implication. If more time and space were available, the argument could easily be extended to cover mobility-training. An inspection of the four conditions which both Professor Turner and I have hypothesized to be pathogenic suggests that only the last two (interpersonal isolation and loss of support, and difficulties in working out a personal value system) are relevant primarily to the experiences of the upwardly mobile; the first two (discrepancies between a level of normative expectations and a level of achievement, and competition for the most desirable occupations) are as relevant to the experiences of maturation and career-progressions generally as they are to those of upward mobility.

It follows that in my decision to limit the discussion primarily to career-training and status-training experiences, I have decided also to concentrate on those two sets of pathogenic conditions which are relevant to both upward mobility and non-mobility. Again, if more time and space were available, the argument could be extended to cover the other two sets of conditions. This emphasis is appropriate to the question whether upward mobility is more likely than non-mobility to be pathogenic in one society than it is in another. The neglected topic of non-mobility becomes crucial for such a comparison, especially in a paper concerned primarily with the effects of variations in the structure of educational systems.

I mentioned in the introduction to this paper that the problem of mobility and non-mobility could not be considered adequately without first discussing the patterns of status rigidity in the society. A comparison of mobility and non-mobility experiences in England with those in the United States would, therefore, involve a comparison of these societies with respect to status rigidity. Further, this task requires an analysis of patterns of status incongruence. Because these cannot be attempted here, any discussion of the effects of variations in educational systems on the consequences of mobility and of non-mobility must be incomplete. I hope only to illustrate the contribution which variations in the structures of educational systems might make to these relationships.

Insofar as an educational system fails to meet the tasks implicated by the structure of its warming-up: cooling-out dilemma, both the mobile and the non-mobile are likely to encounter pathogenic conditions. England is more likely than the United States to meet the cooling-out tasks effectively at *high* and at *low* levels of achievement, but less likely to do so at *middle* levels of achievement. England is more likely than the United States to meet the warming-up tasks effectively at *high* levels of achievement, but less likely to do so at *middle* and *low* levels of achievement. These strengths and weaknesses are manifest in the experiences which are characteristic of the routes through the respective systems.

In conclusion, a selection of the set of hypotheses which pertain to a comparison of England with the United States with respect to the pathogenic quality of patterns of mobility and non-mobility, especially as affected by their respective educational systems, is as follows:

(i) The non-mobile from the lower social classes in England who use initial rejection routes are less likely than their counterparts in the United States to encounter pathogenic conditions.

(ii) Both the upwardly mobile from the lower social classes and the non-mobile from the upper social classes in England who use these routes characterized by initial selection followed by selection through the apex of the system are also less likely than their counterparts in the United States to encounter pathogenic conditions.

(iii) Both the upwardly mobile from the lower social classes and the non-mobile from the lower social classes who use the middle-range routes in England are more likely to encounter pathogenic conditions than are their counterparts in the United States. These are the routes which begin with initial selection but terminate with subsequent rejection at various levels prior to the apex. They are especially likely to be ineffective in both warming-up and cooling-out experiences with respect to career, status, and mobility training. Such routes are an integral part of the educational system in England, but a more nominal part of the American system.

(iv) Upward mobility from the lower social classes through initial rejection routes in England is more likely to be pathogenic than is its analogous pattern in the United States. Upward mobility from the lower social classes in England represents a more serious problem than in the United States. Most of the upward mobility from these social classes occurs through initial rejection routes, and not through initial selection routes, as is usually but incorrectly assumed. These routes provide almost no mobility-training experiences. Their career-training and status-training experiences are for the lower social classes, and are inappropriate for those who become upwardly mobile despite their having been rejected initially (and in effect incorrectly).

(v) Downward mobility in England is more likely to be pathogenic than it is in the United States.

Notes and References:

I am indebted to Joan Raphael, London School of Economics, and Professor Joseph Kahl, Cornell University, for their helpful comments on an earlier draft of this paper.

1. *ASR*, vol. 25, 1960, pp. 855–867. The article had a mixed critical reception, but it has been recognized as one of the few sociological attempts in the field of the comparative study of educational systems to go beyond mere description. The article has now been reprinted in several Readers, often under other titles, and has become a standard reference.

2. Even a cursory inspection of the literature shows that very few researchers fail to mention Turner's work.

3. op. cit., pp. 866–867.

4. *Sociology*, vol. 2, No. 1, January 1968, pp. 29–46.

5. Many of the revised hypotheses which result from this perspective are the basis of my empirical study of some personal and interpersonal consequences of social mobility among men who are now around 35 years of age. These are members of the age cohort who first experienced the restructured educational system in England which followed the 1944 Educational Act. It is impossible in one paper to convey both the theory which underpins this empirical study, its method, and results. I have opted for a portion of the theory but I hope that some empirical illustrations will be appropriate during discussion. Several research assistants

at the London School of Economics have been especially helpful in the analysis of data relevant to the present paper: Adam Pearce, Peter Stone, Carol Hewlet, Liz Atkins, and Lin Hoblyn Clark.

6. Professor Turner was concerned only with the implications of his typology, and did not intend this portion of his article to be a comprehensive statement. In more recent work, he has developed some parts of the thesis, but not others; for example, see *The Social Context of Ambition,* Chandler Press, San Francisco, 1964. However, his few cryptic paragraphs are so suggestive a starting point for more detailed work that I have taken the liberty to expand his thesis slightly— but only in order to draw out its full implications and to clarify its theoretical structure. In conversation and correspondence, Professor Turner has accepted my formulation of his position as expressed in his article.

7. It is important to note the distinction between the concepts of 'pathogenic' and of 'pathological'. I would also stress that the conditions outlined in the text can be formulated in a more sophisticated way, and integrated into a theory of various personal and interpersonal characteristics. I have tried to do this in the study of social mobility mentioned in Note 5. This material is too lengthy to include here. Further, anxiety takes many manifest forms; in a sense, these forms represent different 'types' of anxiety. Some are more aptly described, from a sociologist's point of view, as 'pathological feeling states', e.g., anomia, relative deprivation, etc. It is with such forms of anxiety that I am primarily concerned. It should be noted that most researchers in this field recognize that until longitudinal studies have been undertaken, any relationship between mobility and anxiety is likely to be partly spurious, no matter how many structural conditions are controlled. Consequently, the aim is always to isolate structural conditions under which the likelihood that anxiety will develop is maximized, particularly if predispositions to anxiety already exist.

8. Nonetheless, to understand why Turner's work is uninformed by such considerations of social structure requires comment. The concept of status rigidity refers to various properties of the status hierarchy, its composition, and its relationship to other hierarchies of power. In turn, the notion of status hierarchy refers to the fact that social honour is one kind of power resource, and that groups of people are ranked according to their amount of status power to control their own and other people's life chances and participation in various spheres of interests and activities. This perspective is virtually absent from American sociology, in which status is usually regarded as a ranking based on a system of values and norms, and is treated as the values, norms, and other aspects of the life style which is manifest by a given family or set of families. Although this view might lead to useful methods of measurement of status power, it renders impotent the concept of 'status as a power resource', and relegates the phenomenon to variations in attitudes and beliefs, etc., which might, for example, affect performance and interest in education. It is not surprising, then, that as one of the most prominent American sociologists who writes on stratification and mobility, Turner should exclude from his work what is essentially a European perspective. I tried to make this point in a review of Bendix and Lipset's *Class, Status and Power*; see Earl Hopper, *British Journal of Sociology,* volume XIX, No. 2, June 1968, pp. 214–215.

9. Various texts are available for the United States. With respect to England, see Olive Banks, *The Sociology of Education,* Batsforth, London 1968.

10. Please note that I use the concept of 'functional problem' and not 'functional prerequisites'. I wish to avoid at the outset the usual and largely correct criticisms which are made of the various forms of classical functional analysis. To identify a functional problem is not at the same time to identify the functional

alternatives which might cope with it; nor is it to identify the specific forms of social organization which might arise at a given time and place; nor is it to explain why those forms and not others were developed. It must be stressed, therefore, that in this paper I am not primarily concerned with the many determinants of variations in the structure of educational systems. Nor do I argue that the systems which now exist in any society are necessarily the 'best' in any sense of the word. Nor do I approve of many of the features of these systems. In brief, the notion of 'functional problem' is used to connote a sense of struggle which probably can never be completely successful and which may often be closer to failure than to success.

11. Hopper, 'Typology', op. cit. The present paper offers a more extensive discussion.

12. See the discussion of status rigidity later in this paper.

13. Many sociologists recoil from making these kinds of statements and from the sentiments which are manifest in the social organization which warrants such discussion. But our moral repugnance does not negate the evidence that such processes exist and are essential to the present structure of all industrial societies. For a preliminary discussion of normative expectations of authority and their association with social class positions in England and the United States, see Earl Hopper 'Some Effects of Variation in Supervisory Styles: A Sociological Analysis', *B.J.S.*, vol. 16, No. 3, September 1965.

14. Hopper, 'A typology for the classification of education systems', op. cit.

15. Which is not to say that these two qualities are always related.

16. This is a sociological truism. But for support see Ted Robert Gurr, *Why Men Rebel*, Princeton University Press, Princeton, New Jersey, 1970.

17. This too is a sociological truism. But for a useful review of the literature and helpful discussion of many crucial issues, see David E. Lavin, *The Prediction of Academic Performance*, Russell Sage Foundation, New York, 1965, and David A. Goslin, *The Search for Ability*, Russell Gage Foundation, New York, 1963.

18. Which leads to various kinds of direct and indirect controls of education processes whenever educational institutions have been made responsible for recruitment and/or allocation processes.

19. For example, see J. W. B. Douglas, *The Home and The School*, MacGibbon and Kee, London, 1964; *et al.*, *All our Future*, Peter Davies, London 1964; and James S. Coleman (ed.), *Education and Political Development*, Princeton University Press, Princeton, 1965.

20. ibid.

21. See Joseph A. Kahl, *The Measurement of Modernism: A study of Values in Brazil and Mexico*, The University of Texas Press, Austin, Texas, 1968; and Richard de Charms, *Personal Causation*, Academic Press, London 1968.

22. See Turner, *The Social Context of Ambition*, op. cit.

23. As societies industrialize, their educational systems become the institutionalized source of the preparatory phase of almost all careers. In addition, they become the main source of opportunity for social mobility. All other channels for social mobility, and for careers in general, come to depend on the educational systems for prior screening and preliminary training of candidates. For an early statement on this point see P. Sorokin, *Social and Cultural Mobility*, Collin MacMillan Ltd., London 1964 (first published in 1929). It should be stressed, however, that educational systems do not become just 'mobility routes' —it is rather that they become a source of mobility in so far as they become a source of careers in general.

24. Burton Clark, 'The Sociology of Education', in R. L. Faris (ed.) *Handbook of Modern Sociology*, Rand and McNally, Chicago, 1964.

25. For discussion and bibliography see Coleman, op. cit.

26. For bibliography to support this statement see the recent studies of industrialization and convergence.

27. For example, consider the responsibility of Student Union officers in England and in the United States compared with those of clerical workers or many middle managers.

28. 'Cooling-out' was introduced as a serious concept in sociology by E. Goffman, 'Cooling the Mark Out: Some Aspects of Adaptation to Failure', *Psychiatry*, XV, November, 1952 pp. 451–463. For an application of the concept to certain routes within American higher education, see B. Clark, 'The "Cooling-out" Function in Higher Education', *A.J.S.*, LXV, May 1960, pp. 569–576. I have tried to modify the concept to include not only adaptation to failure but also adaptation to success.

29. Hopper, 'An Expanded Typology for the Classification of Educational Systems', *op. cit.*

30. For a discussion of such a problem see Philip Selznick. *TVA and The Grass Roots,* University of California Press, Berkeley, 1949.

31. For discussion of the determinants of the structure of educational systems, see any of the well known introductory texts. I prefer Banks, op. cit.

32. However, this relationship raises the possibility of a spurious explanation in connection with the effects of status rigidity. It has been shown that variations in status rigidity affect the structure of the dilemma. But it was also shown that variations in the structure of status rigidity have only a minimal effect on the structure of an educational system. (Hopper, 'An Expanded Typology', *op. cit.*) If it is so that the structure of the dilemma is a prime determinant of the structure of an educational system, how can it be that there is so little relationship between variations in status rigidity and the structure of the system? The evidence suggests that although variations in status rigidity are sometimes related to variations in the ideologies of educational selection and of implementation, they are not necessarily related to variations in positions on the other dimension of the typology. Most important, variation in status rigidity is not related to the patterns of positions on all the dimensions. Thus, although variations in the degree of status rigidity have some direct effects on the structure of the system, it is determined by many other factors, only some of which are related to variations in status rigidity. (The structure is defined by a set of co-ordinating points on the various dimensions, including many which are considered by my typology.) In brief, the problem of spuriousness is only apparent, and not real. But this highlights the facts that although the structured emphasis of the dilemma which a society assigns to its educational system may help to explain certain of its most essential and characteristic properties, one cannot thereby hope to explain a great deal of the variation.

33. With reference to the United States, see C. Jenks and D. Riesman, *The Academic Revolution.* Doubleday and Son, New York, 1968.

34. Douglas, op. cit; see also his bibliography for further evidence.

35. For example, see the early works of Prof. Basil Bernstein and his colleagues.

36. Of course, to the extent that routes are ineffective in the cooling-out process, that is, ambition remains high despite the negative assessment of the student by the educational system, some selection errors may subsequently be corrected by achievements which stem primarily from ambition, and, possibly, from undetected 'natural talent' in conjunction with ambition. Further, there is some evidence which suggests that the children of those who were 'incorrectly' rejected at the lower echelons of the system are likely to be among the most ambitious in their cohort; and given the dependence of the system on high levels of ambition, it becomes especially difficult to discuss the functions and dysfunctions of existing methods of selection.

36a. See Reading 11 in the present volume, for a discussion of 'lateral autonomy'. This dimension was not included in my original typology.

37. In very complex systems, there are routes which, for example, begin with an initial rejection, are followed by a subsequent selection, and end with a still subsequent rejection. It is quite likely that a route which contains a phase which is characterized by a rejection followed by a selection will offer special difficulties for the cooling-out process.

38. To discern the hypothetical effects of variation in an ideology on social organization, and more specifically, on social action, is extraordinarily difficult. For one reason, such a task involves the prior solution, at least in assumptive terms, of the classical philosophical questions concerning the issues, for example, of nominalism v.s. realism, and idealism v.s. materialism. However, at this stage in the present study it is in order to side step some of these issues. My position is that variations in ideology are almost always necessary but never sufficient to *explain* variation in social organization or in social action. They help to coordinate random predispositions towards actions, to stabilize existing social organization, and to justify structural changes. Most important is that they limit the perception of alternatives in such a way that other properties of interpersonal relationships and their contexts, both human and non-human, have relatively consistent effects. In brief, variations in ideologies either facilitate or impede the effects of interaction systems. Nonetheless, to facilitate or to impede constitutes a causal process, and, therefore, the effects of ideologies warrant analysis as independent forces.

39. This is certainly not always the case. They are combined here only for purposes of simplification. More detailed analysis would demand that each variation in a combination be examined separately.

40. I make these assertions on the basis of personal experience and observations in English and American schools and Universities, and also from my experience with American students who come to England to study, as well as with German, French, and Italian counterparts.

41. This is one aspect of the process of elite self-perpetuation discussed by C. Wright Mills, *The Power Elite,* Oxford University Press, New York 1957. With respect to educational selection it is now notorious that selection methods which are weighted towards personal recommendations of teachers favour the middle class child relative to the working class child more than do impersonal tests.

42. For example, see J. F. Dusenbury. *Income, Saving and the Theory of Consumer Behaviour*, Harvard University Press, Cambridge, Mass., 1949; and George C. Homans, *Social Behaviour: Its Elementary Forms*, Routledge and Kegan Paul, London, 1962.

43. This raises the point that one should not be too quick to see a Sponsorship ideology rather than a Contest ideology as a source of legitimization for the existing status hierarchy. A Contest ideology may also be used, and to an even better effect. Selection procedures become normatively depersonalized under a Contest ideology; and it is relatively more difficult for members of the lower social classes to feel and believe that they did not have a 'fair chance'. But this does not mean that most of them will acquiesce in the judgement.

44. Hopper, 'Some Effects of Variations in Supervisory Styles', op. cit.

45. Hopper, 'A Typology for the Classification of Educational Systems', op. cit.

46. ibid.

47. See E. G. Dunning and E. I. Hopper, 'Industrialization and the Problem of Convergence: A Critical Note', *Sociological Review,* XIV, July 1966, No. 2.

48. Roger Beard, 'Today, a Degree is just "Passing the 21-Plus" ', *New Statesman,* 20 February 1970.